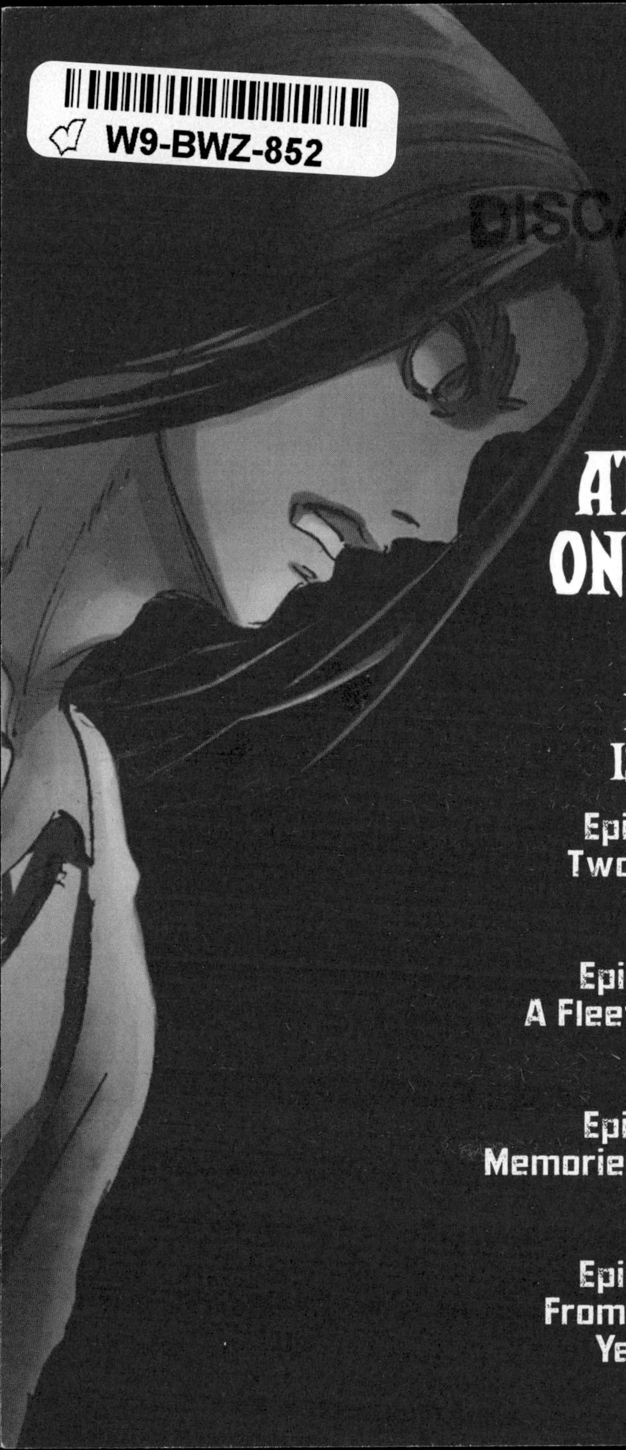

ATTACK ON TITAN 30

HAJIME ISAYAMA

THE CHARACTERS OF ATTACK ON TITAN

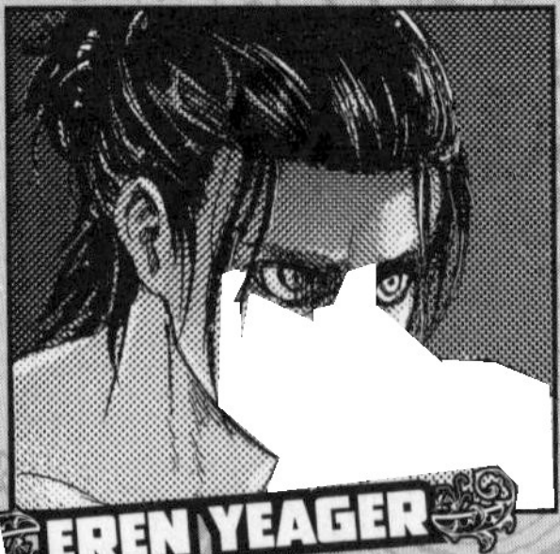

EREN YEAGER

FROM THE 104TH TRAINING CORPS; NOW IN THE SURVEY CORPS. HOLDS THE POWER OF THE ATTACK TITAN AND THE FOUNDING TITAN. BOLDLY INFILTRATED MARLEY ON HIS OWN.

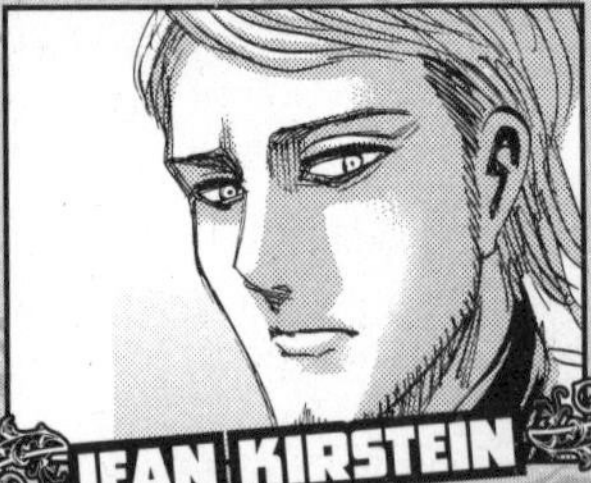

JEAN KIRSTEIN

FROM THE 104TH TRAINING CORPS; NOW IN THE SURVEY CORPS. ONCE KNOWN FOR HIS SARCASTIC PERSONALITY, HE HAS NOW GROWN INTO A LEADER.

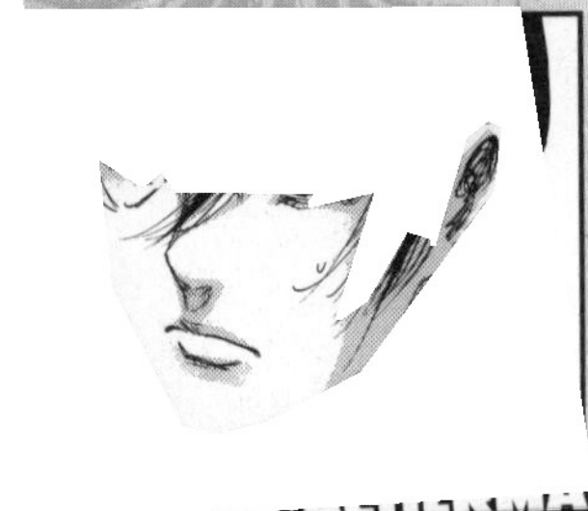

FROM THE 104TH TRAINING CORPS; NOW IN THE SURVEY CORPS. SHE HAS SHOWN INCREDIBLE COMBAT ABILITIES EVER SINCE SHE WAS A RECRUIT. SHE SEES PROTECTING EREN AS HER MISSION.

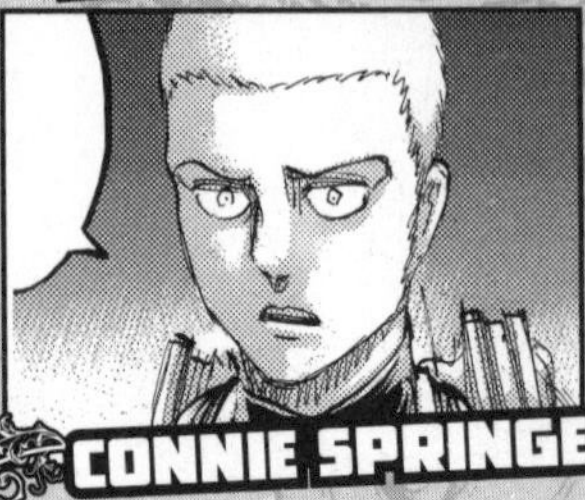

CONNIE SPRINGER

FROM THE 104TH TRAINING CORPS; NOW IN THE SURVEY CORPS. HE IS CHEERFUL IN PERSONALITY, BUT FINDS HIMSELF LOSING EVERYONE IMPORTANT TO HIM... ORIGINALLY FROM RAGAKO VILLAGE.

FROM THE 104TH TRAINING CORPS; NOW IN THE SURVEY CORPS. HOLDS THE POWER OF THE COLOSSUS TITAN. HE HAS SAVED HIS COMRADES COUNTLESS TIMES WITH HIS SHARP INTELLECT AND BRAVERY.

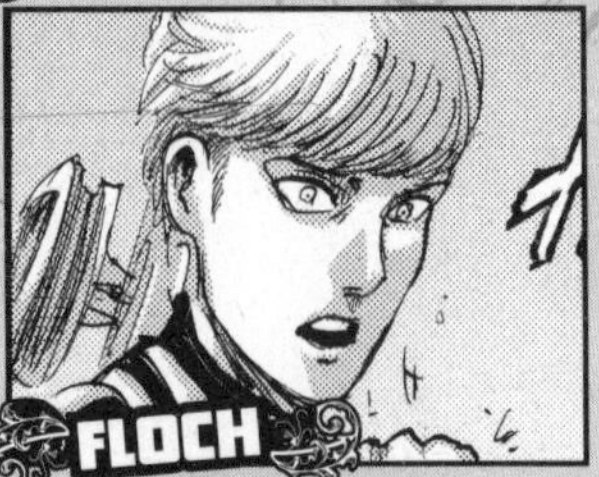

FLOCH

A MEMBER OF THE SURVEY CORPS. A SURVIVOR OF THE DECISIVE BATTLE FOR SHIGANSHINA DISTRICT, WHICH CLAIMED MANY LIVES, INCLUDING ERWIN'S.

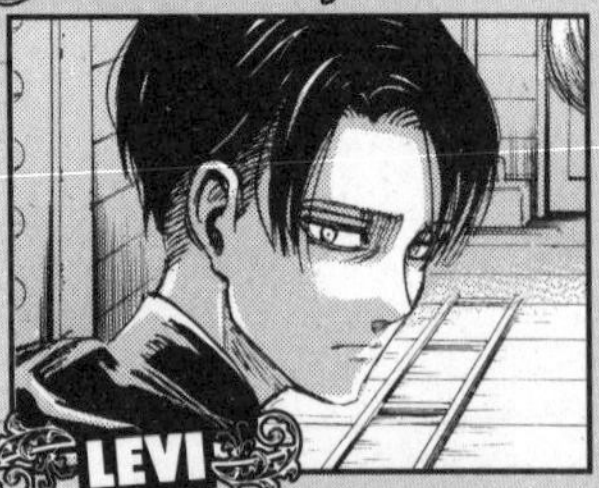

LEVI

CAPTAIN OF THE SURVEY CORPS. KNOWN AS "HUMANITY'S STRONGEST SOLDIER." HE FIGHTS THROUGH HIS STRUGGLES IN ORDER TO CARRY ON HIS GOOD FRIEND ERWIN'S DYING WISHES.

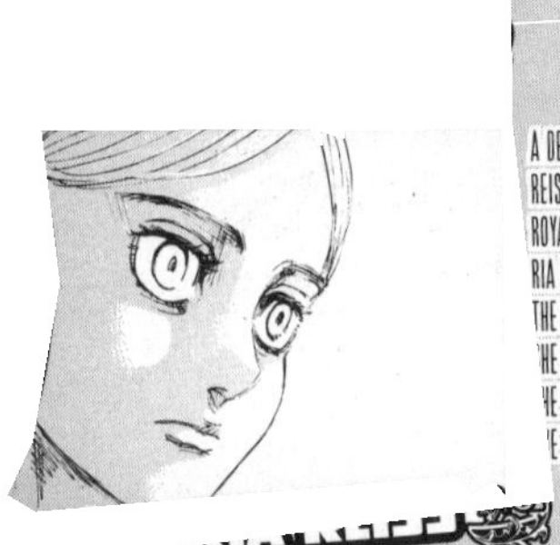

A DESCENDANT OF THE REISS FAMILY, THE TRUE ROYAL BLOODLINE, HISTORIA HAS ASCENDED TO THE THRONE AS QUEEN. HE ONCE BELONGED TO HE SURVEY CORPS UNDER E NAME KRISTA LENZ.

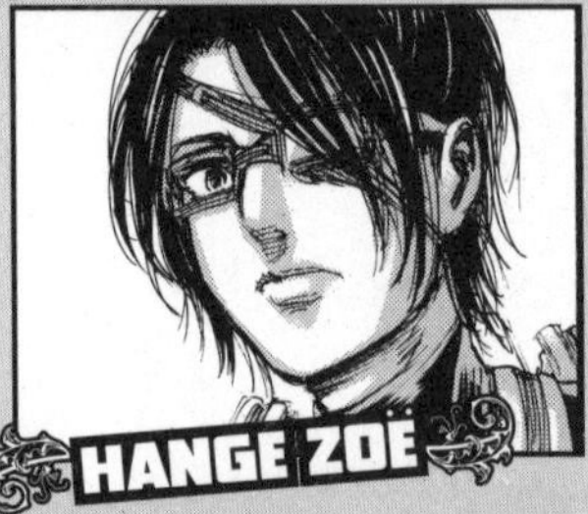

HANGE ZOË

COMMANDER OF THE SURVEY CORPS. THEIR KEEN POWERS OF OBSERVATION LED ERWIN TO NAME HANGE HIS SUCCESSOR DESPITE THEIR OBVIOUS ECCENTRICITIES.

THE NATION OF ELDIA [THE ISLAND OF PARADIS]

THE ELDIAN WARRIORS OF THE MARLEYAN ARMY

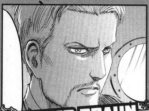

REINER BRAUN

HOLDS THE ARMORED TITAN WITHIN HIM. SINCE HE WAS THE ONLY ONE TO MAKE IT BACK FROM THE MISSION ON PARADIS, HE SUFFERS FROM A GUILTY CONSCIENCE.

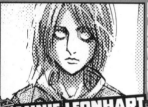

ANNIE LEONHART

HOLDS THE FEMALE TITAN WITHIN HER. A MEMBER OF THE 104TH. SHE HAS BEEN SLEEPING WITHIN A HARDENED CRYSTAL EVER SINCE HER TRUE IDENTITY WAS DISCOVERED.

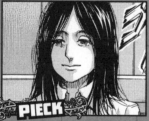

PIECK

HOLDS THE CART TITAN WITHIN HER, CARRYING THE PANZER UNIT ON THE BACK OF THE "CARTMAN" TO FIGHT. HIGHLY PERCEPTIVE.

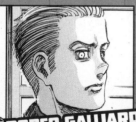

PORCO GALLIARD

HOLDS THE JAW TITAN WITHIN HIM. THERE IS STRIFE BETWEEN HIM AND REINER OVER BOTH THE INHERITANCE OF THE ARMORED TITAN AND THE DEATH OF HIS OLDER BROTHER, MARCEL.

THE ANTI-MARLEYAN VOLUNTEERS

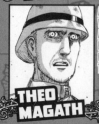

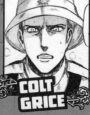

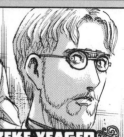

ZEKE YEAGER

HOLDS THE POWER OF THE BEAST TITAN. A LEADER OF THE WARRIORS, HE WAS ONCE KNOWN AS THE "WONDER CHILD." HIS MOTHER IS A DESCENDANT OF THE ROYAL BLOODLINE. HE IS ALSO EREN'S HALF-BROTHER.

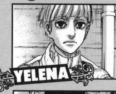

YELENA

YELENA COMMANDS THE VOLUNTEERS AND FOLLOWS ZEKE. SHE DRESSED AS A MAN DURING THE EXPEDITION TO MARLEY IN ORDER TO WORK IN SECRET.

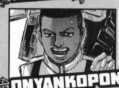

ONYANKOPON

AFTER TRAVELING TO PARADIS WITH YELENA, HE TELLS ITS INHABITANTS OF MARLEY'S ADVANCED CULTURE.

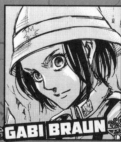

GABI BRAUN

BOLD DESPITE HER SMALL SIZE, GABI IS A DYNAMIC WARRIOR CANDIDATE. HER GOAL IS TO EVENTUALLY INHERIT THE ARMORED TITAN. REINER'S COUSIN.

THEO MAGATH

A MARLEYAN WHO LEADS A UNIT OF ELDIANS. PROMOTED TO GENERAL.

COLT GRICE

FALCO'S OLDER BROTHER, THE OLDEST OF THE WARRIOR CANDIDATES, AND, IN EFFECT, THEIR LEADER.

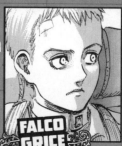

FALCO GRICE

A WARRIOR CANDIDAT HE HAS AFFECTION FOR GABI AND WANTS TO PROTECT HER. DURING EREN'S TIME INFILTRATING MARLEY FALCO CAME IN CONTA WITH EREN WITHOUT REALIZING HIS TRUE IDENTITY.

ATTACK ON TITAN

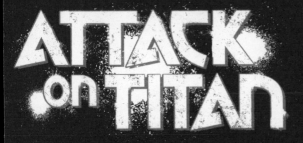

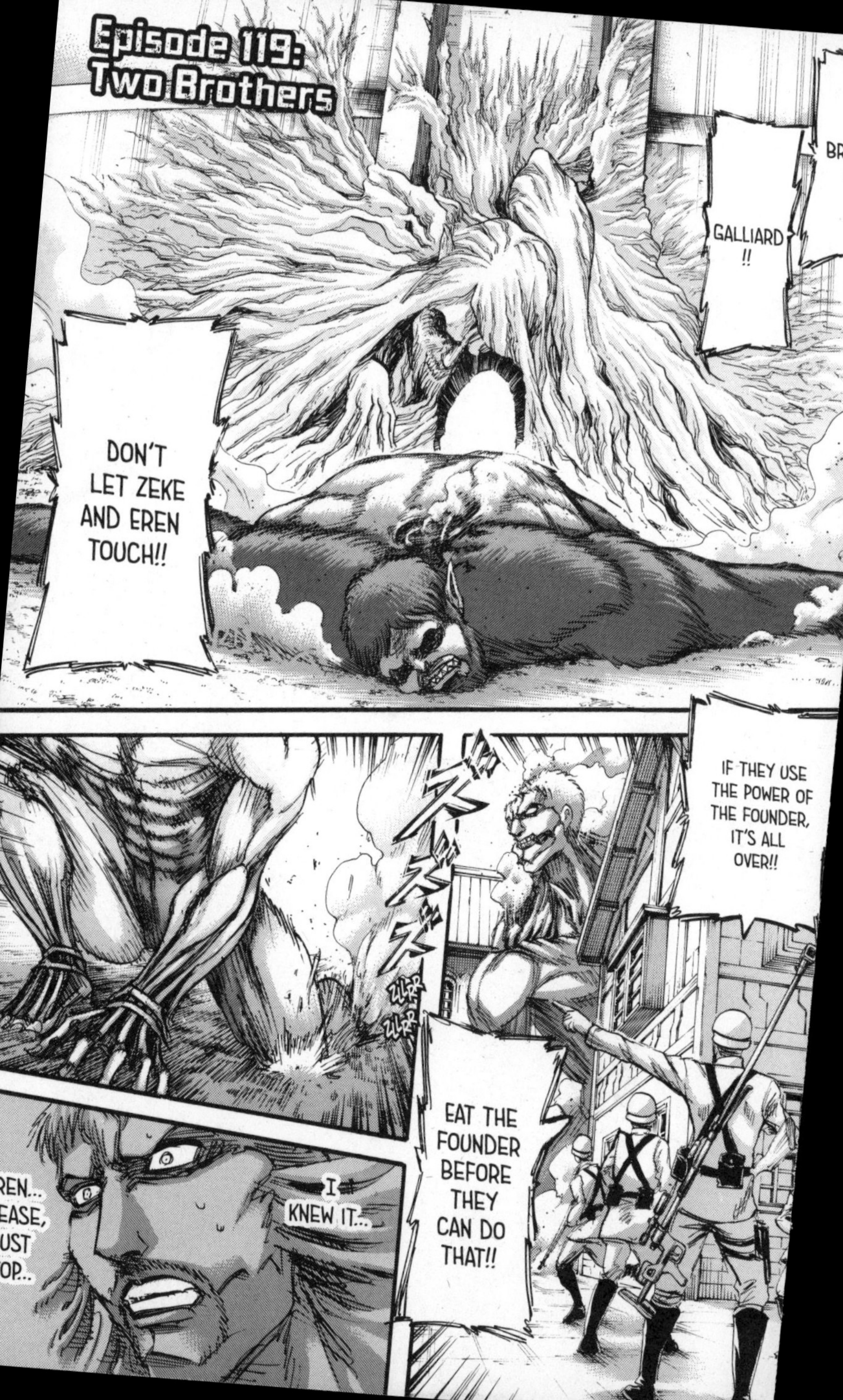
Episode 119: Two Brothers
BR
GALLIARD!!
DON'T LET ZEKE AND EREN TOUCH!!
IF THEY USE THE POWER OF THE FOUNDER, IT'S ALL OVER!!
EAT THE FOUNDER BEFORE THEY CAN DO THAT!!
ZLLRR
ZLLRR
I KNEW IT...
REN... EASE, UST OP...

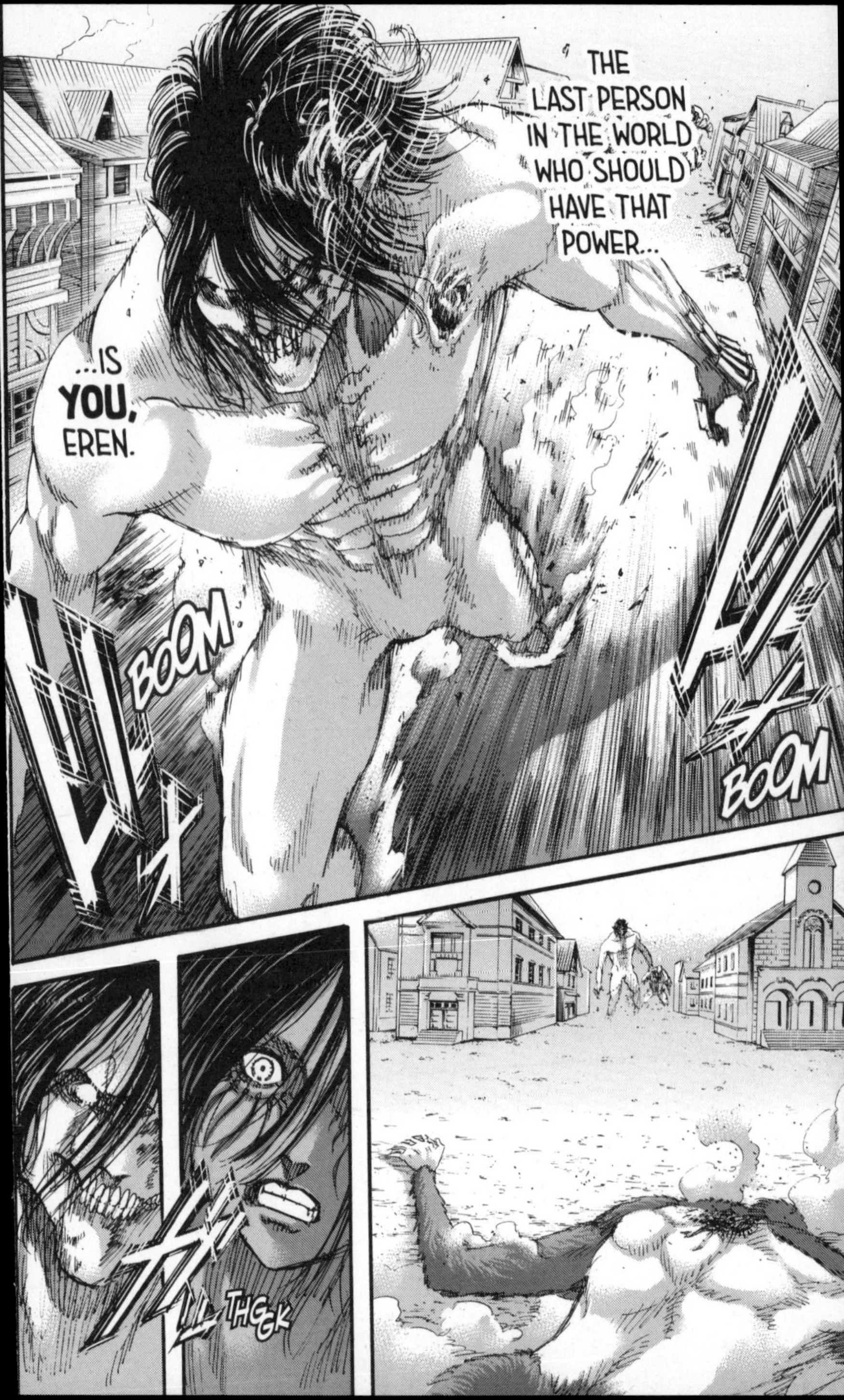
THE LAST PERSON IN THE WORLD WHO SHOULD HAVE THAT POWER...
...IS **YOU,** EREN.
BOOM
BOOM
THGGK

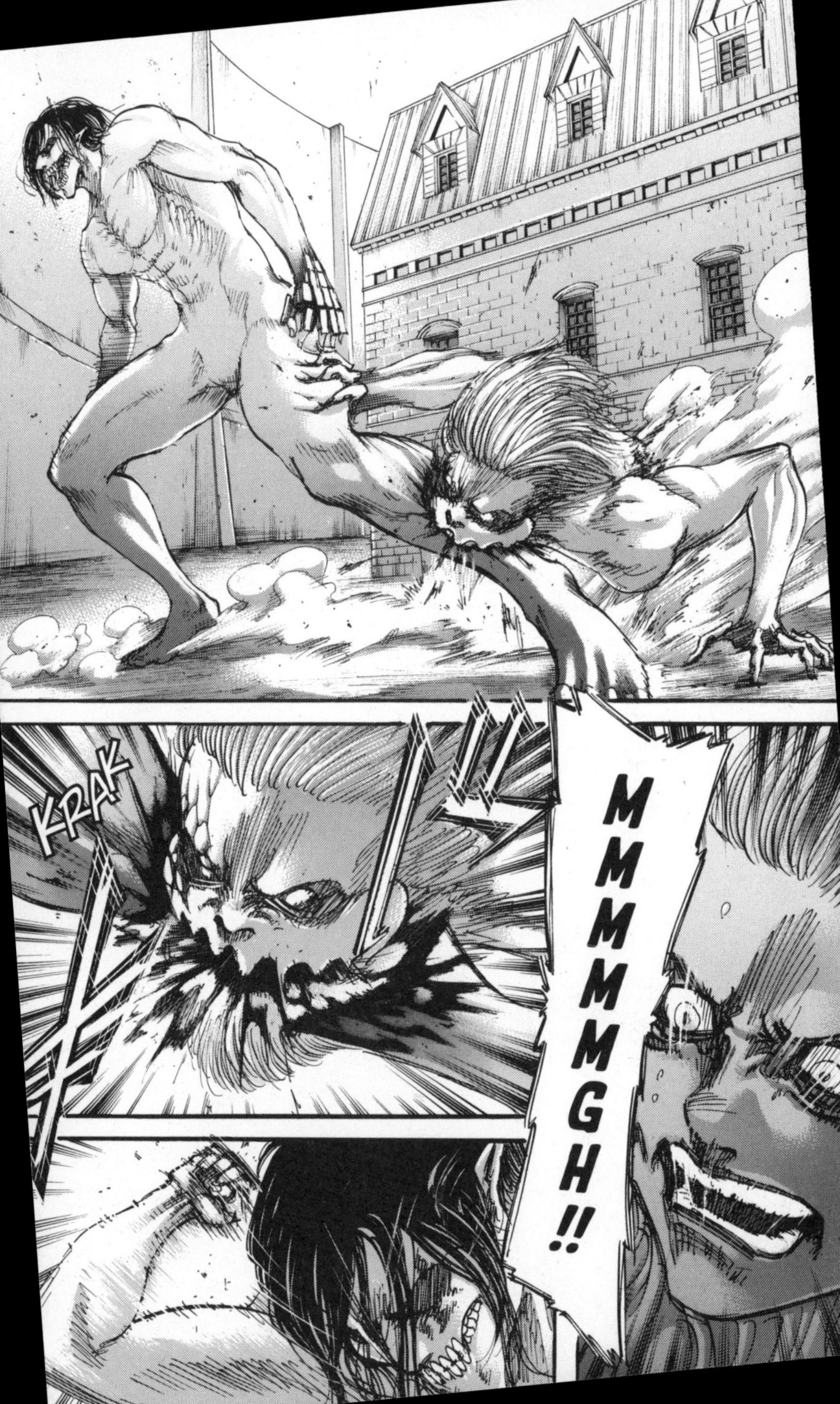
MMMMMGH!!
KRAK

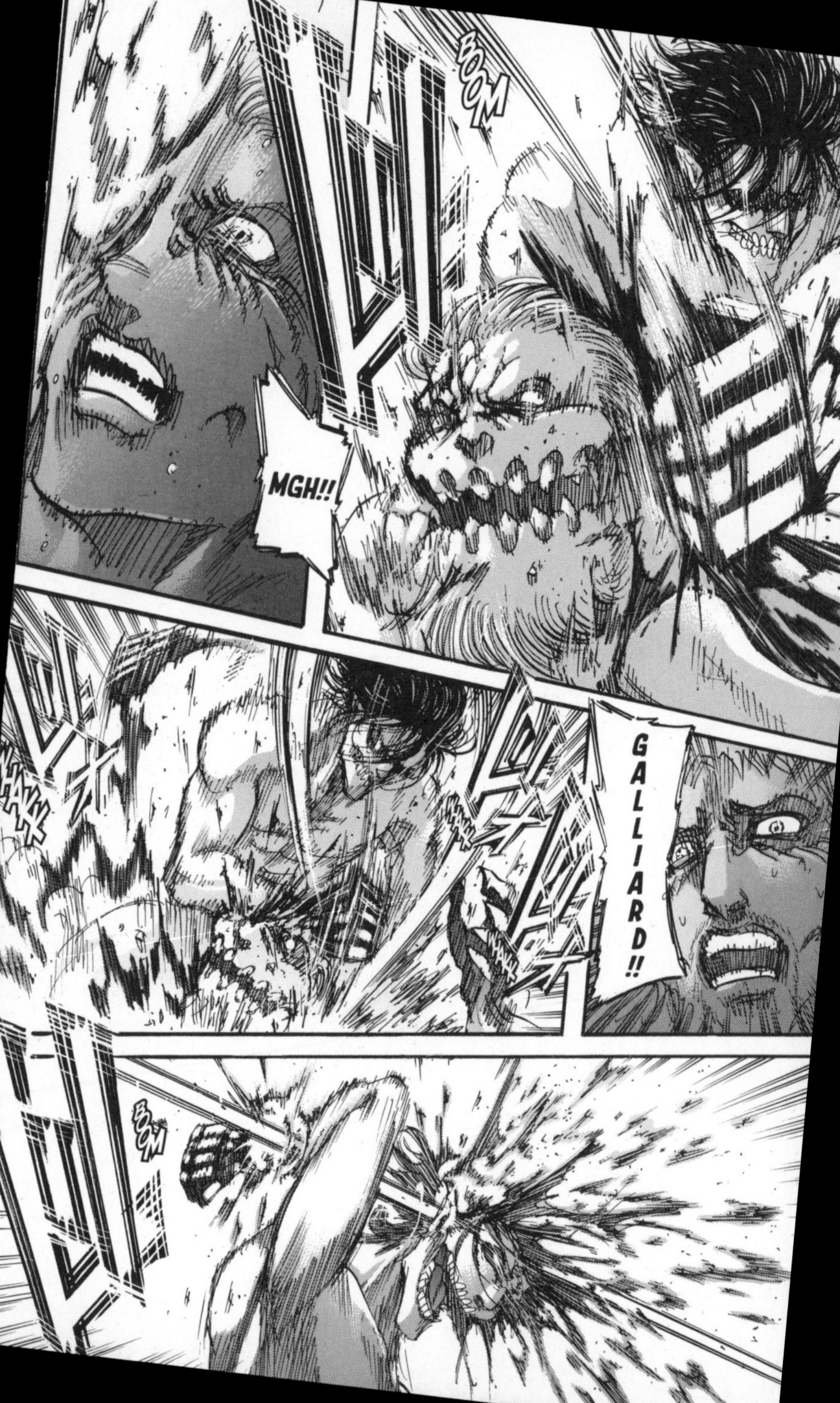
BOOM
MGH!!
GALLIARD!!
WHAK
WHAK
WHAK
BOOM

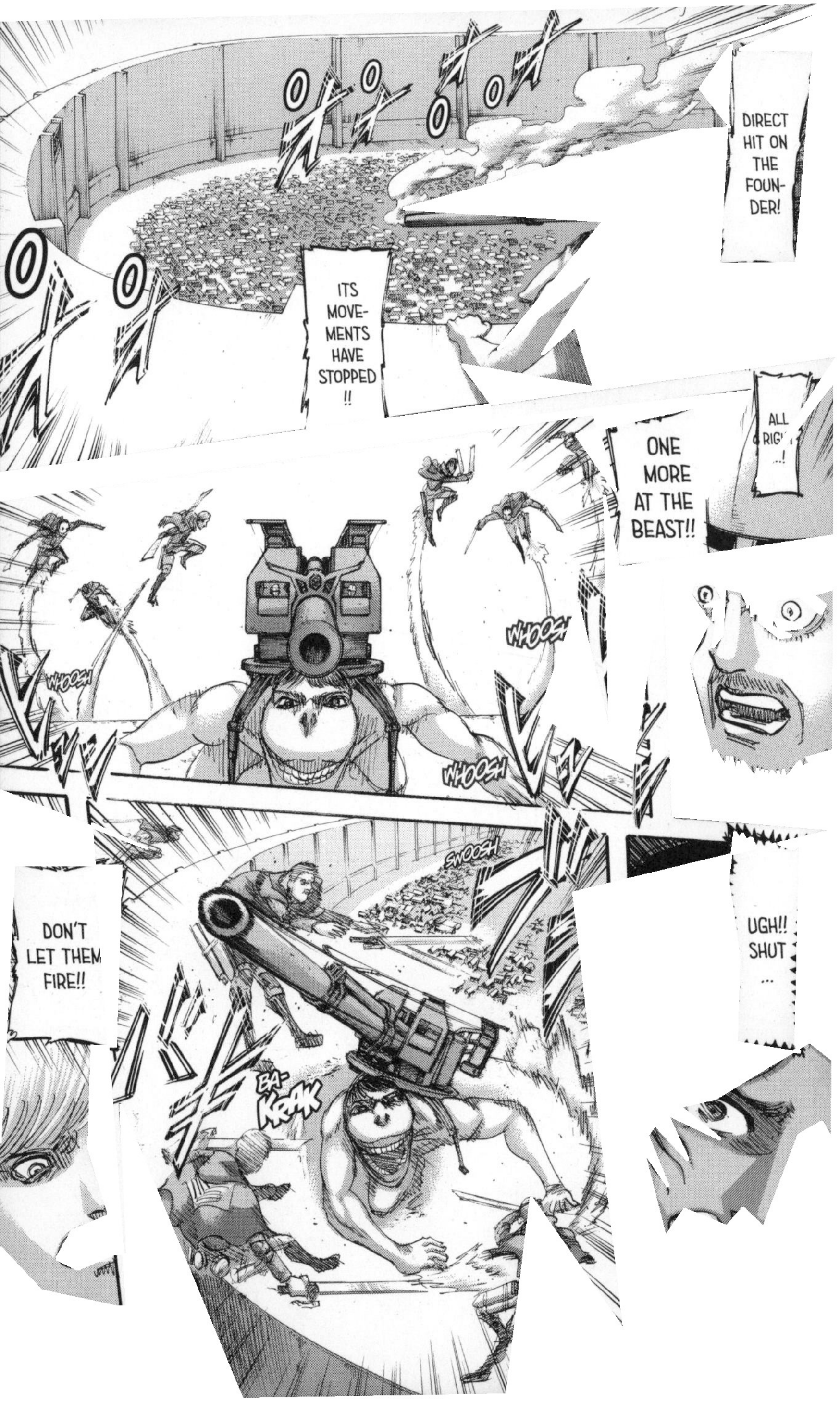
DIRECT HIT ON THE FOUNDER!
ITS MOVEMENTS HAVE STOPPED!!
ALL RIG ...!
ONE MORE AT THE BEAST!!
WHOOSH
WHOOSH
WHOOSH
UGH!! SHUT ...
DON'T LET THEM FIRE!!
SWOOSH
BA-KRAK

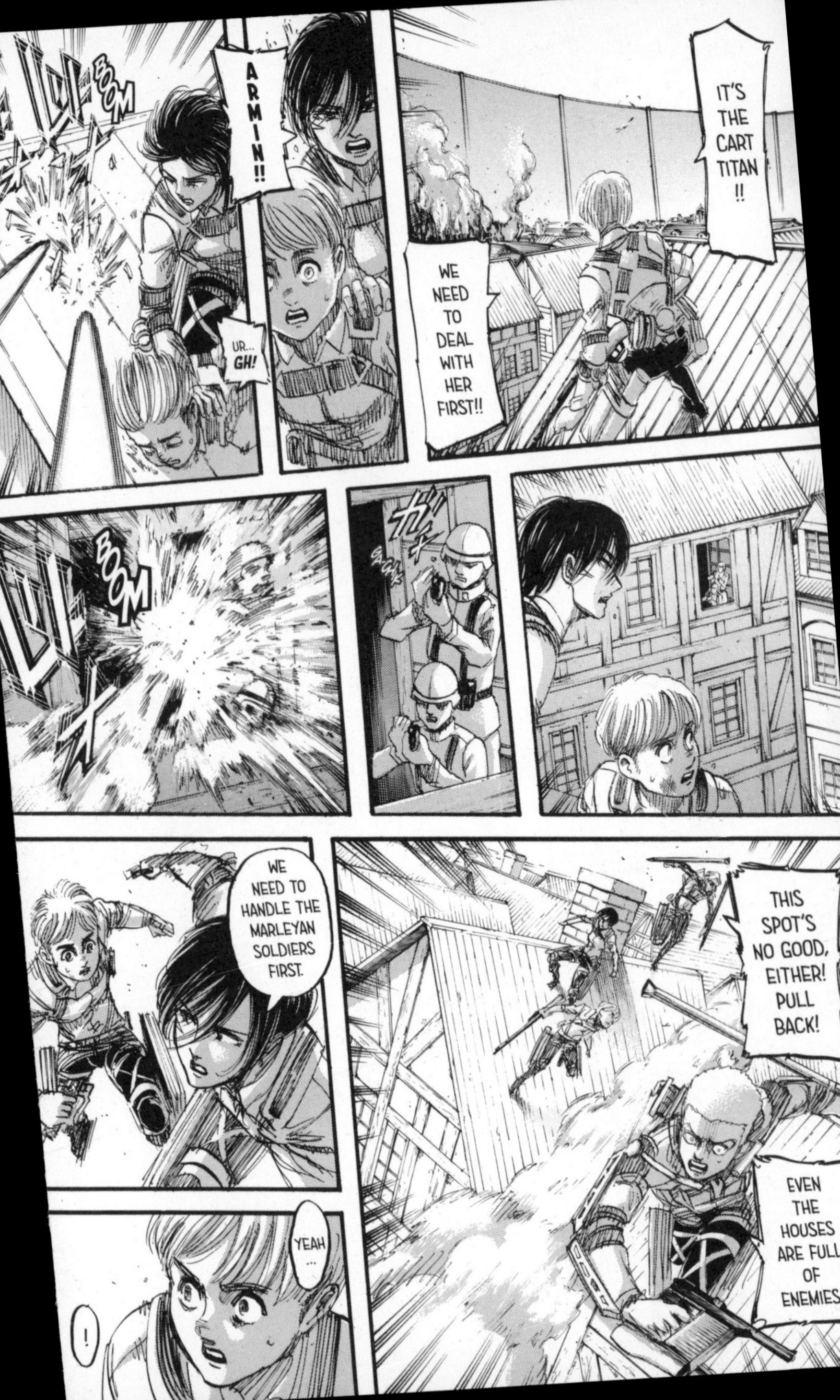
IT'S THE CART TITAN!!
WE NEED TO DEAL WITH HER FIRST!!
ARMIN!!
BOOM
UR... GH!
BOOM
THIS SPOT'S NO GOOD, EITHER! PULL BACK!
EVEN THE HOUSES ARE FULL OF ENEMIES
WE NEED TO HANDLE THE MARLEYAN SOLDIERS FIRST.
YEAH...
!

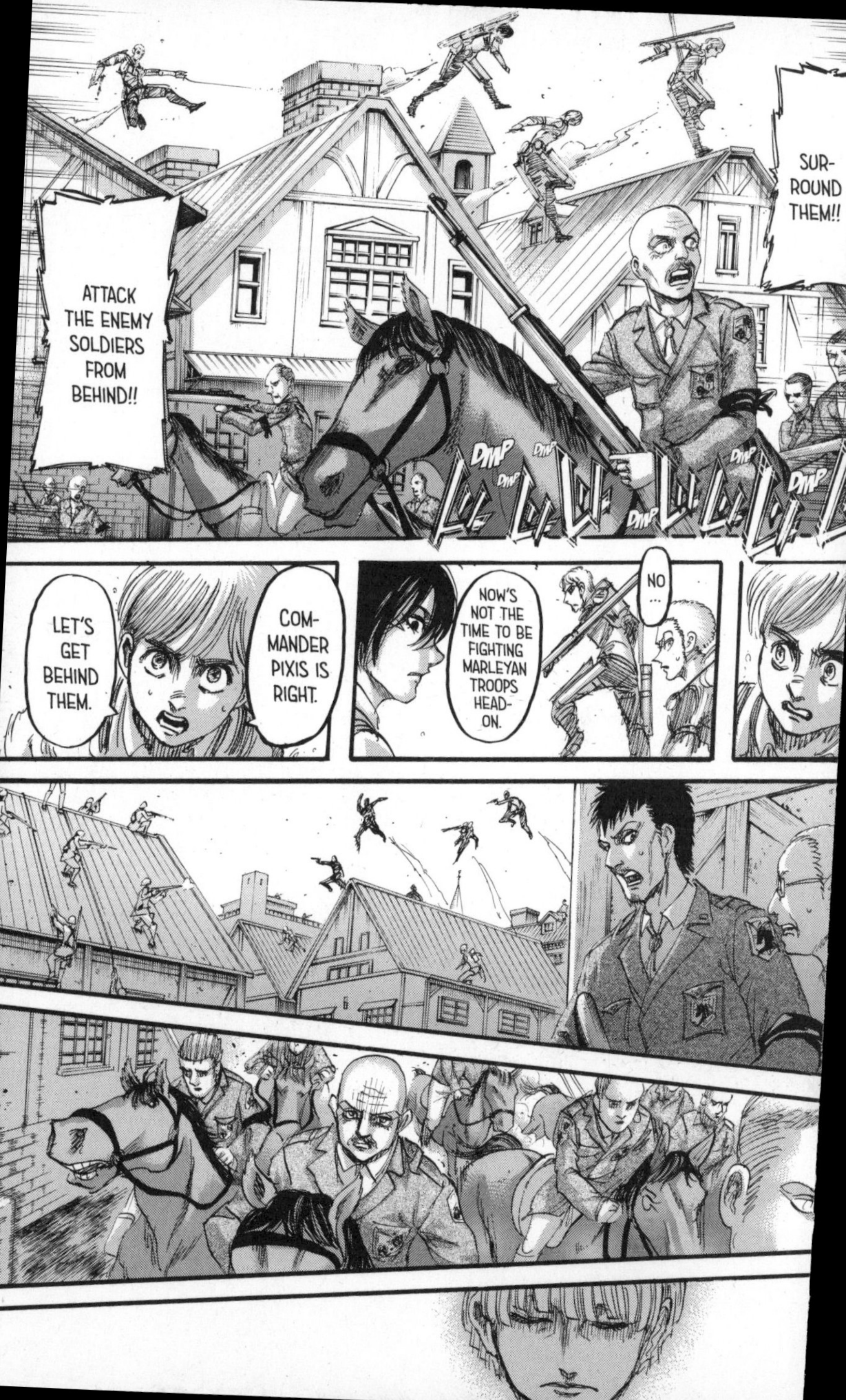
SUR-
ROUND
THEM!!
ATTACK
THE ENEMY
SOLDIERS
FROM
BEHIND!!
DMP DMP DMP DMP DMP DMP
NO
...
NOW'S
NOT THE
TIME TO BE
FIGHTING
MARLEYAN
TROOPS
HEAD-
ON.
COM-
MANDER
PIXIS IS
RIGHT.
LET'S
GET
BEHIND
THEM.

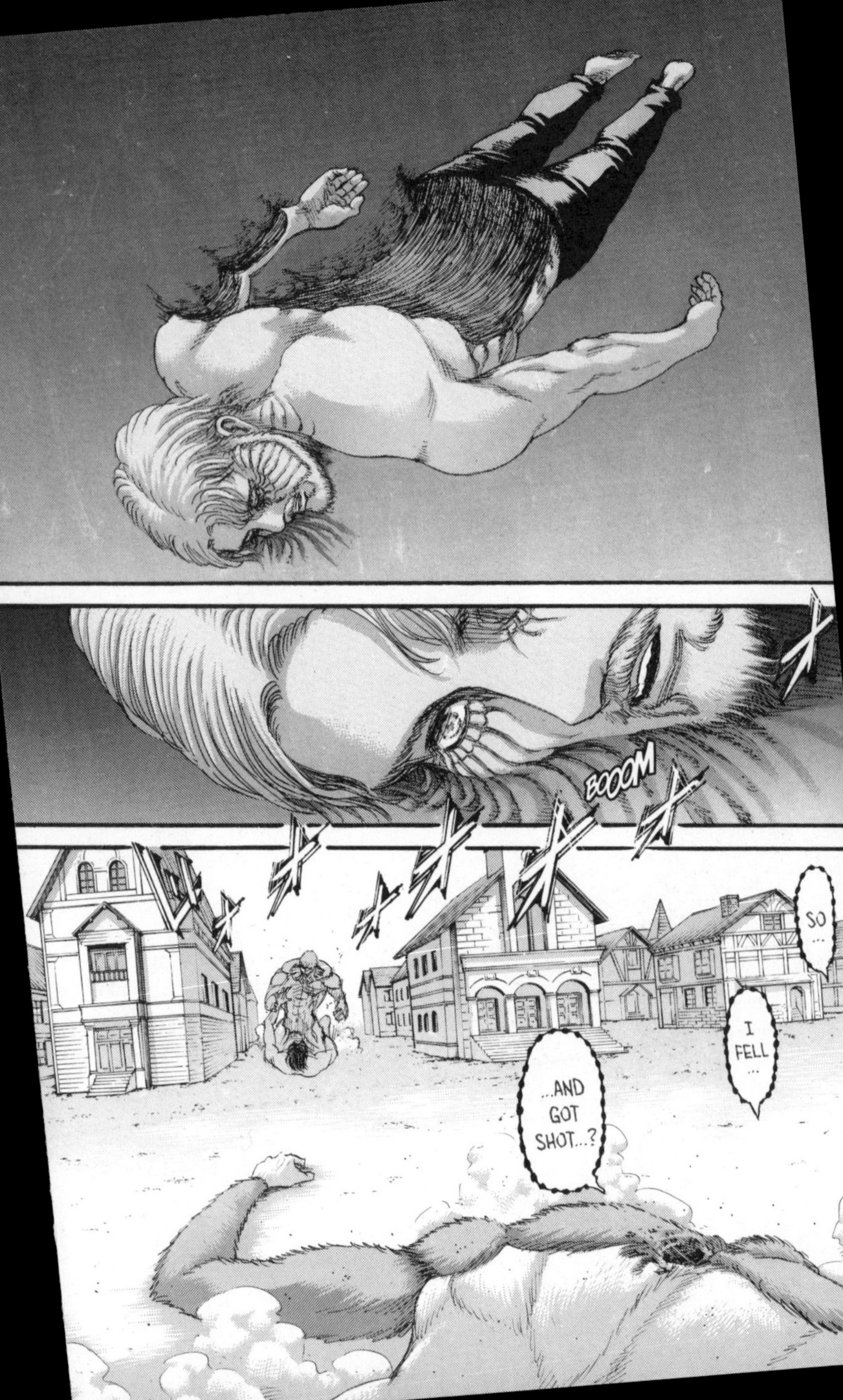
BOOOM
SO...
I FELL...
...AND GOT SHOT...?

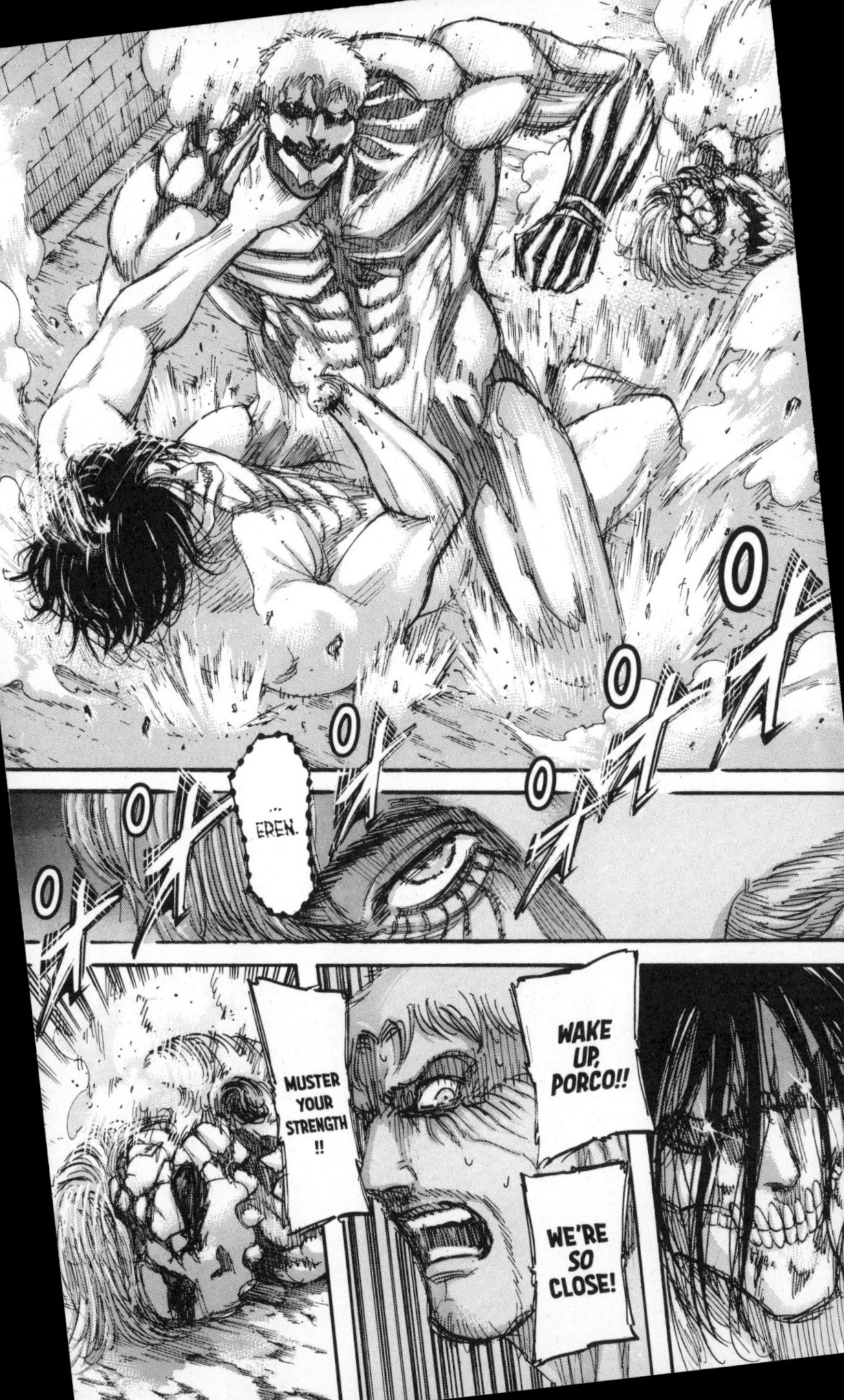
... EREN.
WAKE UP, PORCO!!
WE'RE SO CLOSE!
MUSTER YOUR STRENGTH !!

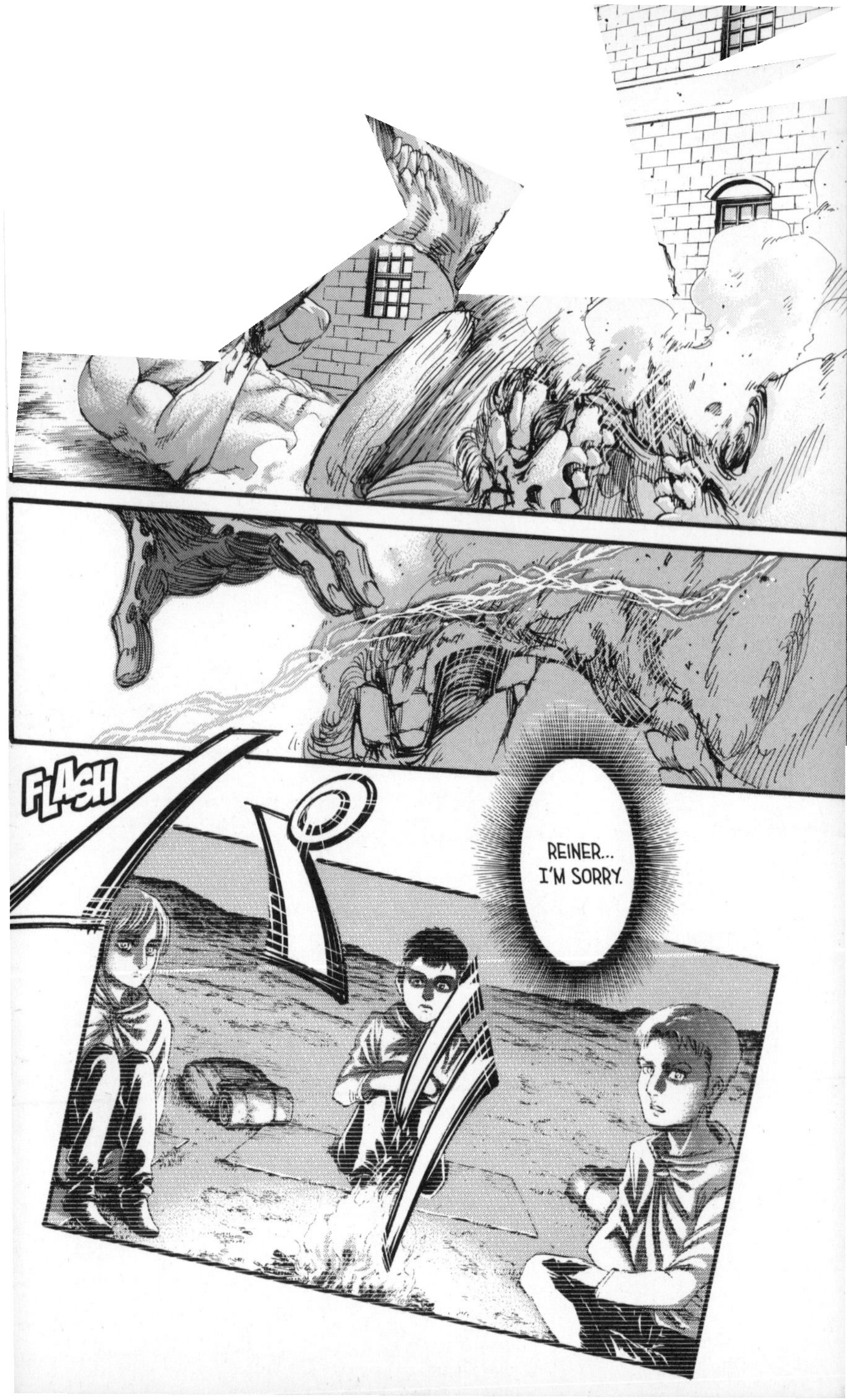
FLASH
REINER... I'M SORRY.

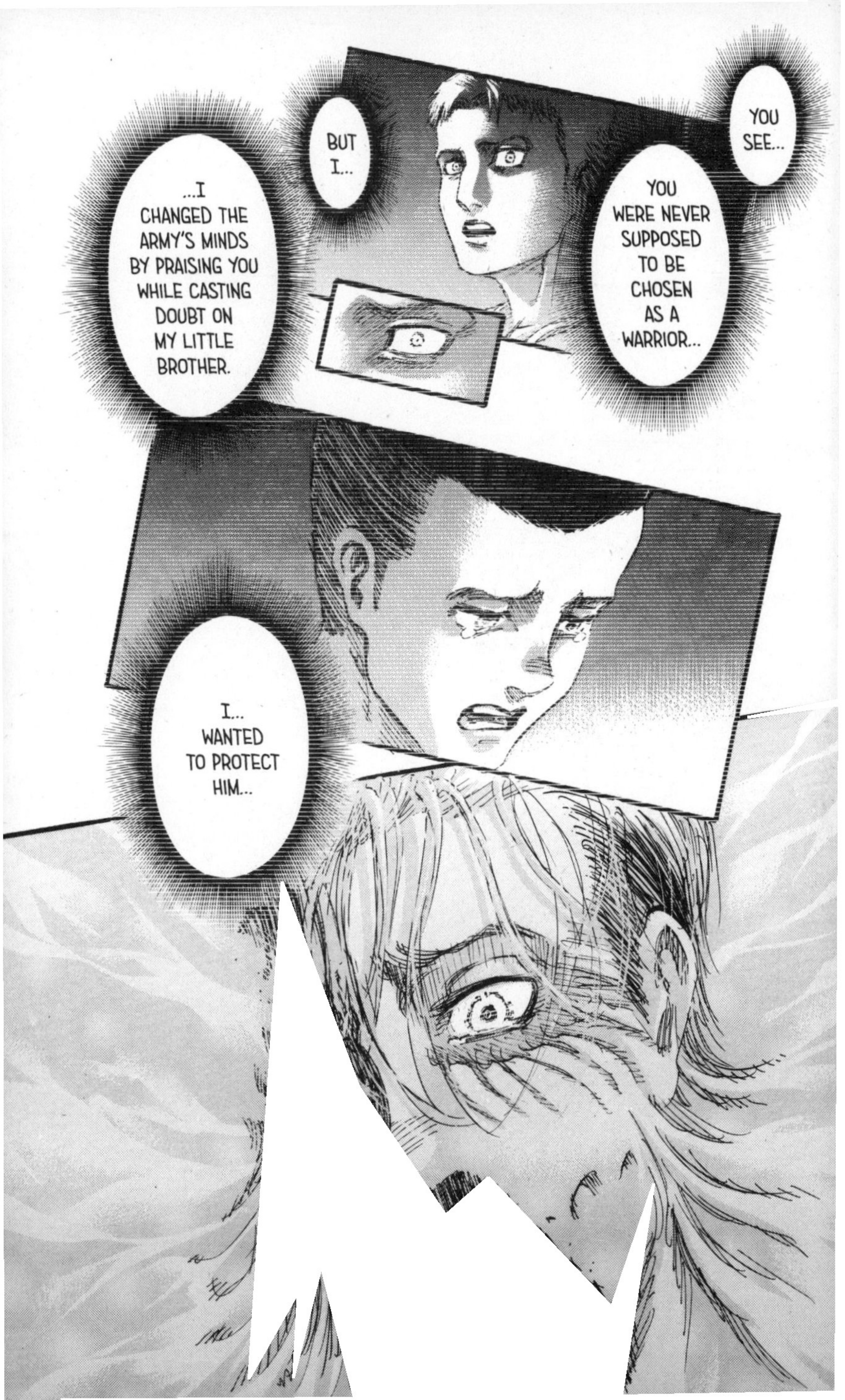
YOU SEE...
YOU WERE NEVER SUPPOSED TO BE CHOSEN AS A WARRIOR...
BUT I...
...I CHANGED THE ARMY'S MINDS BY PRAISING YOU WHILE CASTING DOUBT ON MY LITTLE BROTHER.
I... WANTED TO PROTECT HIM...

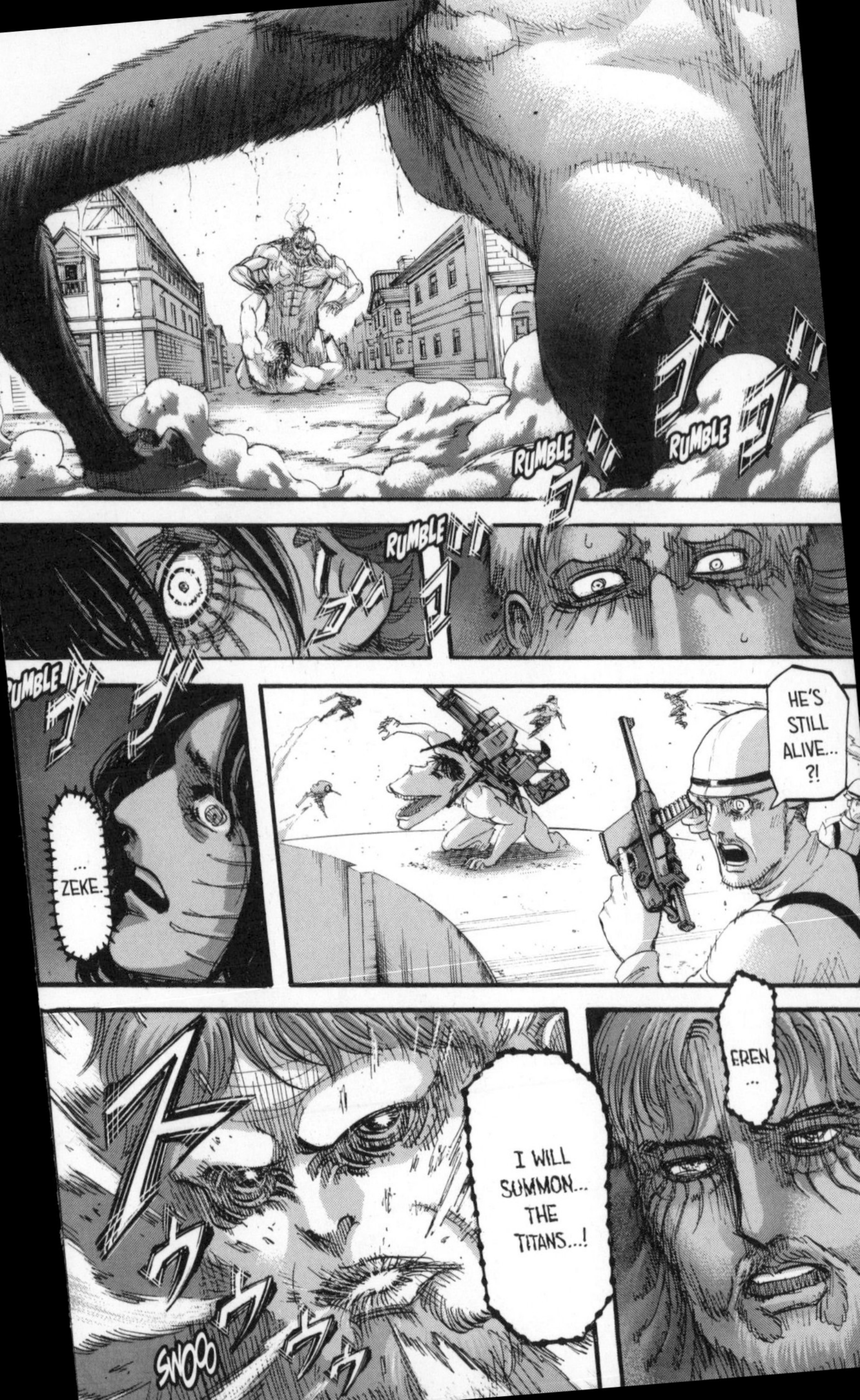
RUMBLE
RUMBLE
RUMBLE
HE'S STILL ALIVE... ?!
RUMBLE
... ZEKE.
EREN ...
I WILL SUMMON... THE TITANS...!
SWOOO

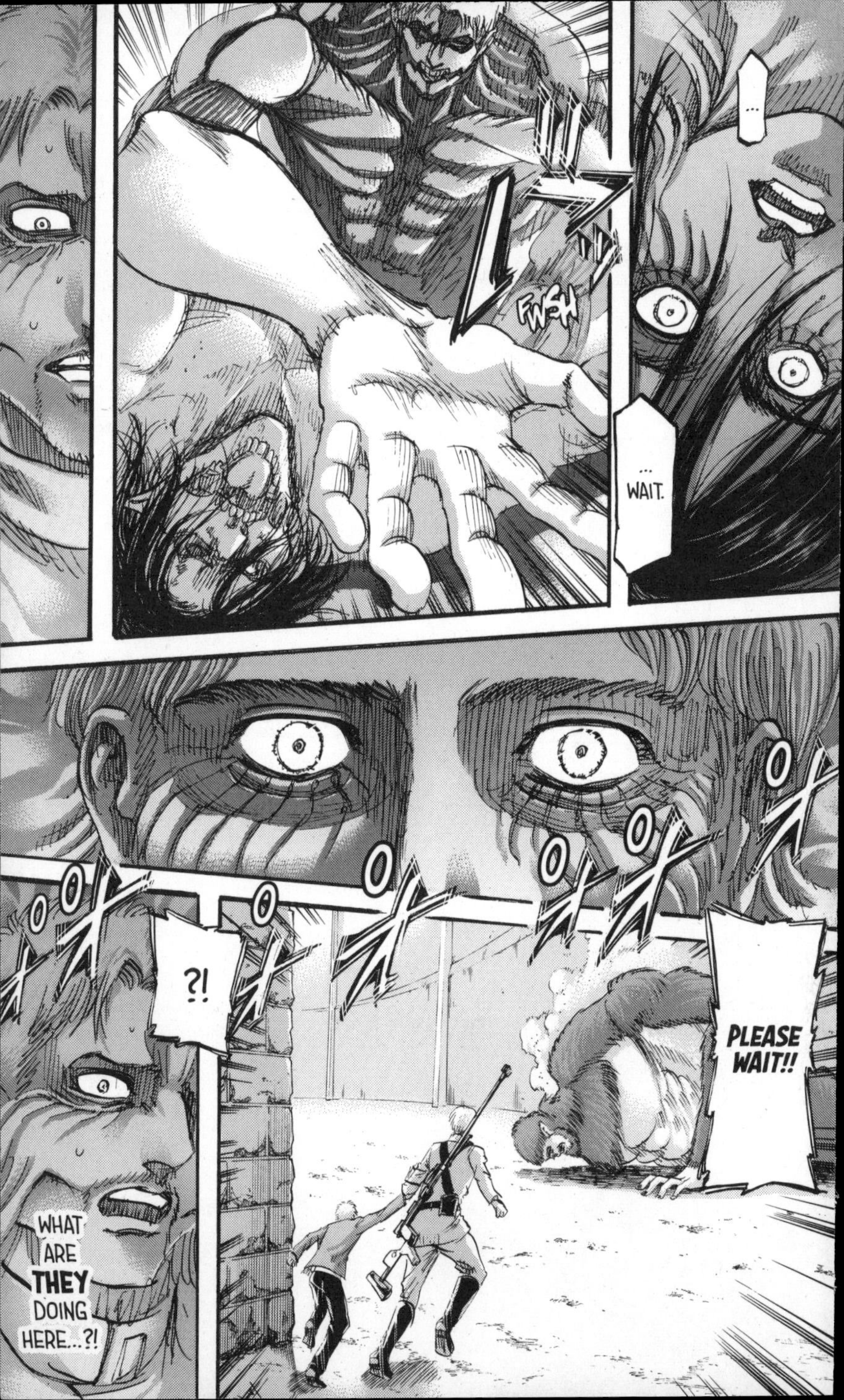

...
... WAIT.
FWSH
PLEASE WAIT!!
?!
WHAT ARE THEY DOING HERE...?!

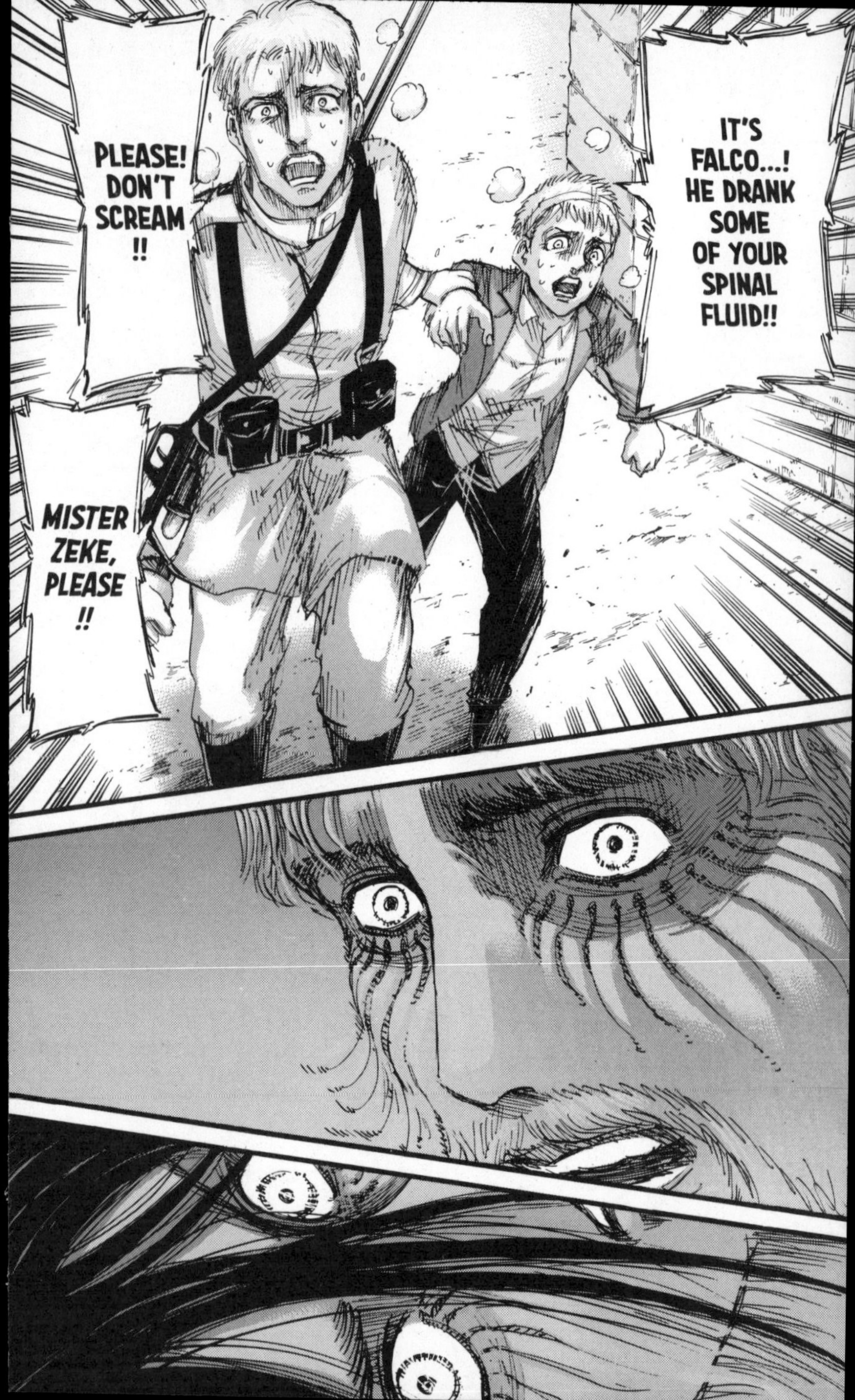
IT'S FALCO...! HE DRANK SOME OF YOUR SPINAL FLUID!!
PLEASE! DON'T SCREAM !!
MISTER ZEKE, PLEASE !!

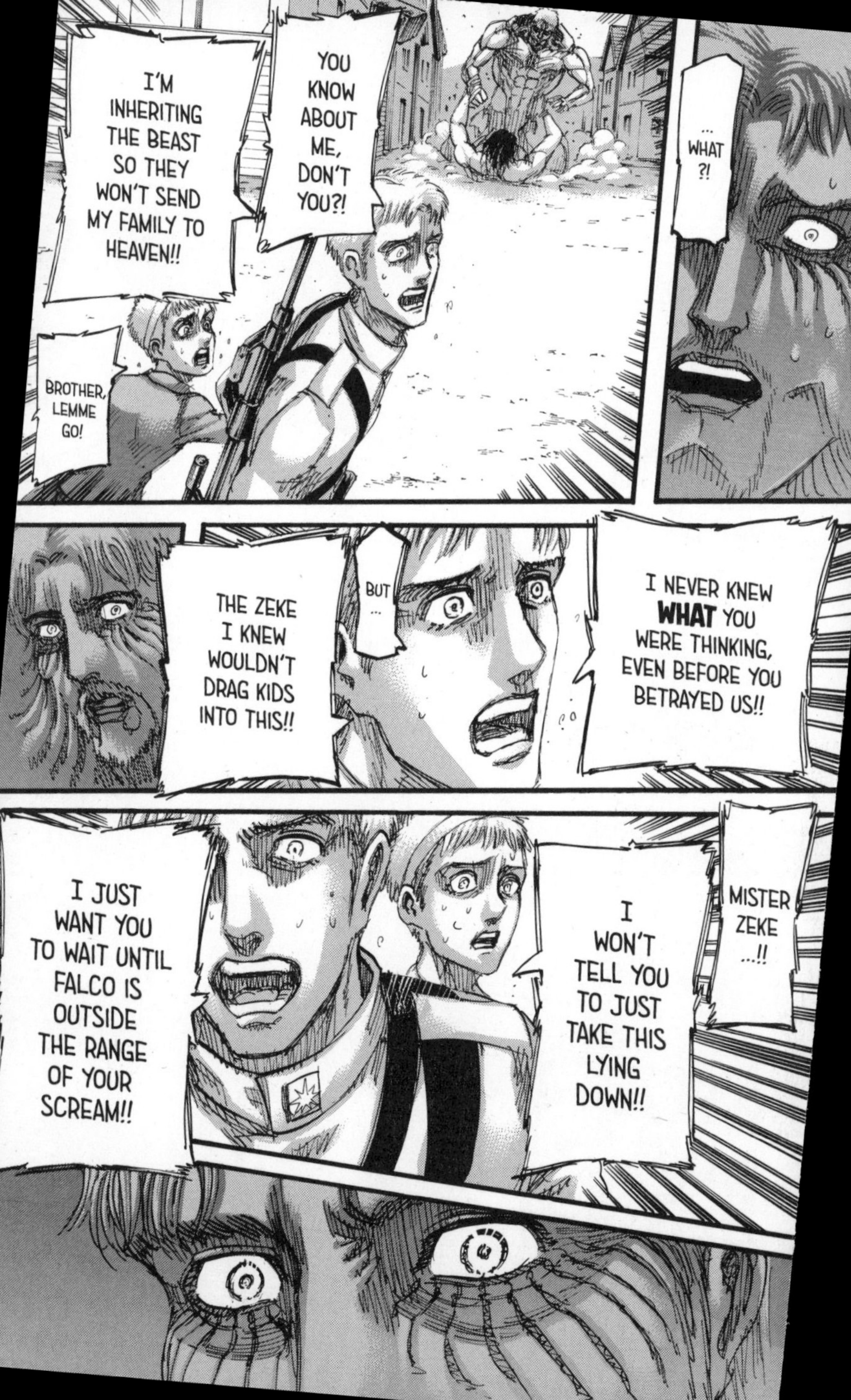
...WHAT?!
YOU KNOW ABOUT ME, DON'T YOU?!
I'M INHERITING THE BEAST SO THEY WON'T SEND MY FAMILY TO HEAVEN!!
BROTHER, LEMME GO!
I NEVER KNEW **WHAT** YOU WERE THINKING, EVEN BEFORE YOU BETRAYED US!!
BUT ...
THE ZEKE I KNEW WOULDN'T DRAG KIDS INTO THIS!!
MISTER ZEKE ...!!
I WON'T TELL YOU TO JUST TAKE THIS LYING DOWN!!
I JUST WANT YOU TO WAIT UNTIL FALCO IS OUTSIDE THE RANGE OF YOUR SCREAM!!

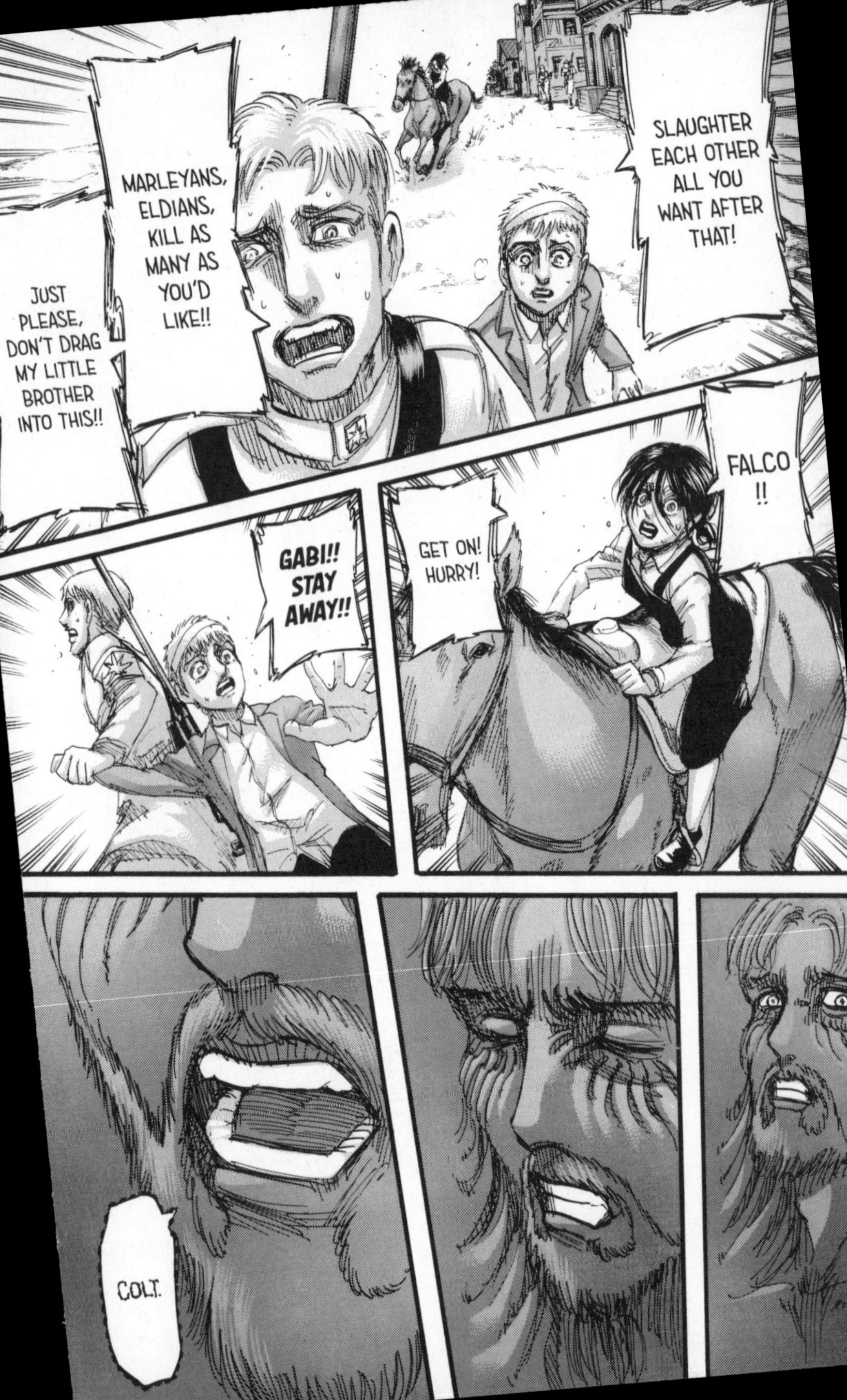
SLAUGHTER EACH OTHER ALL YOU WANT AFTER THAT!
MARLEYANS, ELDIANS, KILL AS MANY AS YOU'D LIKE!!
JUST PLEASE, DON'T DRAG MY LITTLE BROTHER INTO THIS!!
FALCO !!
GET ON! HURRY!
GABI!! STAY AWAY!!
COLT.

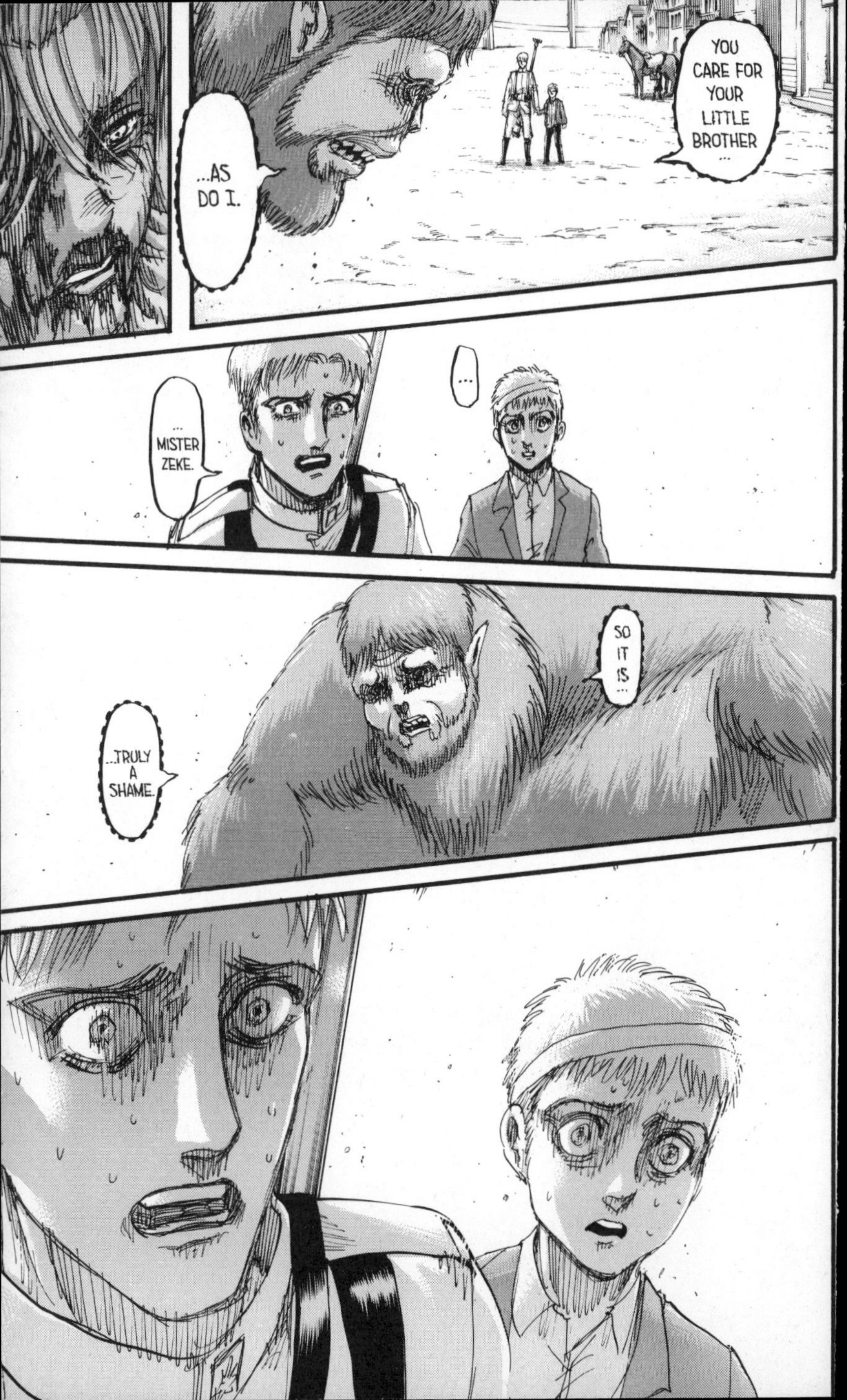
YOU CARE FOR YOUR LITTLE BROTHER ...
...AS DO I.
...
... MISTER ZEKE.
SO IT IS ...
...TRULY A SHAME.

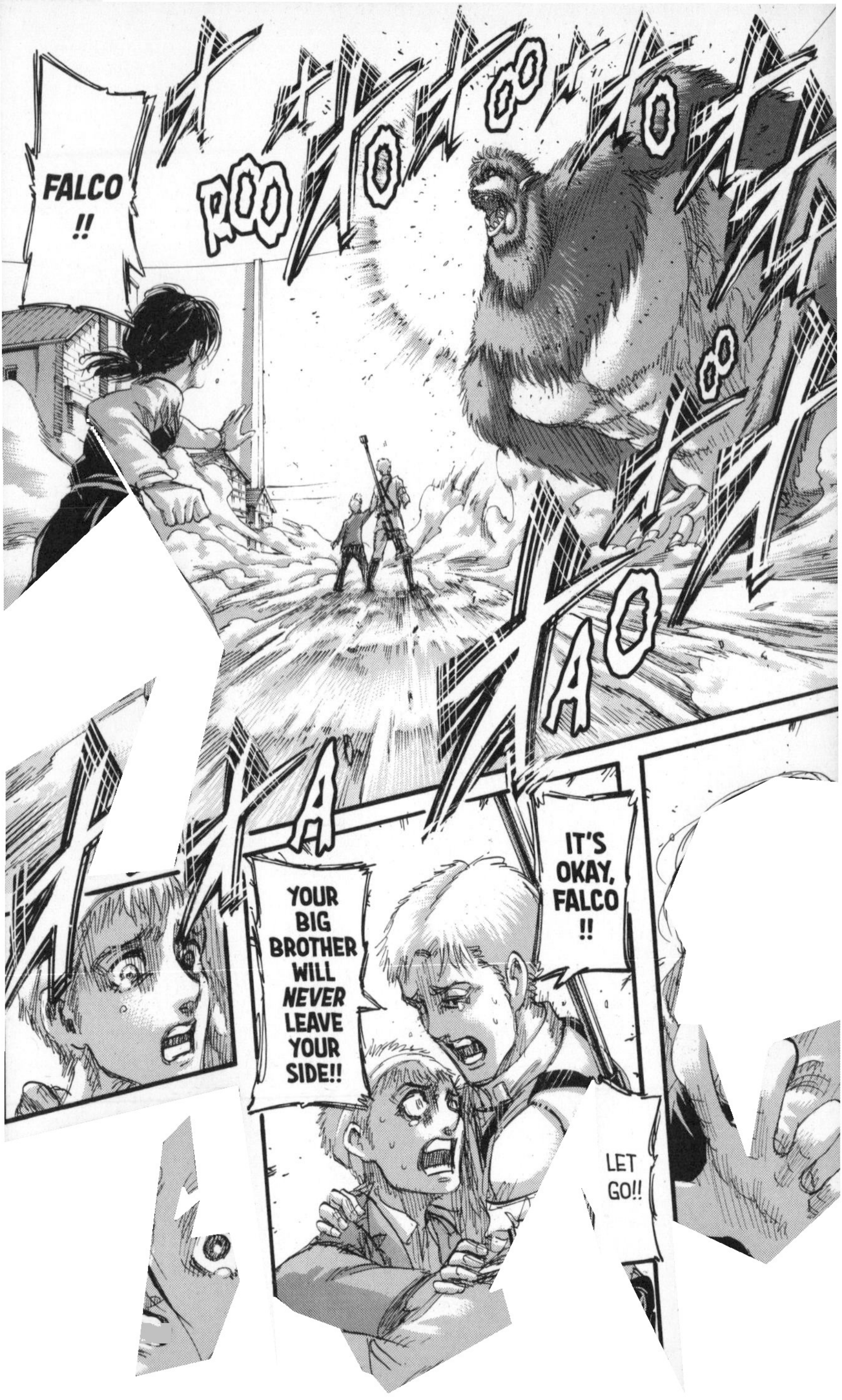
ROOOOOOOAAA
FALCO!!
IT'S OKAY, FALCO!!
YOUR BIG BROTHER WILL NEVER LEAVE YOUR SIDE!!
LET GO!!

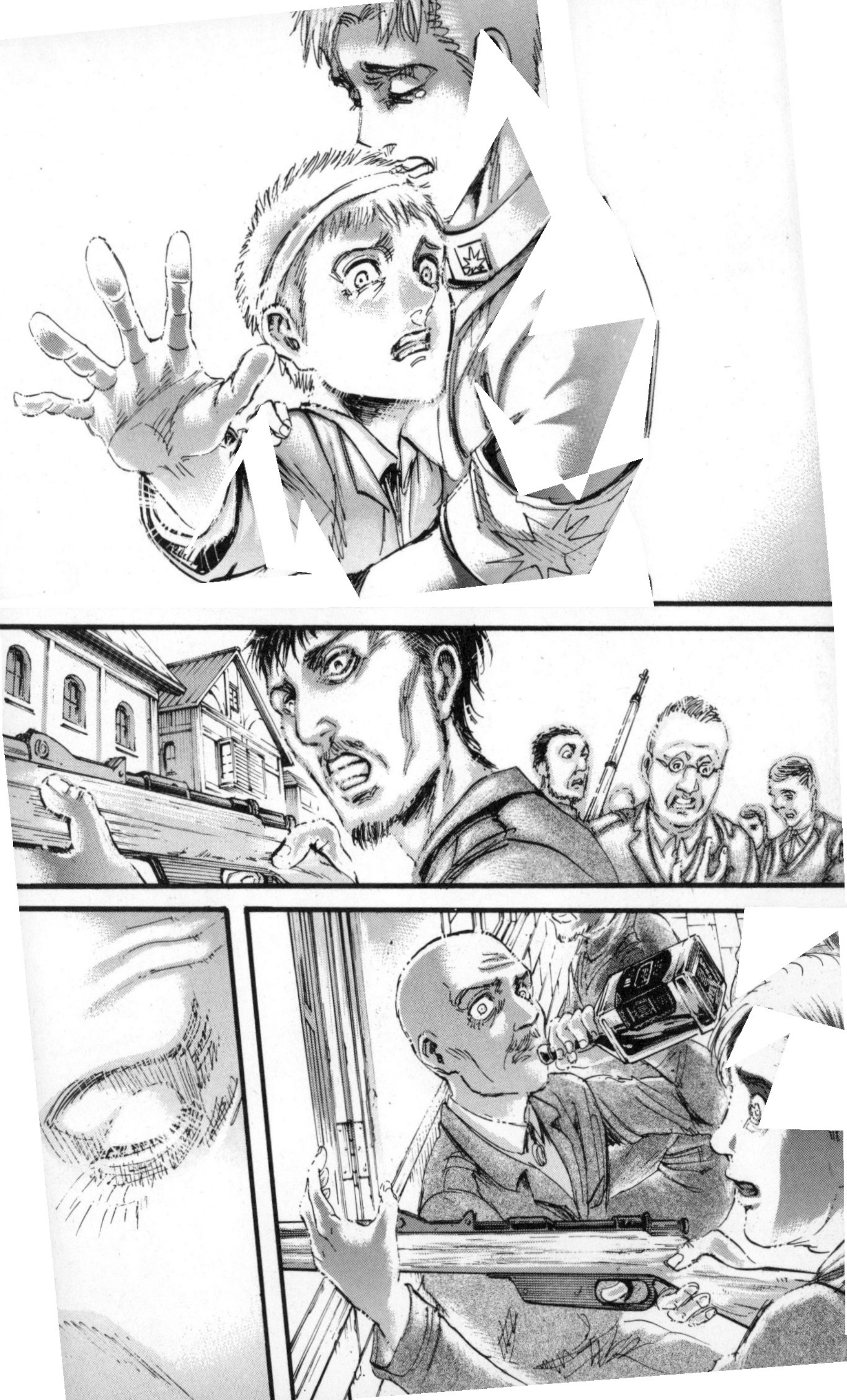

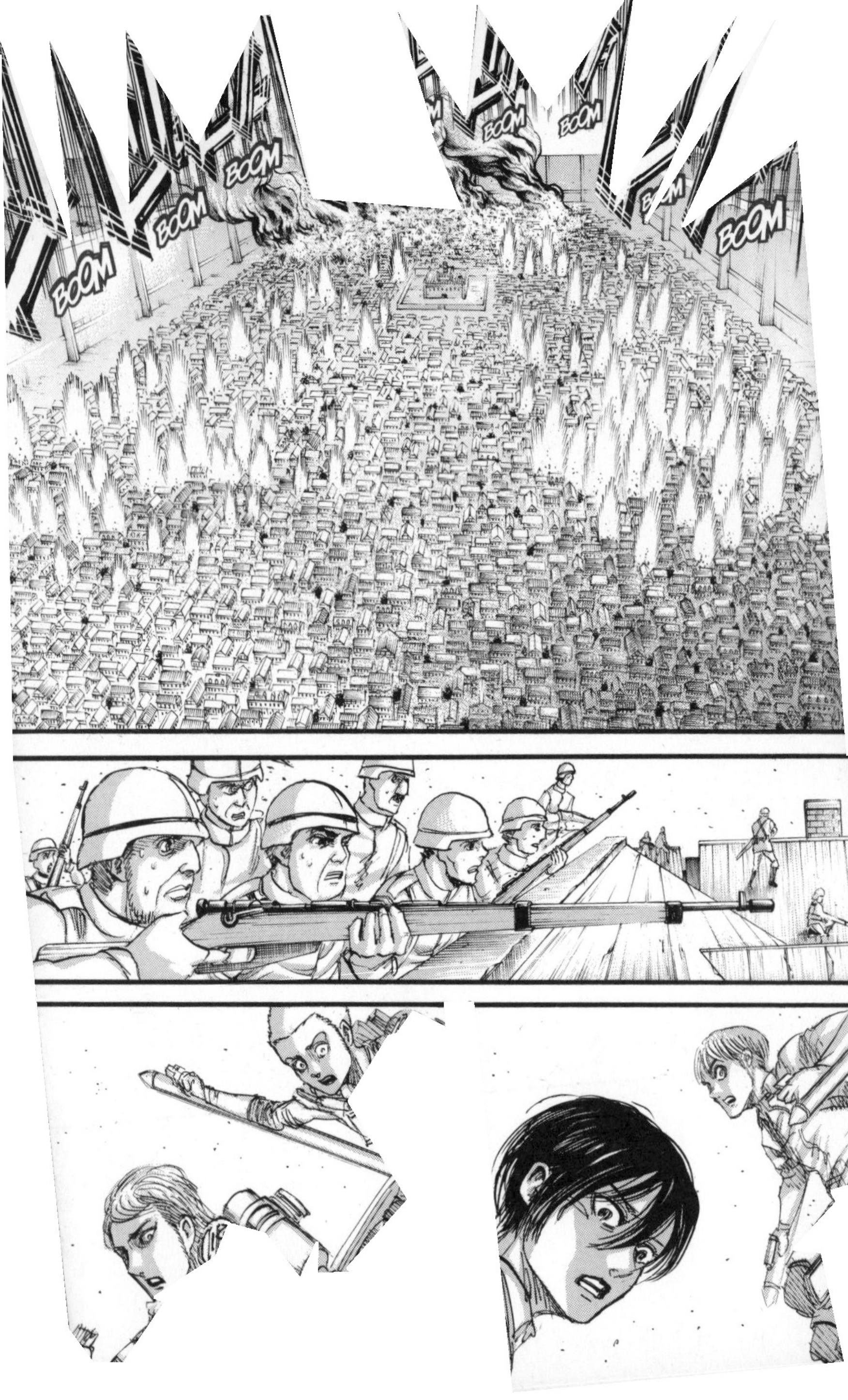
BOOM
BOOM
BOOM
BOOM
BOOM
BOOM
BOOM

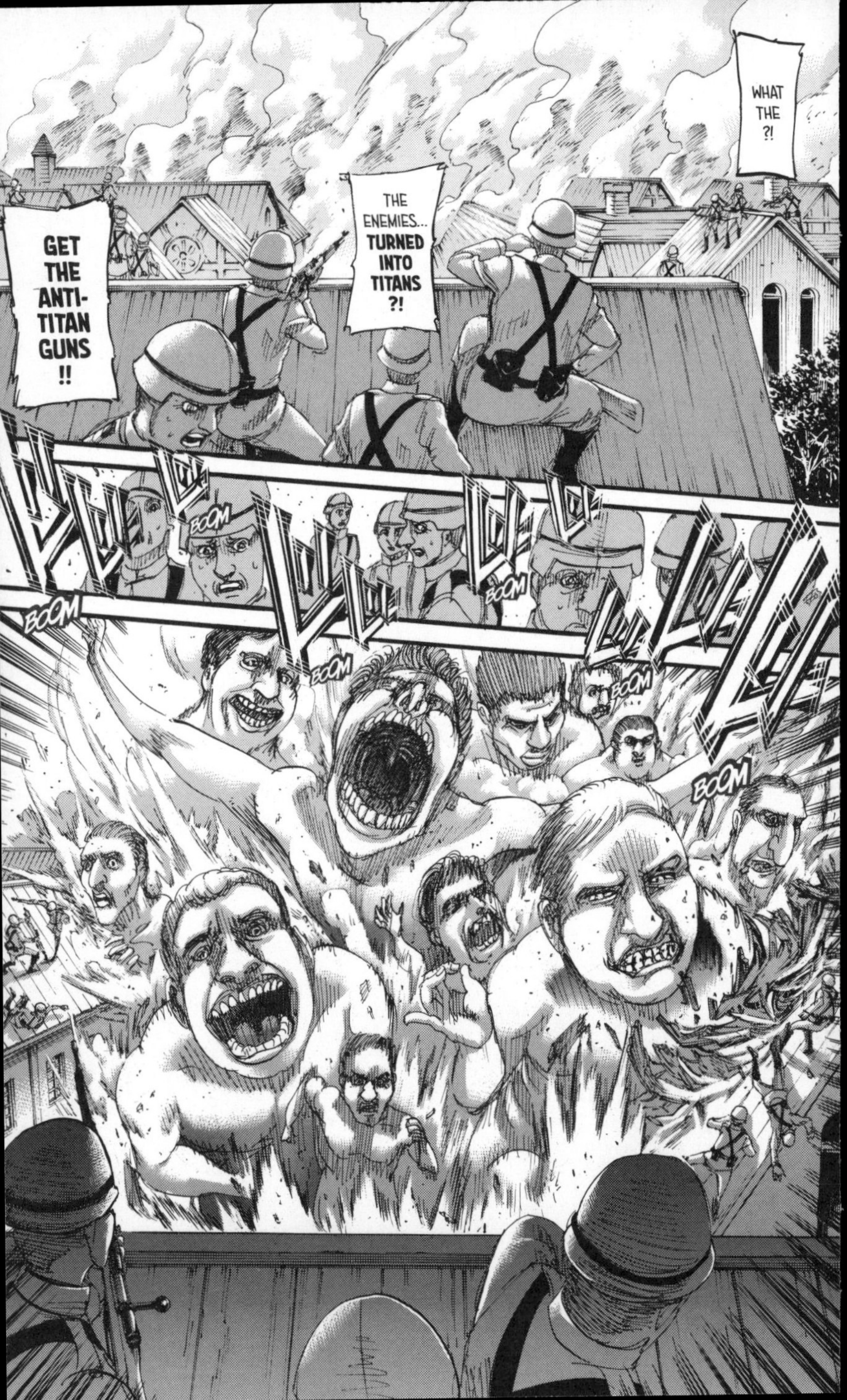
WHAT THE ?!
THE ENEMIES... TURNED INTO TITANS ?!
GET THE ANTI-TITAN GUNS !!
BOOM
BOOM
BOOM
BOOM
BOOM
BOOM

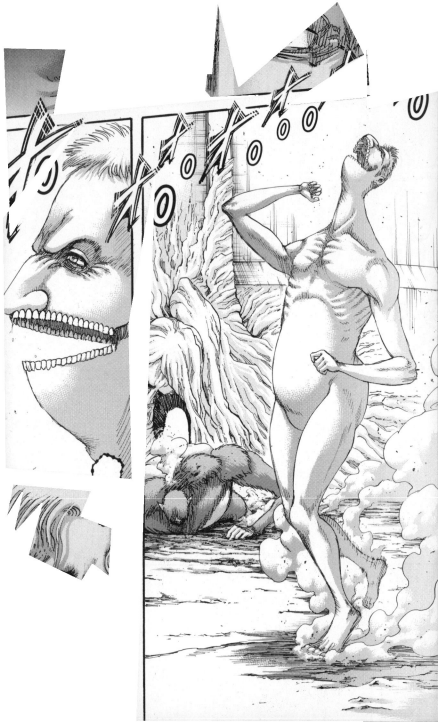

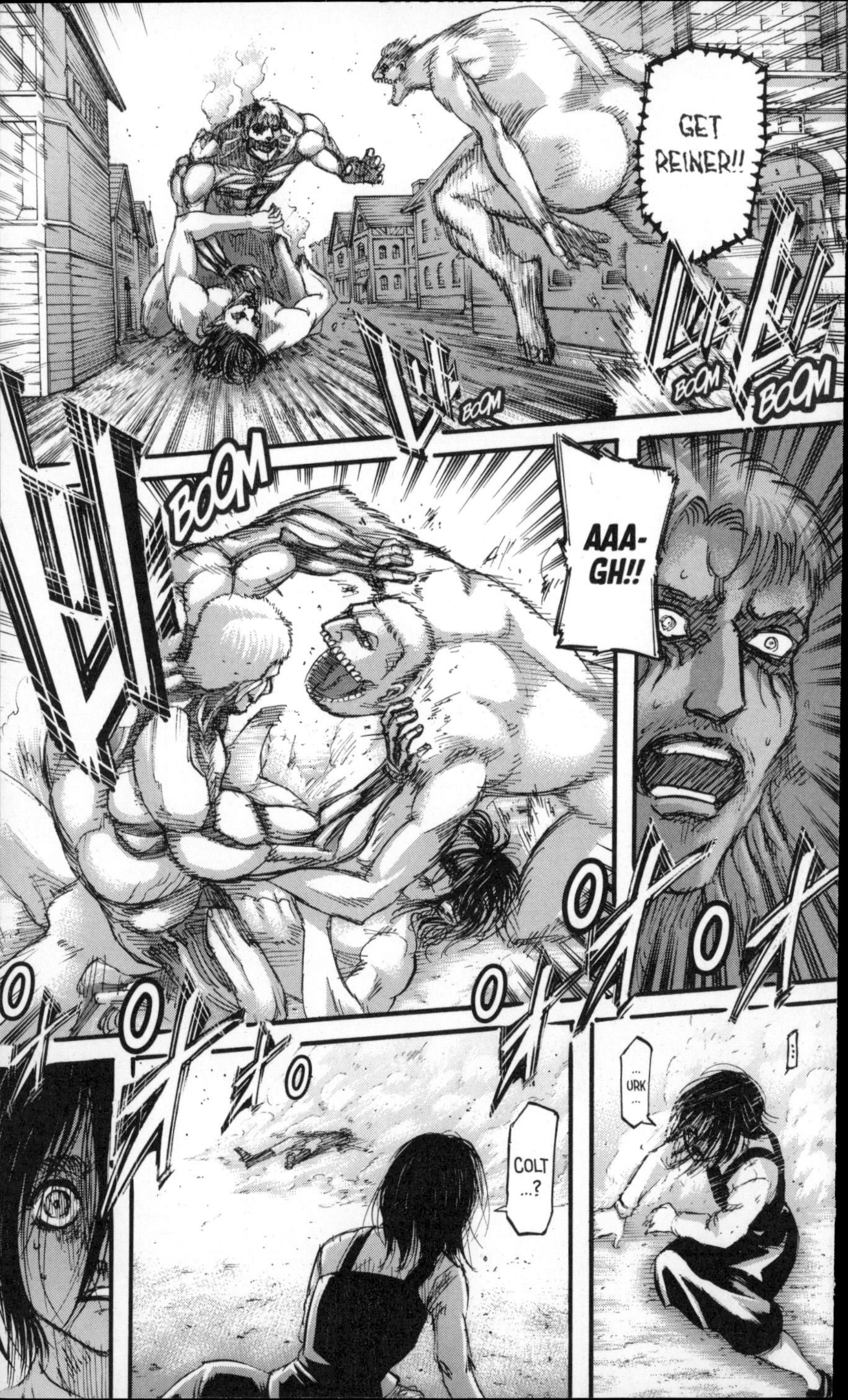
GET REINER!!
BOOM
BOOM
BOOM
BOOM
AAA-GH!!
BOOM
...URK...
!
COLT ...?

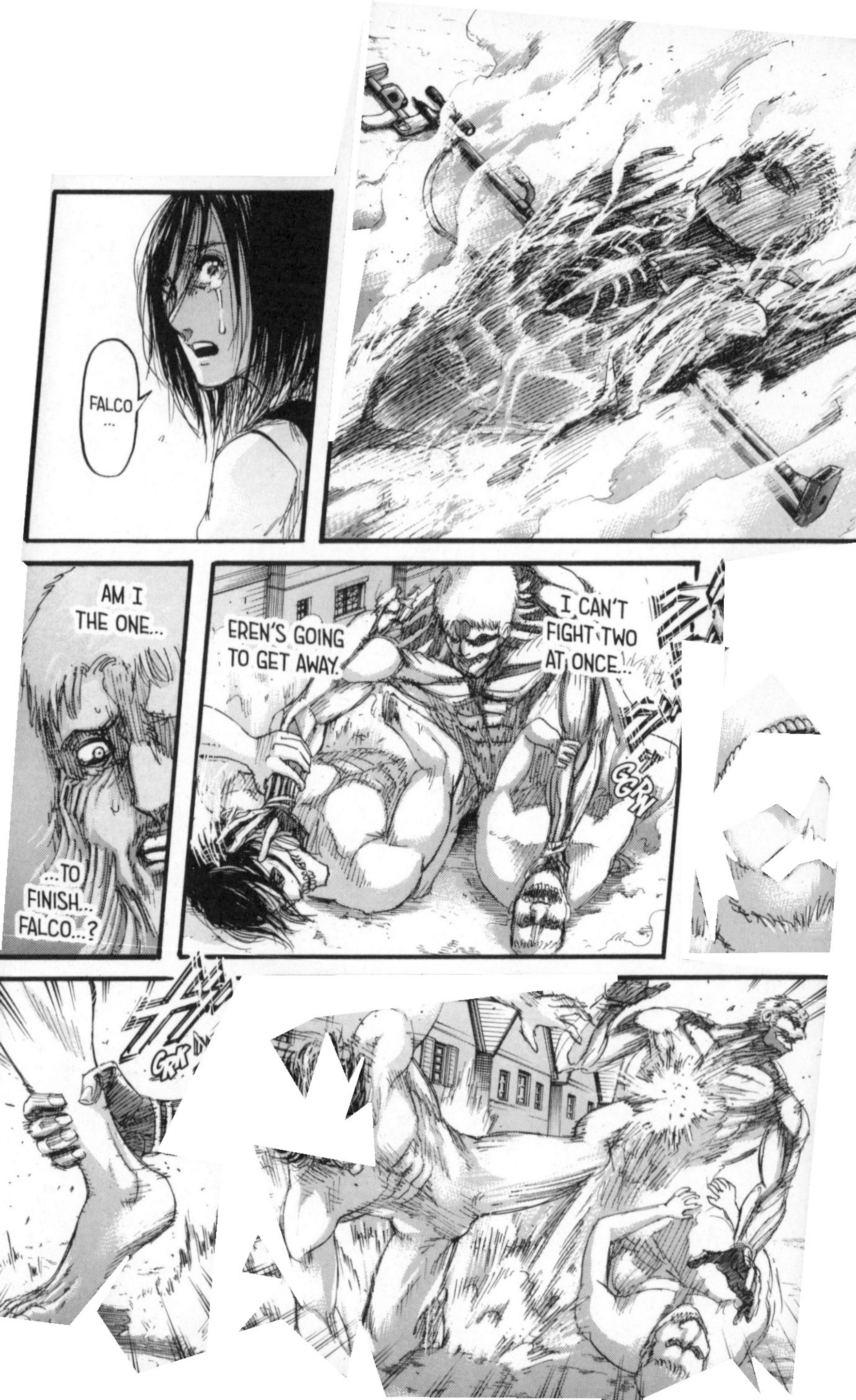
FALCO...
I CAN'T FIGHT TWO AT ONCE...
EREN'S GOING TO GET AWAY.
AM I THE ONE...
...TO FINISH... FALCO...?

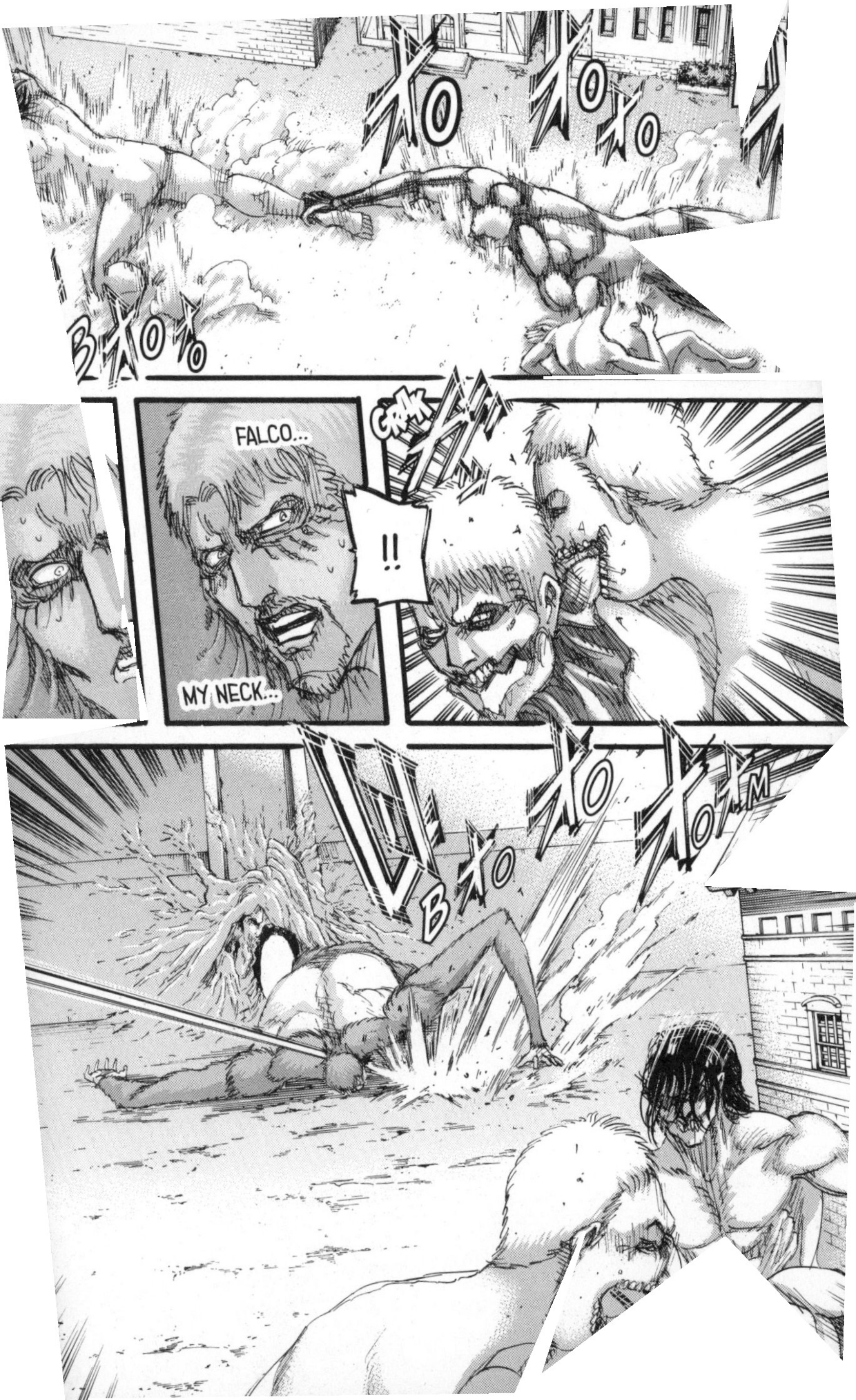
GRAK
!!
FALCO...
MY NECK...

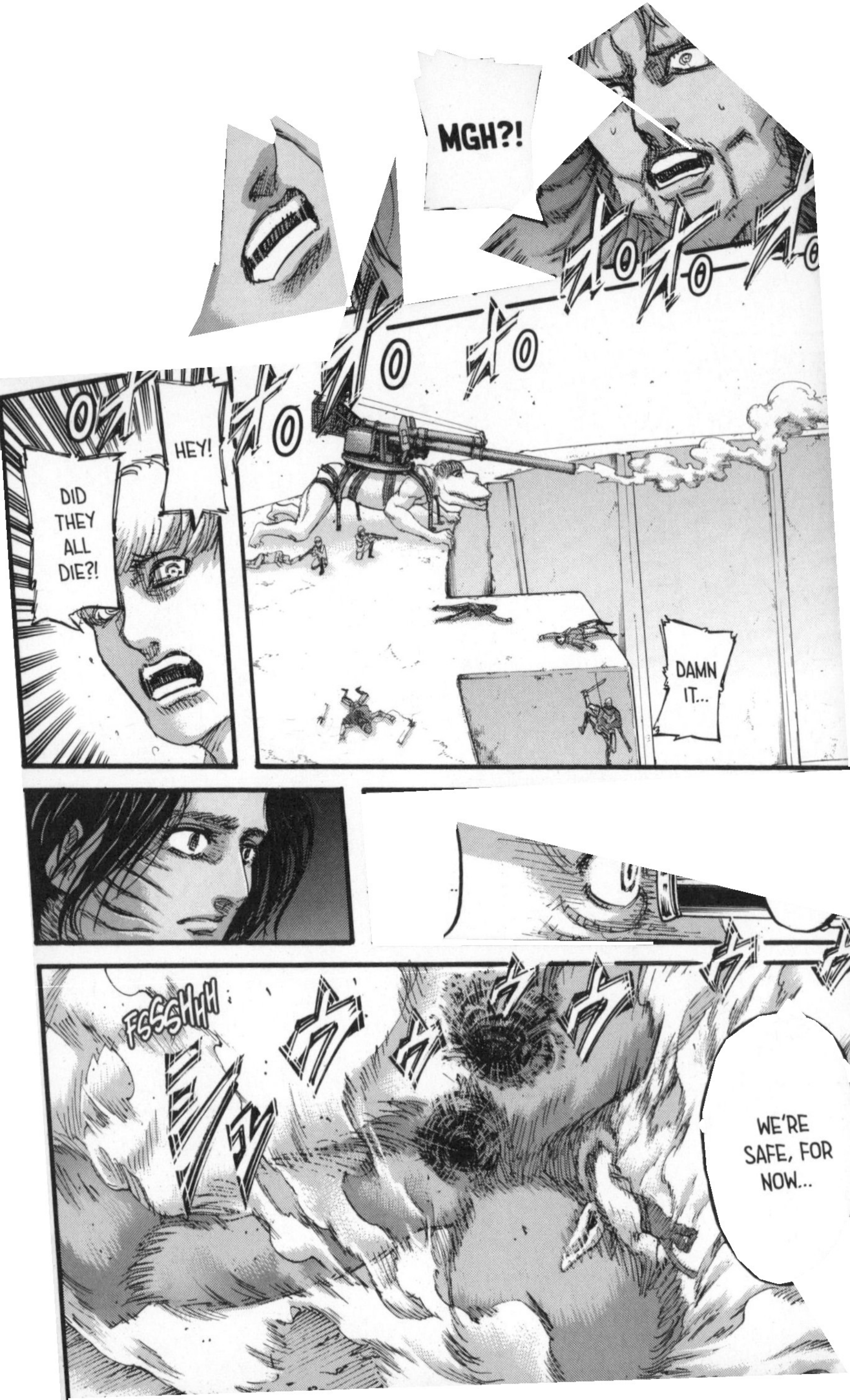
MGH?!
DAMN IT...
HEY!
DID THEY ALL DIE?!
FSSSHHH
WE'RE SAFE, FOR NOW...

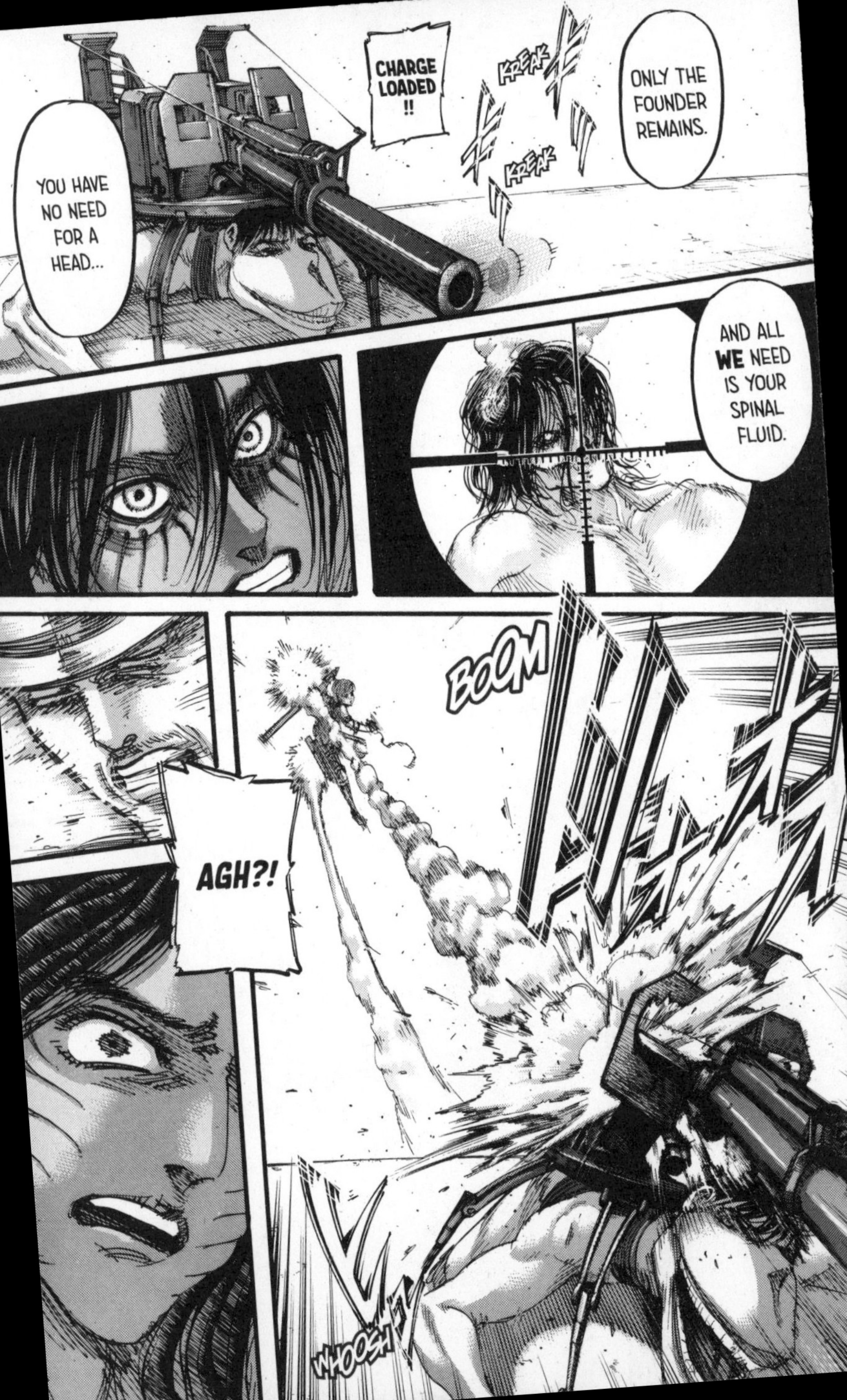
ONLY THE FOUNDER REMAINS.
KREAK
KREAK
CHARGE LOADED !!
YOU HAVE NO NEED FOR A HEAD...
AND ALL WE NEED IS YOUR SPINAL FLUID.
BOOM
WHOOSH
AGH?!

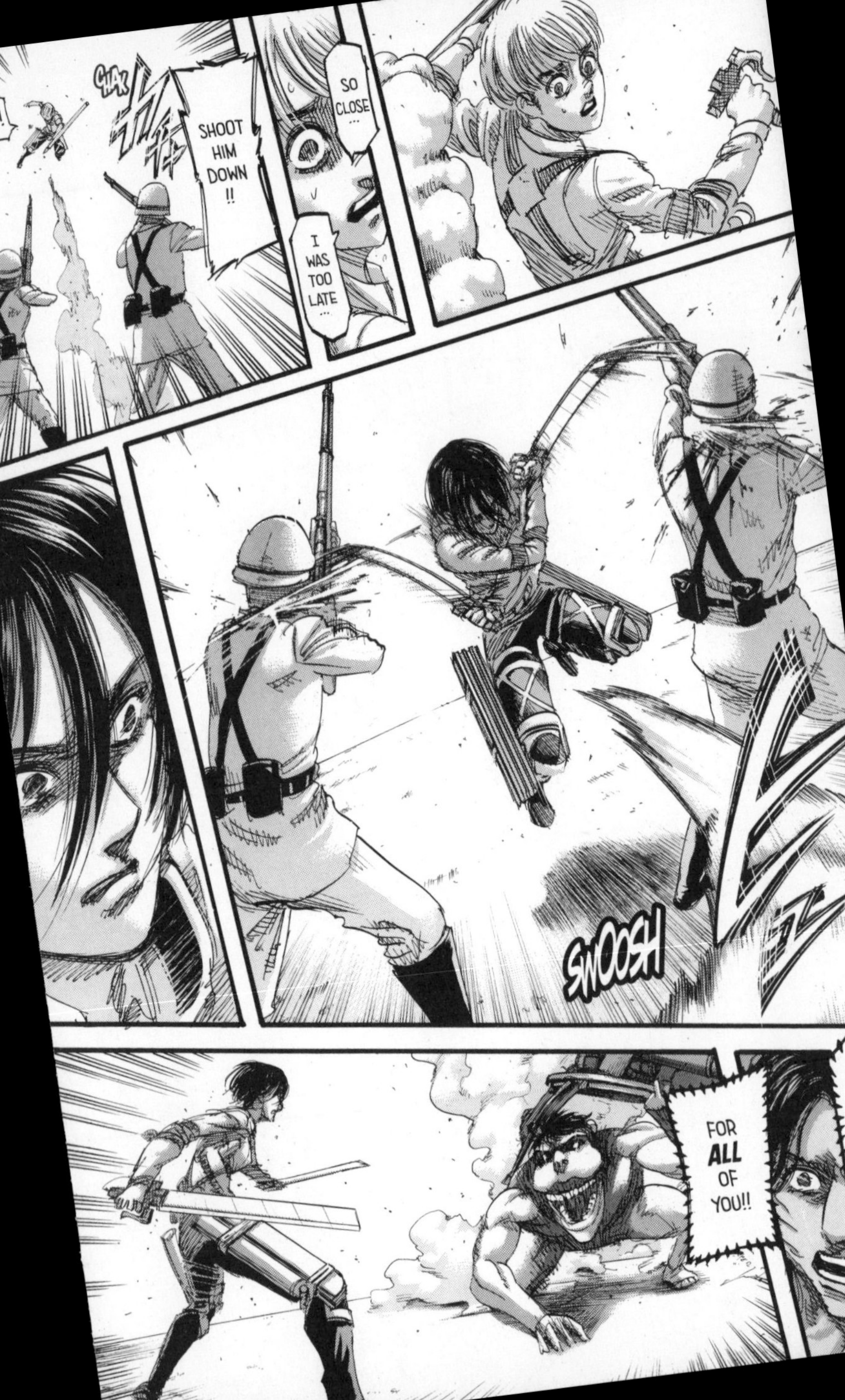
SO CLOSE ...
I WAS TOO LATE ...
SHOOT HIM DOWN !!
CHAK
SWOOSH
FOR ALL OF YOU!!

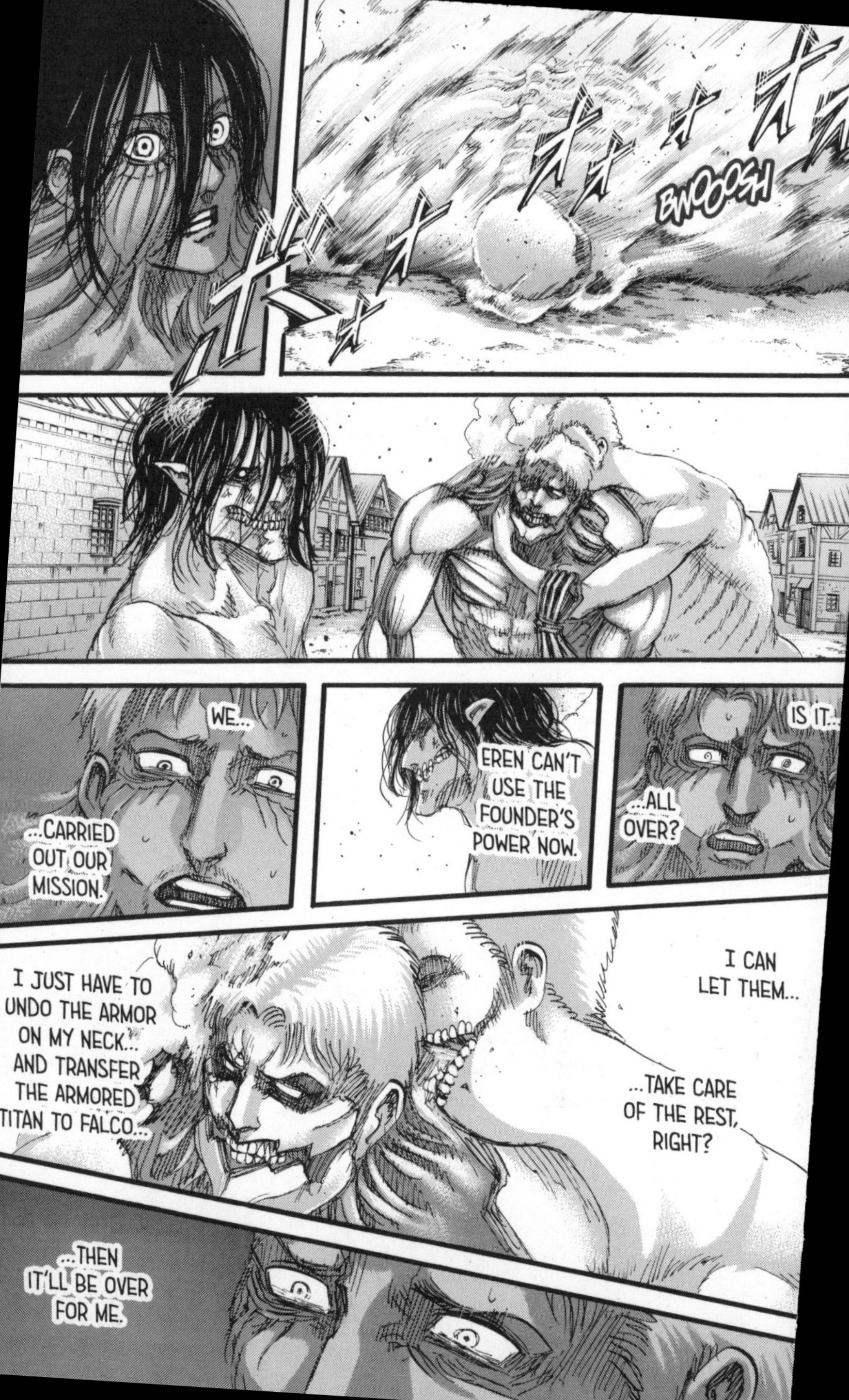
BWOOOSH
IS IT...
...ALL OVER?
EREN CAN'T USE THE FOUNDER'S POWER NOW.
WE...
...CARRIED OUT OUR MISSION.
I CAN LET THEM...
...TAKE CARE OF THE REST, RIGHT?
I JUST HAVE TO UNDO THE ARMOR ON MY NECK... AND TRANSFER THE ARMORED TITAN TO FALCO...
...THEN IT'LL BE OVER FOR ME.

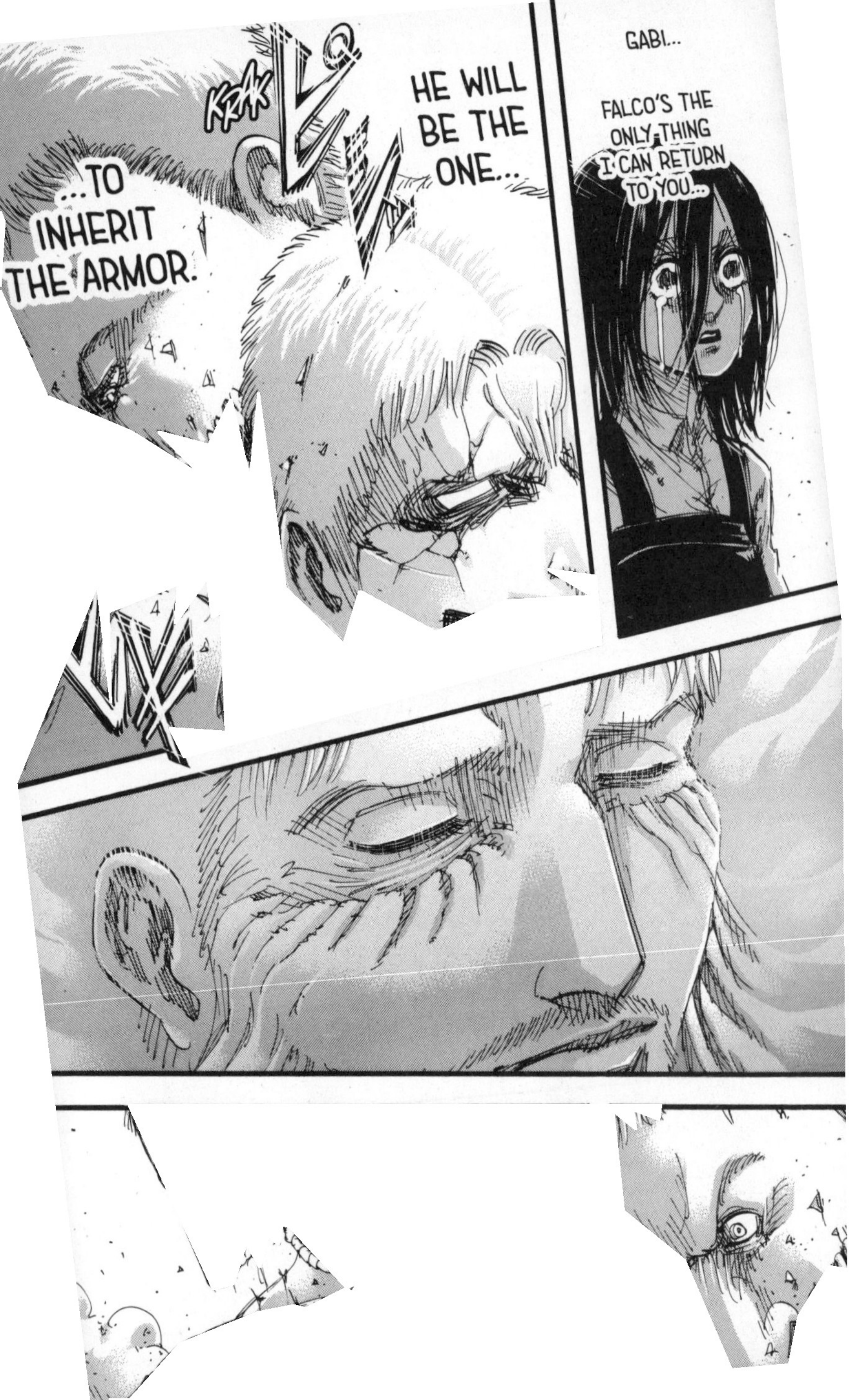
GABI...
FALCO'S THE ONLY THING I CAN RETURN TO YOU...
HE WILL BE THE ONE...
KRAK
...TO INHERIT THE ARMOR.

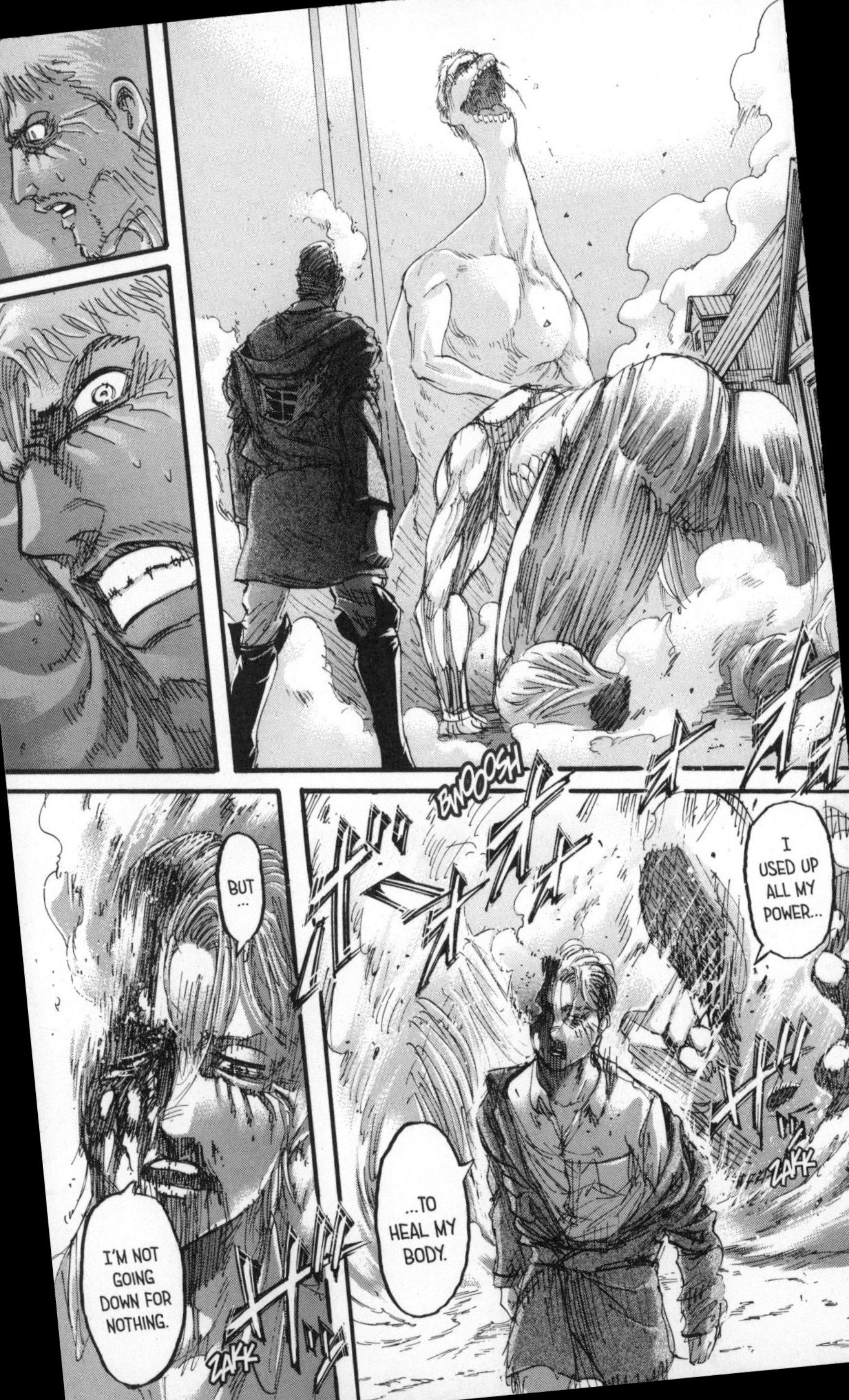
BWOOOSH
I USED UP ALL MY POWER...
...TO HEAL MY BODY.
ZAKK
BUT ...
I'M NOT GOING DOWN FOR NOTHING.
ZAKK

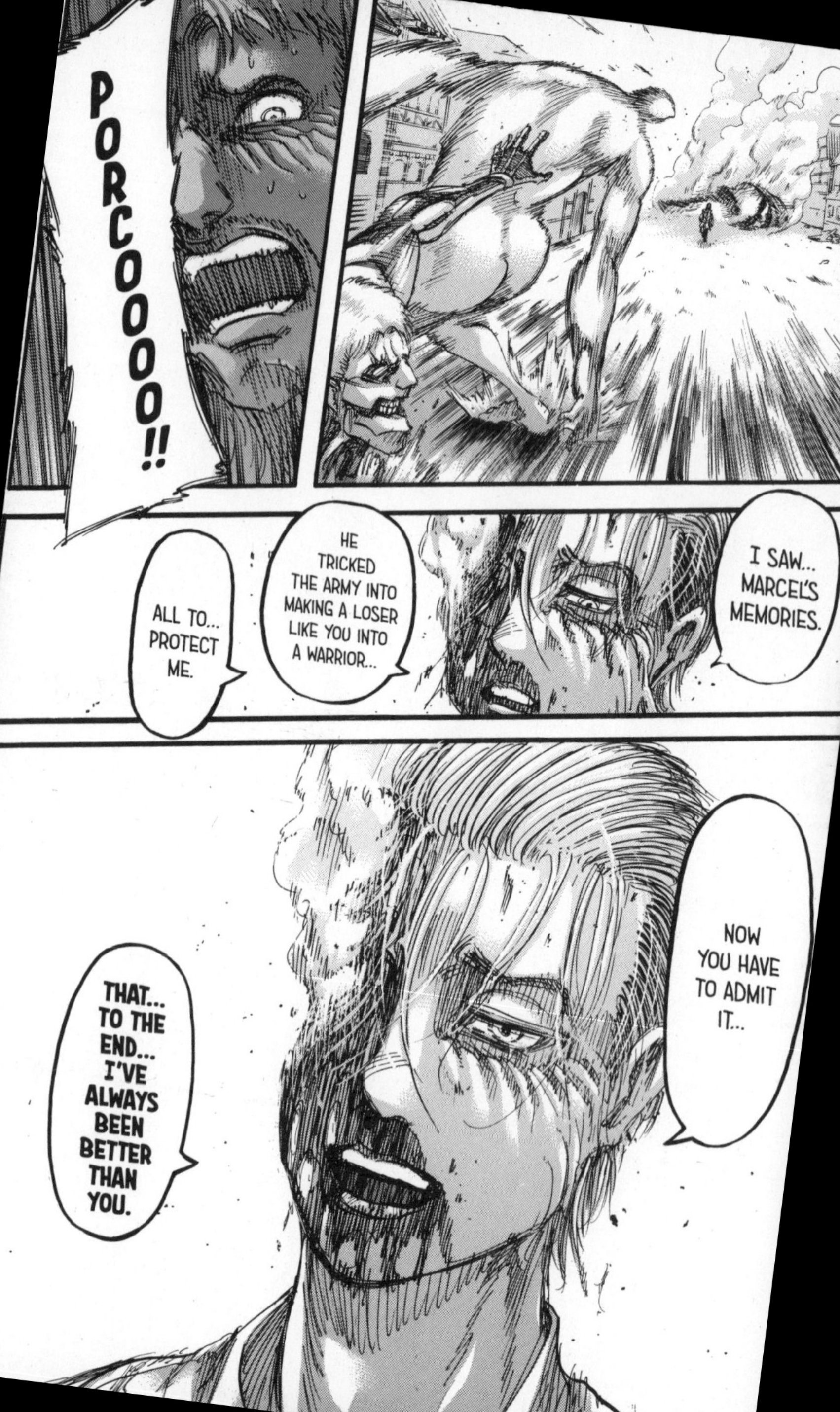
PORCOOOOO!!
I SAW... MARCEL'S MEMORIES.
HE TRICKED THE ARMY INTO MAKING A LOSER LIKE YOU INTO A WARRIOR...
ALL TO... PROTECT ME.
NOW YOU HAVE TO ADMIT IT...
THAT... TO THE END... I'VE ALWAYS BEEN BETTER THAN YOU.

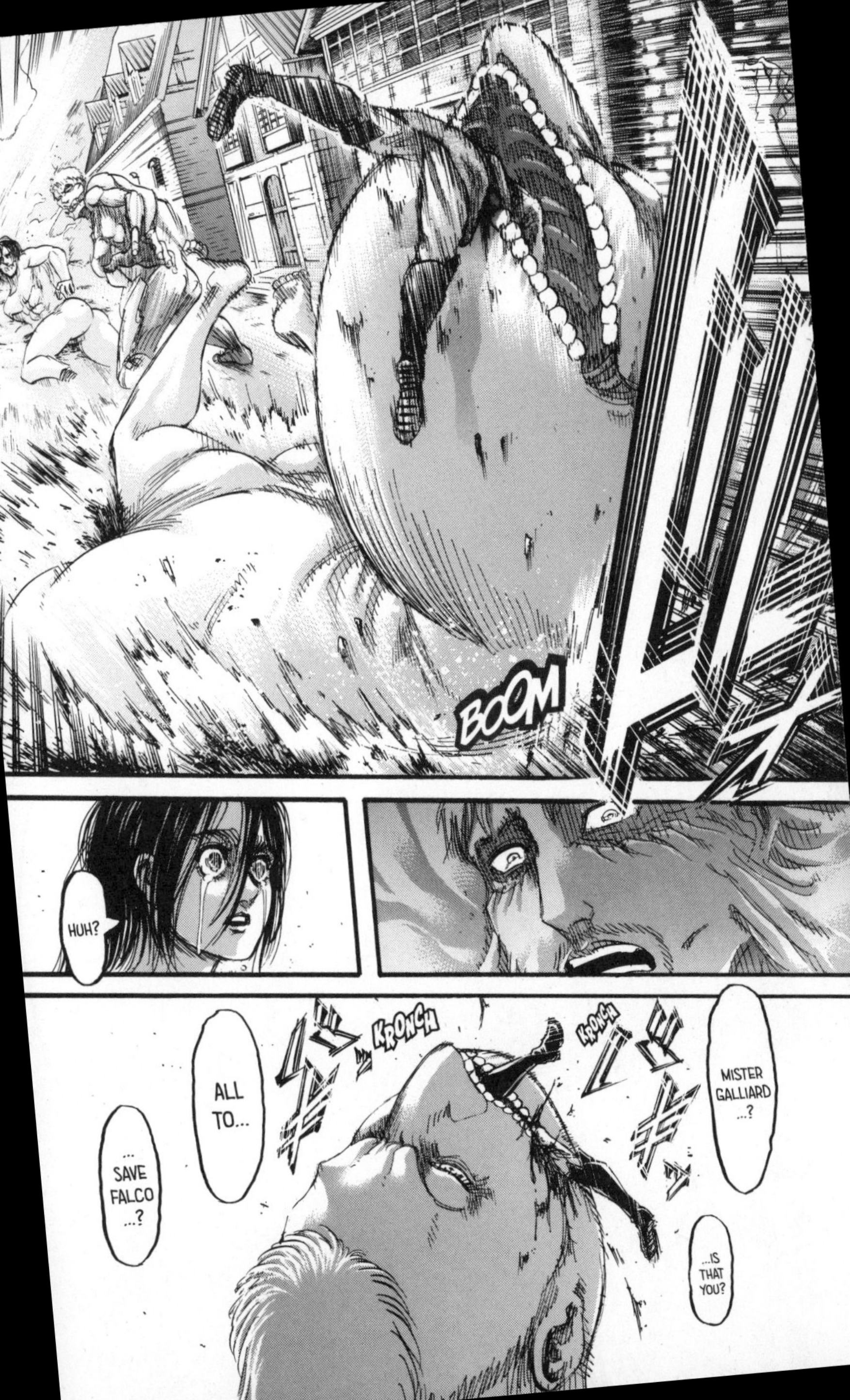
BOOM
HUH?
MISTER GALLIARD ...?
KRONCH
KRONCH
ALL TO...
...IS THAT YOU?
... SAVE FALCO ...?

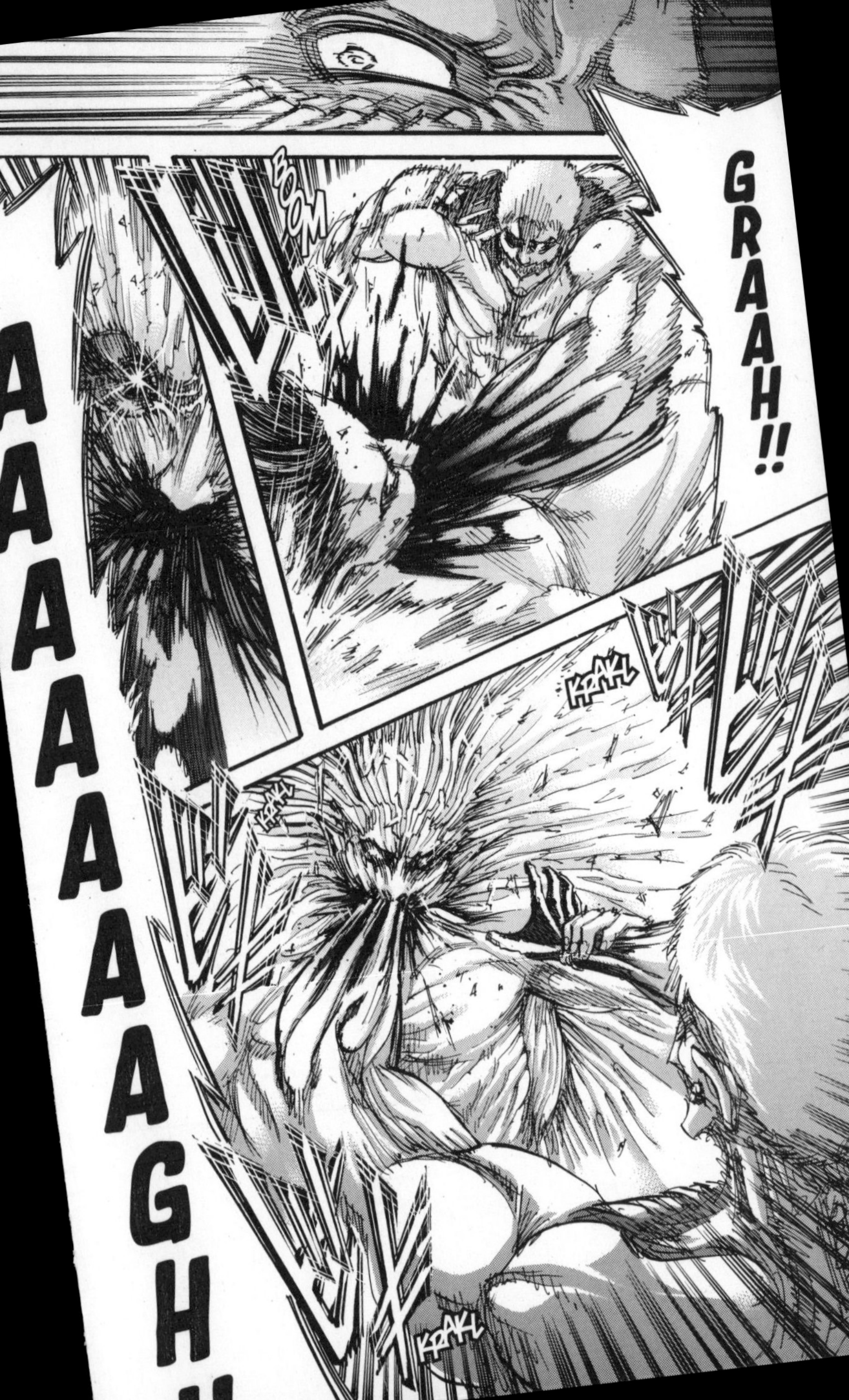
GRAAAH!!
BOOM
AAAAAAAGH!!
KRAKL
KRAKL
KRAKL

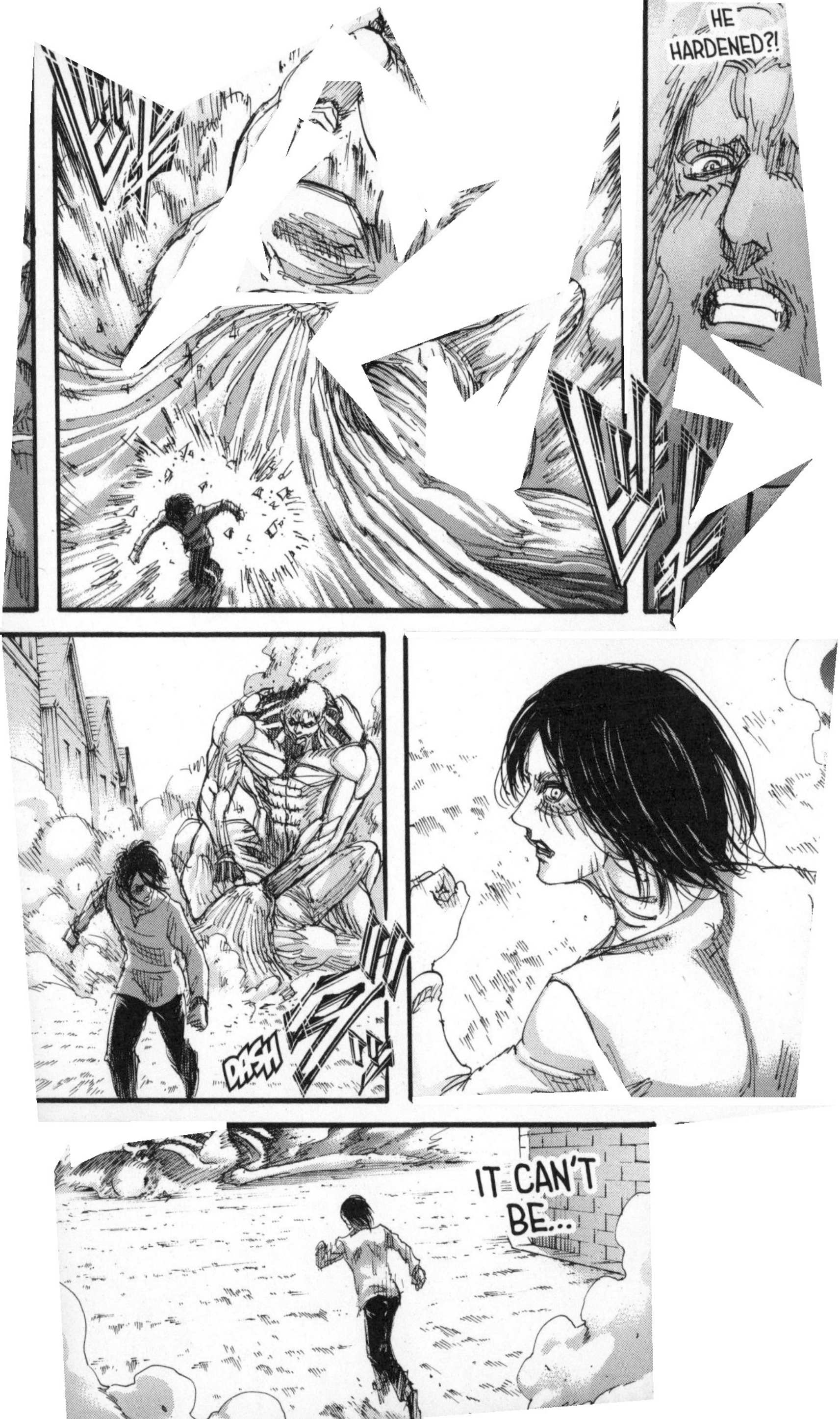
HE HARDENED?!
DASH
IT CAN'T BE...

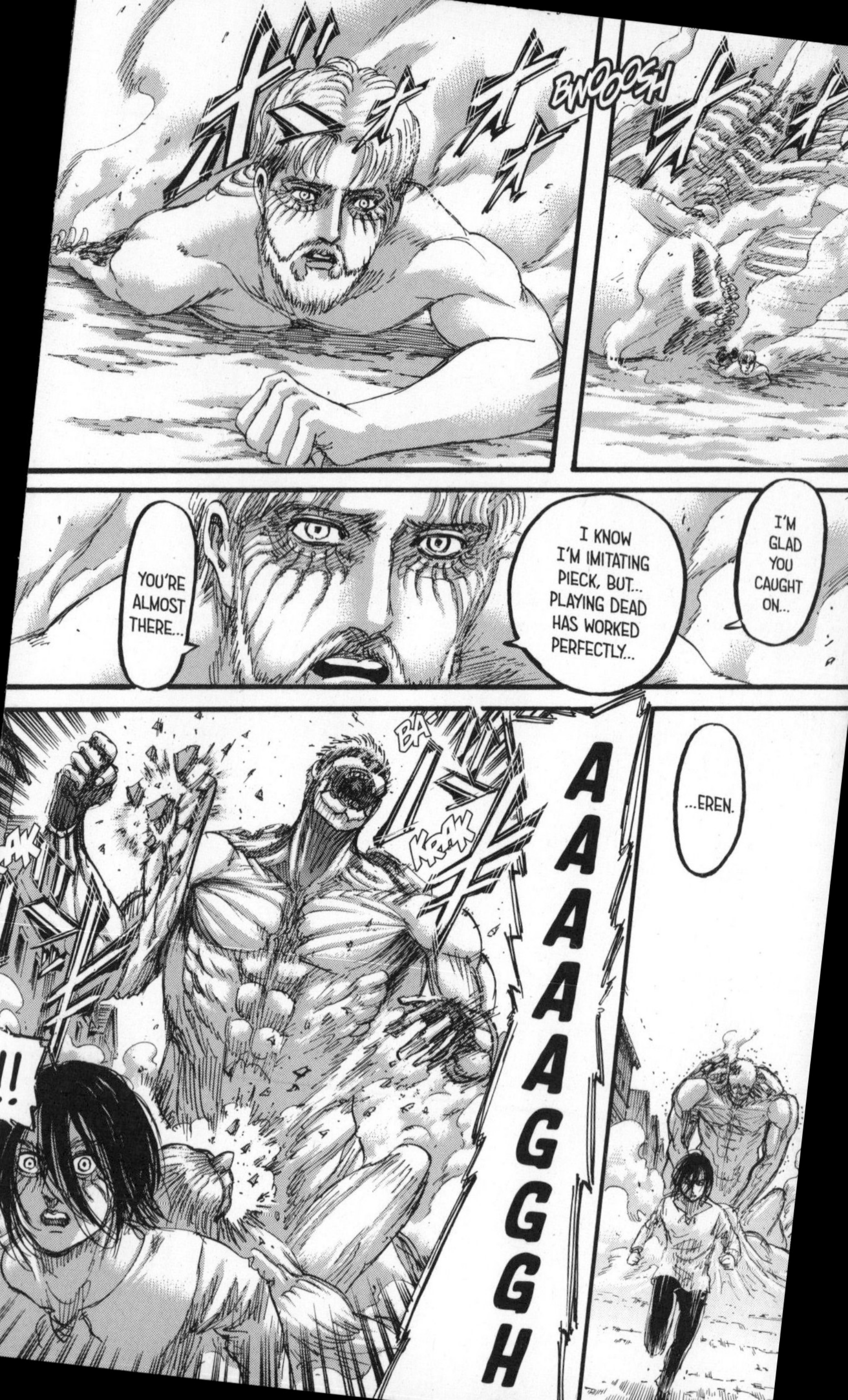
BWOOOSH
I'M GLAD YOU CAUGHT ON...
I KNOW I'M IMITATING PIECK, BUT... PLAYING DEAD HAS WORKED PERFECTLY...
YOU'RE ALMOST THERE...
...EREN.
BA-
KRAK
AAAAAGGGH

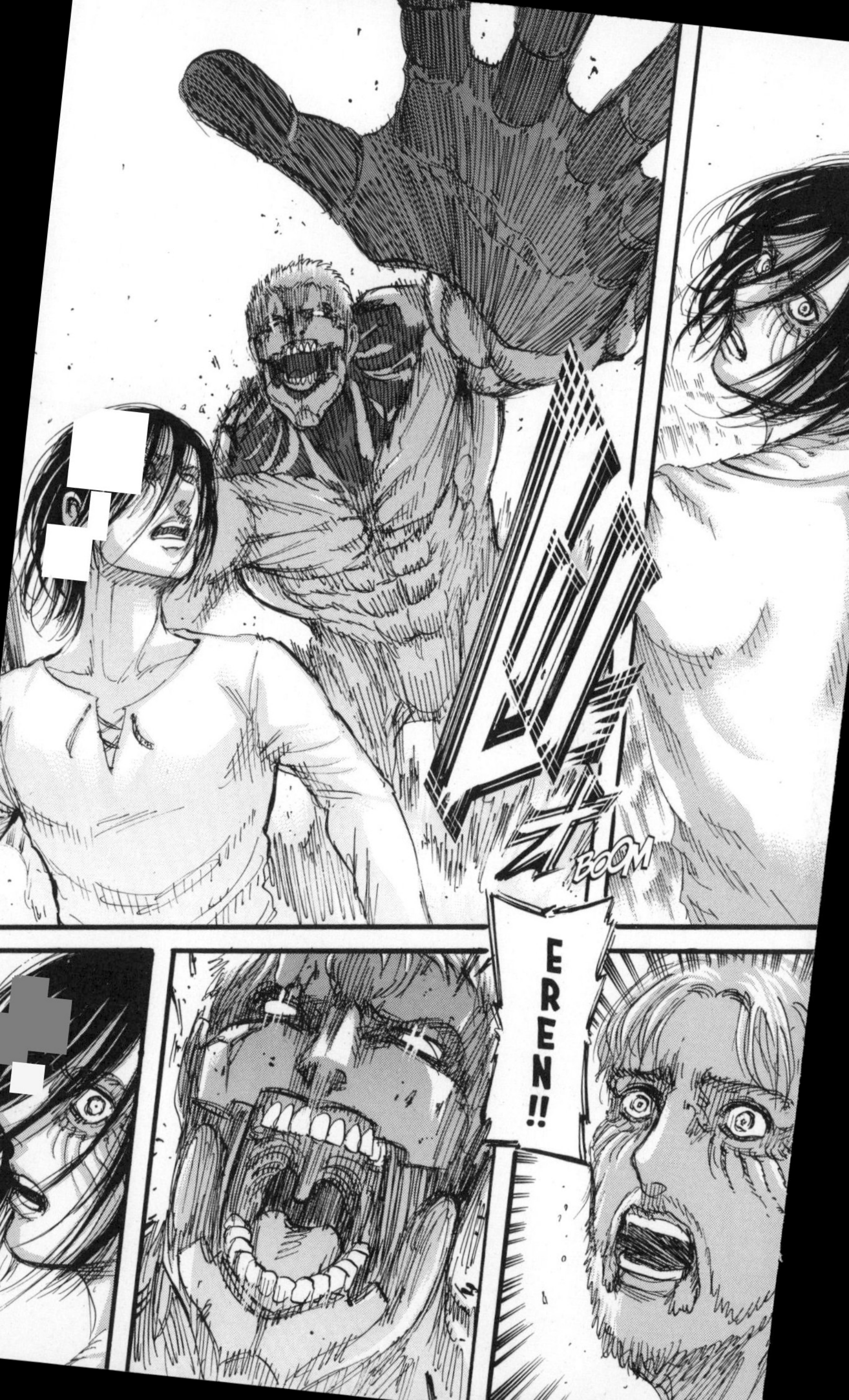
BOOM
EREN!!

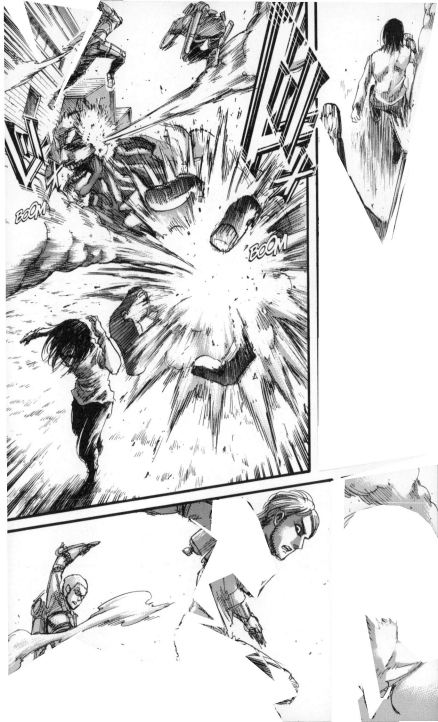

BOOM

BOOM

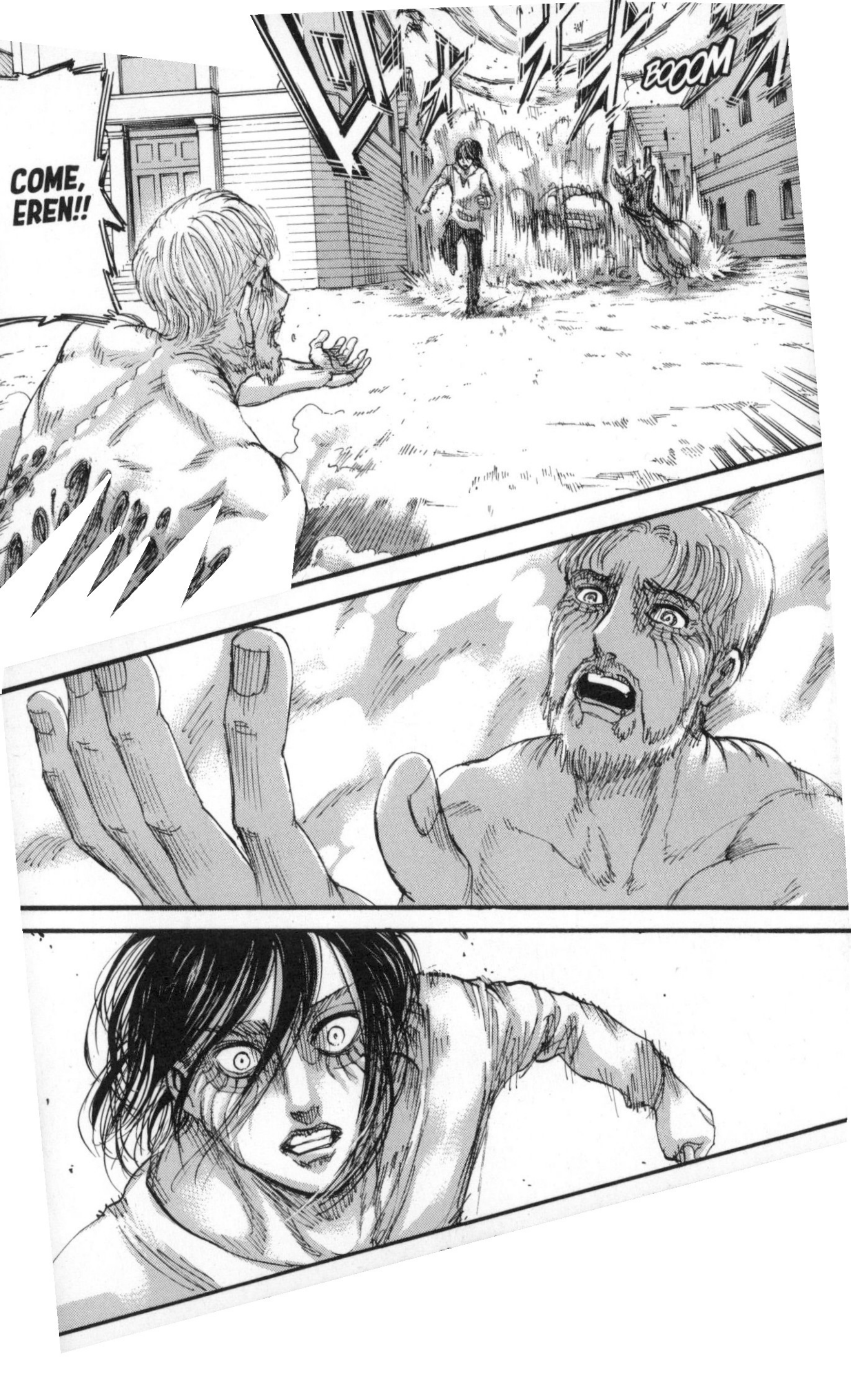
BOOOM
COME, EREN!!

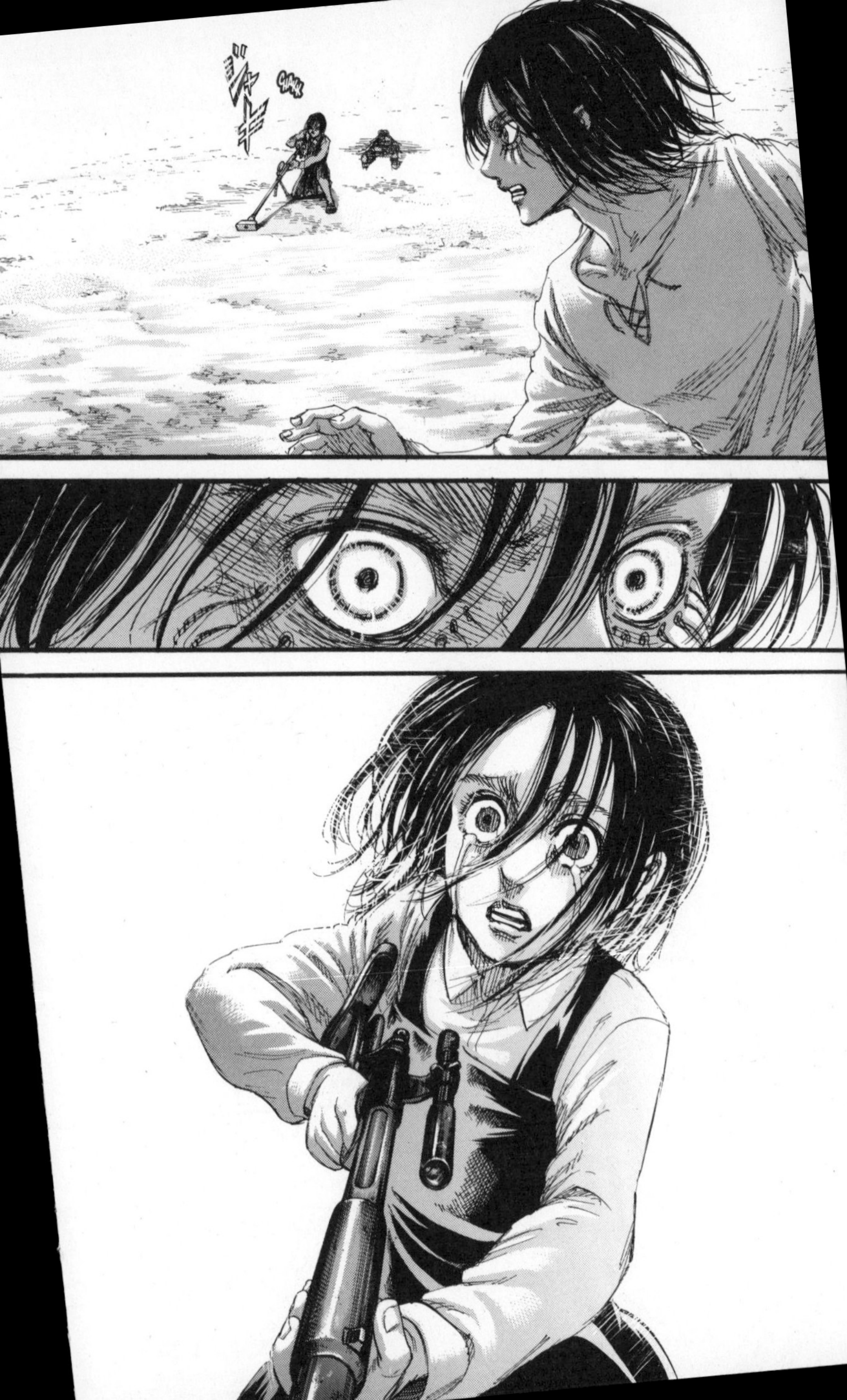
ジャキ
CHAKK

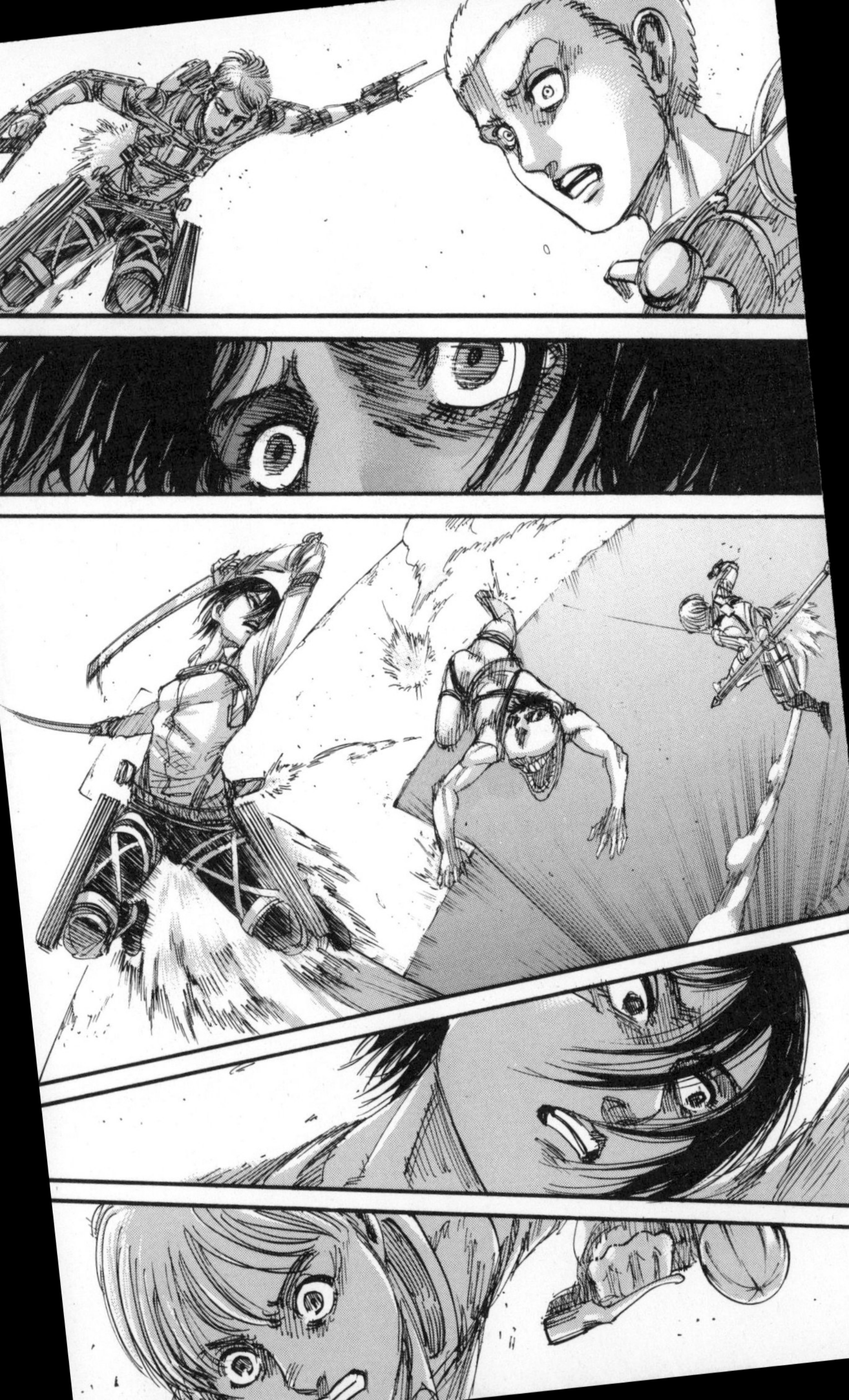

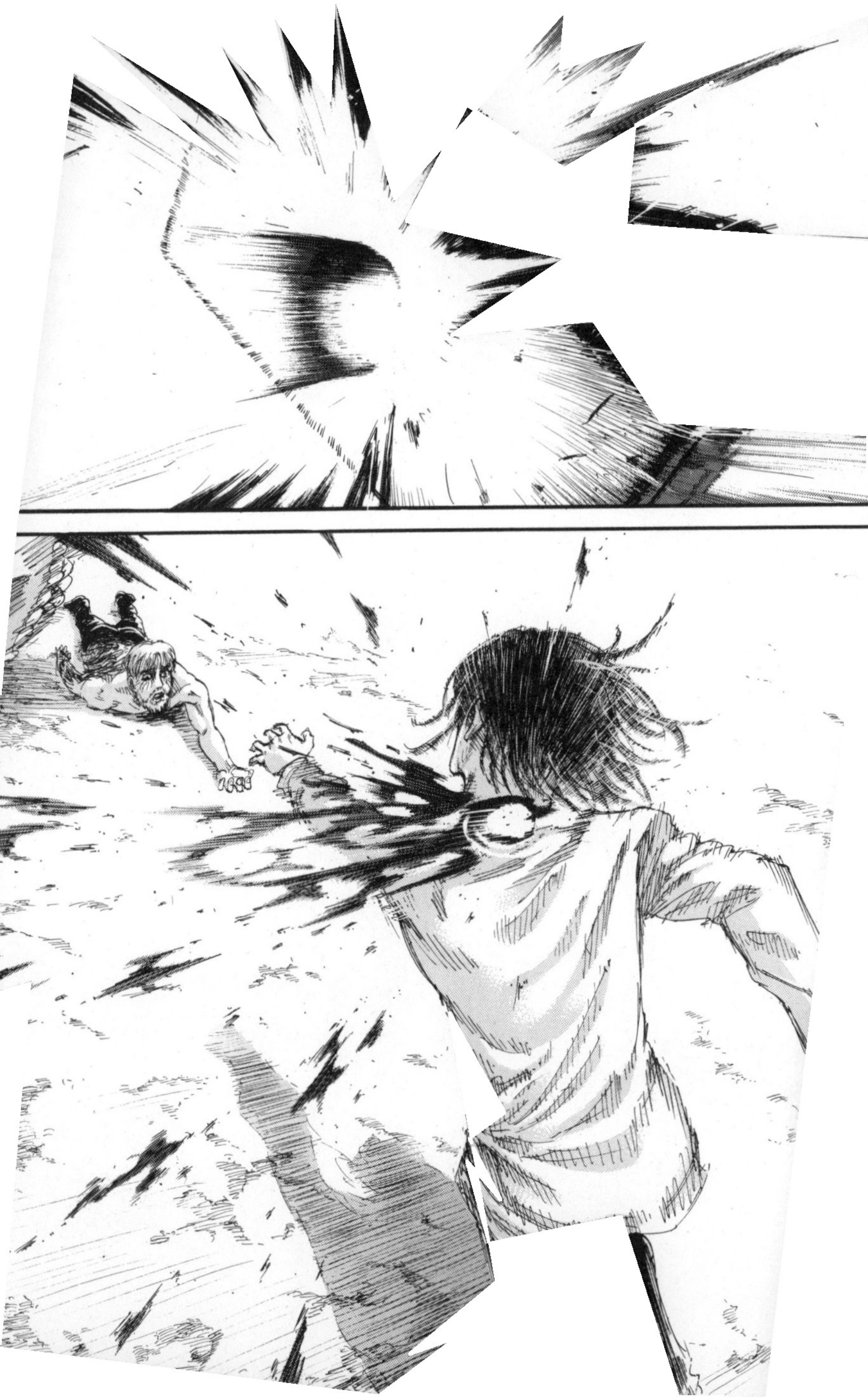

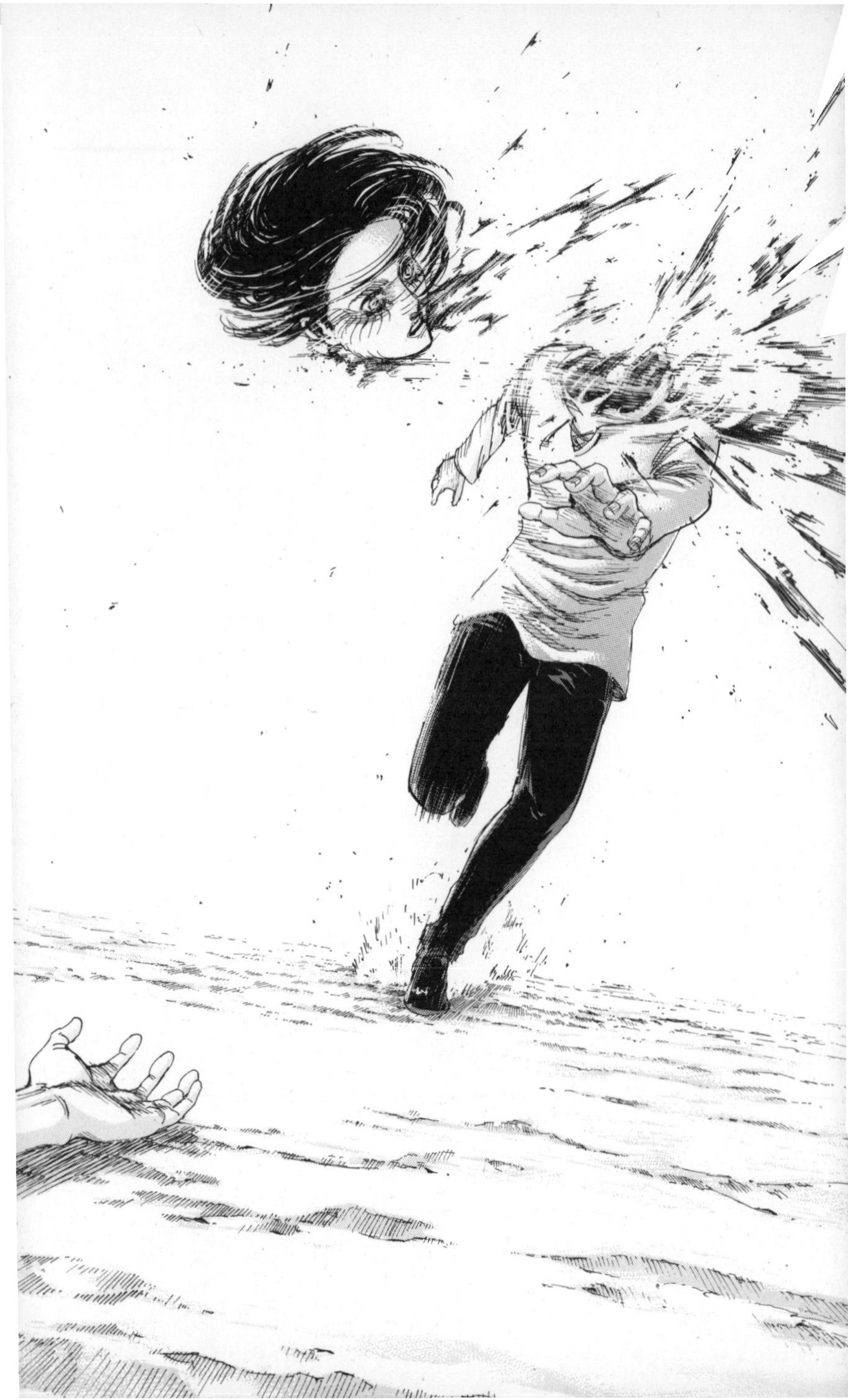

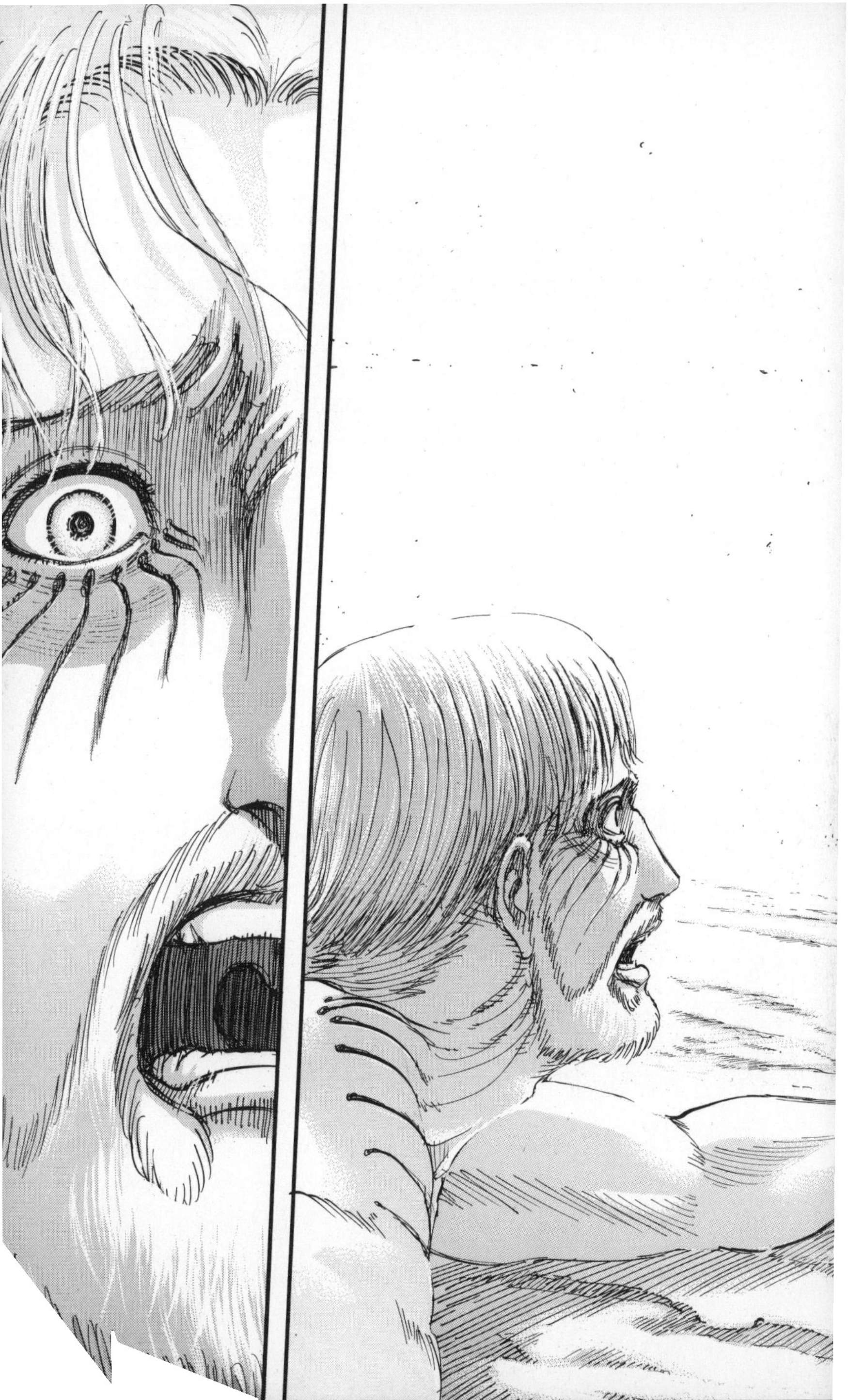

ATTACK on TITAN

Episode 120: A Fleeting Moment

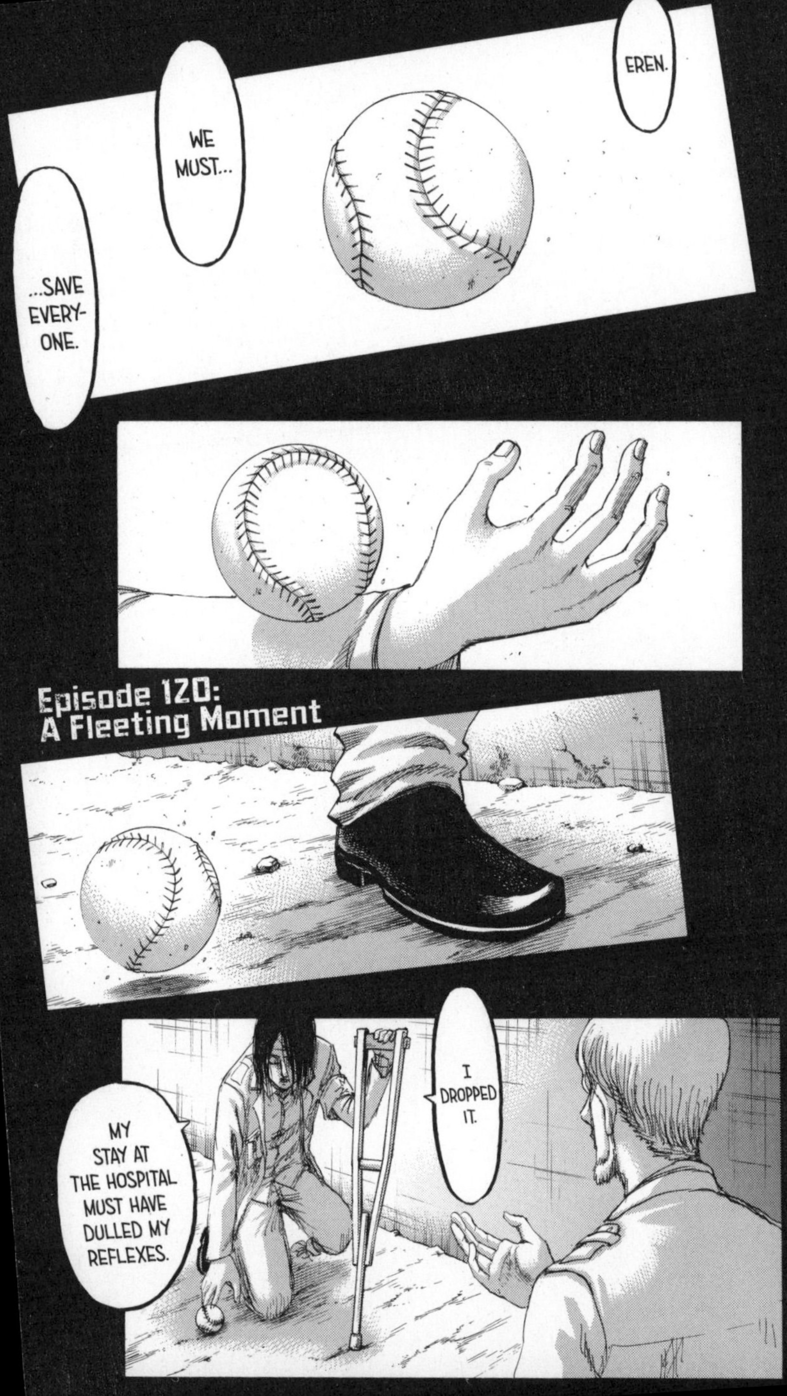
EREN.
WE MUST...
...SAVE EVERY-ONE.
I DROPPED IT.
MY STAY AT THE HOSPITAL MUST HAVE DULLED MY REFLEXES.

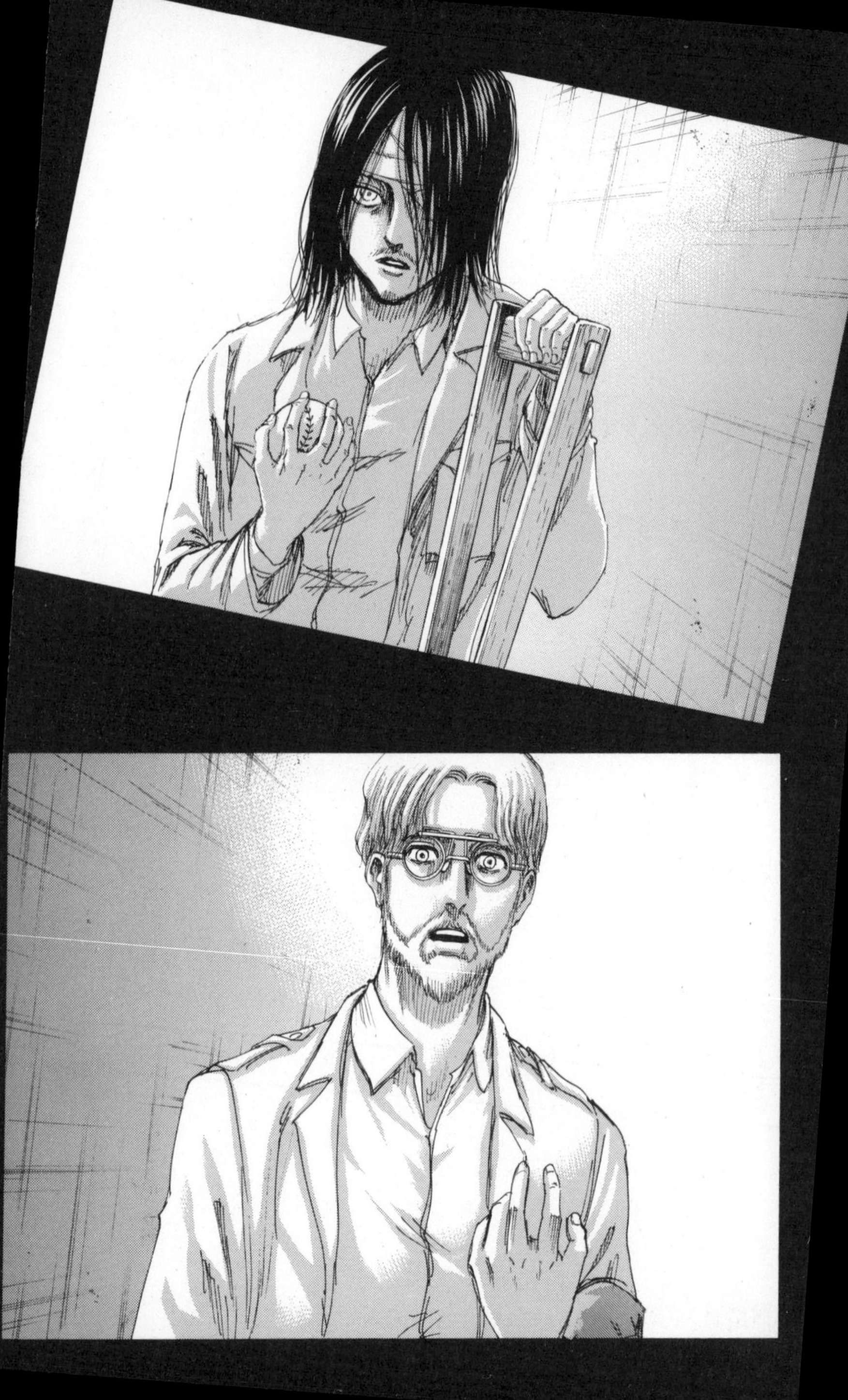

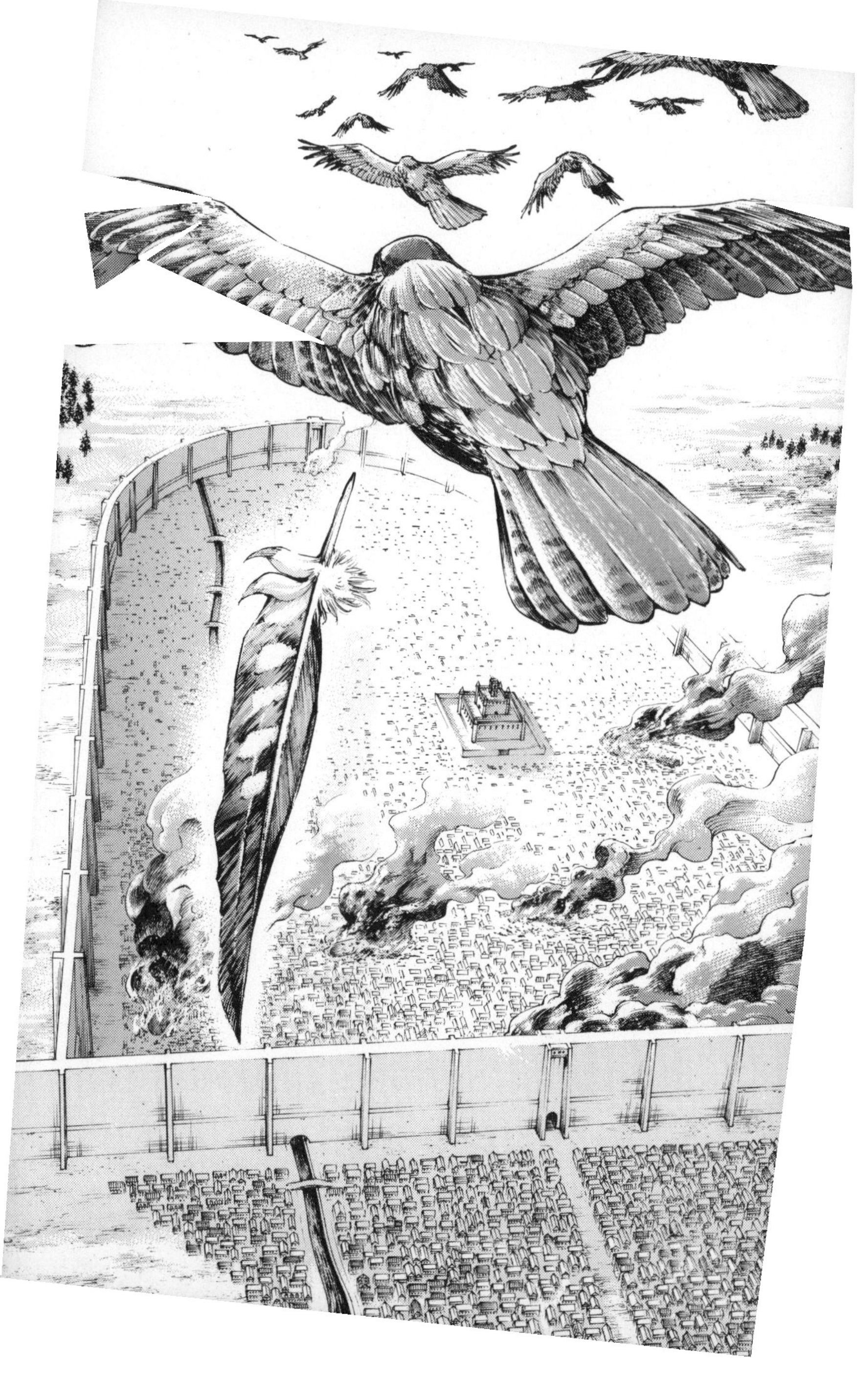

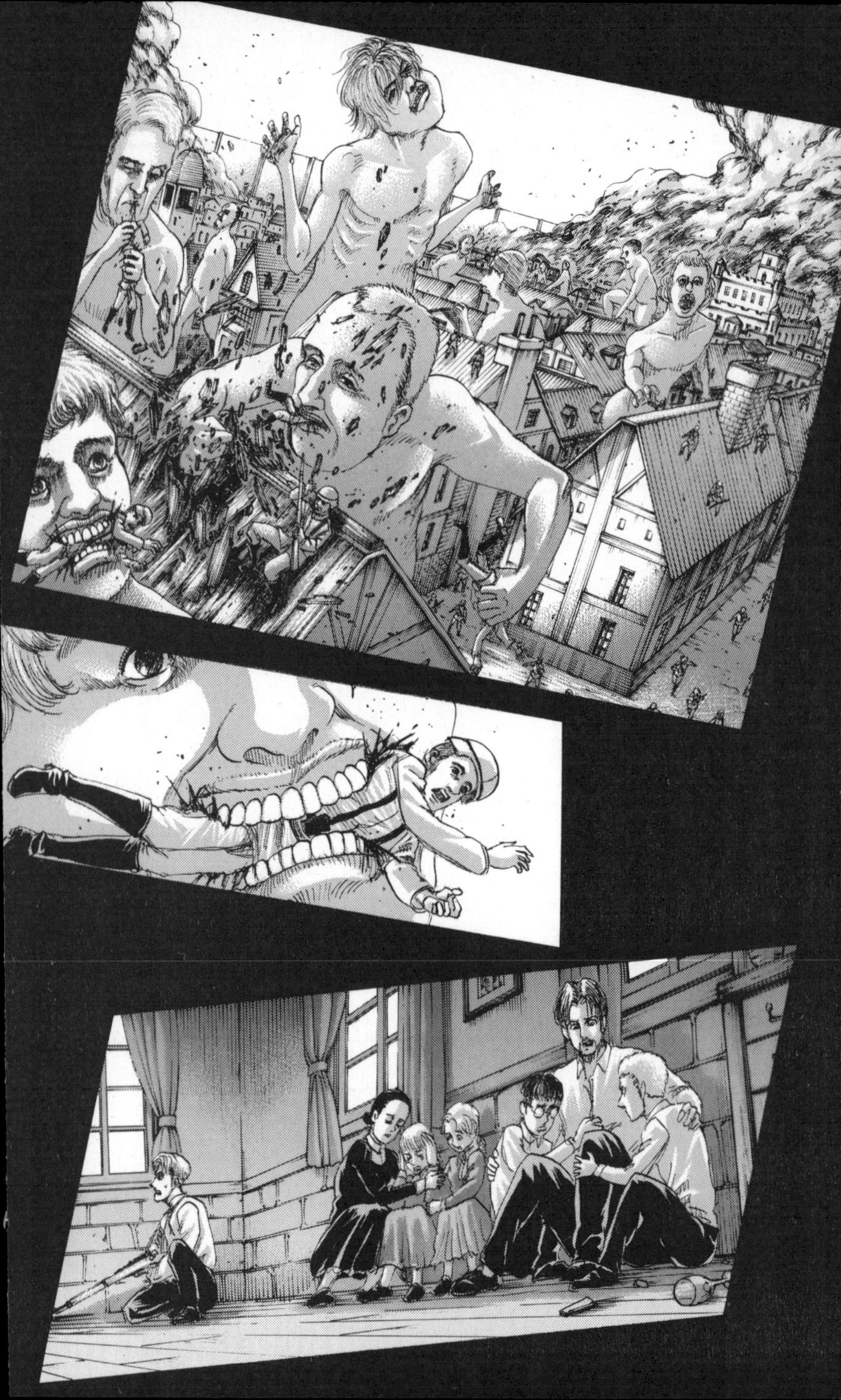

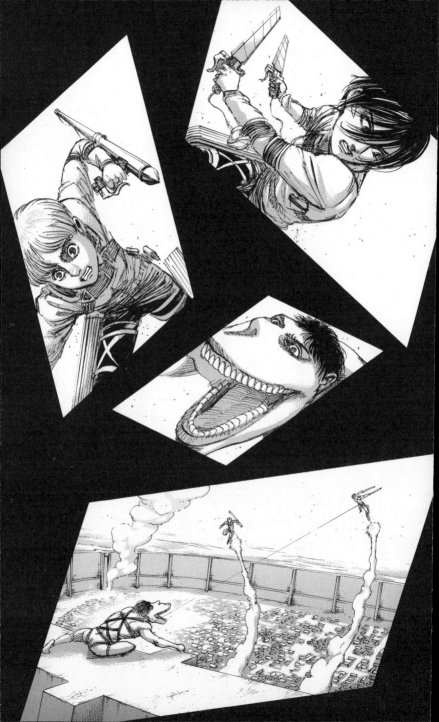

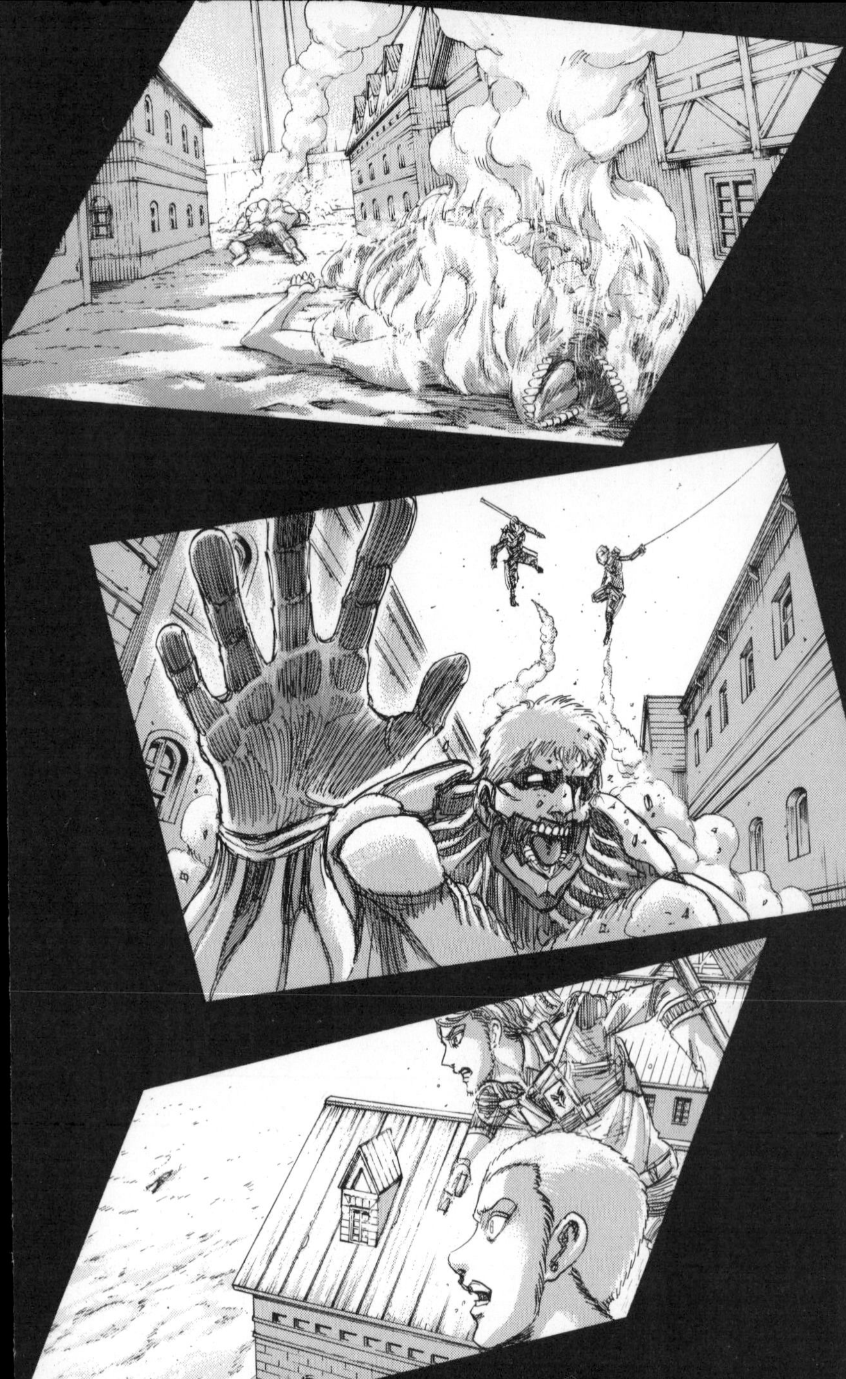

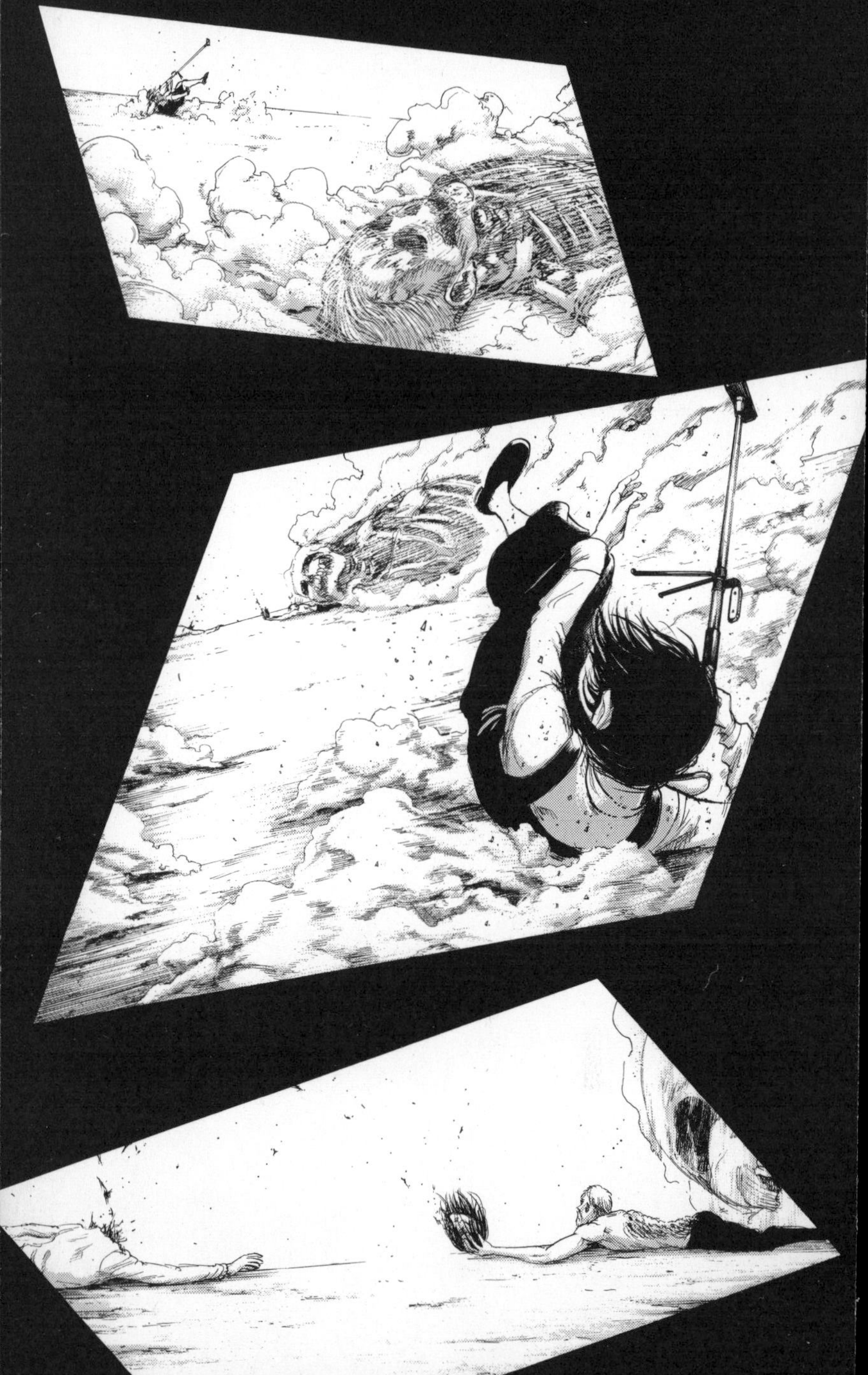

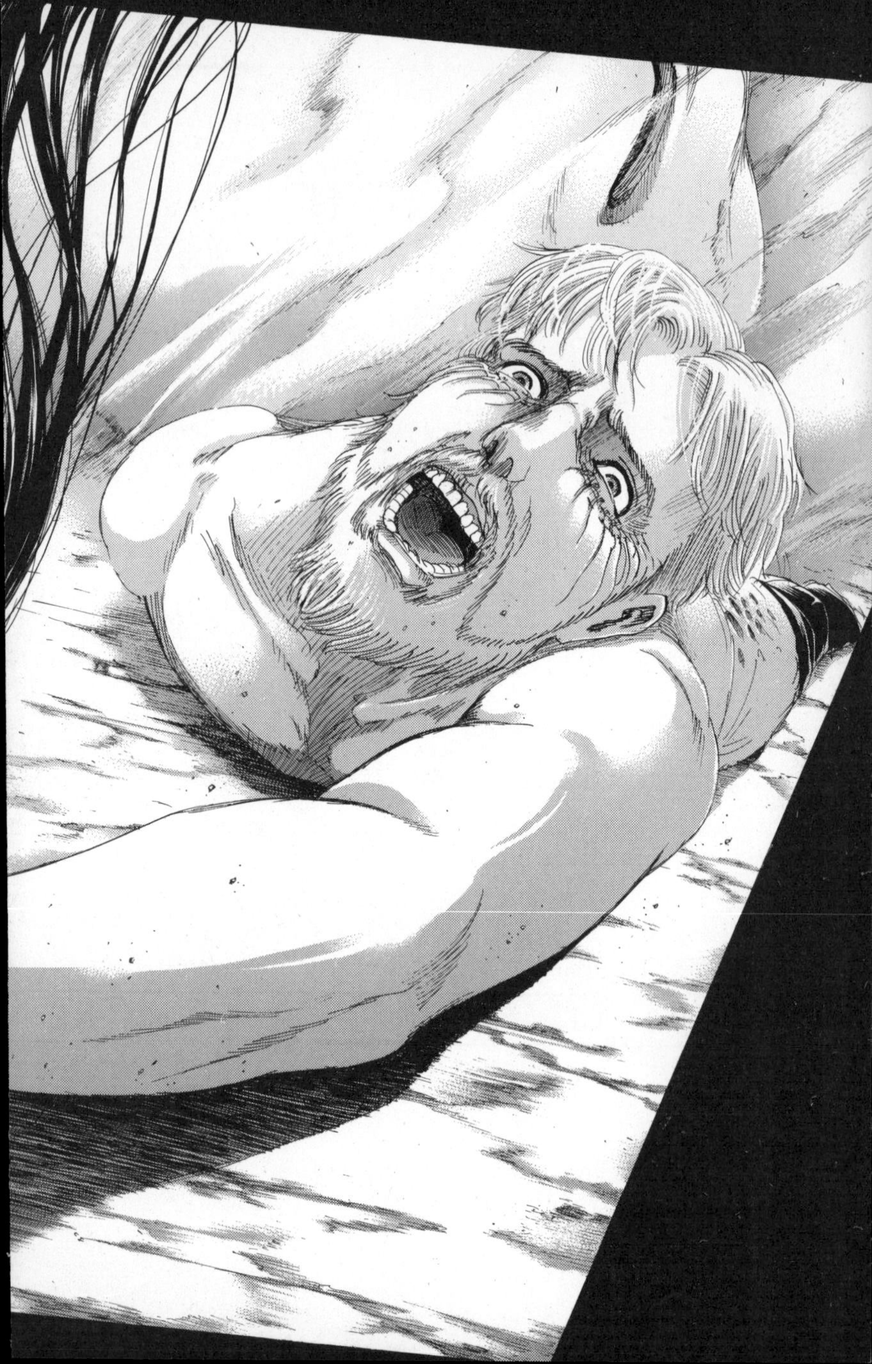

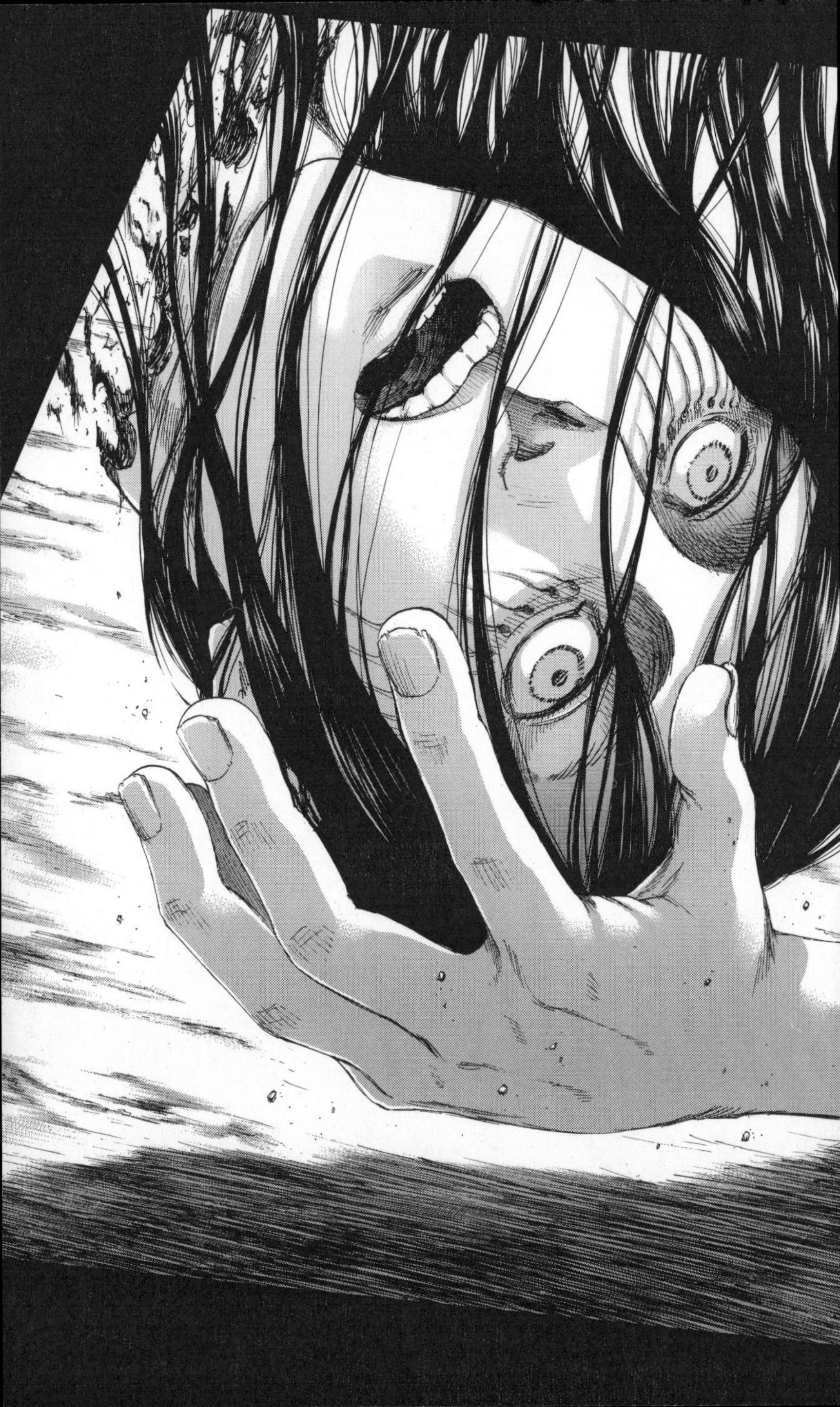

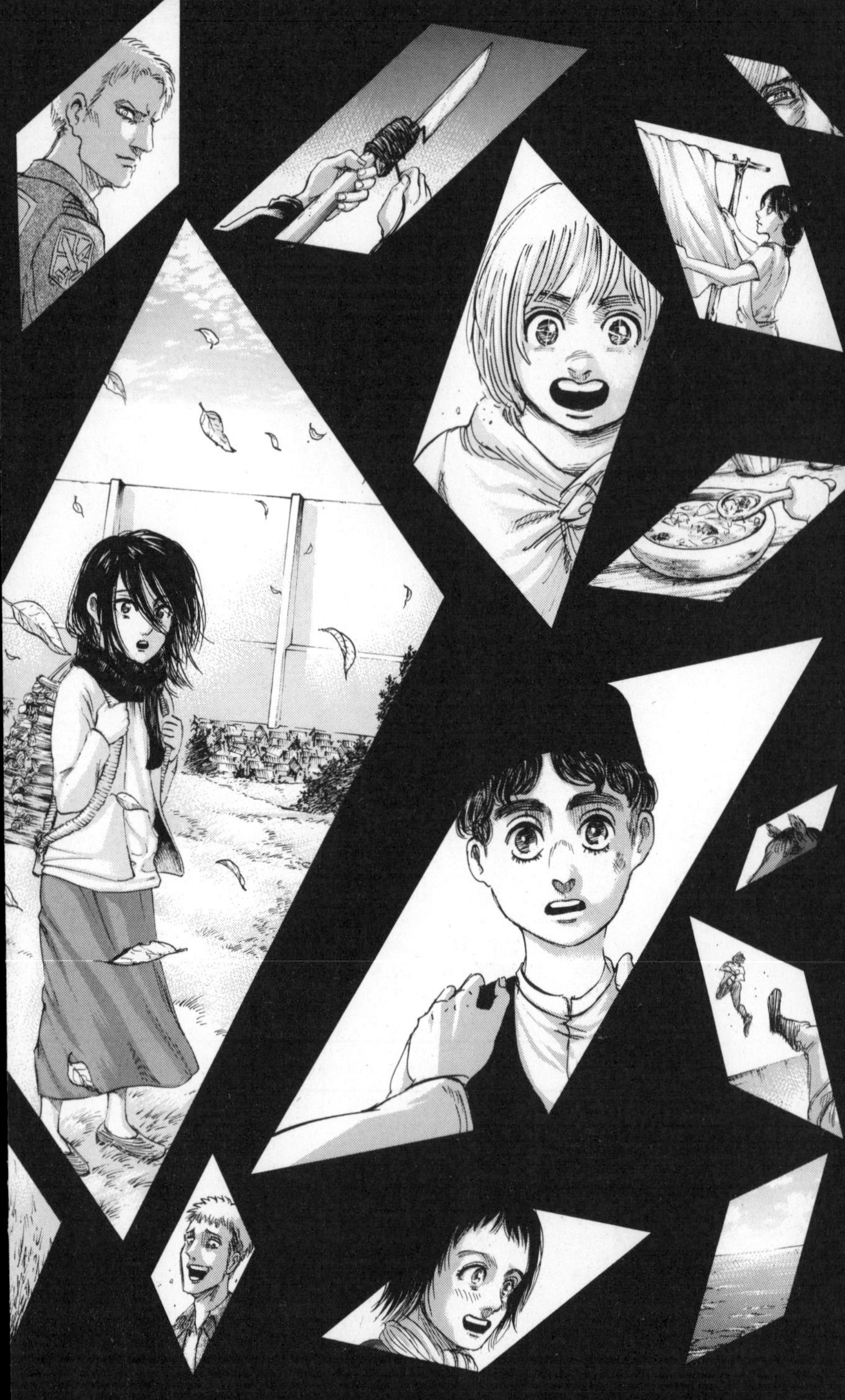

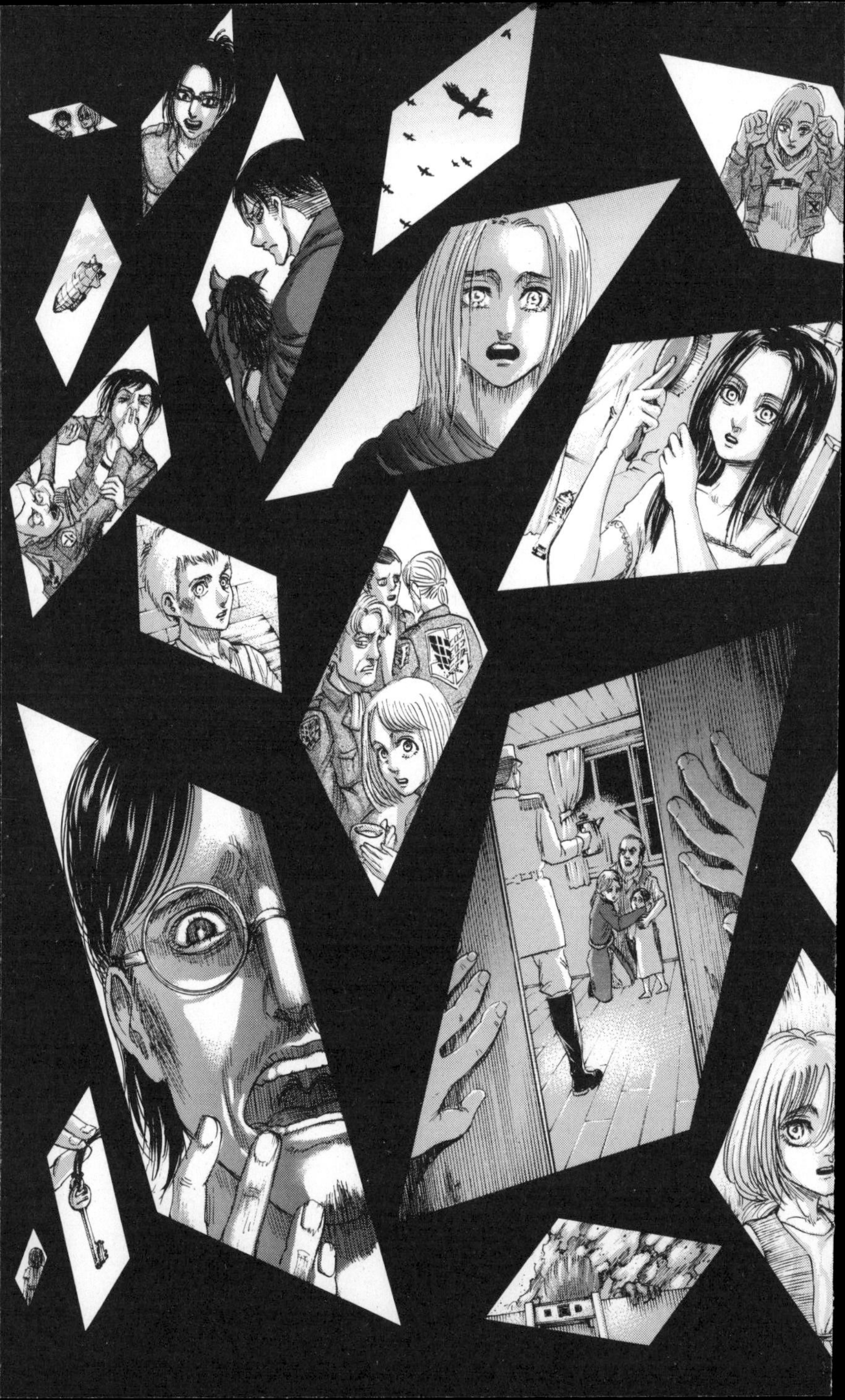

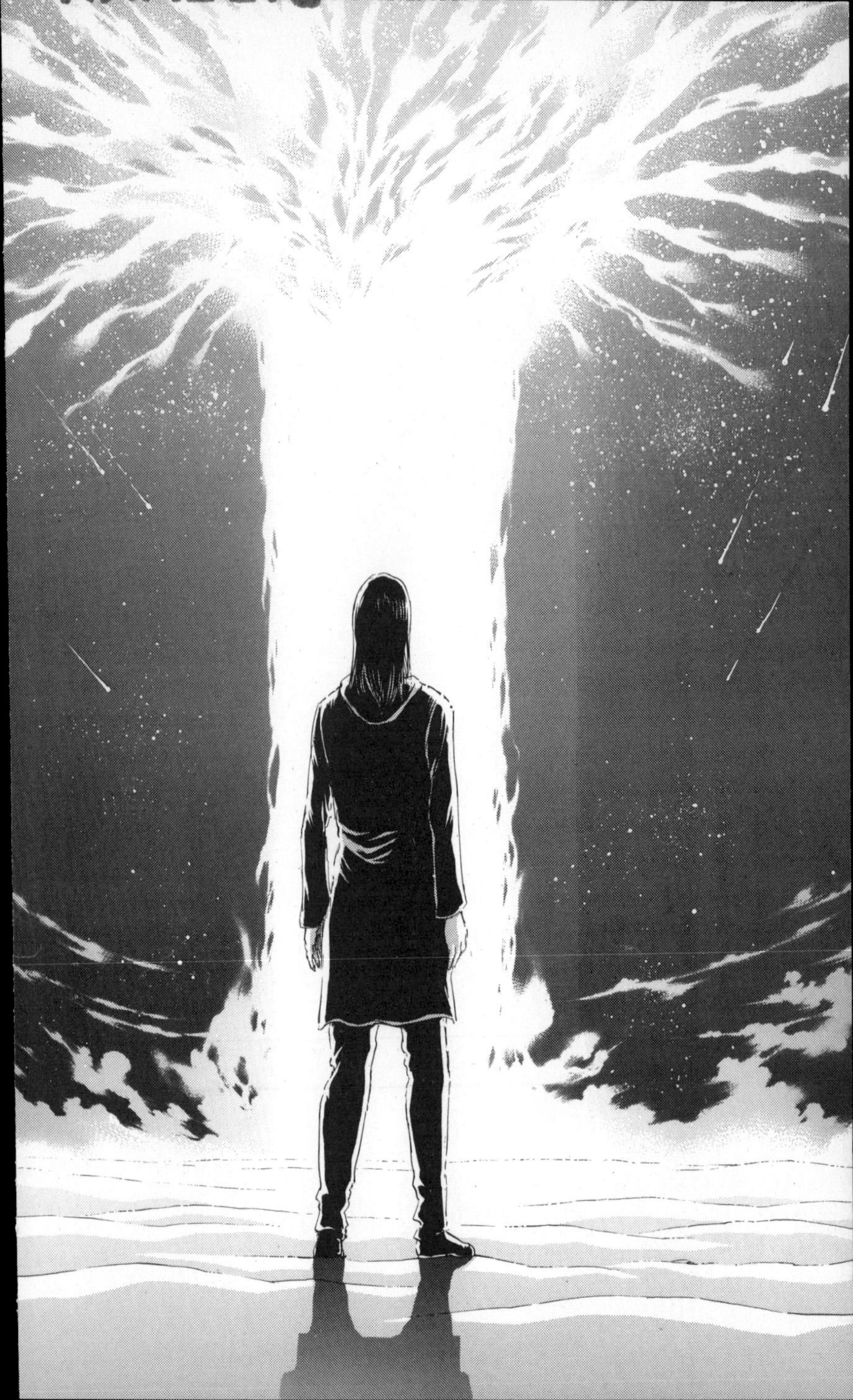

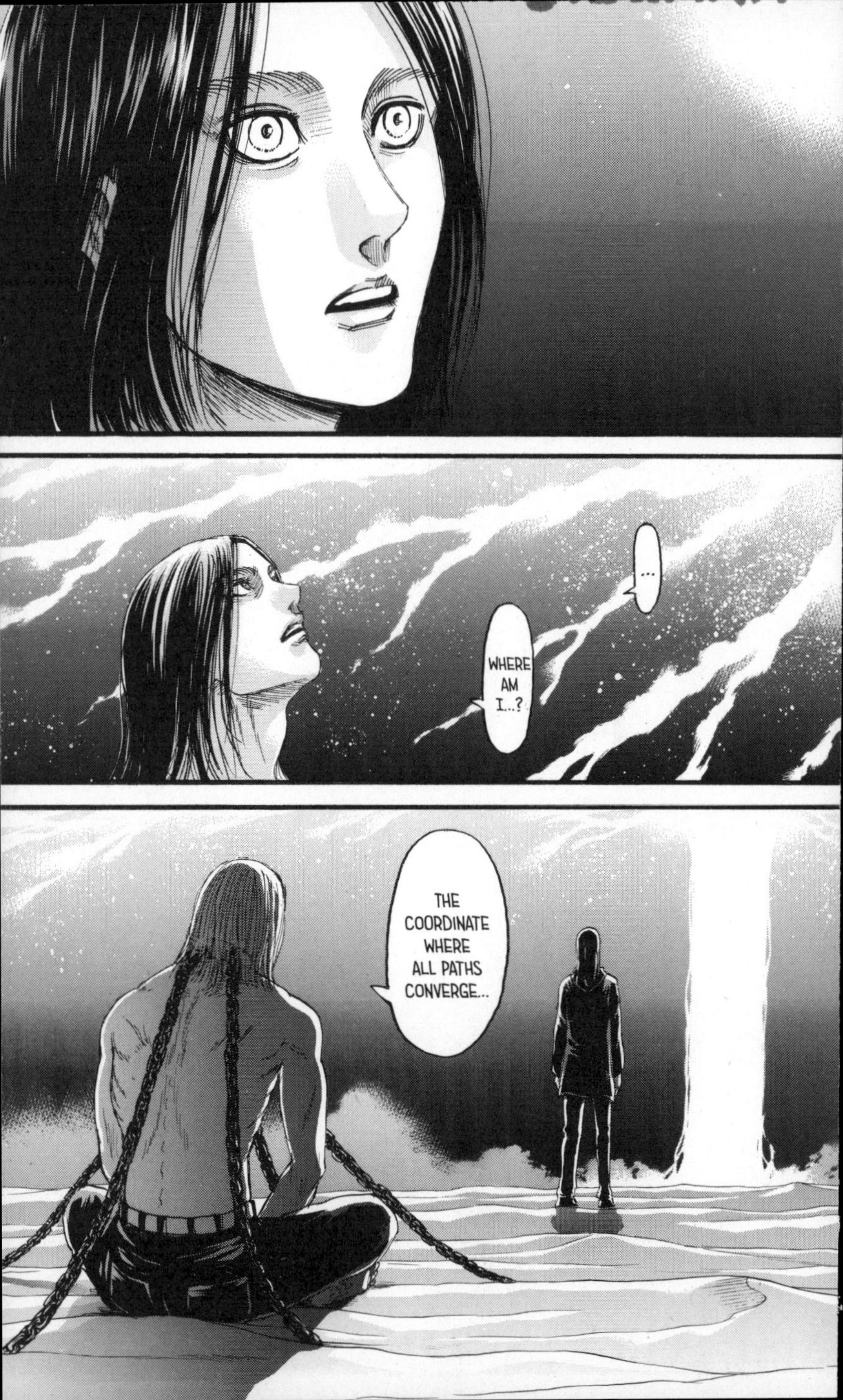
...
WHERE AM I...?
THE COORDINATE WHERE ALL PATHS CONVERGE...

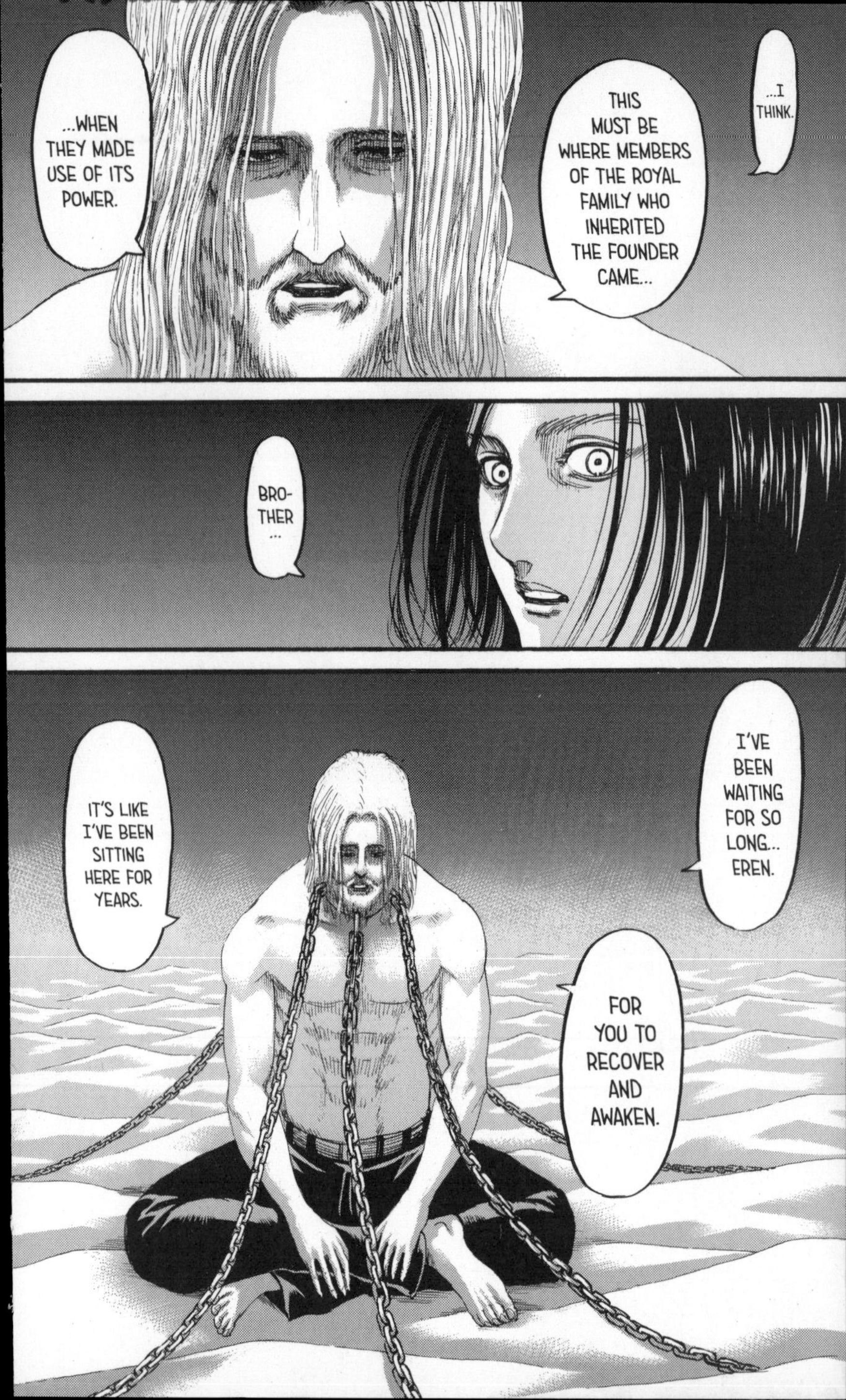
THIS MUST BE WHERE MEMBERS OF THE ROYAL FAMILY WHO INHERITED THE FOUNDER CAME...
...I THINK.
...WHEN THEY MADE USE OF ITS POWER.
BRO-THER...
I'VE BEEN WAITING FOR SO LONG... EREN.
FOR YOU TO RECOVER AND AWAKEN.
IT'S LIKE I'VE BEEN SITTING HERE FOR YEARS.

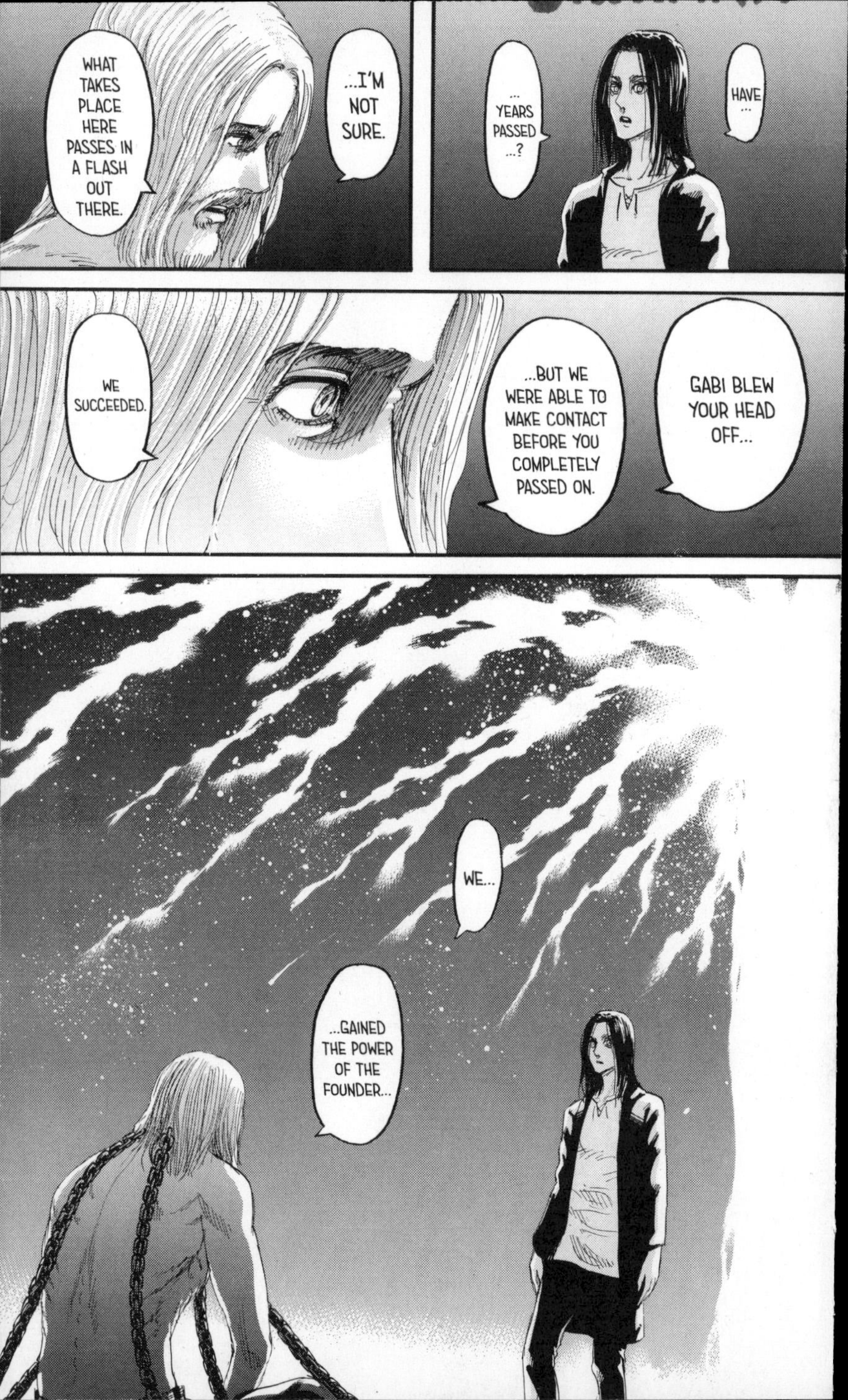
HAVE ...
... YEARS PASSED ...?
...I'M NOT SURE.
WHAT TAKES PLACE HERE PASSES IN A FLASH OUT THERE.
GABI BLEW YOUR HEAD OFF...
...BUT WE WERE ABLE TO MAKE CONTACT BEFORE YOU COMPLETELY PASSED ON.
WE SUCCEEDED.
WE...
...GAINED THE POWER OF THE FOUNDER...

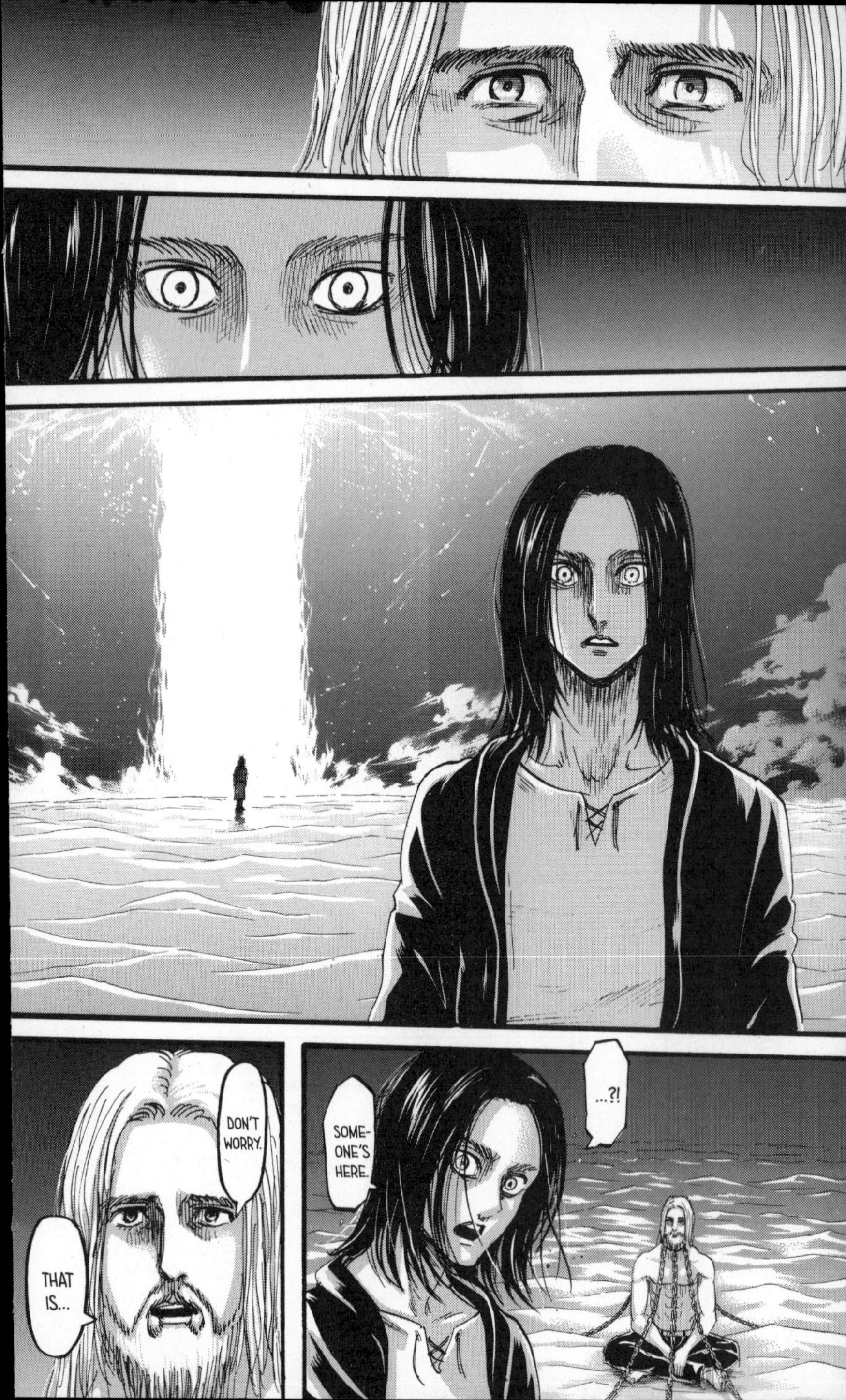
...?!
SOME-ONE'S HERE.
DON'T WORRY.
THAT IS...

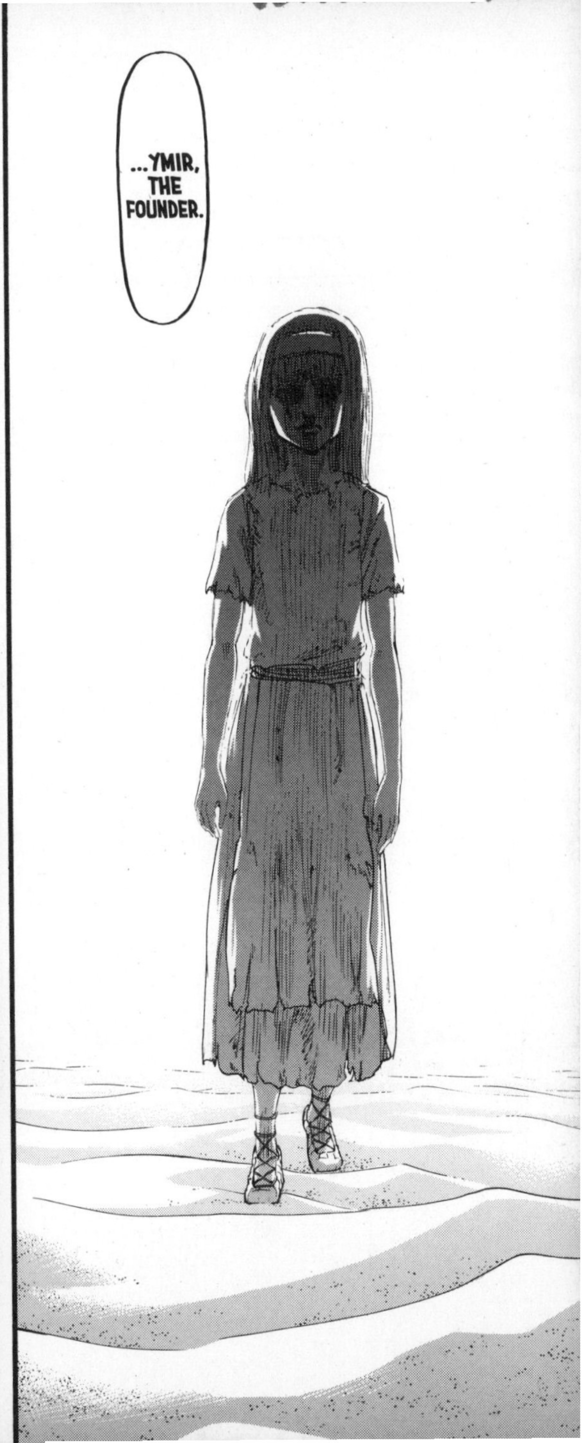
...YMIR, THE FOUNDER.

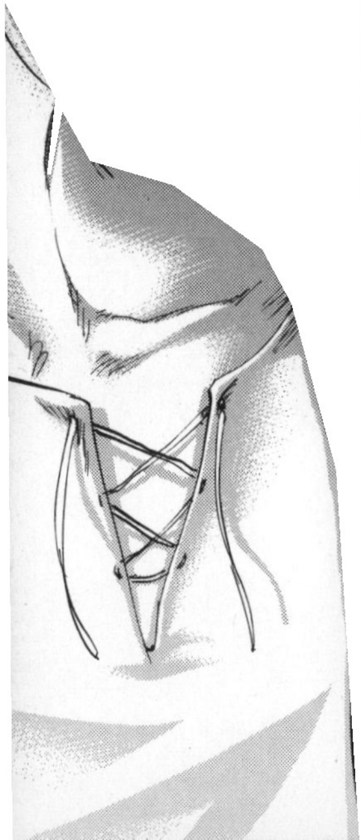

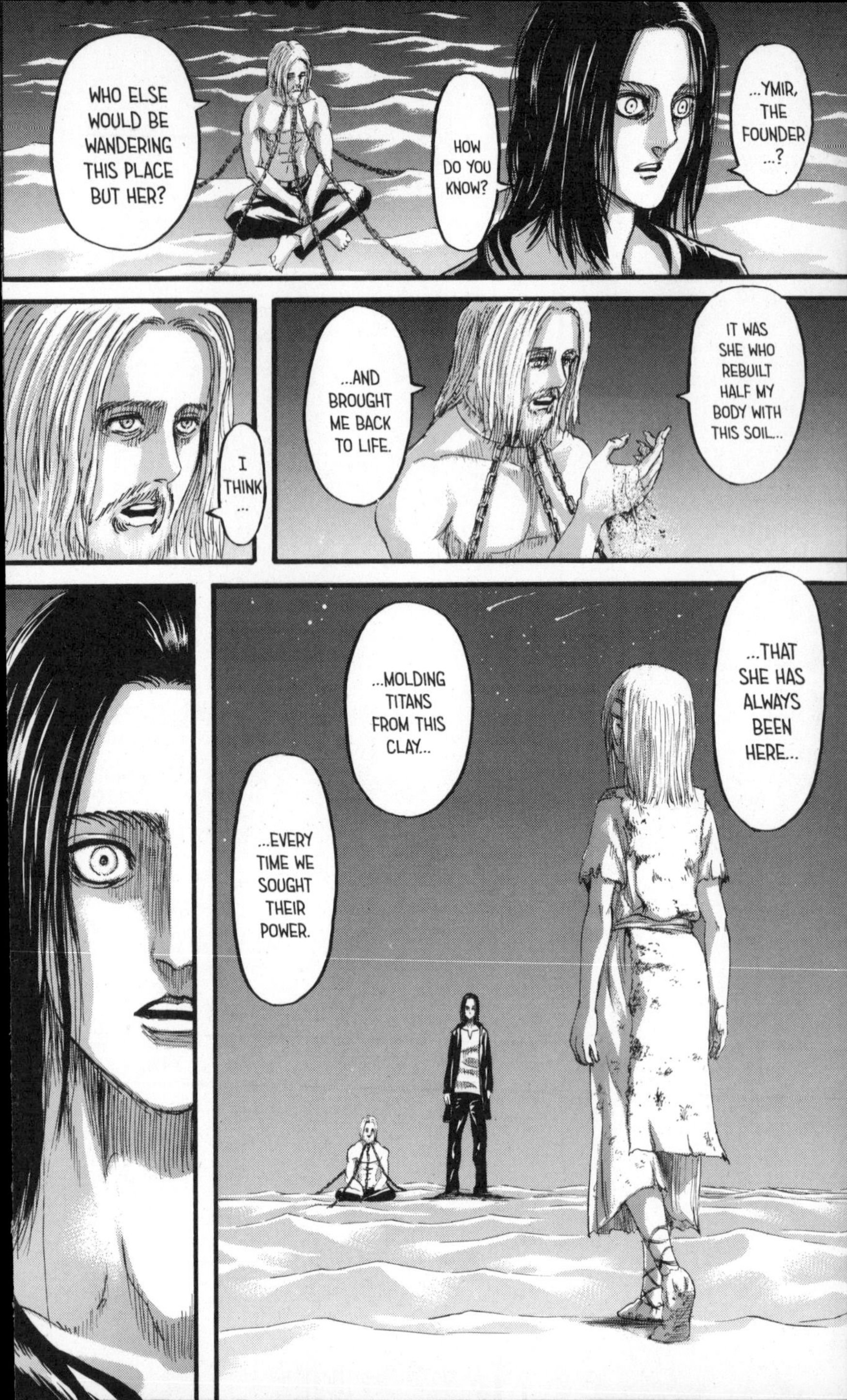
...YMIR, THE FOUNDER ...?
HOW DO YOU KNOW?
WHO ELSE WOULD BE WANDERING THIS PLACE BUT HER?
IT WAS SHE WHO REBUILT HALF MY BODY WITH THIS SOIL...
...AND BROUGHT ME BACK TO LIFE.
I THINK ...
...THAT SHE HAS ALWAYS BEEN HERE...
...MOLDING TITANS FROM THIS CLAY...
...EVERY TIME WE SOUGHT THEIR POWER.

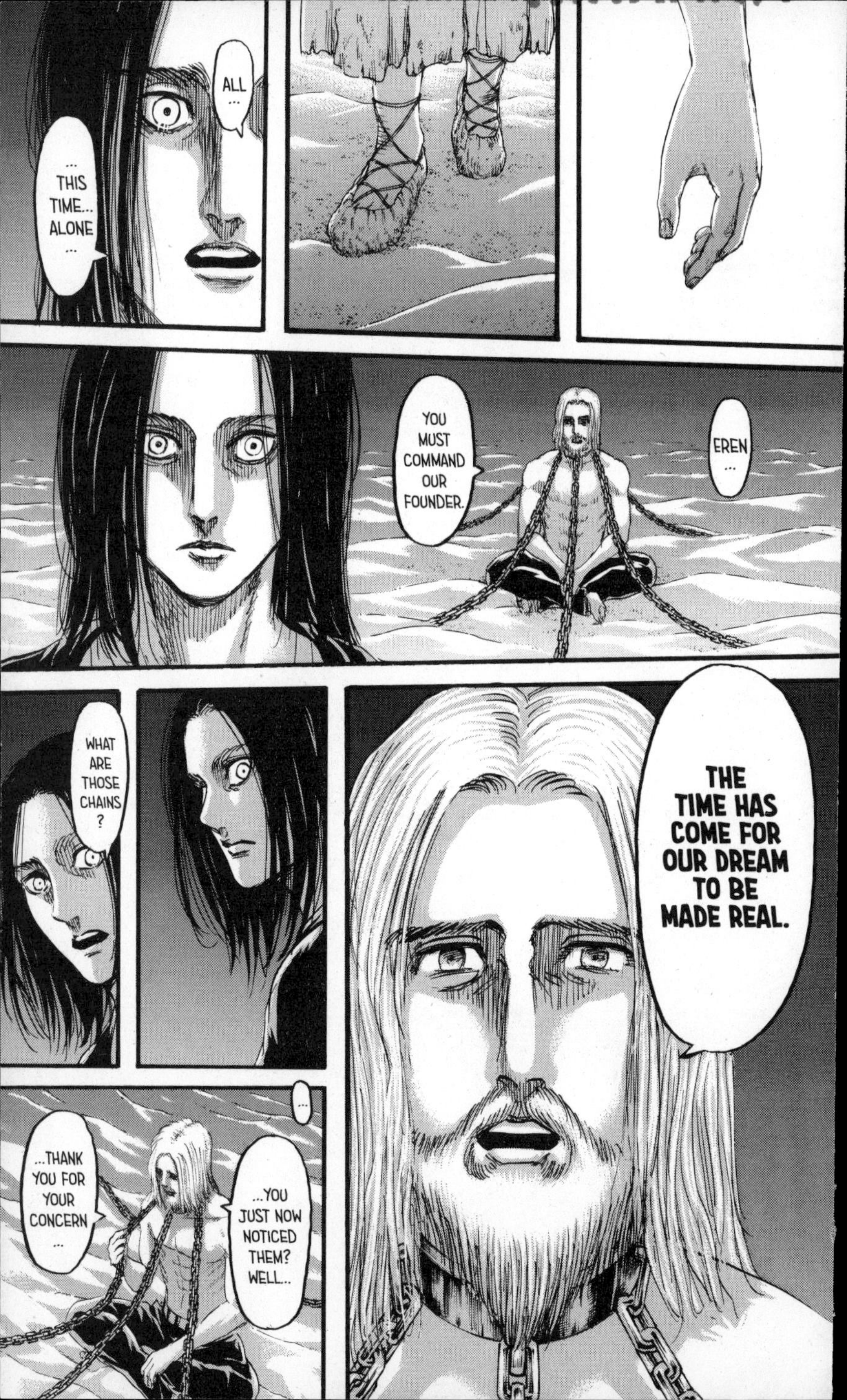
ALL ...
... THIS TIME... ALONE ...
EREN ...
YOU MUST COMMAND OUR FOUNDER.
THE TIME HAS COME FOR OUR DREAM TO BE MADE REAL.
WHAT ARE THOSE CHAINS ?
...
...YOU JUST NOW NOTICED THEM? WELL...
...THANK YOU FOR YOUR CONCERN ...

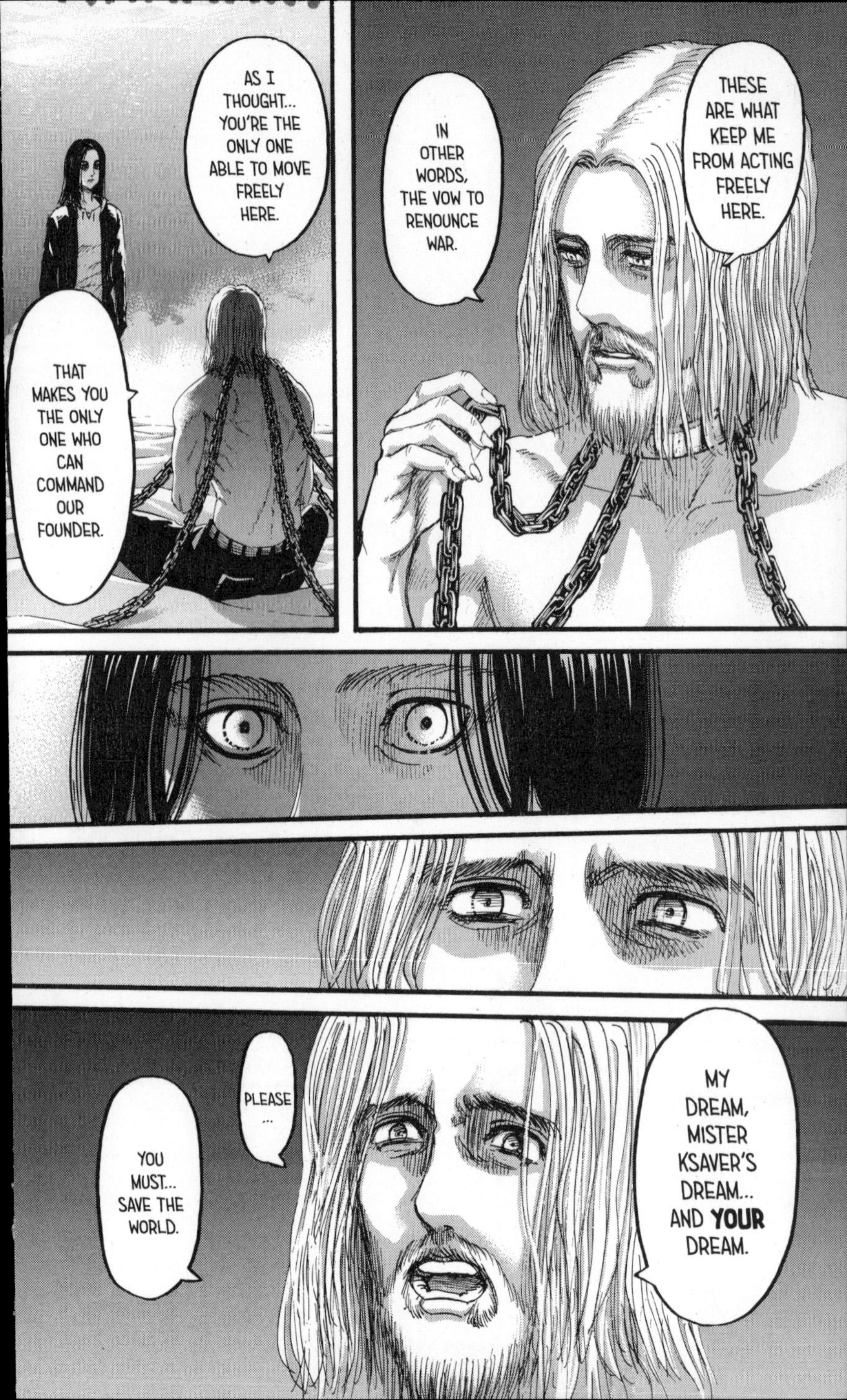
THESE ARE WHAT KEEP ME FROM ACTING FREELY HERE.
IN OTHER WORDS, THE VOW TO RENOUNCE WAR.
AS I THOUGHT... YOU'RE THE ONLY ONE ABLE TO MOVE FREELY HERE.
THAT MAKES YOU THE ONLY ONE WHO CAN COMMAND OUR FOUNDER.
MY DREAM, MISTER KSAVER'S DREAM... AND **YOUR** DREAM.
PLEASE...
YOU MUST... SAVE THE WORLD.

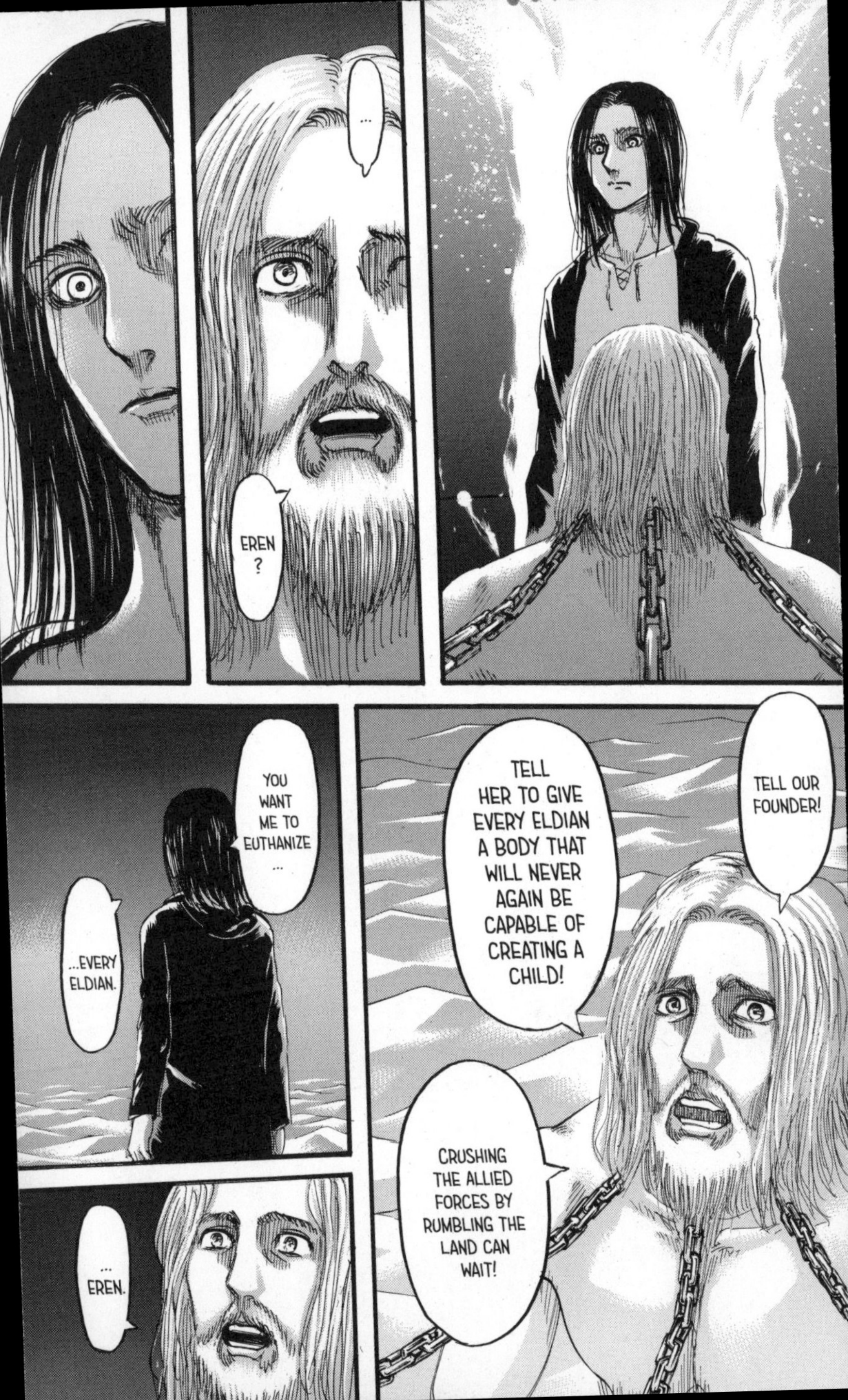
...
EREN?
TELL OUR FOUNDER!
TELL HER TO GIVE EVERY ELDIAN A BODY THAT WILL NEVER AGAIN BE CAPABLE OF CREATING A CHILD!
CRUSHING THE ALLIED FORCES BY RUMBLING THE LAND CAN WAIT!
YOU WANT ME TO EUTHANIZE ...
...EVERY ELDIAN.
... EREN.

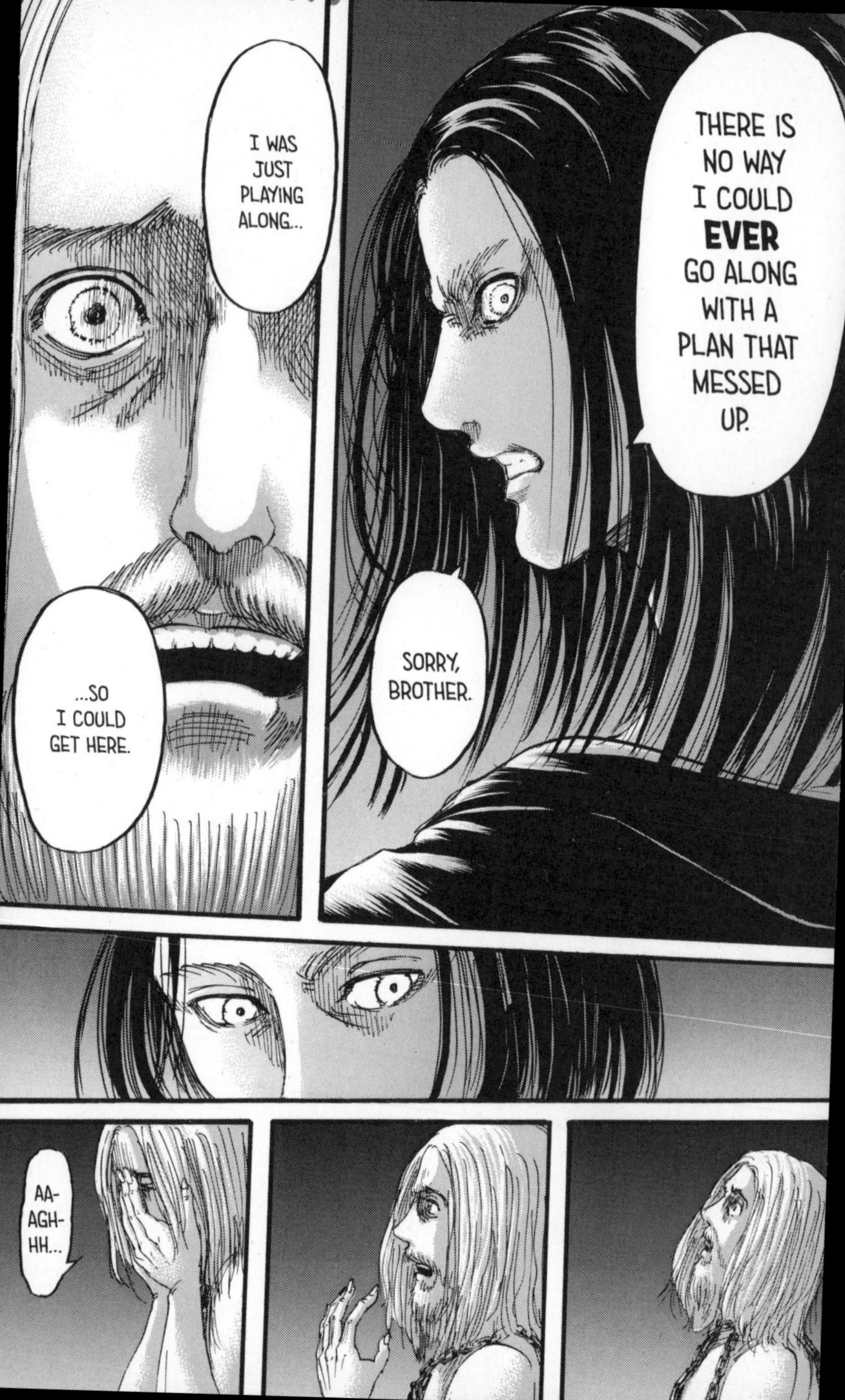
THERE IS NO WAY I COULD **EVER** GO ALONG WITH A PLAN THAT MESSED UP.
SORRY, BROTHER.
I WAS JUST PLAYING ALONG...
...SO I COULD GET HERE.
AA-AGH-HH...

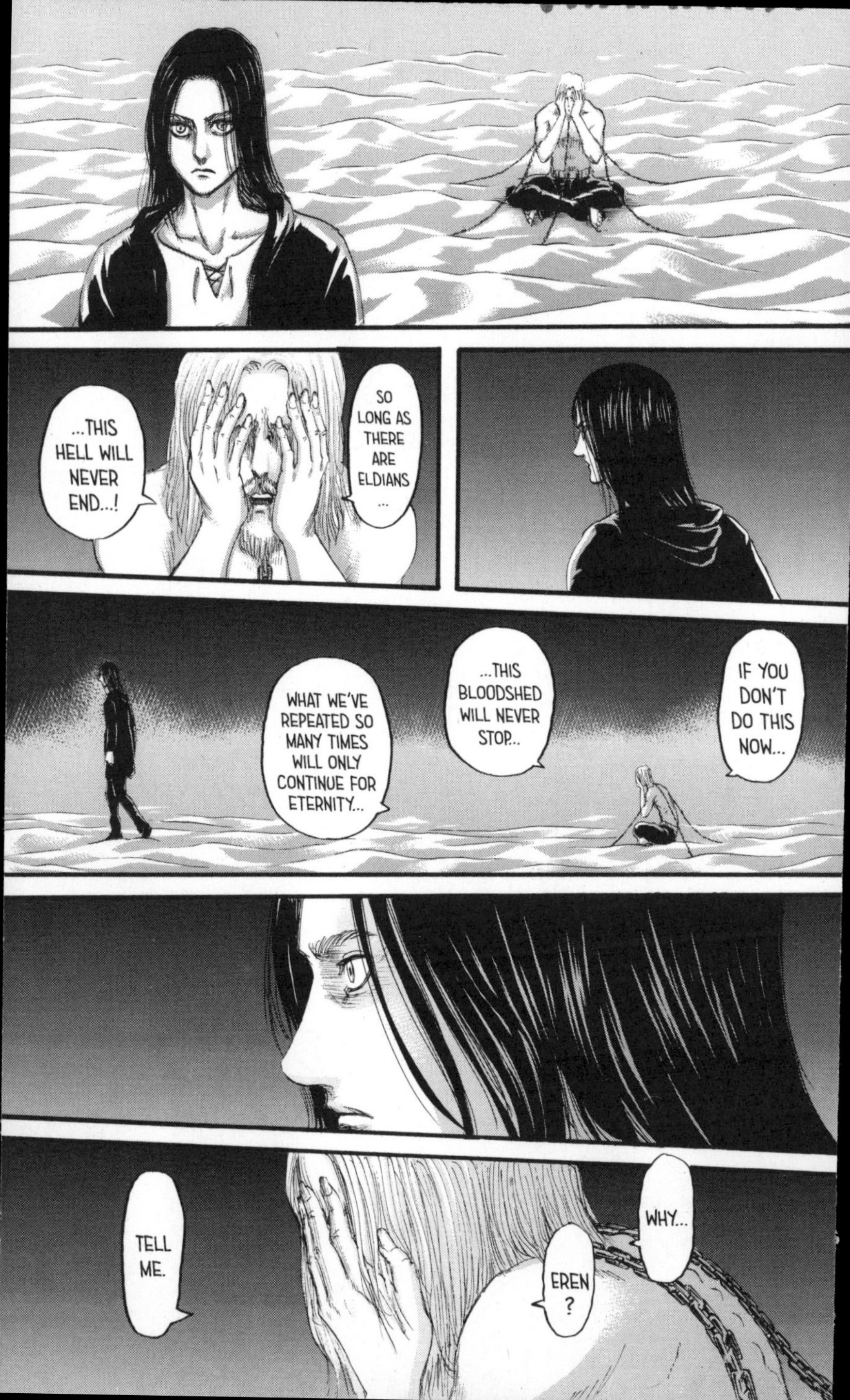
SO LONG AS THERE ARE ELDIANS ...
...THIS HELL WILL NEVER END...!
IF YOU DON'T DO THIS NOW...
...THIS BLOODSHED WILL NEVER STOP..
WHAT WE'VE REPEATED SO MANY TIMES WILL ONLY CONTINUE FOR ETERNITY...
WHY...
EREN ?
TELL ME.

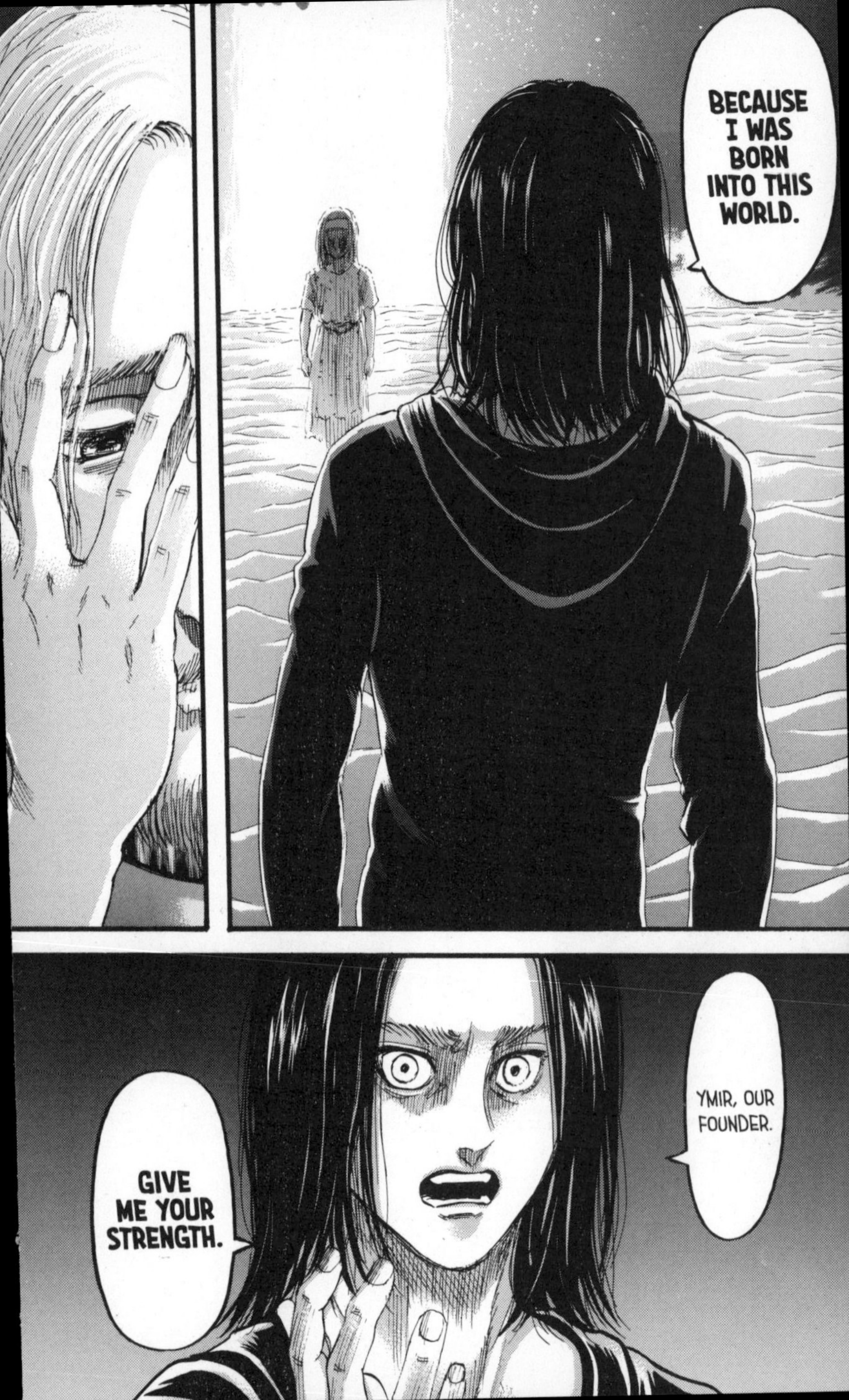
BECAUSE I WAS BORN INTO THIS WORLD.
YMIR, OUR FOUNDER.
GIVE ME YOUR STRENGTH.

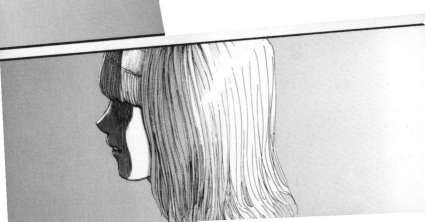

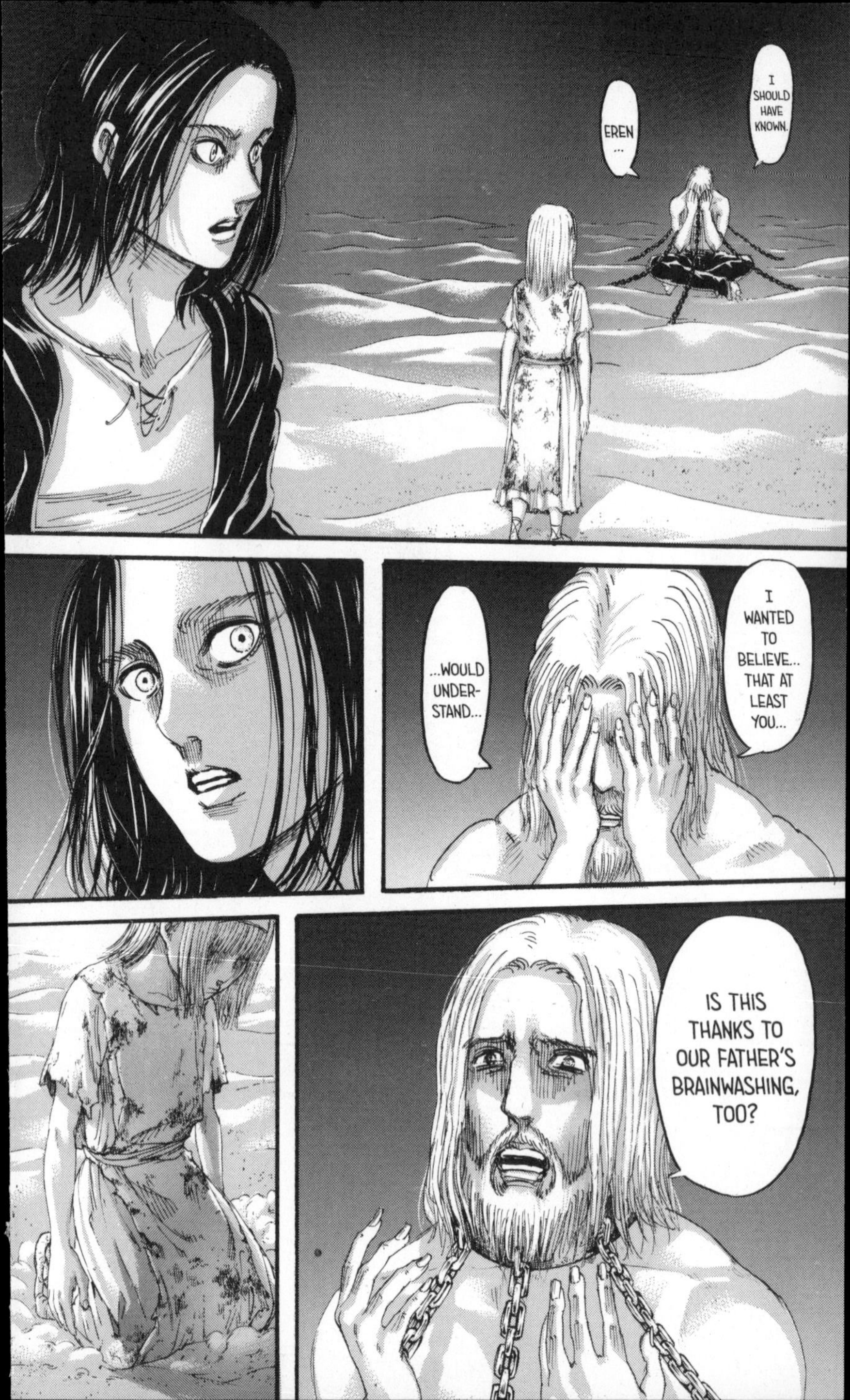
I SHOULD HAVE KNOWN.
EREN ...
I WANTED TO BELIEVE... THAT AT LEAST YOU...
...WOULD UNDER-STAND...
IS THIS THANKS TO OUR FATHER'S BRAINWASHING, TOO?

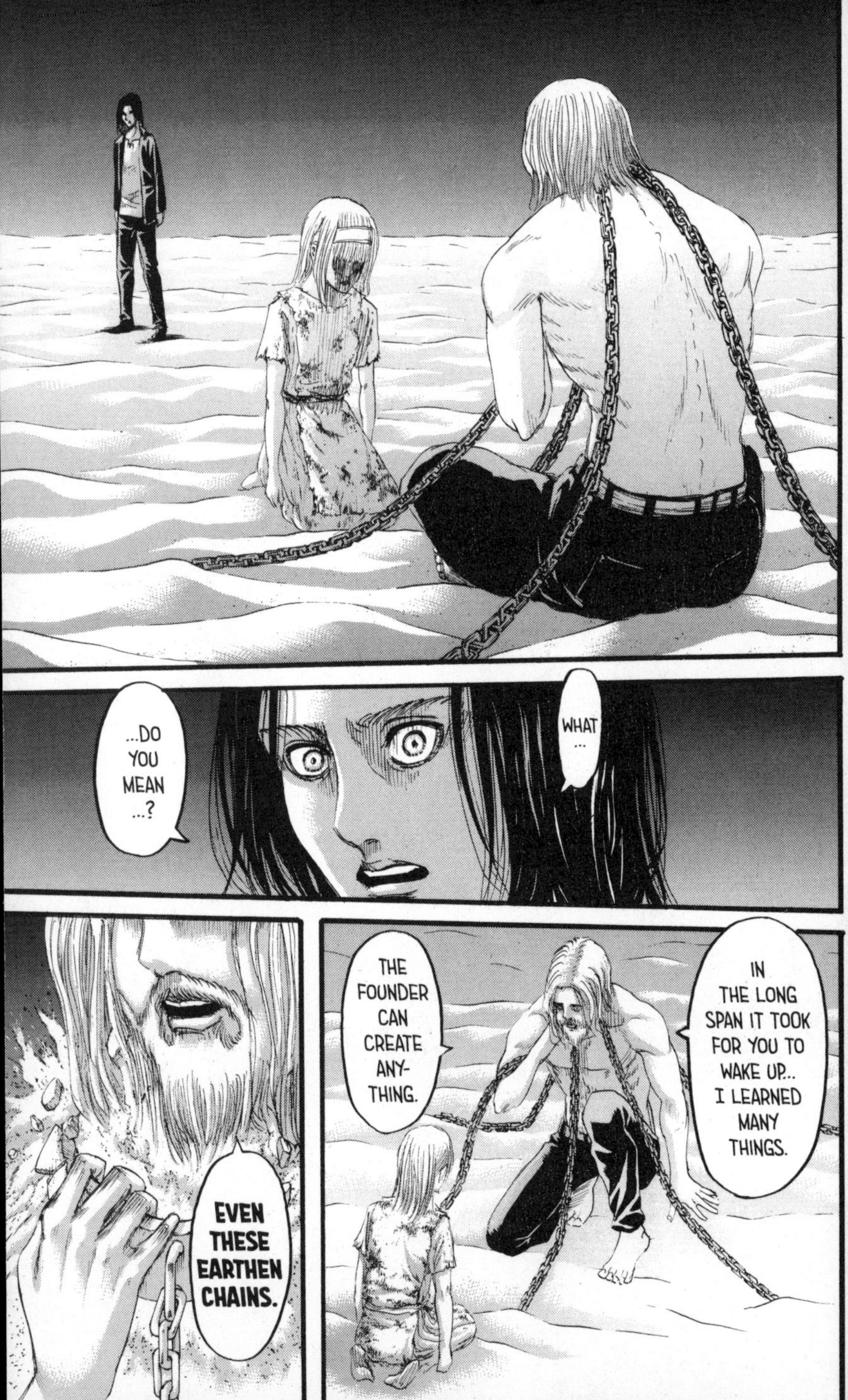
WHAT...
...DO YOU MEAN...?
IN THE LONG SPAN IT TOOK FOR YOU TO WAKE UP... I LEARNED MANY THINGS.
THE FOUNDER CAN CREATE ANYTHING.
EVEN THESE EARTHEN CHAINS.

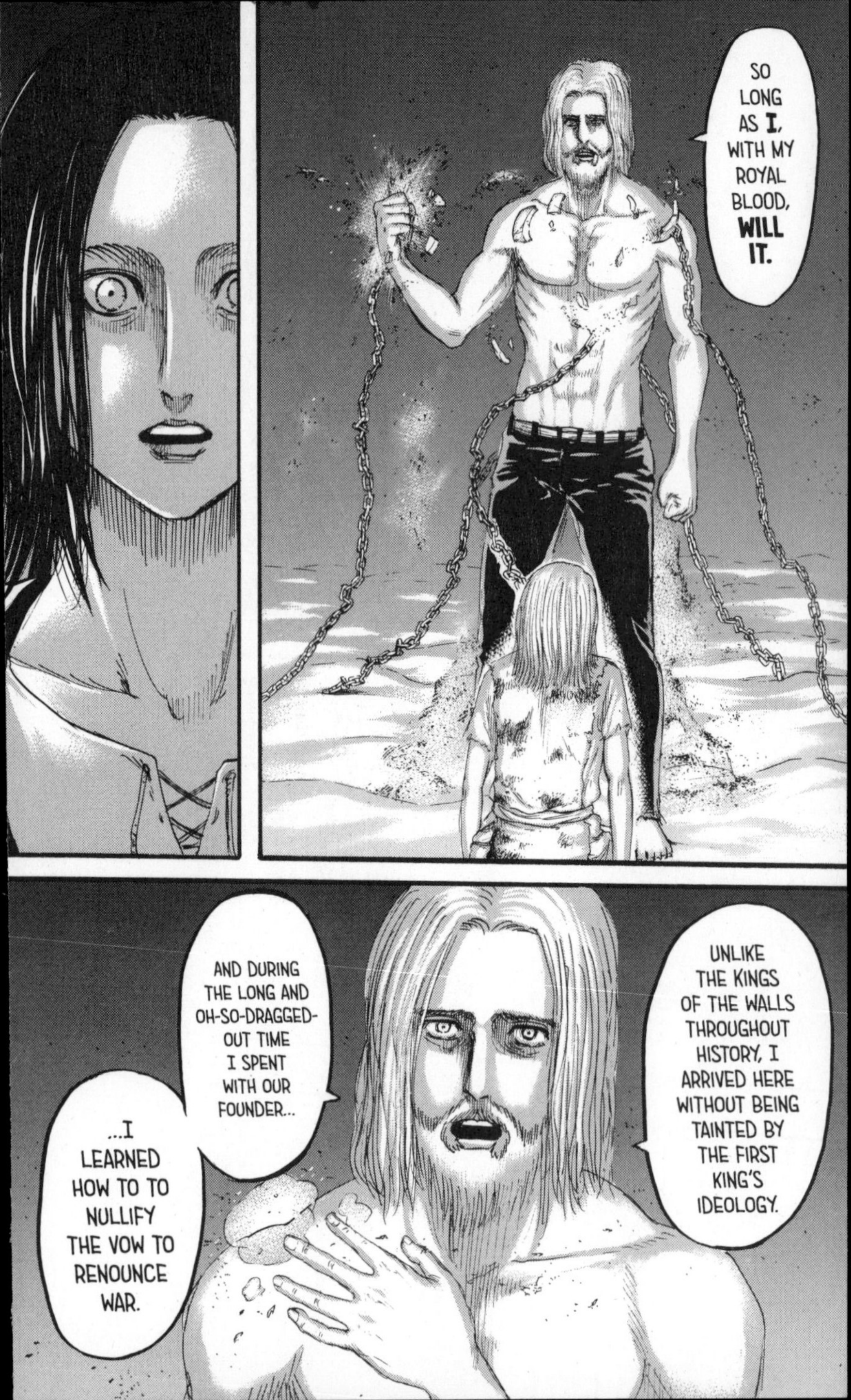
SO LONG AS I, WITH MY ROYAL BLOOD, WILL IT.
UNLIKE THE KINGS OF THE WALLS THROUGHOUT HISTORY, I ARRIVED HERE WITHOUT BEING TAINTED BY THE FIRST KING'S IDEOLOGY.
AND DURING THE LONG AND OH-SO-DRAGGED-OUT TIME I SPENT WITH OUR FOUNDER...
...I LEARNED HOW TO TO NULLIFY THE VOW TO RENOUNCE WAR.

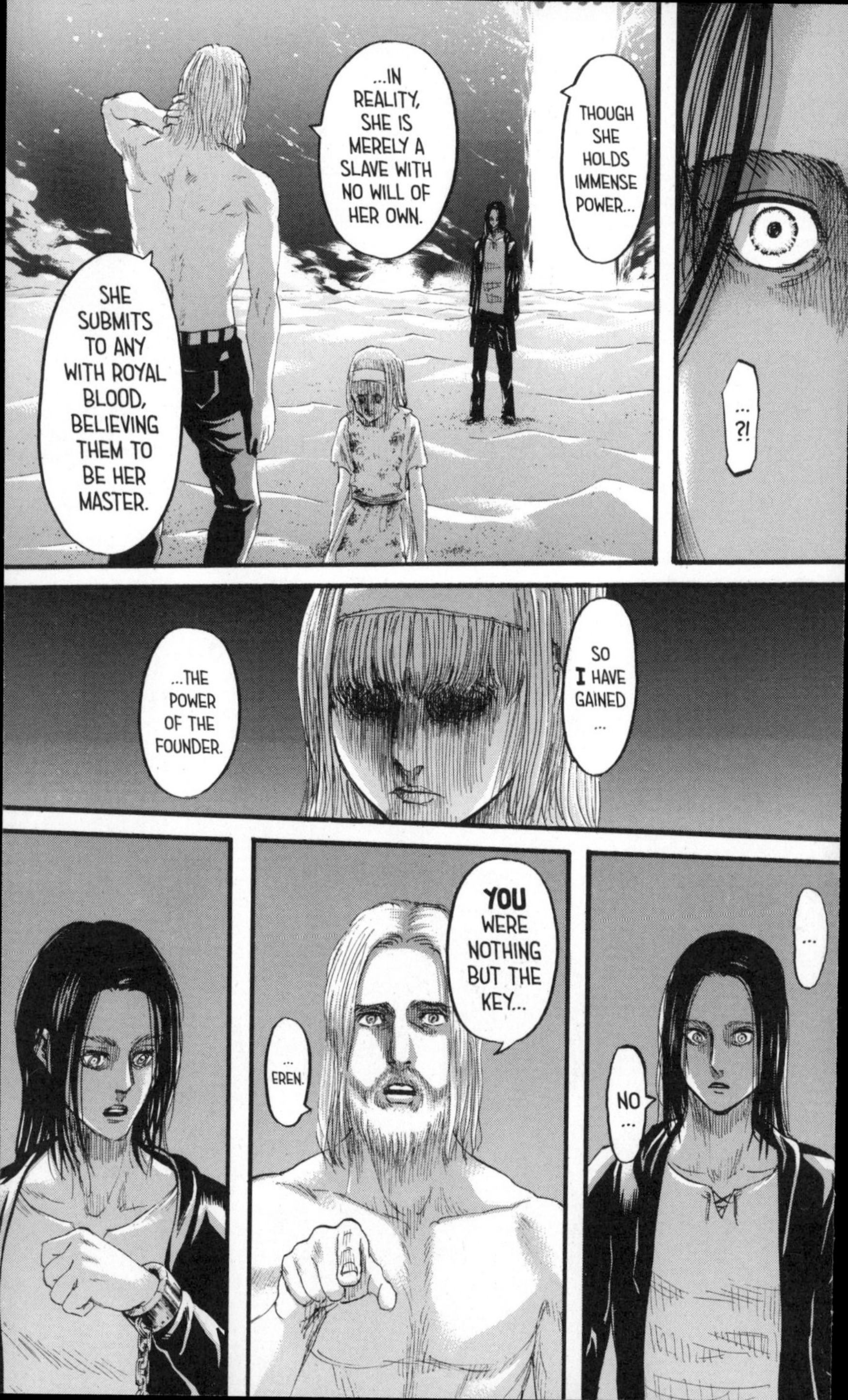
...?!
THOUGH SHE HOLDS IMMENSE POWER...
...IN REALITY, SHE IS MERELY A SLAVE WITH NO WILL OF HER OWN.
SHE SUBMITS TO ANY WITH ROYAL BLOOD, BELIEVING THEM TO BE HER MASTER.
SO **I** HAVE GAINED ...
...THE POWER OF THE FOUNDER.
...
NO ...
YOU WERE NOTHING BUT THE KEY...
... EREN.

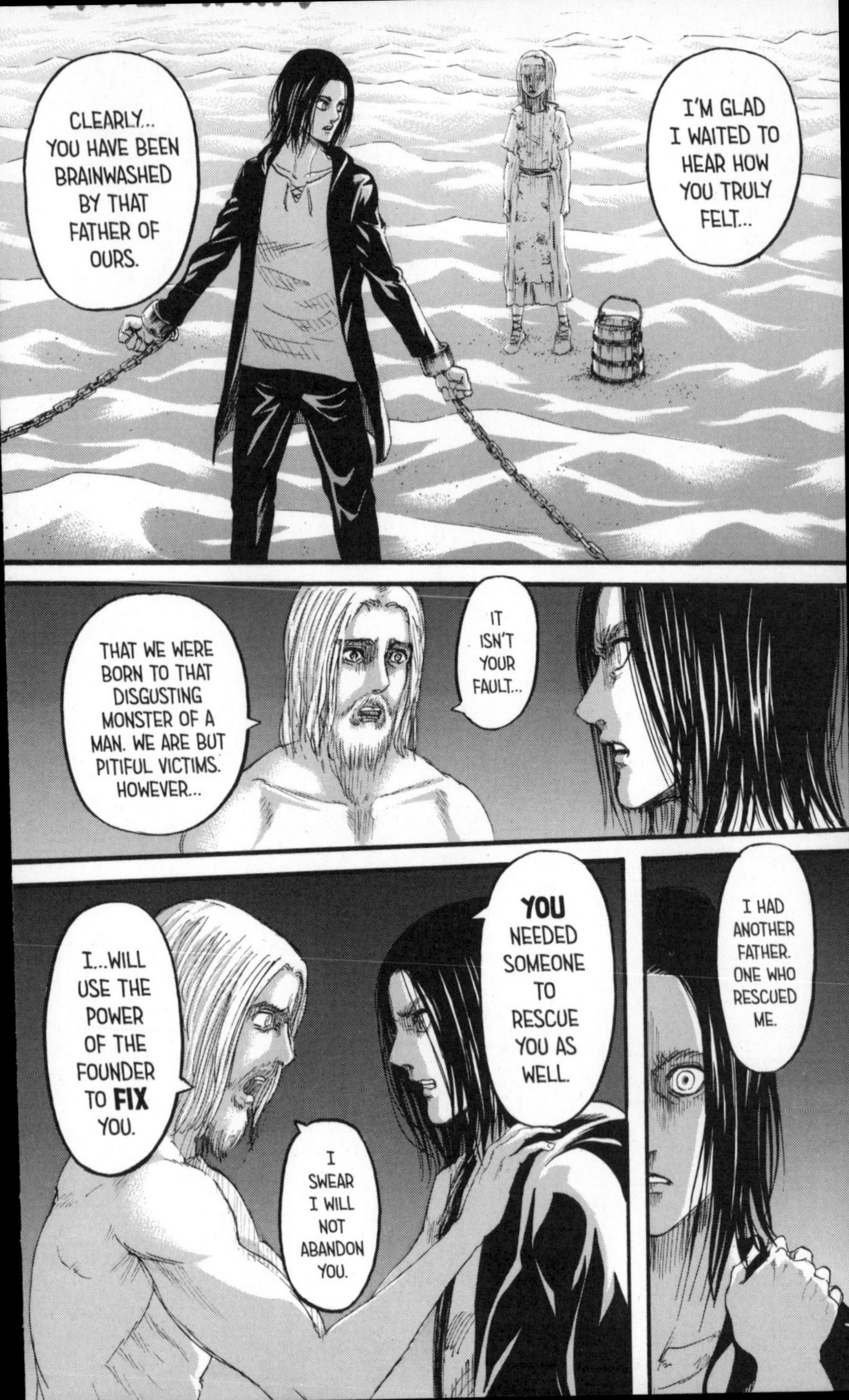
I'M GLAD I WAITED TO HEAR HOW YOU TRULY FELT...
CLEARLY... YOU HAVE BEEN BRAINWASHED BY THAT FATHER OF OURS.
IT ISN'T YOUR FAULT...
THAT WE WERE BORN TO THAT DISGUSTING MONSTER OF A MAN. WE ARE BUT PITIFUL VICTIMS. HOWEVER...
I HAD ANOTHER FATHER. ONE WHO RESCUED ME.
YOU NEEDED SOMEONE TO RESCUE YOU AS WELL.
I...WILL USE THE POWER OF THE FOUNDER TO **FIX** YOU.
I SWEAR I WILL NOT ABANDON YOU.

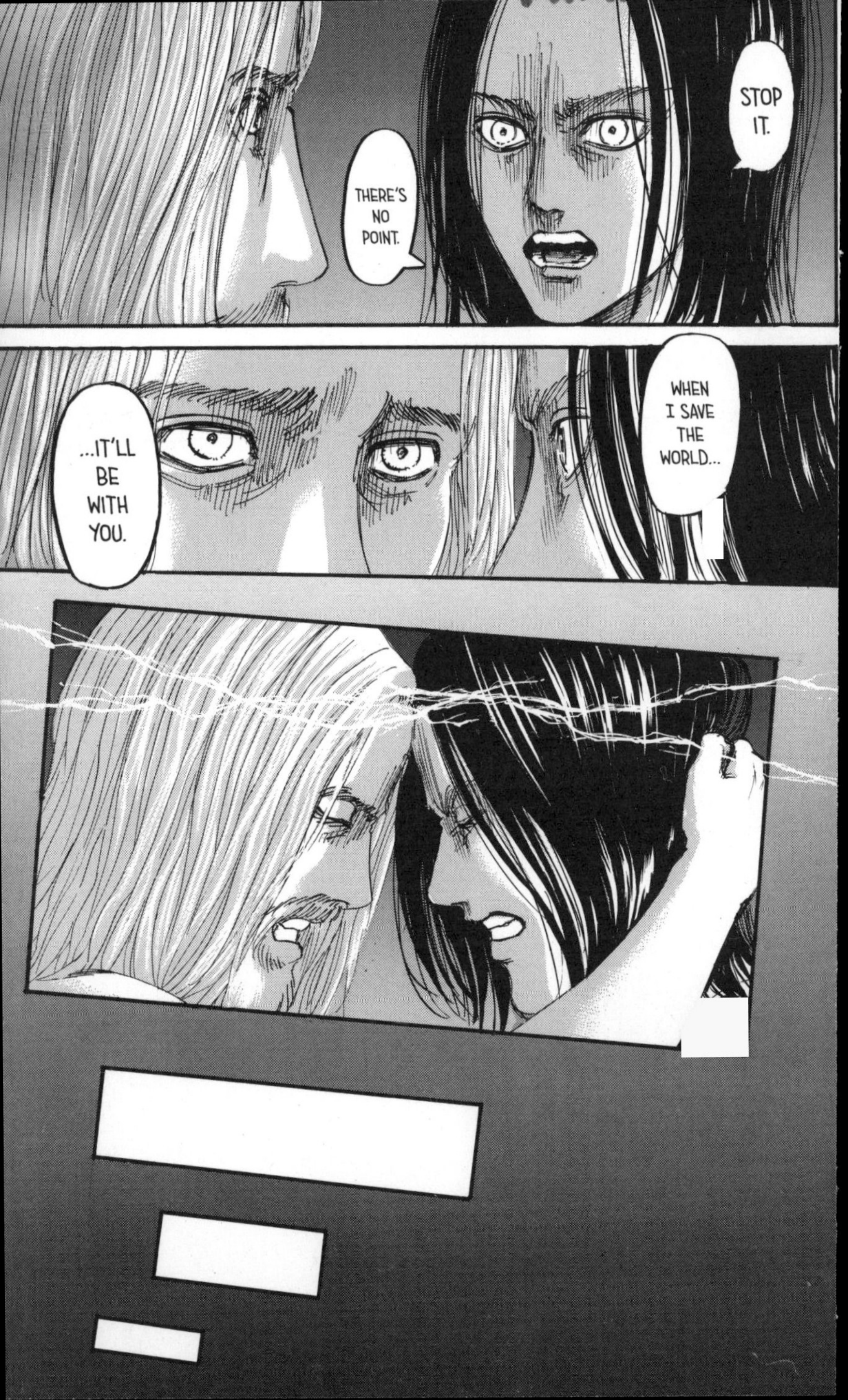
STOP IT.
THERE'S NO POINT.
WHEN I SAVE THE WORLD...
...IT'LL BE WITH YOU.

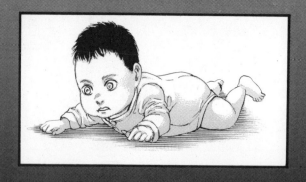

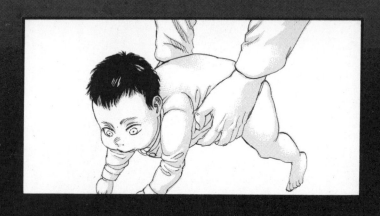

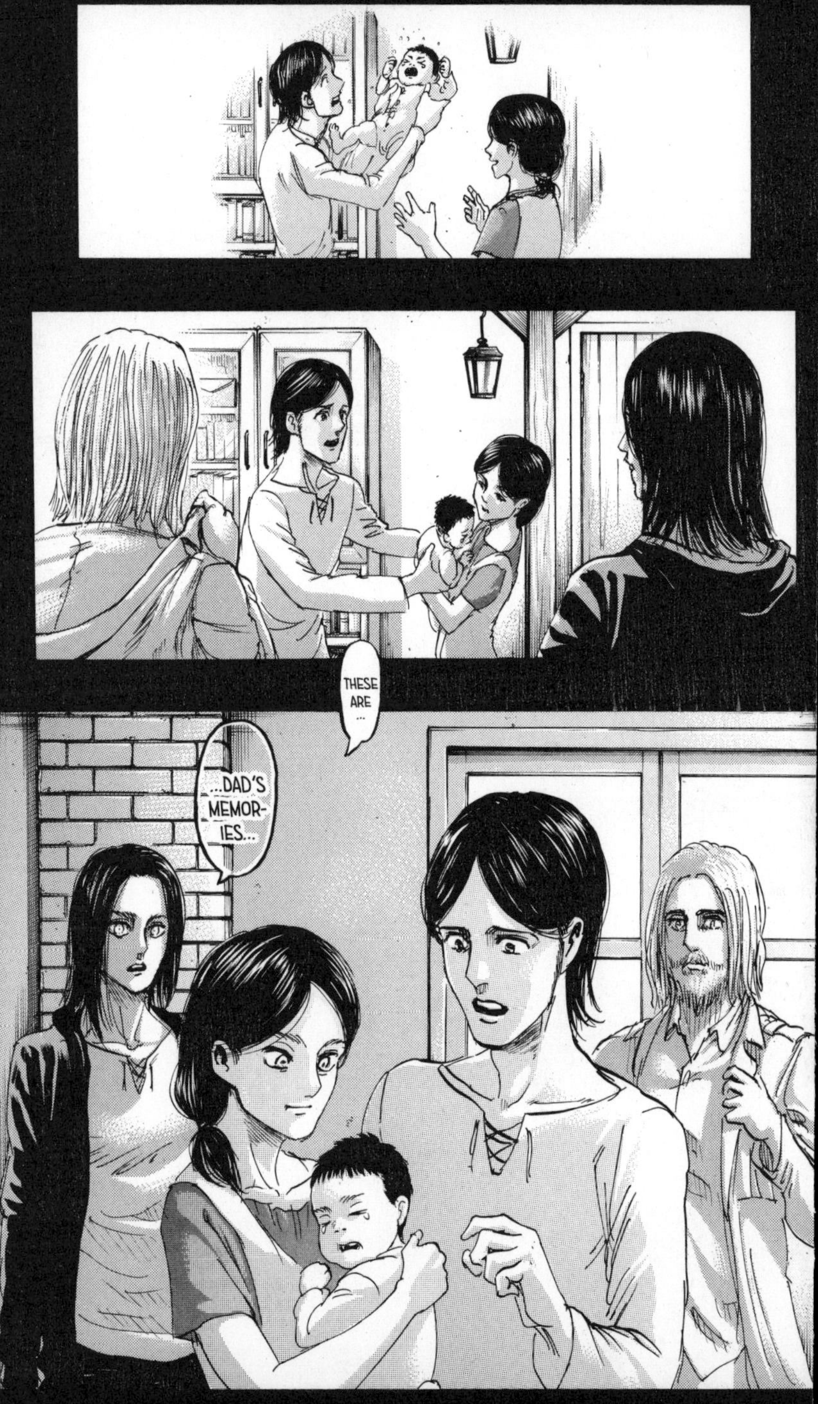
THESE ARE ...
...DAD'S MEMOR-IES...

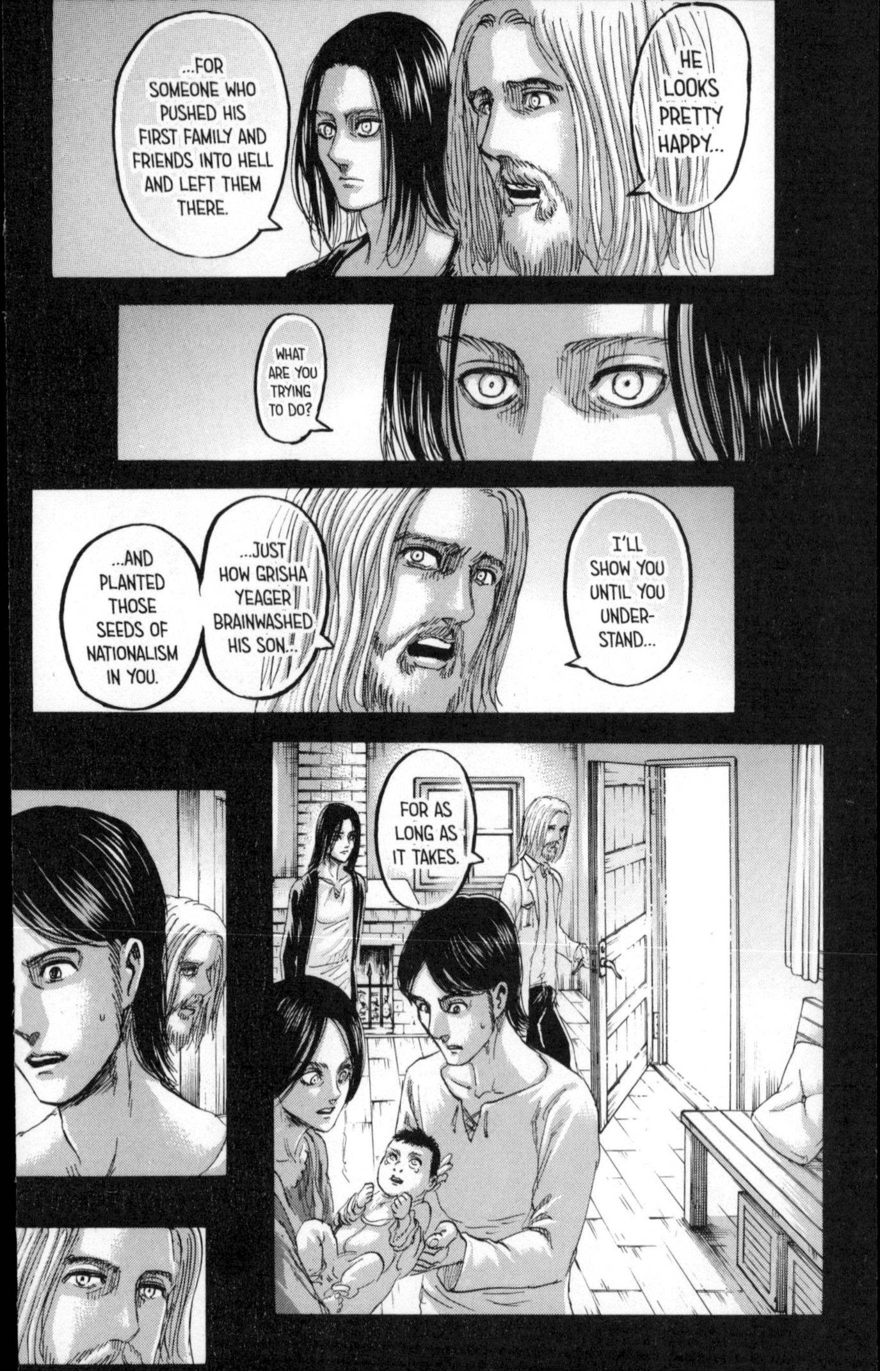

HE LOOKS PRETTY HAPPY...
...FOR SOMEONE WHO PUSHED HIS FIRST FAMILY AND FRIENDS INTO HELL AND LEFT THEM THERE.
WHAT ARE YOU TRYING TO DO?
I'LL SHOW YOU UNTIL YOU UNDER-STAND...
...JUST HOW GRISHA YEAGER BRAINWASHED HIS SON...
...AND PLANTED THOSE SEEDS OF NATIONALISM IN YOU.
FOR AS LONG AS IT TAKES.

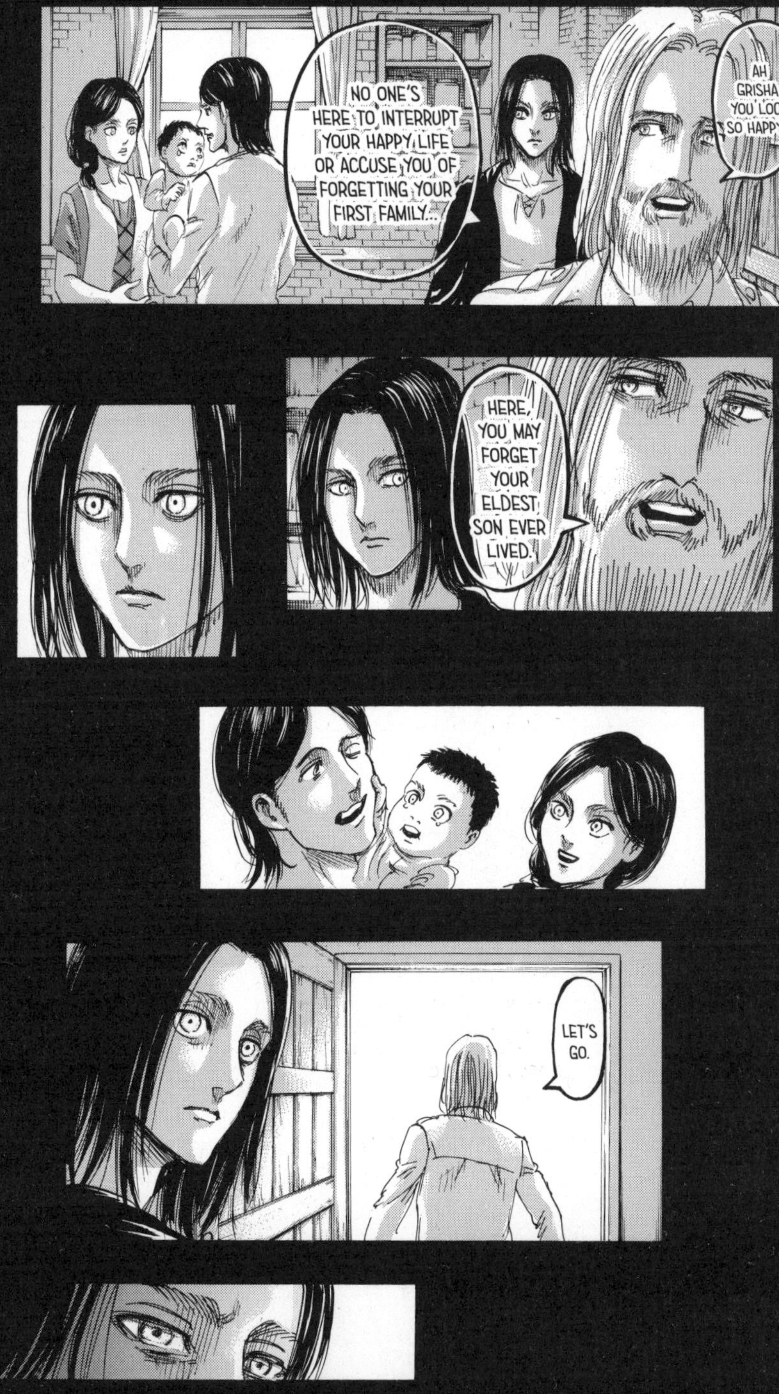
AH GRISHA, YOU LOOK SO HAPPY...
NO ONE'S HERE TO INTERRUPT YOUR HAPPY LIFE OR ACCUSE YOU OF FORGETTING YOUR FIRST FAMILY...
HERE, YOU MAY FORGET YOUR ELDEST SON EVER LIVED.
LET'S GO.

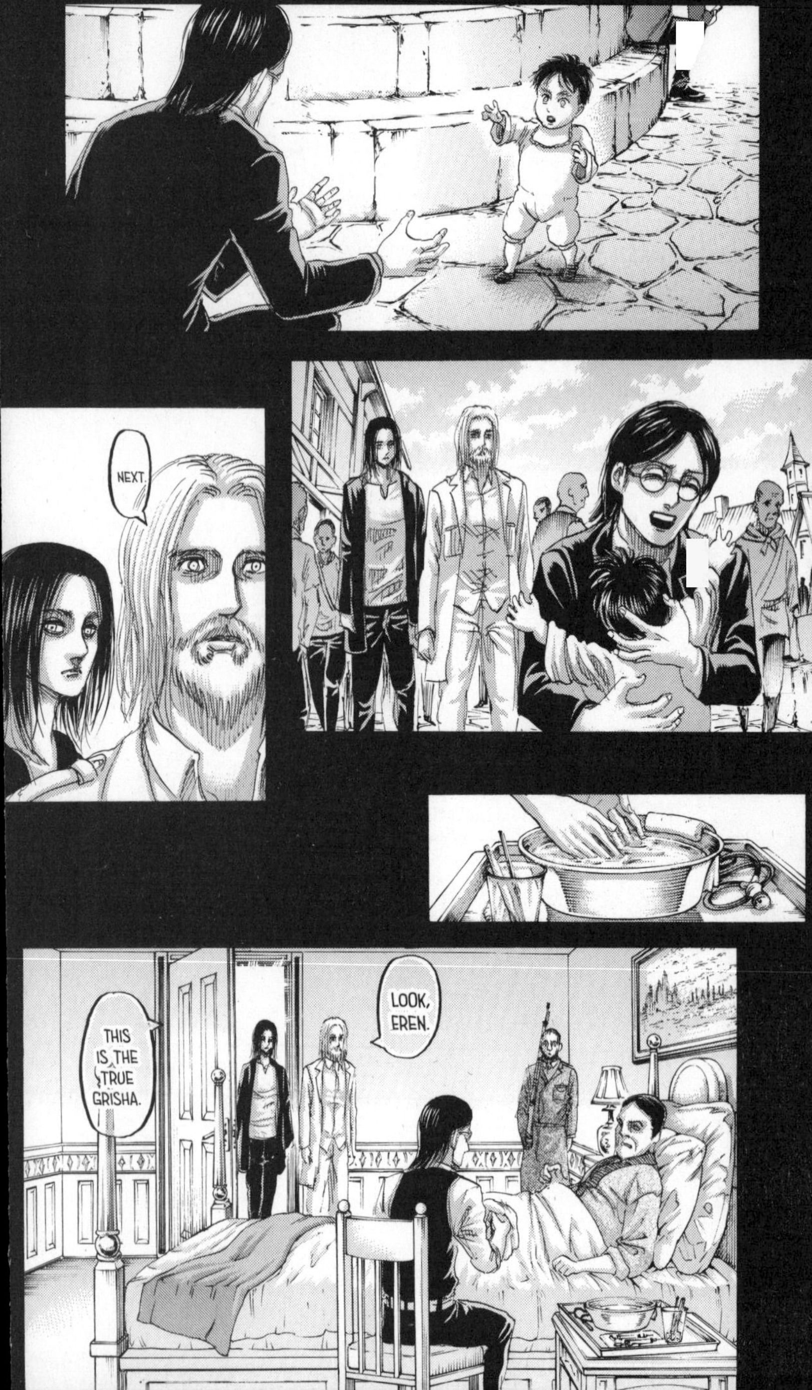
NEXT.
LOOK, EREN.
THIS IS THE TRUE GRISHA.

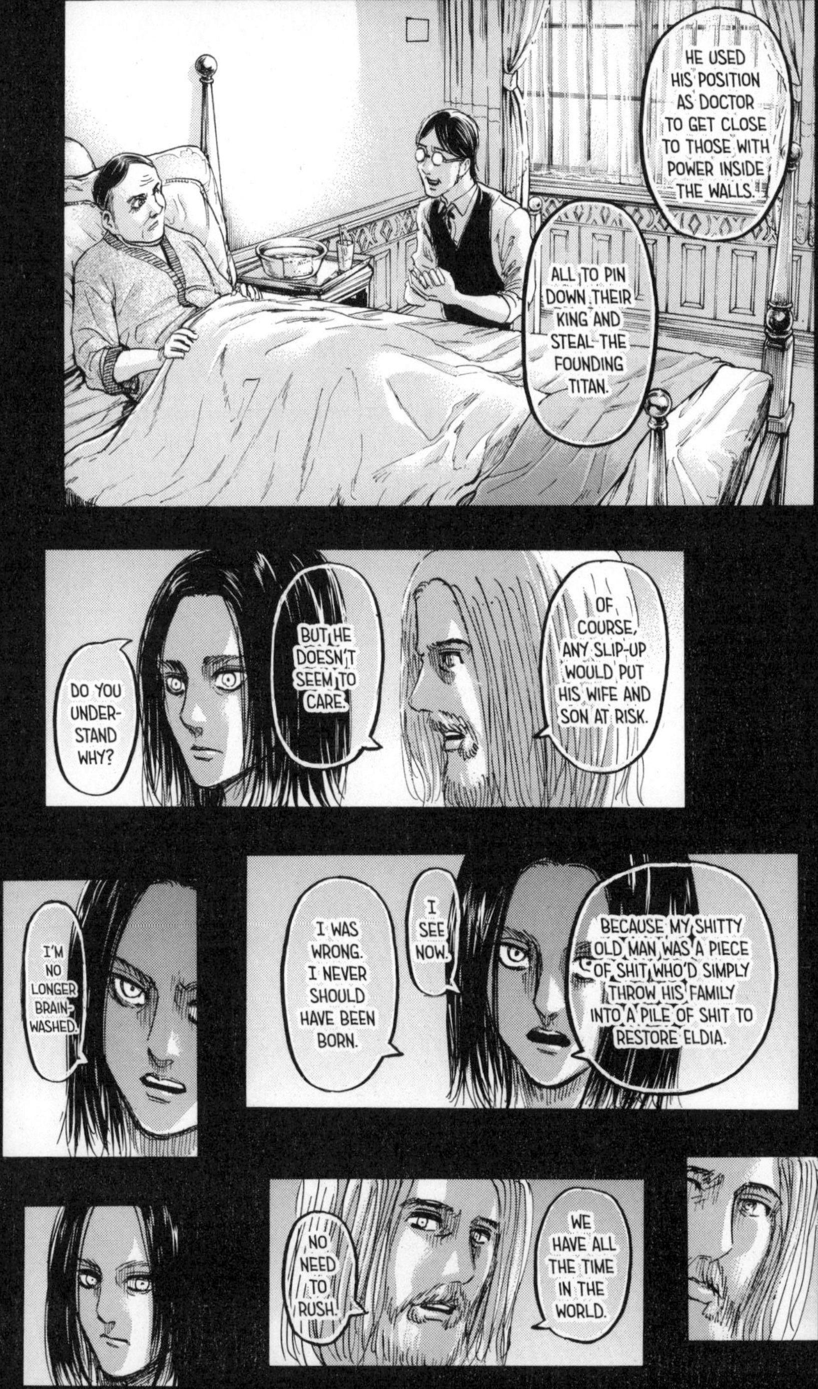
HE USED HIS POSITION AS DOCTOR TO GET CLOSE TO THOSE WITH POWER INSIDE THE WALLS.
ALL TO PIN DOWN THEIR KING AND STEAL THE FOUNDING TITAN.
OF COURSE, ANY SLIP-UP WOULD PUT HIS WIFE AND SON AT RISK.
BUT HE DOESN'T SEEM TO CARE.
DO YOU UNDERSTAND WHY?
BECAUSE MY SHITTY OLD MAN WAS A PIECE OF SHIT WHO'D SIMPLY THROW HIS FAMILY INTO A PILE OF SHIT TO RESTORE ELDIA.
I SEE NOW.
I WAS WRONG. I NEVER SHOULD HAVE BEEN BORN.
I'M NO LONGER BRAINWASHED.
WE HAVE ALL THE TIME IN THE WORLD.
NO NEED TO RUSH.

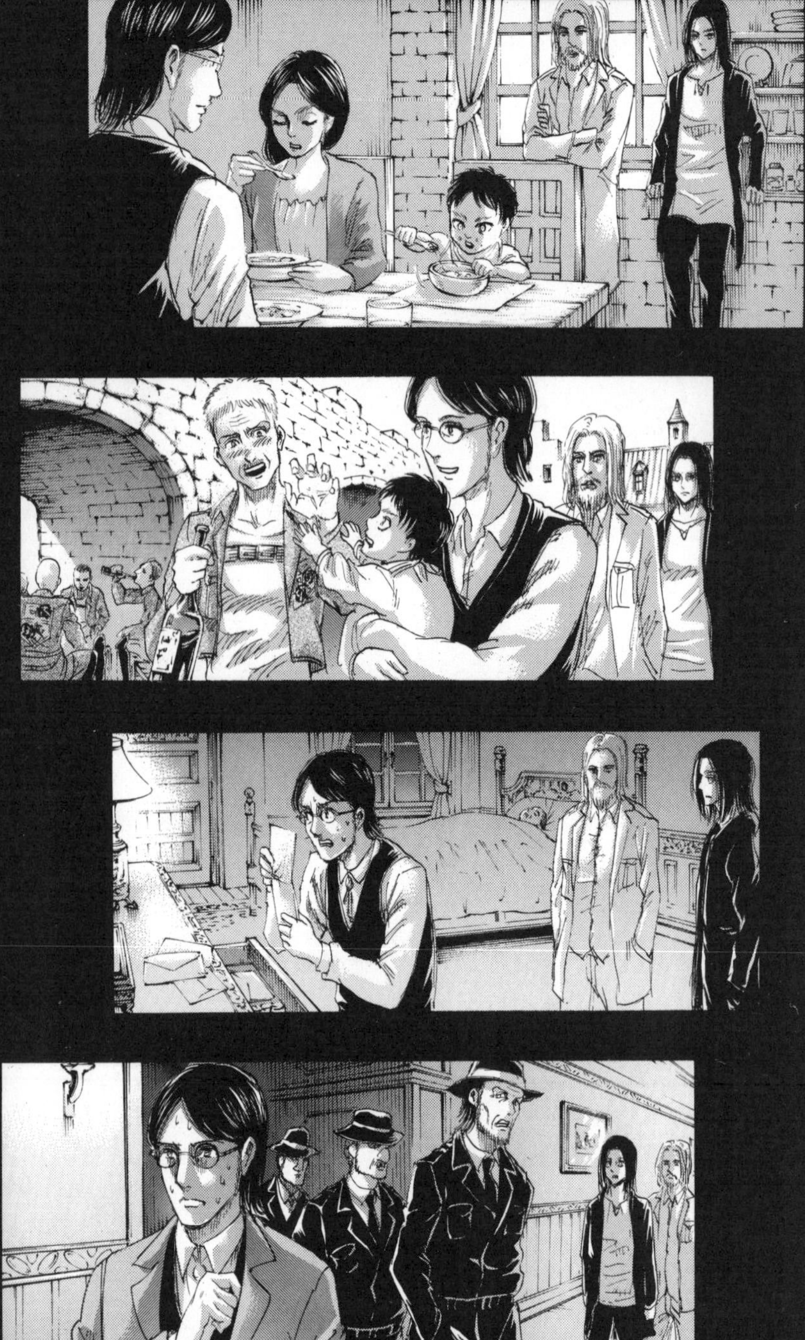

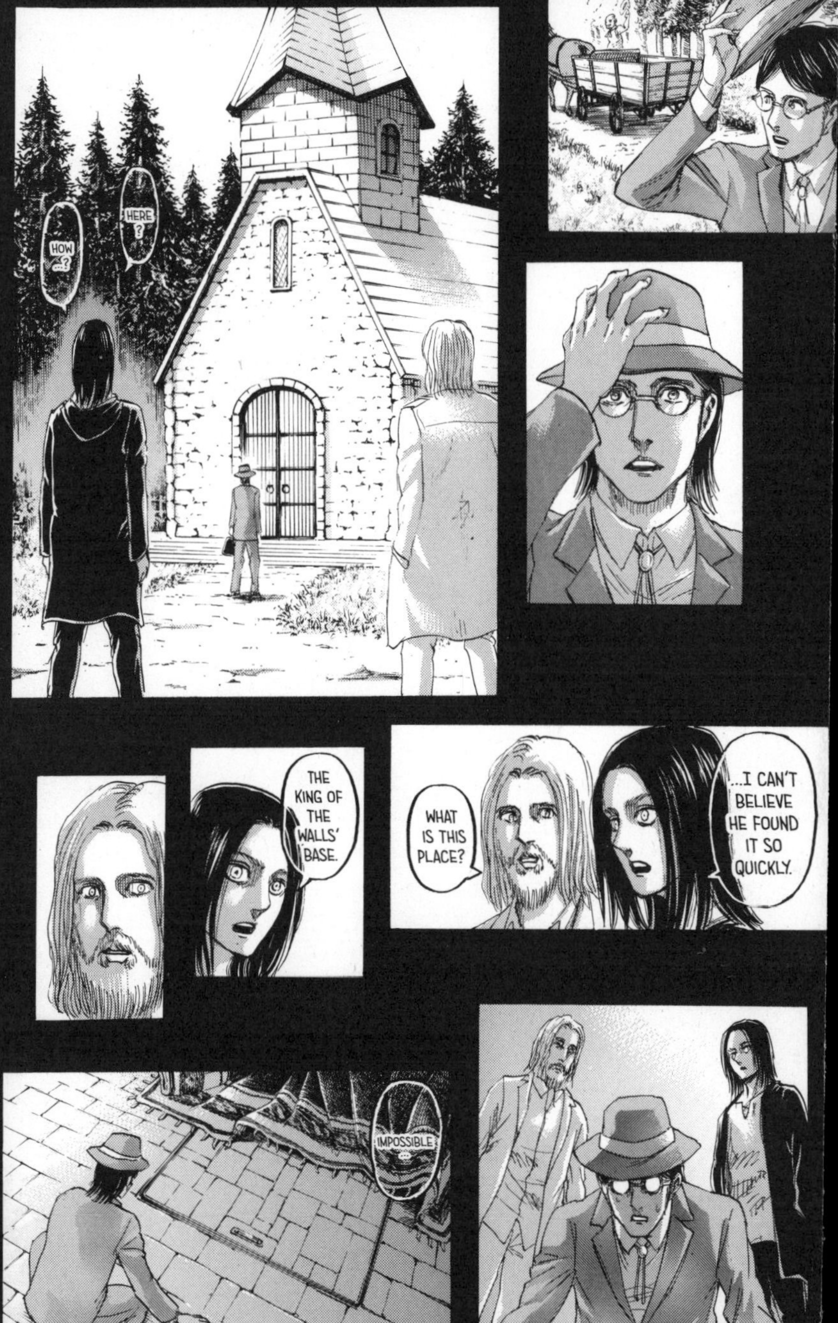
HERE?
HOW...?
...I CAN'T BELIEVE HE FOUND IT SO QUICKLY.
WHAT IS THIS PLACE?
THE KING OF THE WALLS' BASE.
IMPOSSIBLE...

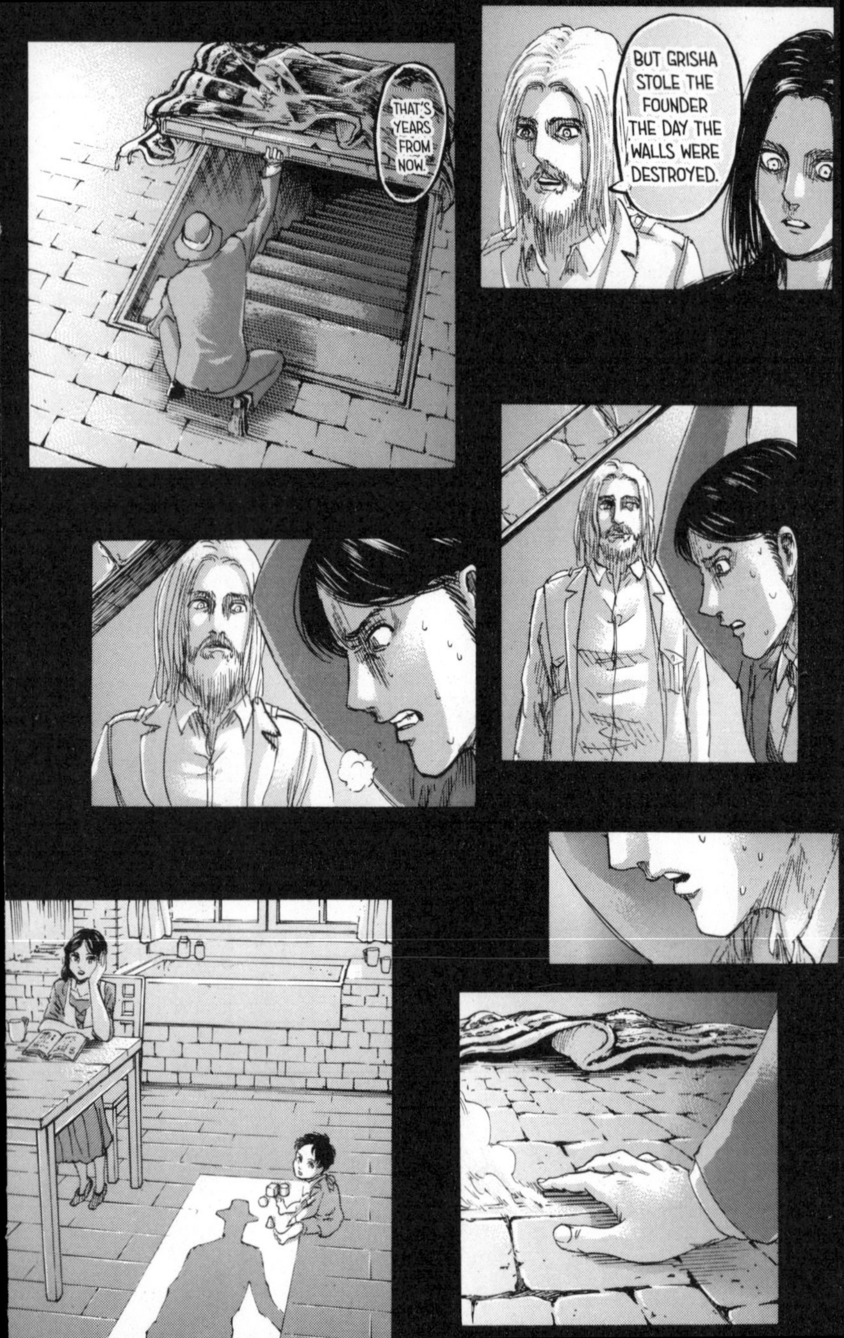
BUT GRISHA STOLE THE FOUNDER THE DAY THE WALLS WERE DESTROYED.
THAT'S YEARS FROM NOW.

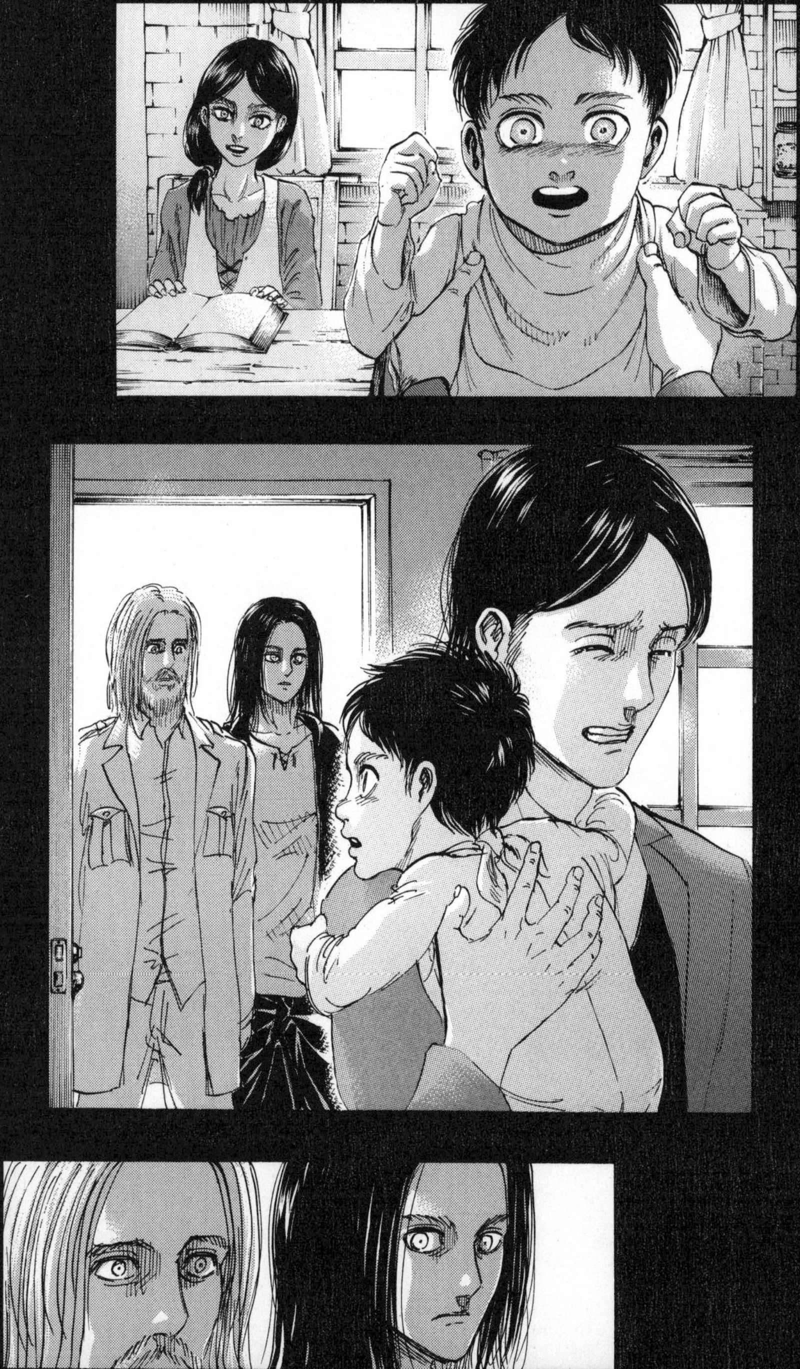

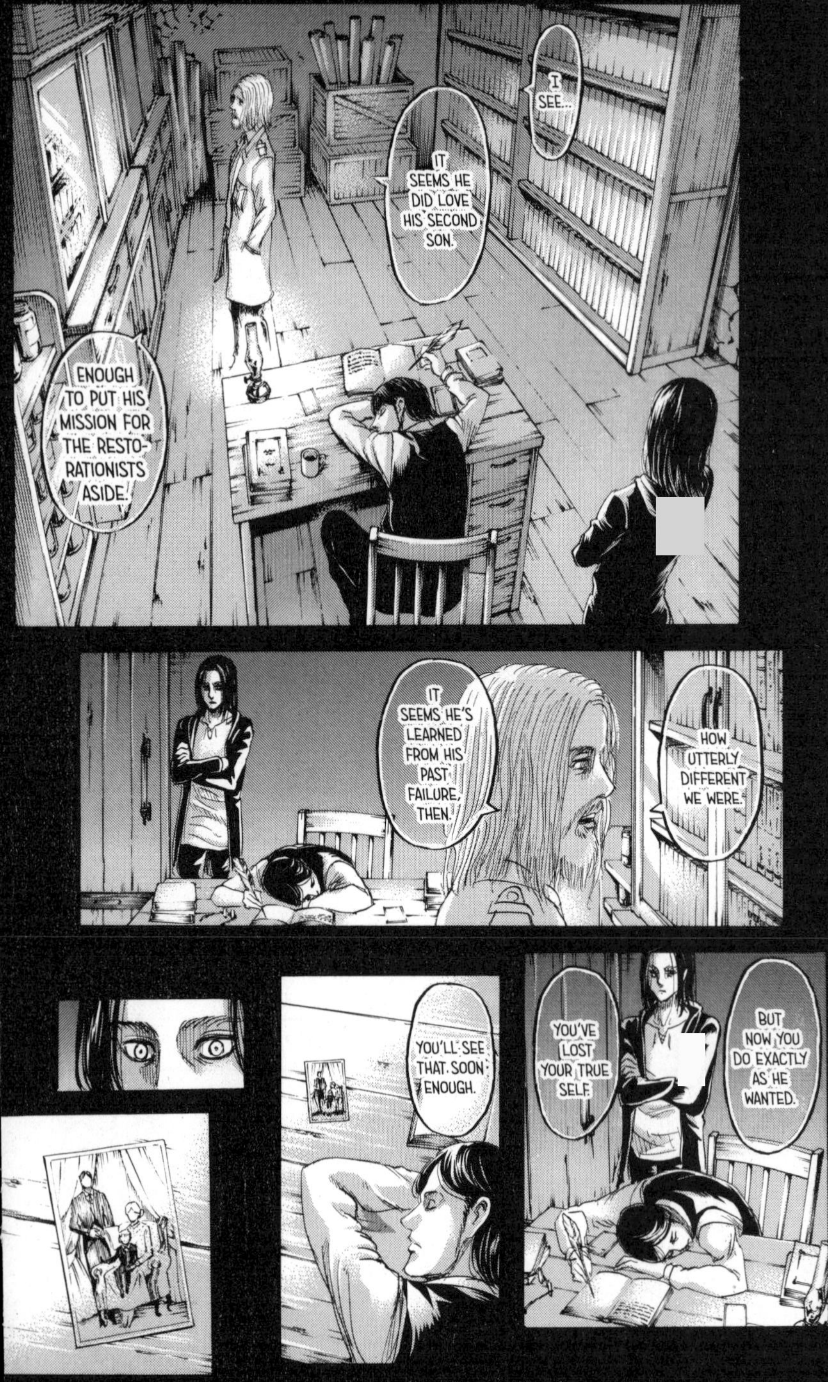
I SEE...
IT SEEMS HE DID LOVE HIS SECOND SON.
ENOUGH TO PUT HIS MISSION FOR THE RESTO-RATIONISTS ASIDE.
HOW UTTERLY DIFFERENT WE WERE.
IT SEEMS HE'S LEARNED FROM HIS PAST FAILURE, THEN.
BUT NOW YOU DO EXACTLY AS HE WANTED.
YOU'VE LOST YOUR TRUE SELF.
YOU'LL SEE THAT SOON ENOUGH.

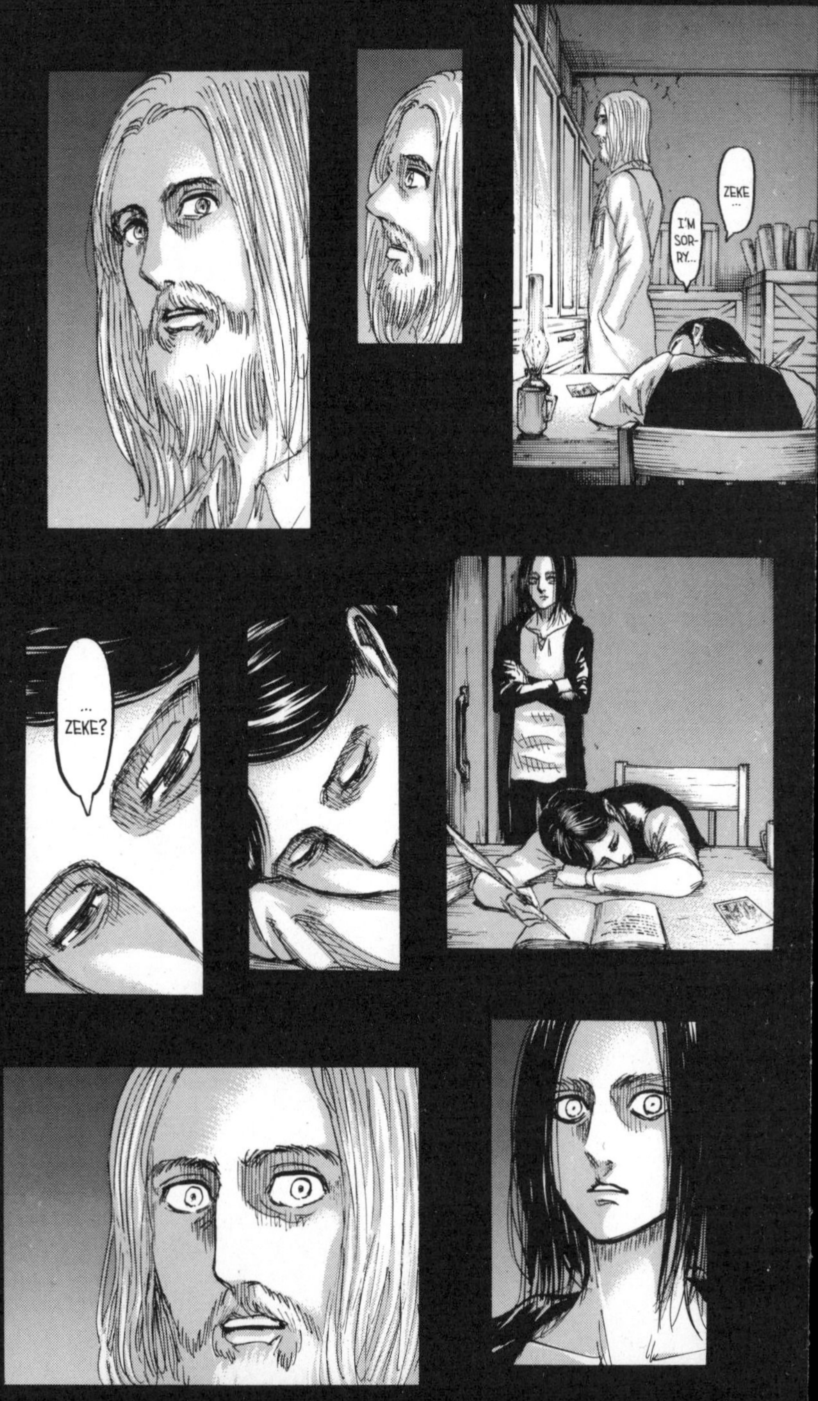
ZEKE ...
I'M SORRY...
... ZEKE?

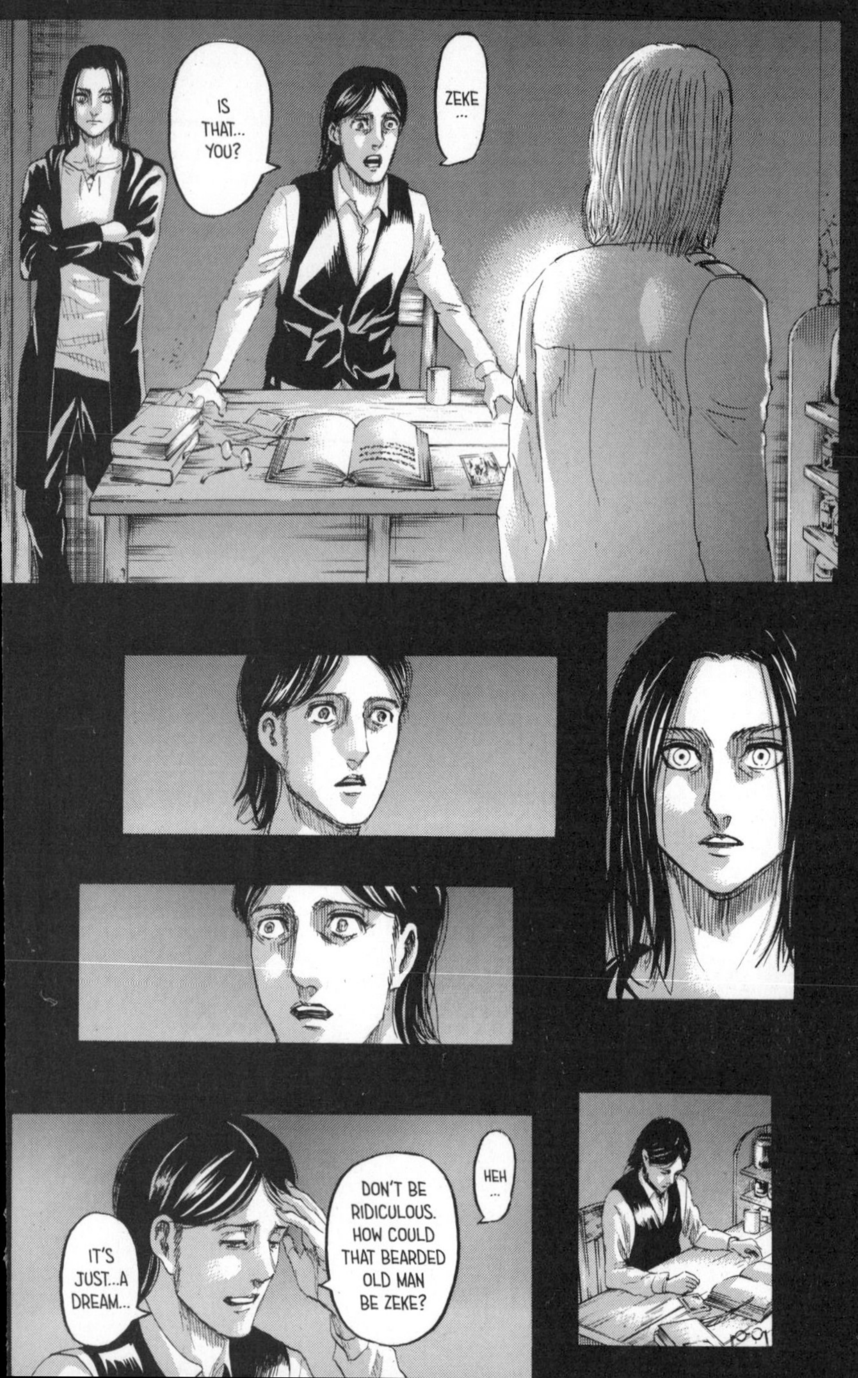
ZEKE ...
IS THAT... YOU?
HEH ...
DON'T BE RIDICULOUS. HOW COULD THAT BEARDED OLD MAN BE ZEKE?
IT'S JUST...A DREAM...

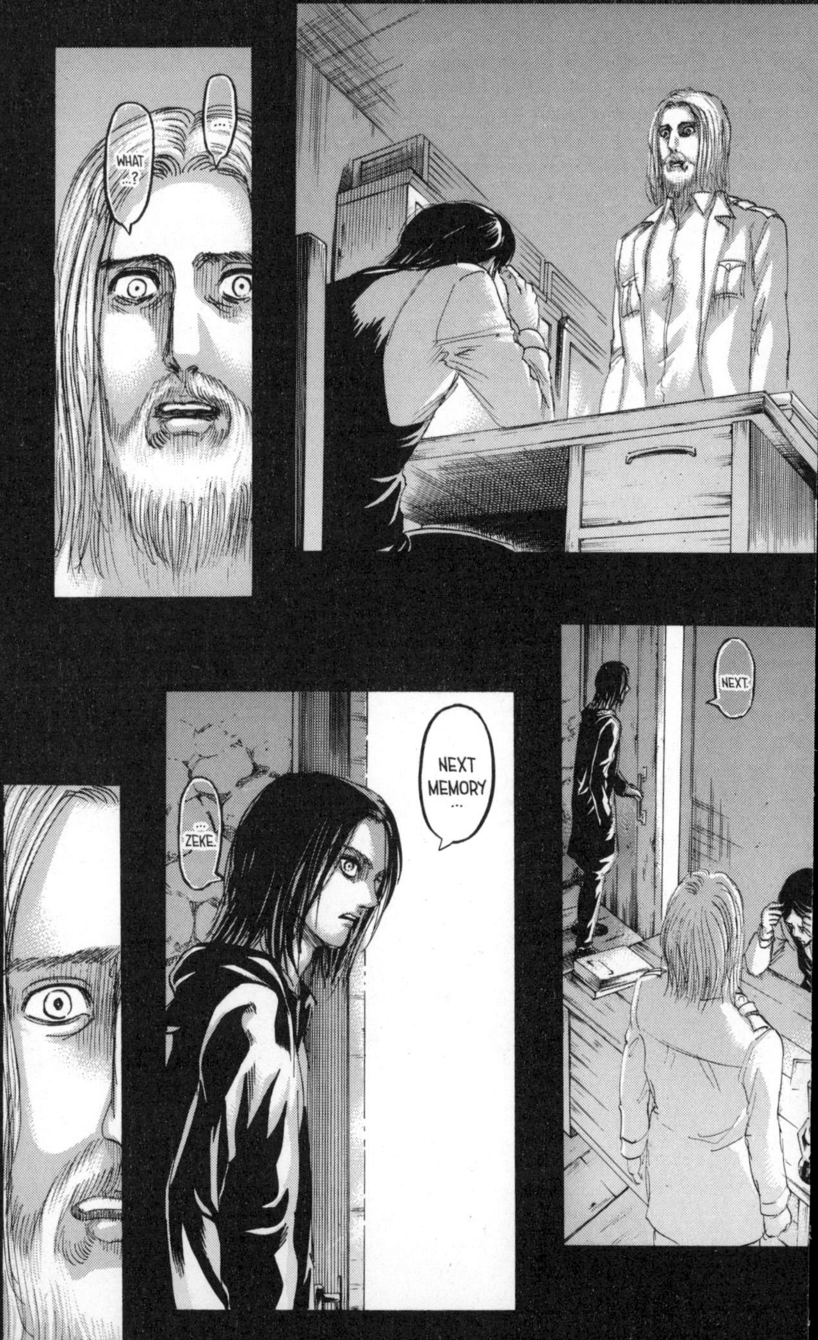
...
WHAT ...?
NEXT.
NEXT MEMORY ...
... ZEKE.

ATTACK on TITAN

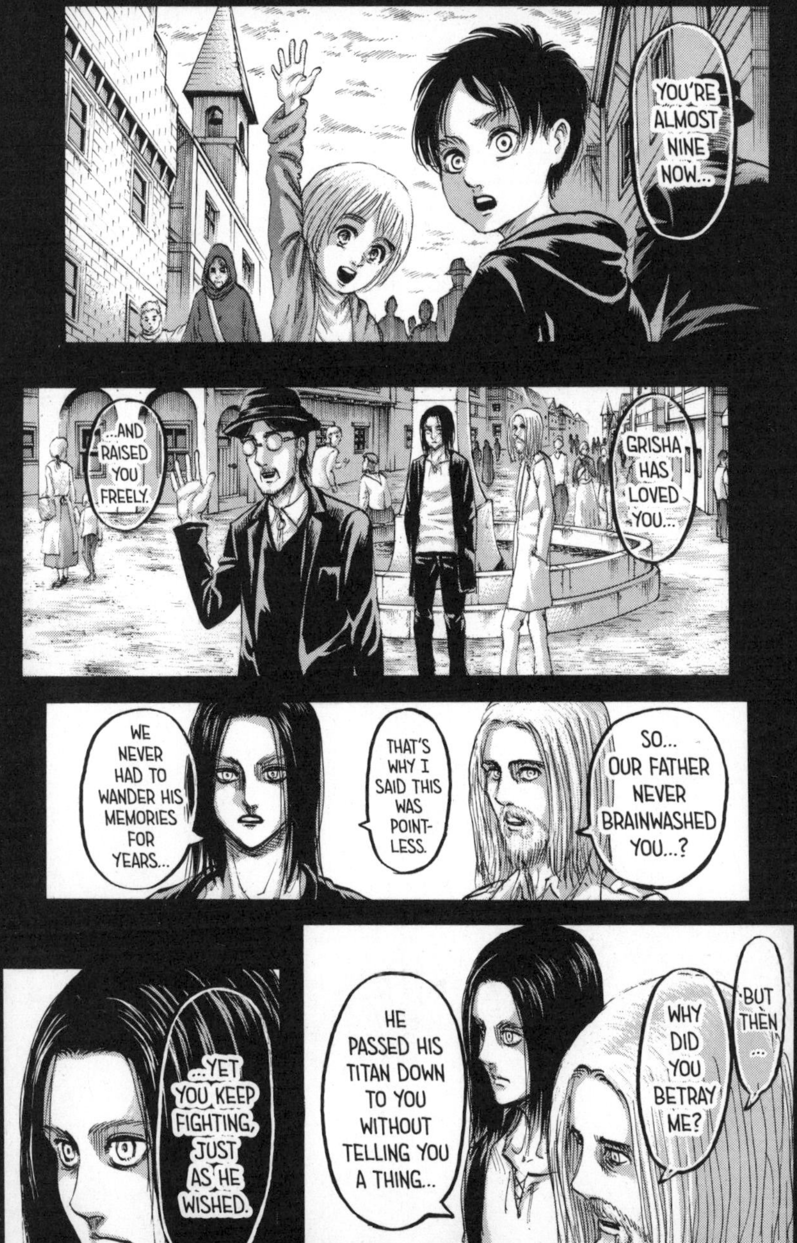
YOU'RE ALMOST NINE NOW...
GRISHA HAS LOVED YOU...
...AND RAISED YOU FREELY.
SO... OUR FATHER NEVER BRAINWASHED YOU...?
THAT'S WHY I SAID THIS WAS POINT-LESS.
WE NEVER HAD TO WANDER HIS MEMORIES FOR YEARS...
BUT THEN...
WHY DID YOU BETRAY ME?
HE PASSED HIS TITAN DOWN TO YOU WITHOUT TELLING YOU A THING...
...YET YOU KEEP FIGHTING, JUST AS HE WISHED.

Episode 121: Memories of the Future

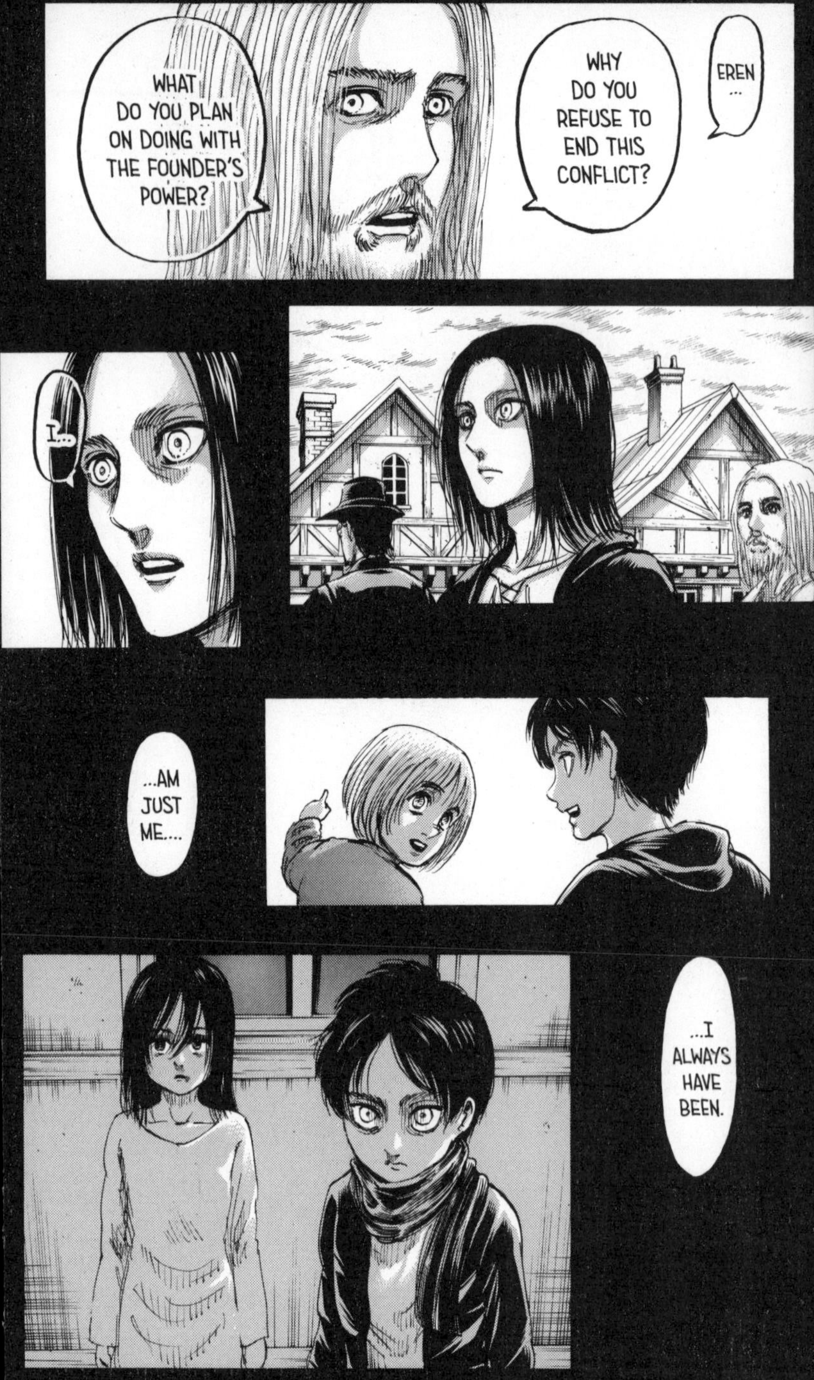
EREN ...
WHY DO YOU REFUSE TO END THIS CONFLICT?
WHAT DO YOU PLAN ON DOING WITH THE FOUNDER'S POWER?
I...
...AM JUST ME....
...I ALWAYS HAVE BEEN.

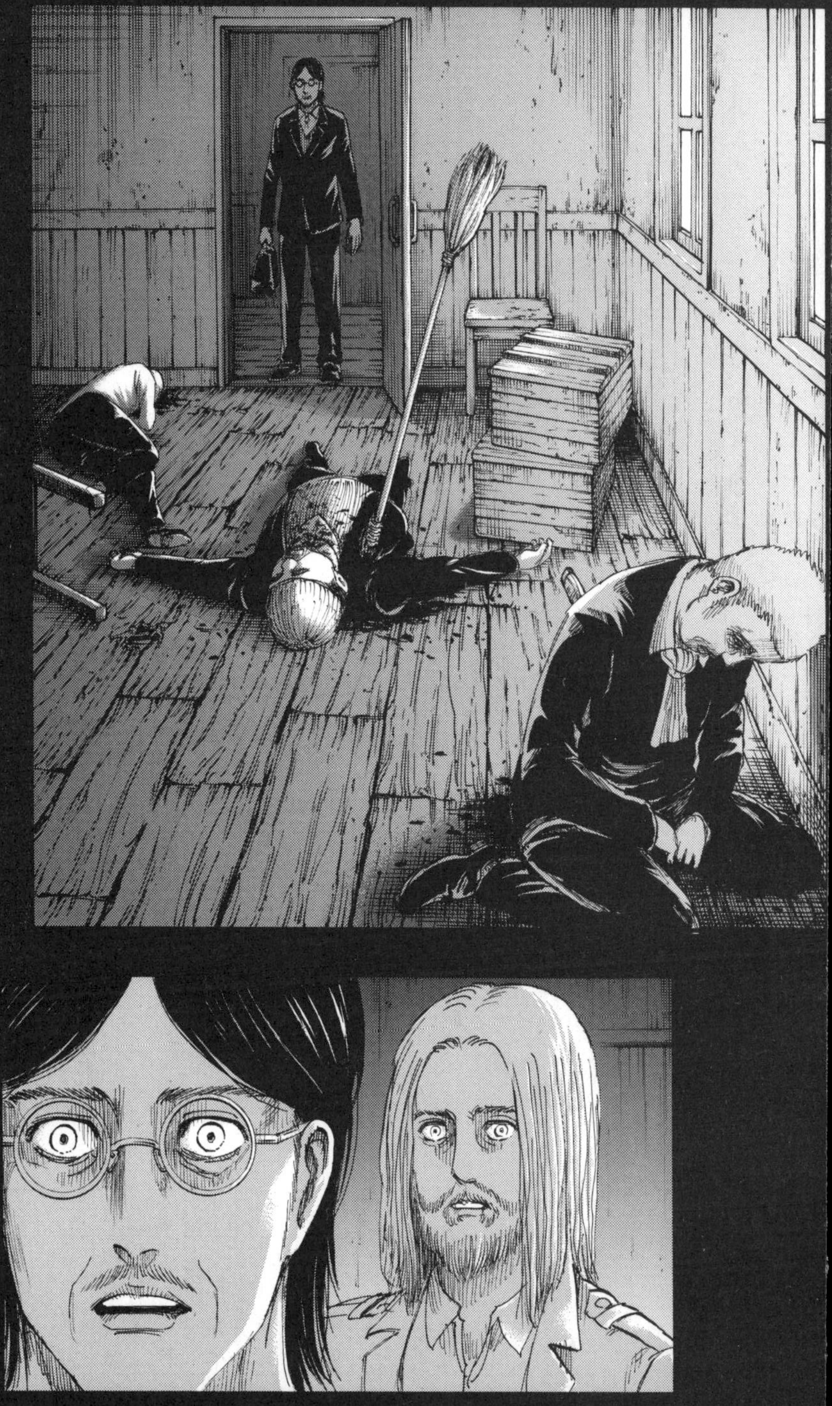

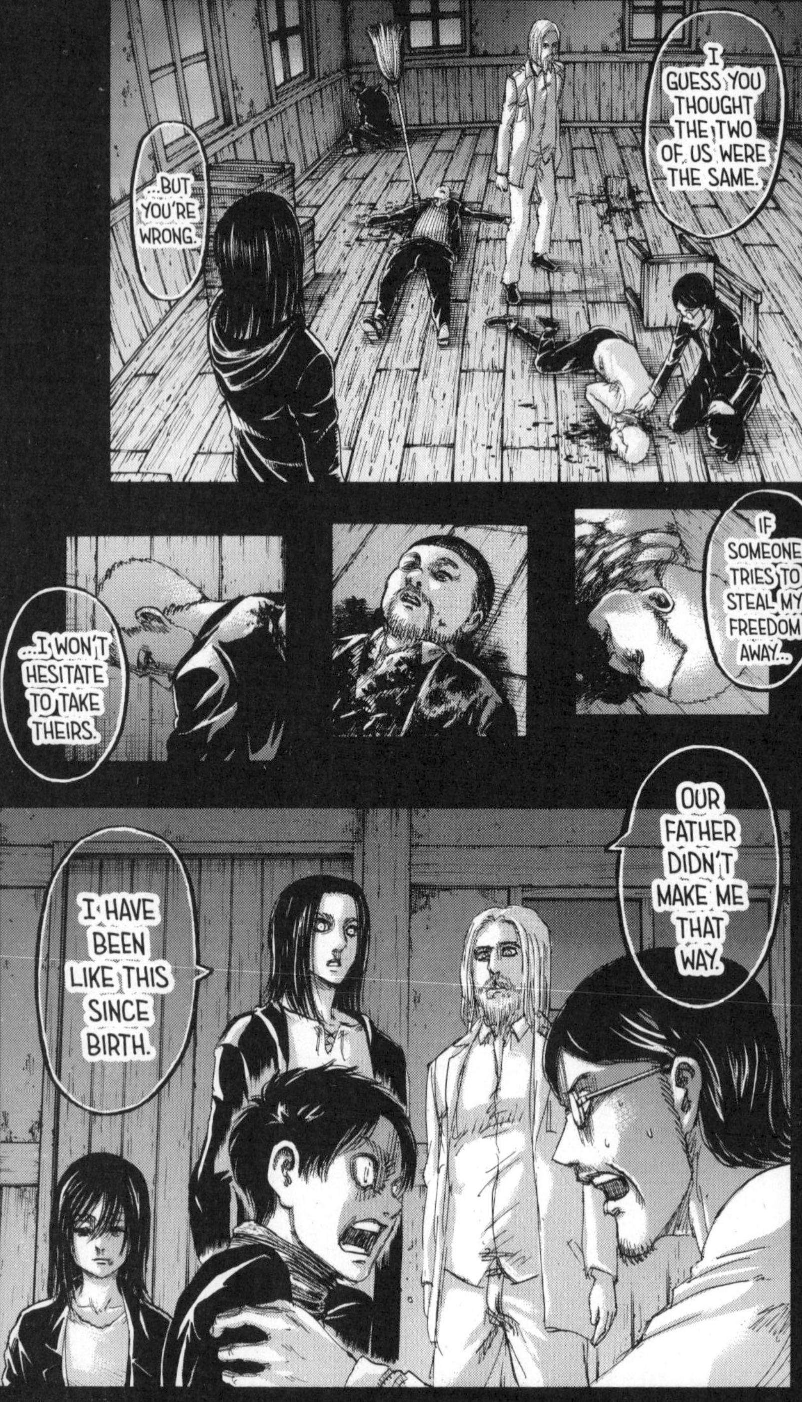
I GUESS YOU THOUGHT THE TWO OF US WERE THE SAME.
...BUT YOU'RE WRONG.
IF SOMEONE TRIES TO STEAL MY FREEDOM AWAY...
...I WON'T HESITATE TO TAKE THEIRS.
OUR FATHER DIDN'T MAKE ME THAT WAY.
I HAVE BEEN LIKE THIS SINCE BIRTH.

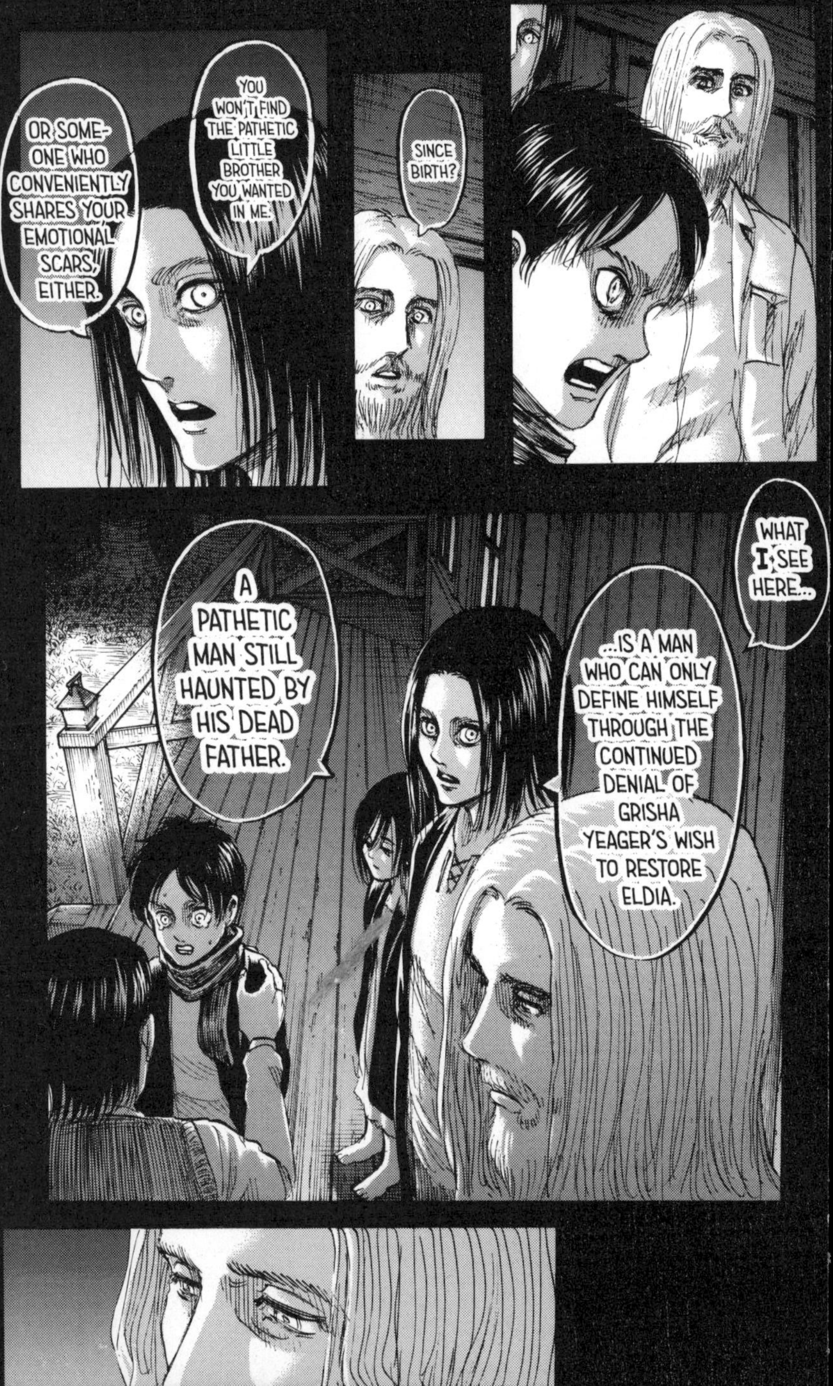
SINCE BIRTH?
YOU WON'T FIND THE PATHETIC LITTLE BROTHER YOU WANTED IN ME.
OR SOME-ONE WHO CONVENIENTLY SHARES YOUR EMOTIONAL SCARS, EITHER.
WHAT I SEE HERE...
...IS A MAN WHO CAN ONLY DEFINE HIMSELF THROUGH THE CONTINUED DENIAL OF GRISHA YEAGER'S WISH TO RESTORE ELDIA.
A PATHETIC MAN STILL HAUNTED BY HIS DEAD FATHER.

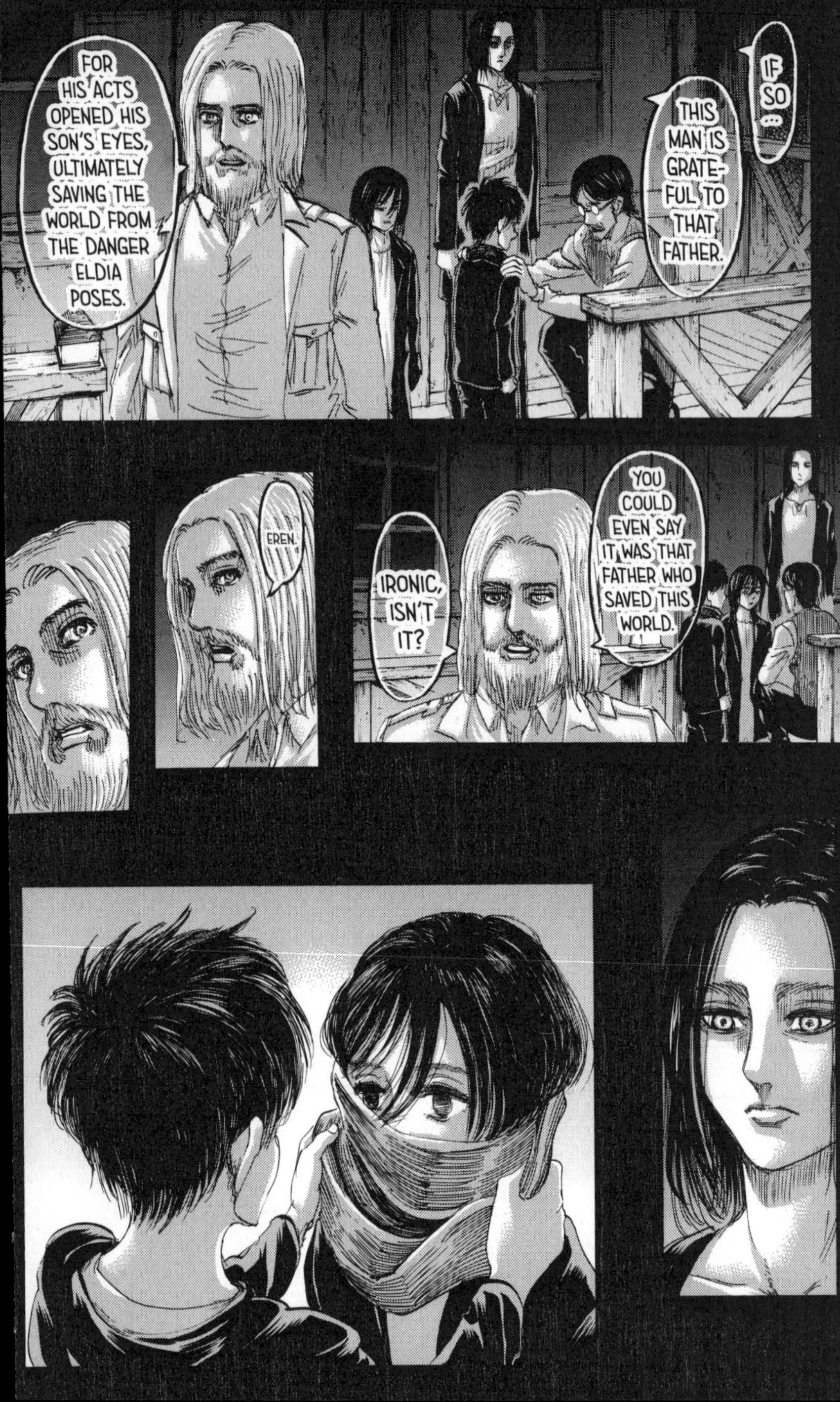
IF SO...
THIS MAN IS GRATEFUL TO THAT FATHER.
FOR HIS ACTS OPENED HIS SON'S EYES, ULTIMATELY SAVING THE WORLD FROM THE DANGER ELDIA POSES.
YOU COULD EVEN SAY IT WAS THAT FATHER WHO SAVED THIS WORLD.
IRONIC, ISN'T IT?
EREN.

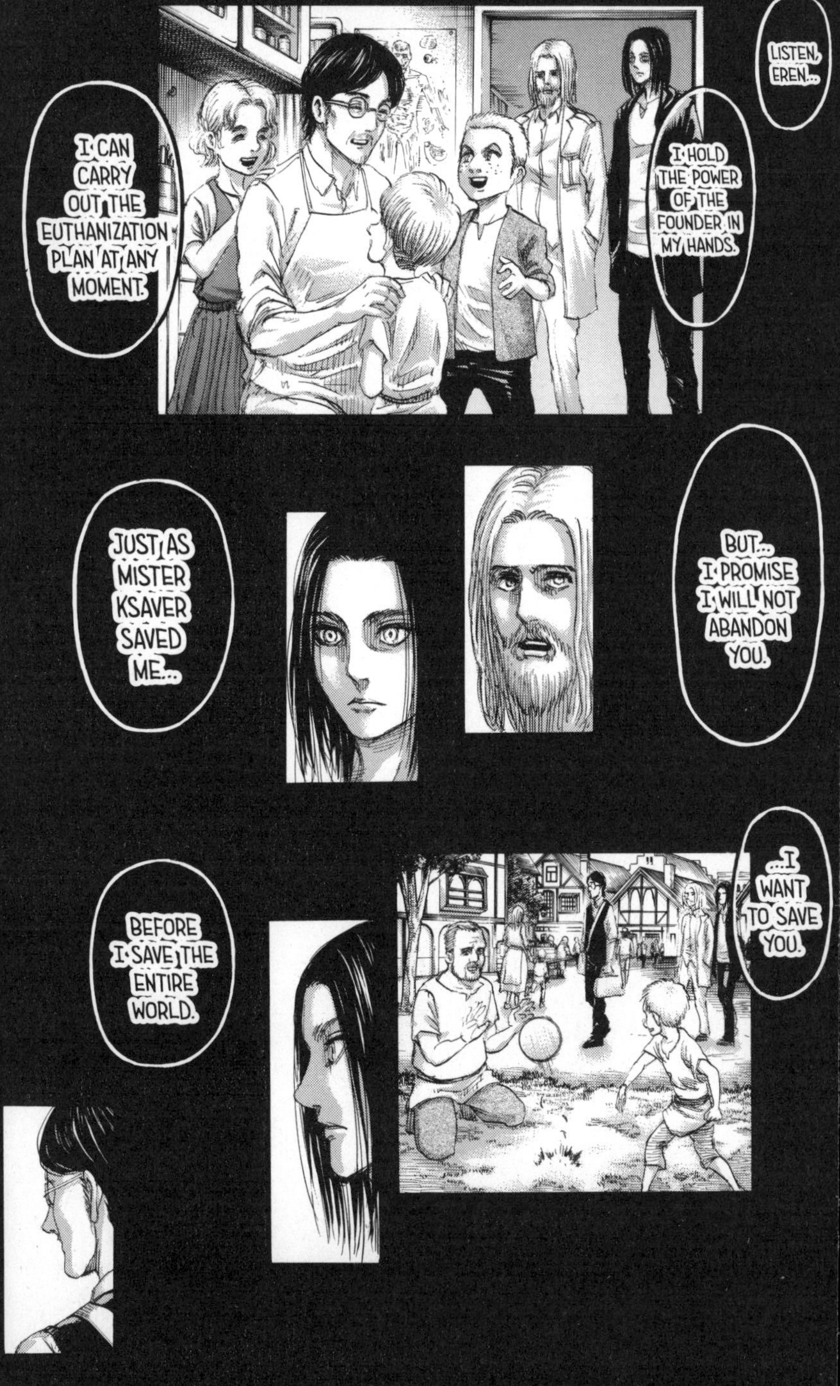
LISTEN, EREN...
I HOLD THE POWER OF THE FOUNDER IN MY HANDS.
I CAN CARRY OUT THE EUTHANIZATION PLAN AT ANY MOMENT.
BUT... I PROMISE I WILL NOT ABANDON YOU.
JUST AS MISTER KSAVER SAVED ME...
...I WANT TO SAVE YOU.
BEFORE I SAVE THE ENTIRE WORLD.

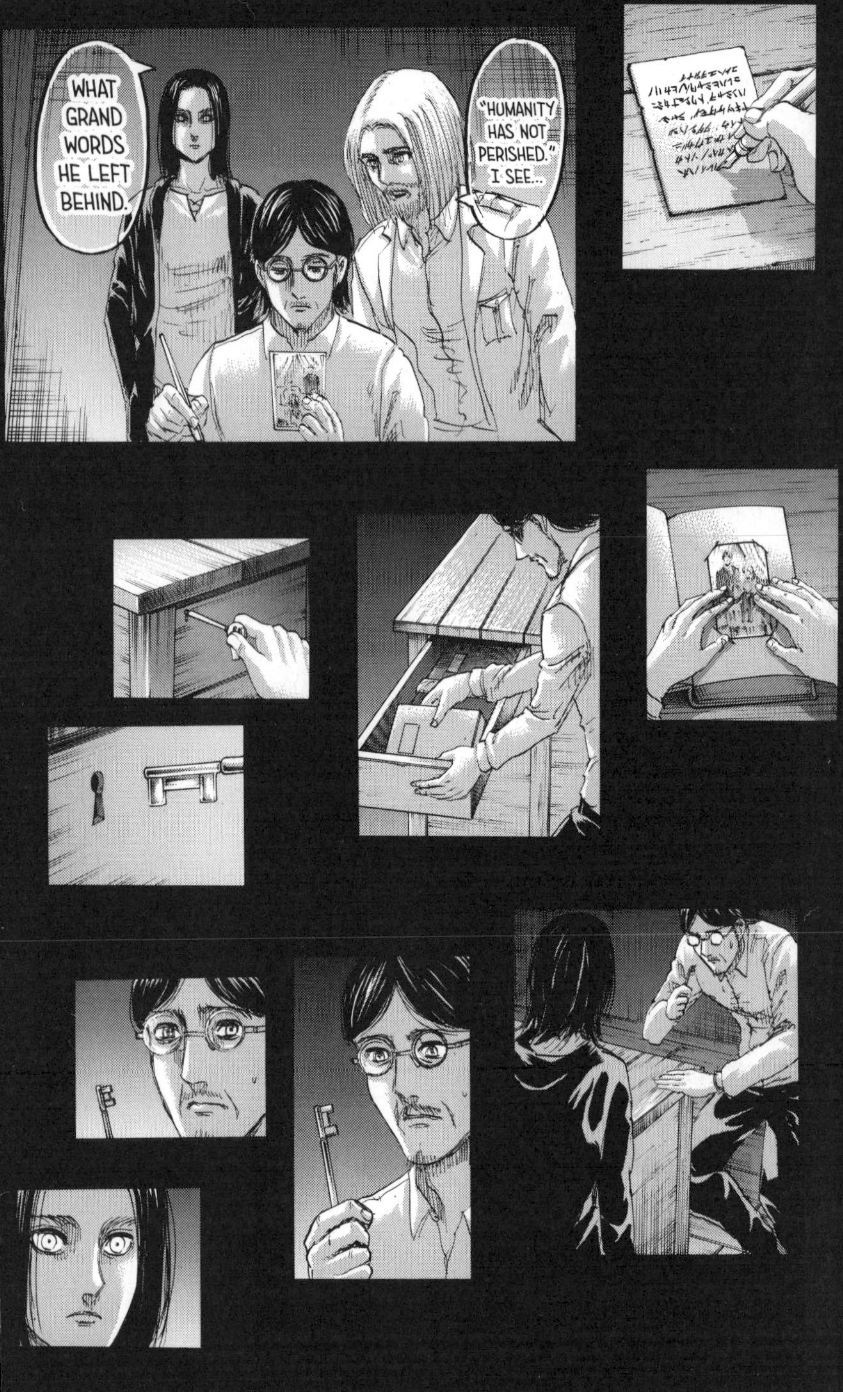

"HUMANITY HAS NOT PERISHED." I SEE...
WHAT GRAND WORDS HE LEFT BEHIND.

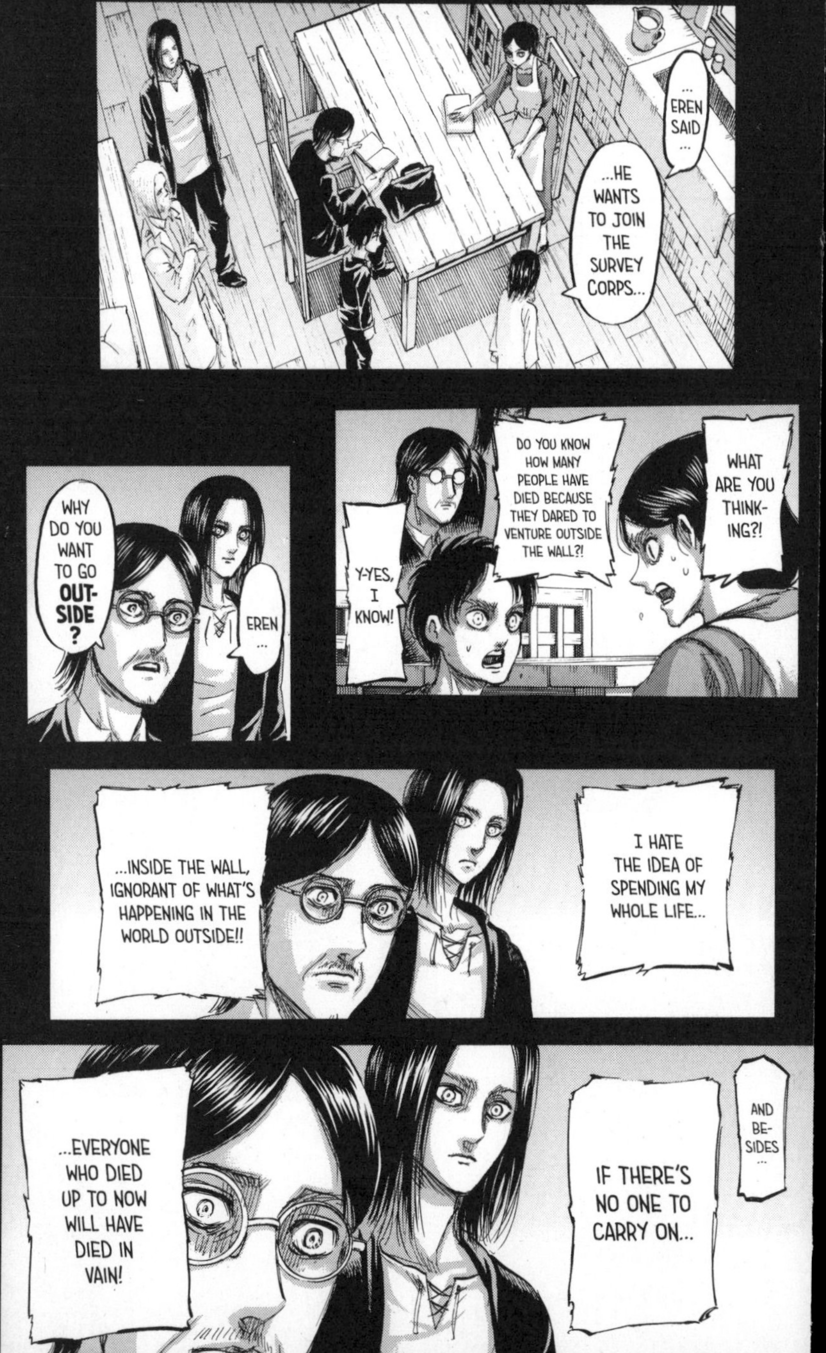

...EREN SAID...
...HE WANTS TO JOIN THE SURVEY CORPS...
WHAT ARE YOU THINKING?!
DO YOU KNOW HOW MANY PEOPLE HAVE DIED BECAUSE THEY DARED TO VENTURE OUTSIDE THE WALL?!
Y-YES, I KNOW!
WHY DO YOU WANT TO GO **OUTSIDE?**
EREN...
I HATE THE IDEA OF SPENDING MY WHOLE LIFE...
...INSIDE THE WALL, IGNORANT OF WHAT'S HAPPENING IN THE WORLD OUTSIDE!!
AND BESIDES...
IF THERE'S NO ONE TO CARRY ON...
...EVERYONE WHO DIED UP TO NOW WILL HAVE DIED IN VAIN!

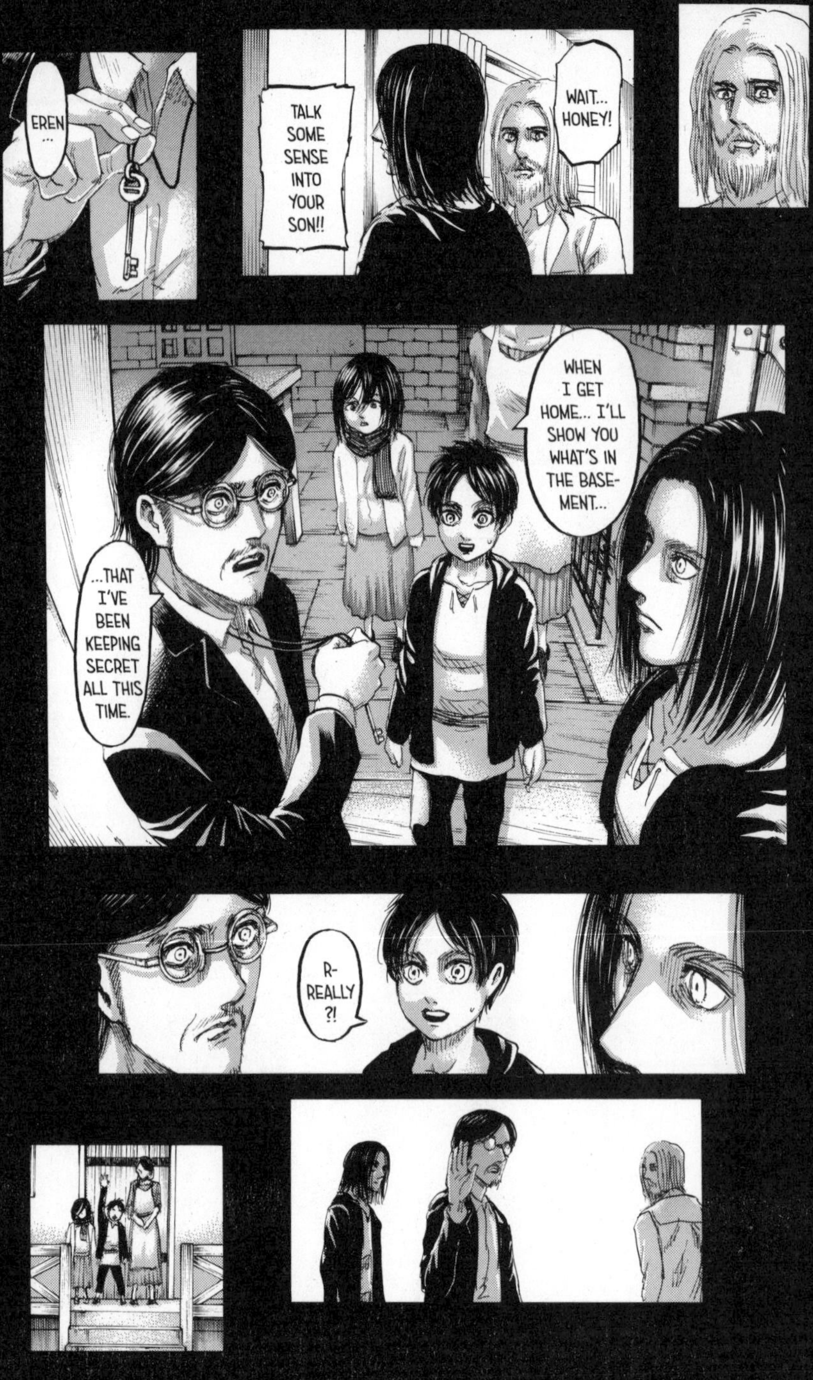
WAIT... HONEY!
TALK SOME SENSE INTO YOUR SON!!
EREN...
WHEN I GET HOME... I'LL SHOW YOU WHAT'S IN THE BASEMENT...
...THAT I'VE BEEN KEEPING SECRET ALL THIS TIME.
R-REALLY?!

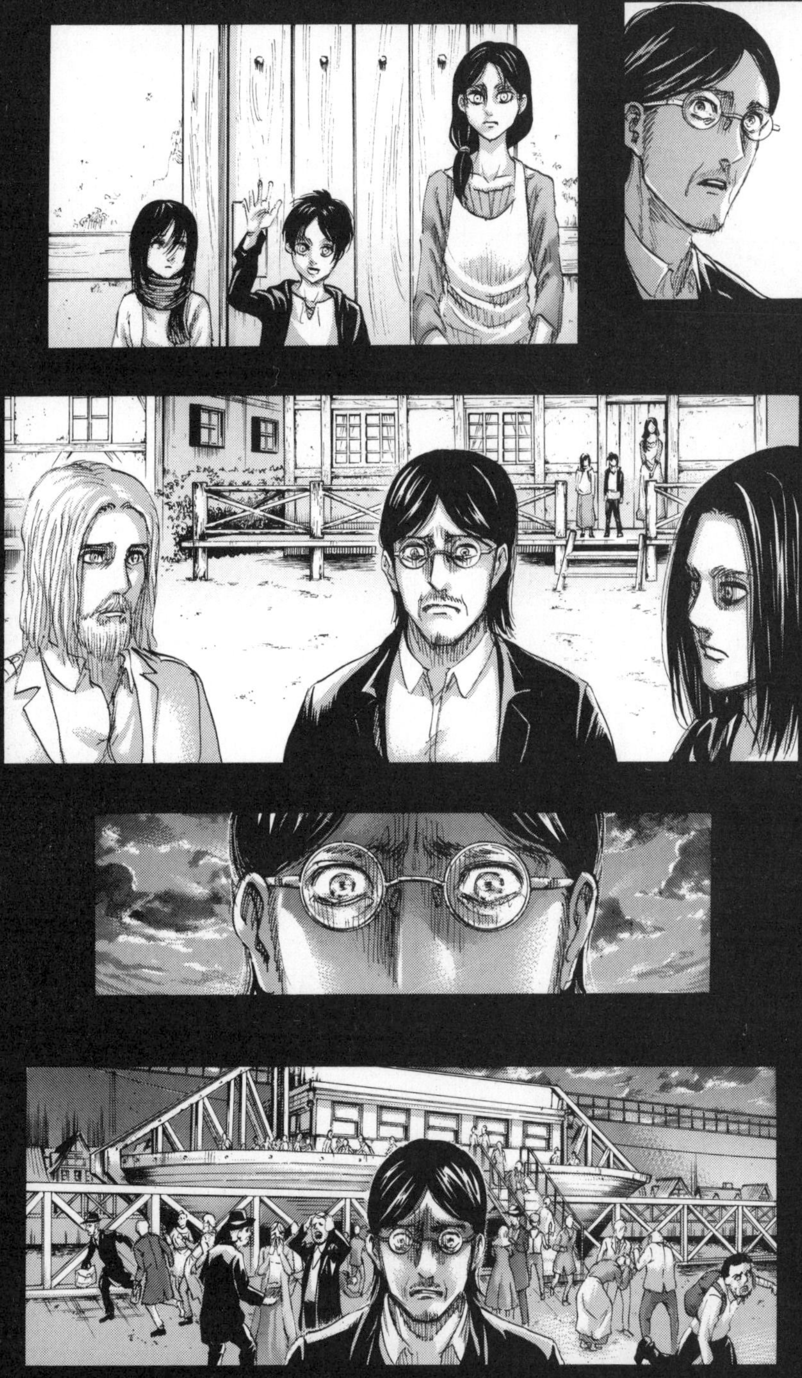

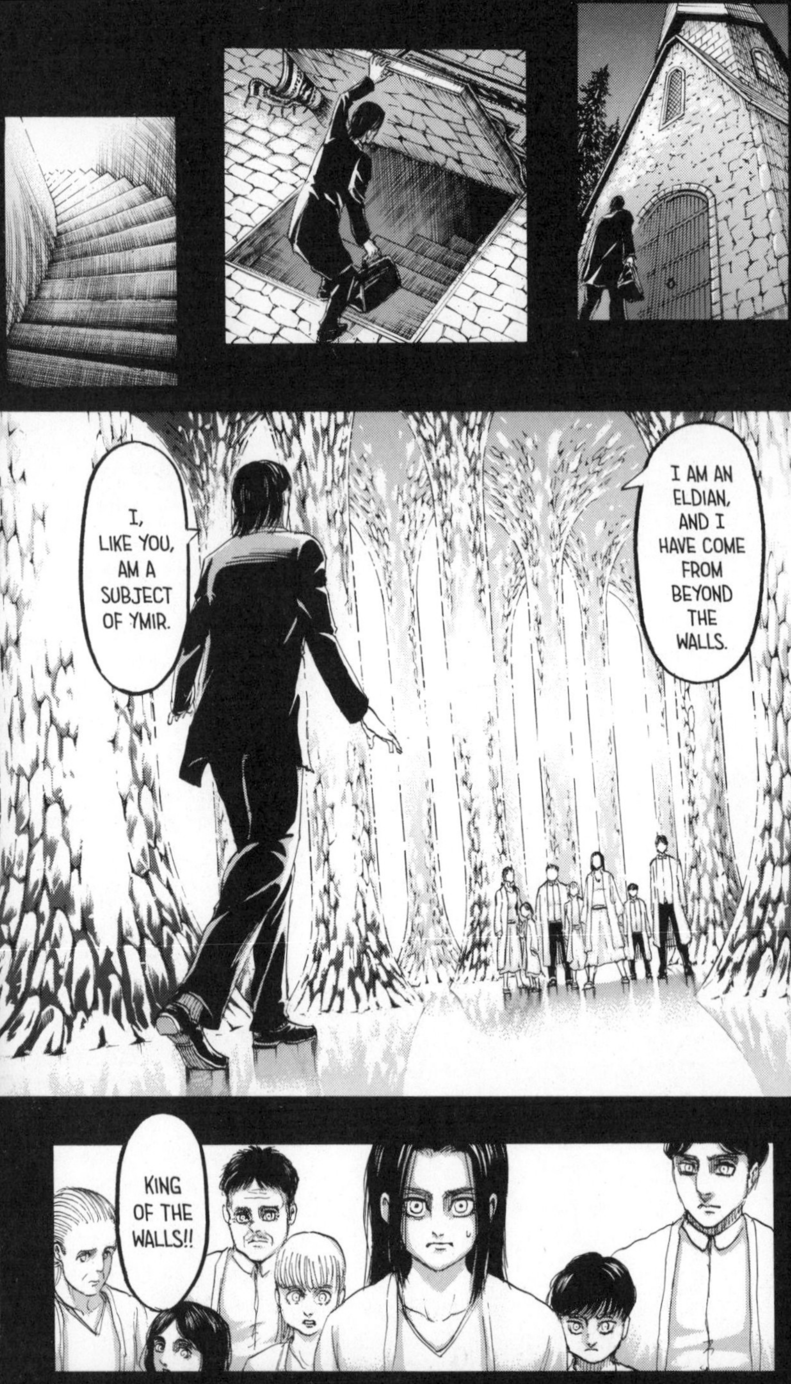

I AM AN ELDIAN, AND I HAVE COME FROM BEYOND THE WALLS.
I, LIKE YOU, AM A SUBJECT OF YMIR.
KING OF THE WALLS!!

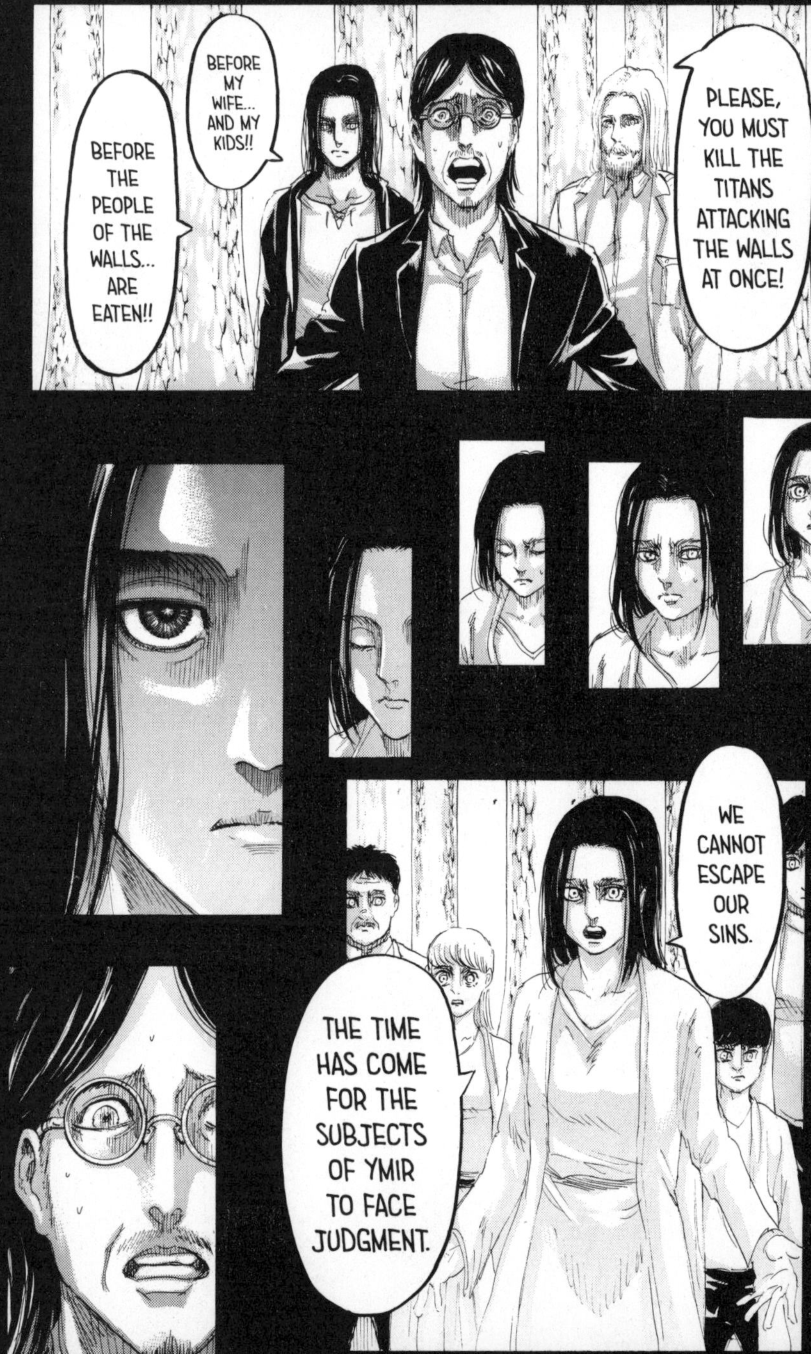
PLEASE, YOU MUST KILL THE TITANS ATTACKING THE WALLS AT ONCE!
BEFORE MY WIFE... AND MY KIDS!!
BEFORE THE PEOPLE OF THE WALLS... ARE EATEN!!
WE CANNOT ESCAPE OUR SINS.
THE TIME HAS COME FOR THE SUBJECTS OF YMIR TO FACE JUDGMENT.

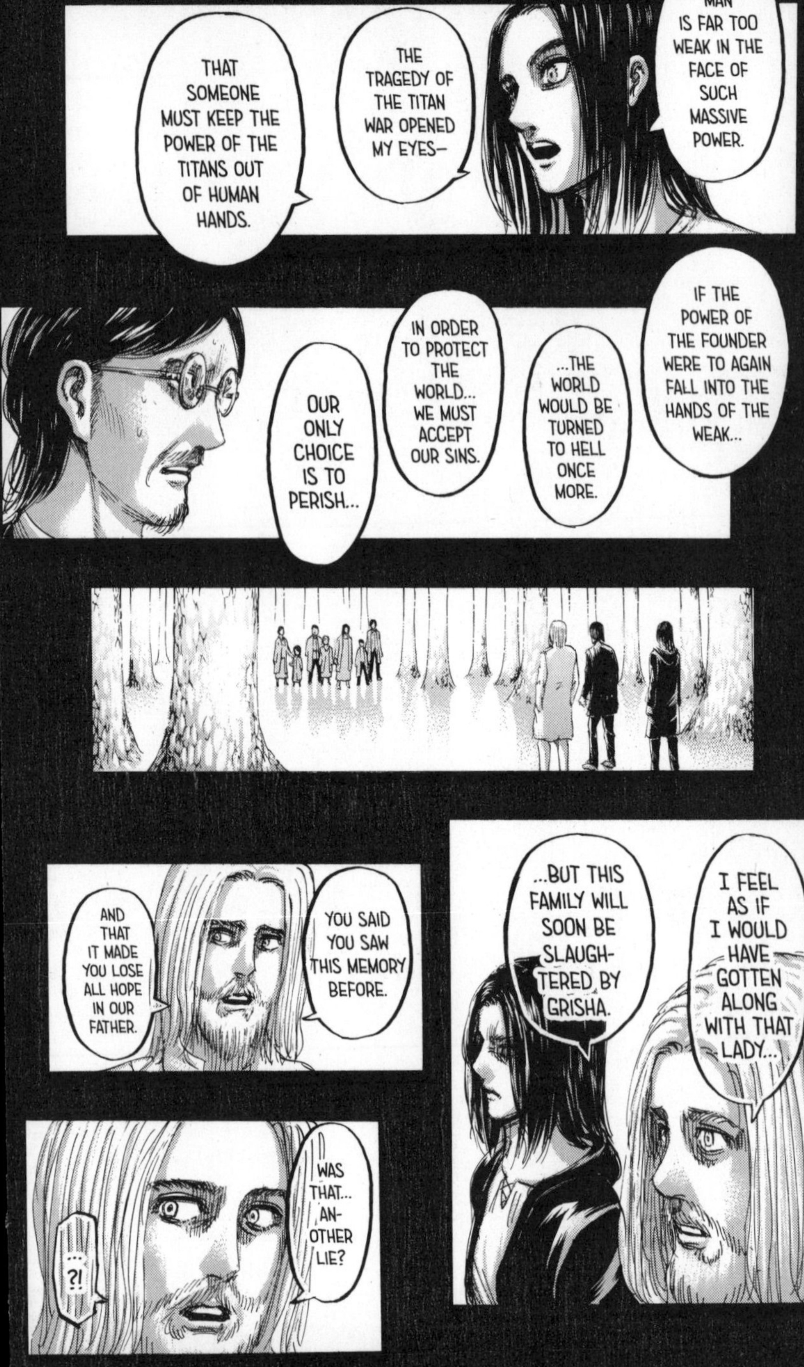
MAN IS FAR TOO WEAK IN THE FACE OF SUCH MASSIVE POWER.
THE TRAGEDY OF THE TITAN WAR OPENED MY EYES—
THAT SOMEONE MUST KEEP THE POWER OF THE TITANS OUT OF HUMAN HANDS.
IF THE POWER OF THE FOUNDER WERE TO AGAIN FALL INTO THE HANDS OF THE WEAK...
...THE WORLD WOULD BE TURNED TO HELL ONCE MORE.
IN ORDER TO PROTECT THE WORLD... WE MUST ACCEPT OUR SINS.
OUR ONLY CHOICE IS TO PERISH...
I FEEL AS IF I WOULD HAVE GOTTEN ALONG WITH THAT LADY...
...BUT THIS FAMILY WILL SOON BE SLAUGH-TERED BY GRISHA.
YOU SAID YOU SAW THIS MEMORY BEFORE.
AND THAT IT MADE YOU LOSE ALL HOPE IN OUR FATHER.
WAS THAT... AN-OTHER LIE?
...?!

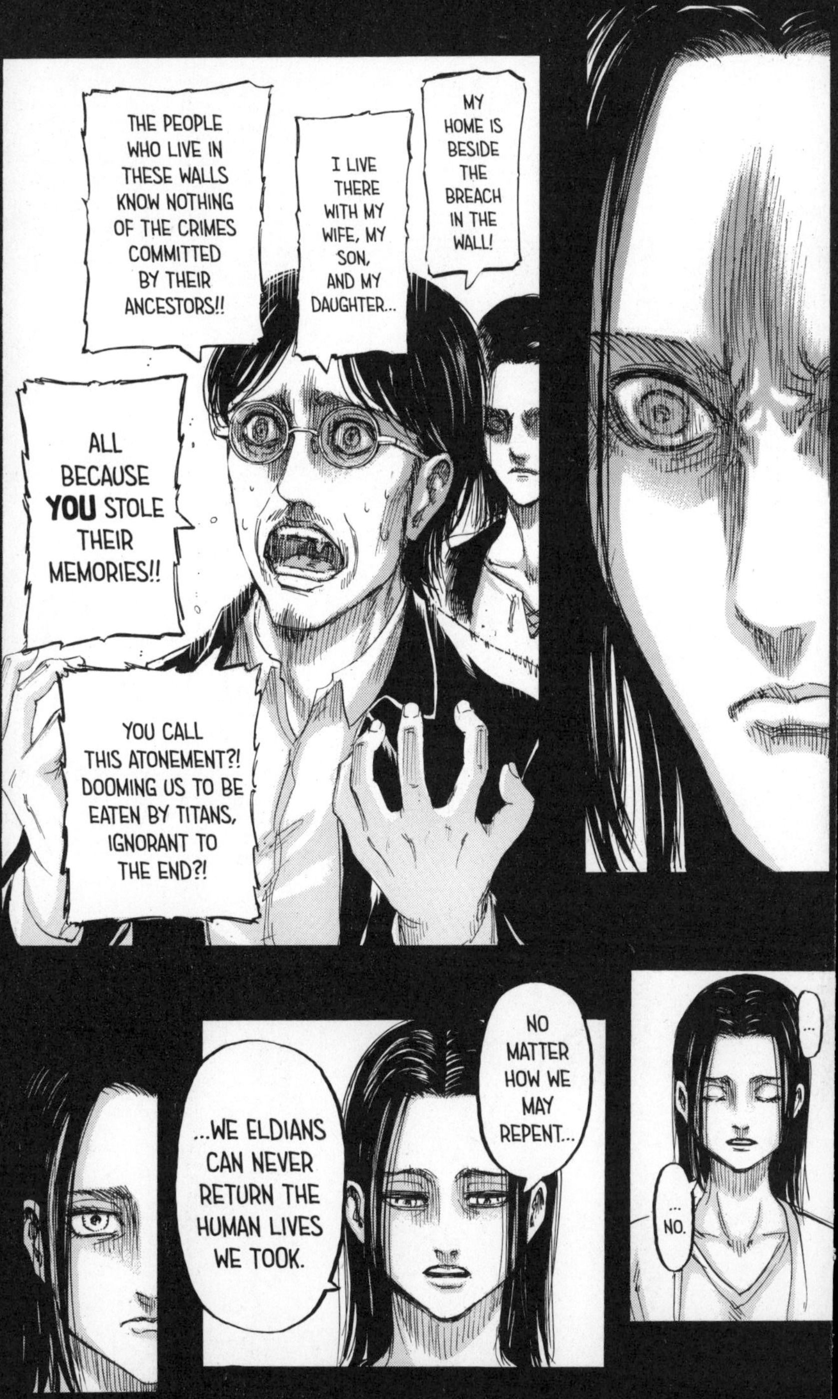
MY HOME IS BESIDE THE BREACH IN THE WALL!
I LIVE THERE WITH MY WIFE, MY SON, AND MY DAUGHTER...
THE PEOPLE WHO LIVE IN THESE WALLS KNOW NOTHING OF THE CRIMES COMMITTED BY THEIR ANCESTORS!!
ALL BECAUSE **YOU** STOLE THEIR MEMORIES!!
YOU CALL THIS ATONEMENT?! DOOMING US TO BE EATEN BY TITANS, IGNORANT TO THE END?!
...
... NO.
NO MATTER HOW WE MAY REPENT...
...WE ELDIANS CAN NEVER RETURN THE HUMAN LIVES WE TOOK.

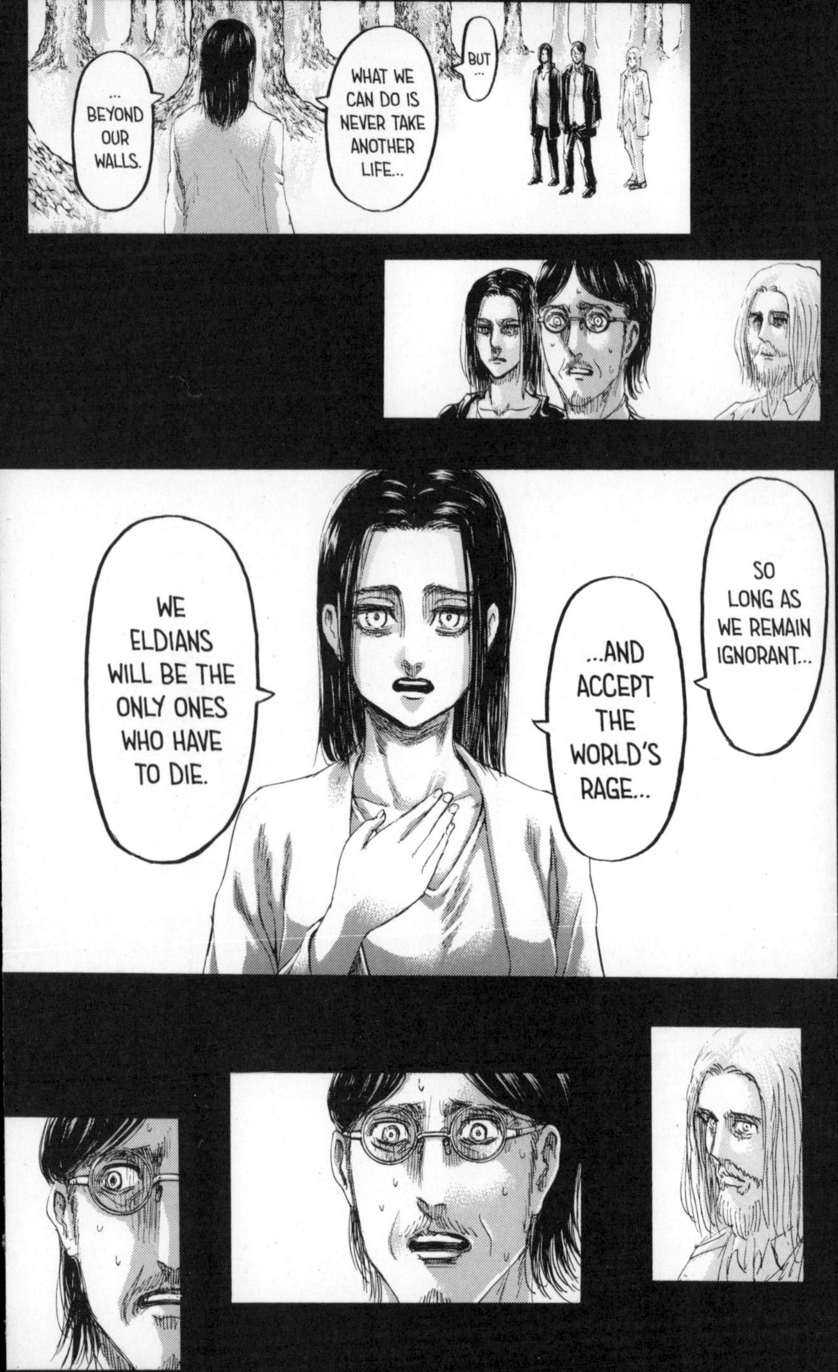
BUT ...
WHAT WE CAN DO IS NEVER TAKE ANOTHER LIFE...
... BEYOND OUR WALLS.
SO LONG AS WE REMAIN IGNORANT...
...AND ACCEPT THE WORLD'S RAGE...
WE ELDIANS WILL BE THE ONLY ONES WHO HAVE TO DIE.

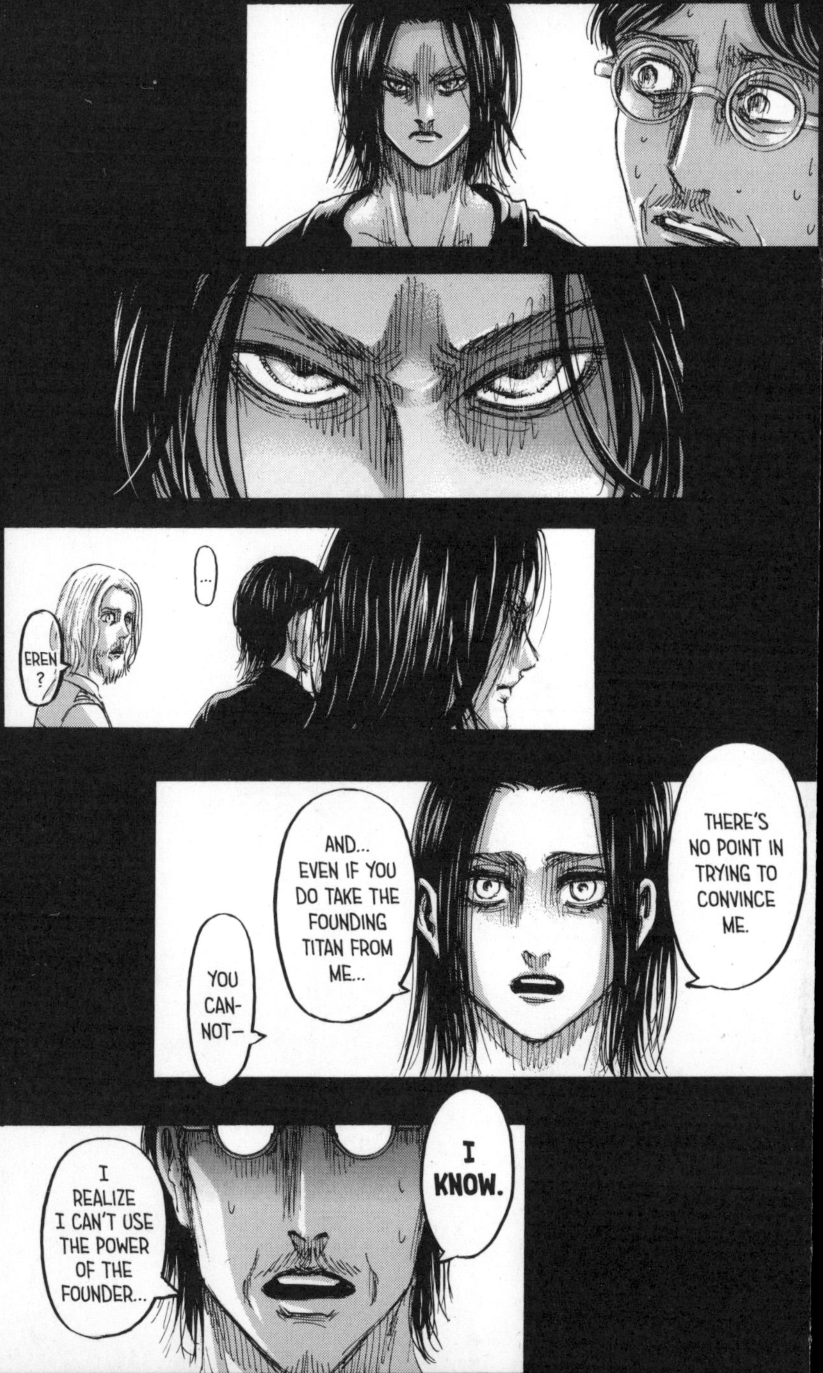
...
EREN?
THERE'S NO POINT IN TRYING TO CONVINCE ME.
AND... EVEN IF YOU DO TAKE THE FOUNDING TITAN FROM ME...
YOU CAN-NOT—
I KNOW.
I REALIZE I CAN'T USE THE POWER OF THE FOUNDER...

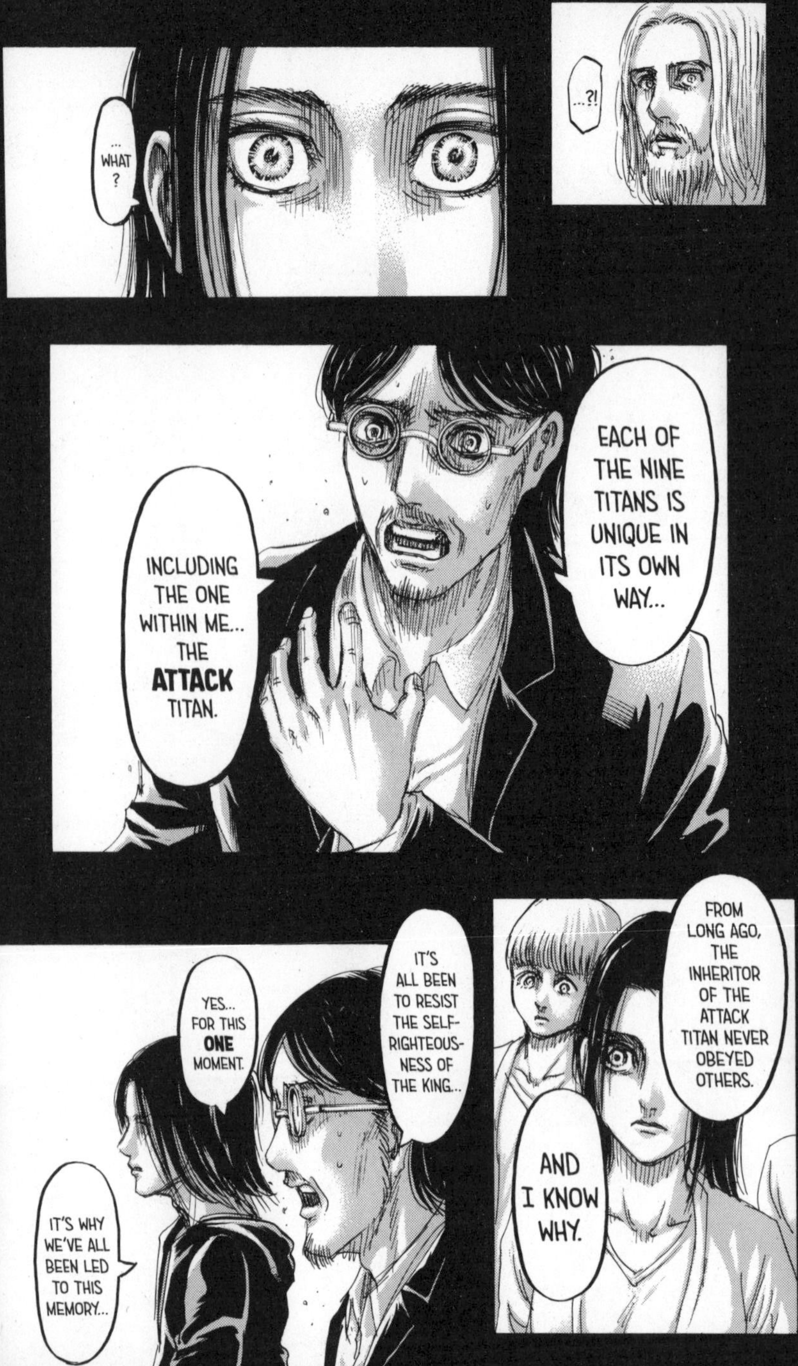
...?!
... WHAT ?
EACH OF THE NINE TITANS IS UNIQUE IN ITS OWN WAY...
INCLUDING THE ONE WITHIN ME... THE **ATTACK** TITAN.
FROM LONG AGO, THE INHERITOR OF THE ATTACK TITAN NEVER OBEYED OTHERS.
AND I KNOW WHY.
IT'S ALL BEEN TO RESIST THE SELF-RIGHTEOUSNESS OF THE KING...
YES... FOR THIS **ONE** MOMENT.
IT'S WHY WE'VE ALL BEEN LED TO THIS MEMORY...

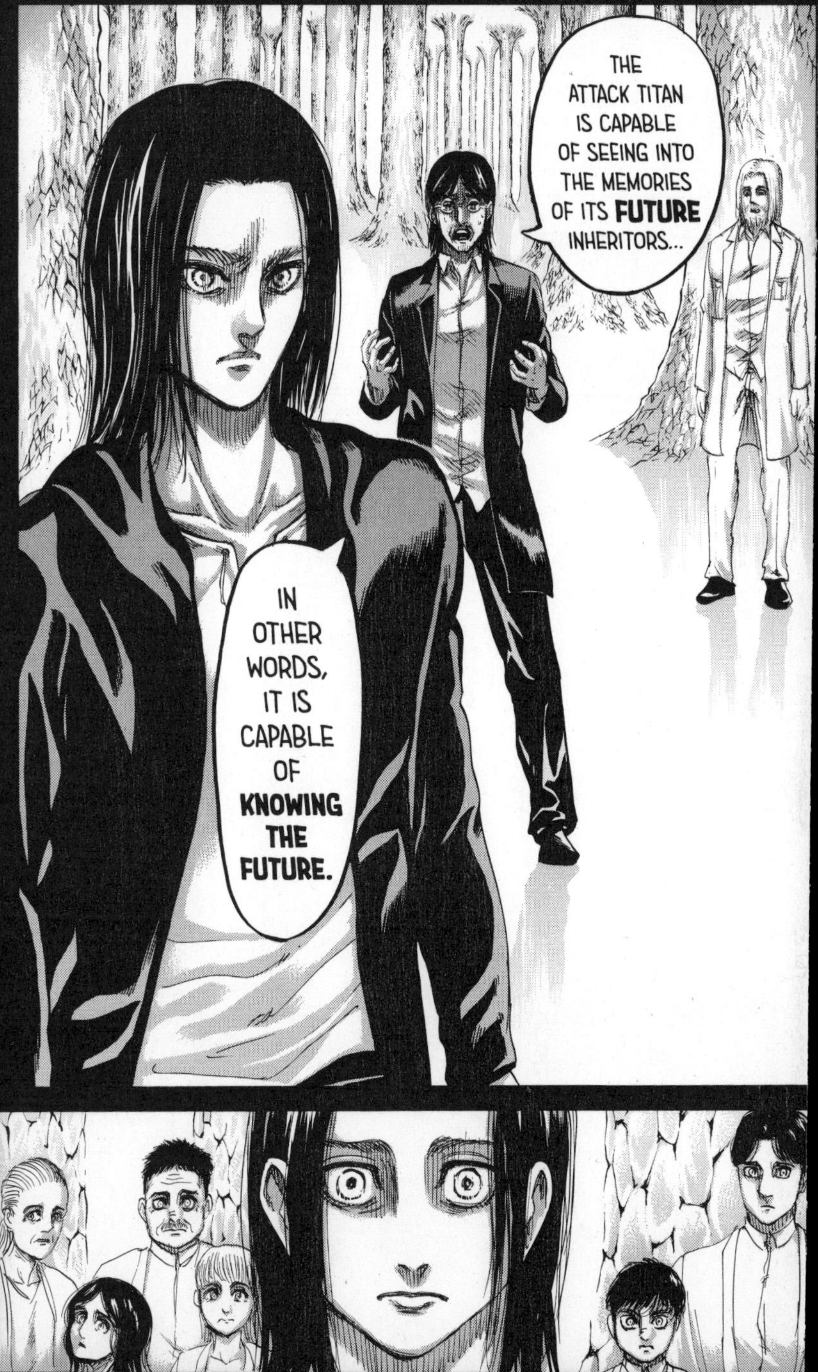
THE ATTACK TITAN IS CAPABLE OF SEEING INTO THE MEMORIES OF ITS **FUTURE** INHERITORS...
IN OTHER WORDS, IT IS CAPABLE OF **KNOWING THE FUTURE.**

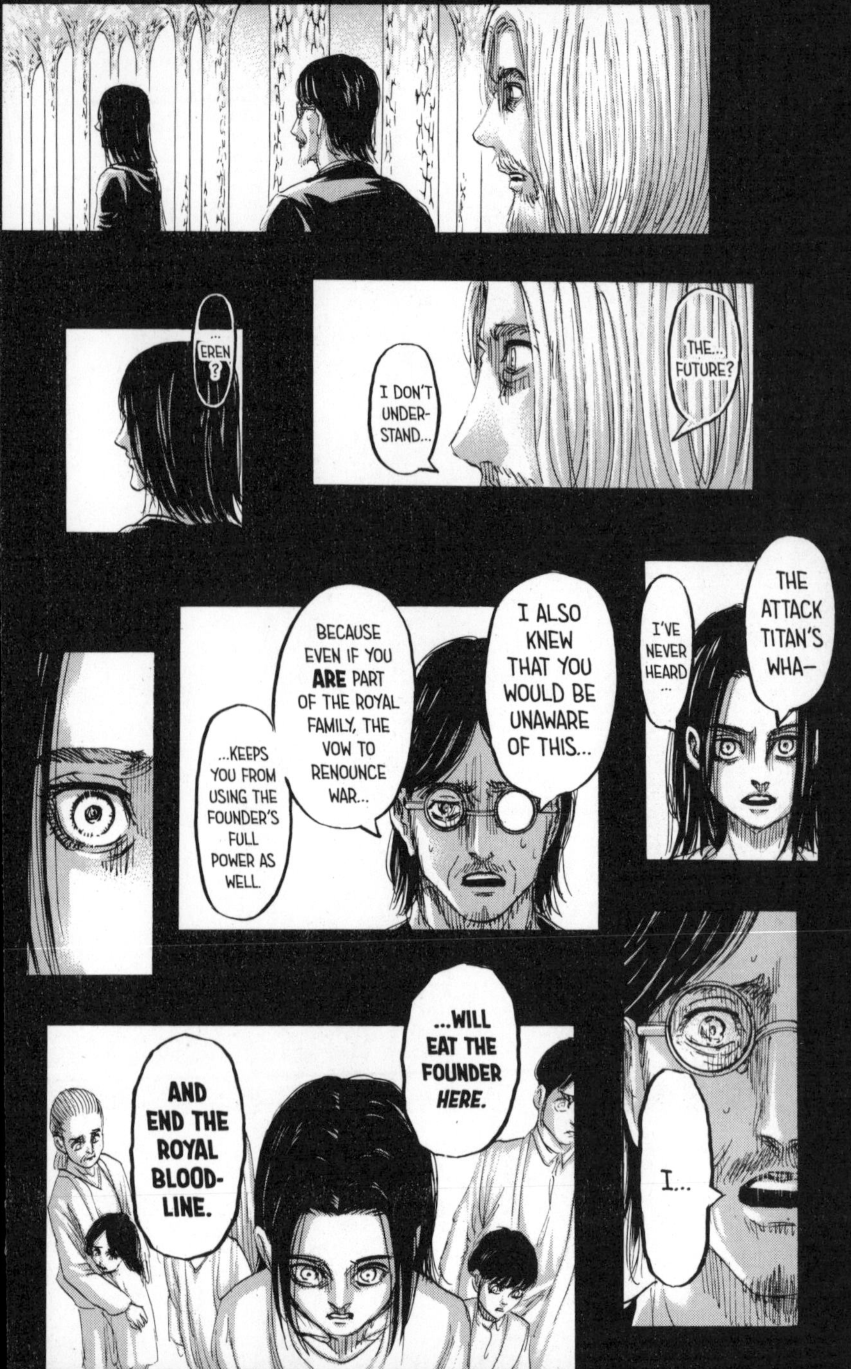
THE... FUTURE?
I DON'T UNDER-STAND...
... EREN ?
THE ATTACK TITAN'S WHA—
I'VE NEVER HEARD ...
I ALSO KNEW THAT YOU WOULD BE UNAWARE OF THIS...
BECAUSE EVEN IF YOU **ARE** PART OF THE ROYAL FAMILY, THE VOW TO RENOUNCE WAR...
...KEEPS YOU FROM USING THE FOUNDER'S FULL POWER AS WELL.
I...
...WILL EAT THE FOUNDER *HERE.*
AND END THE ROYAL BLOOD-LINE.

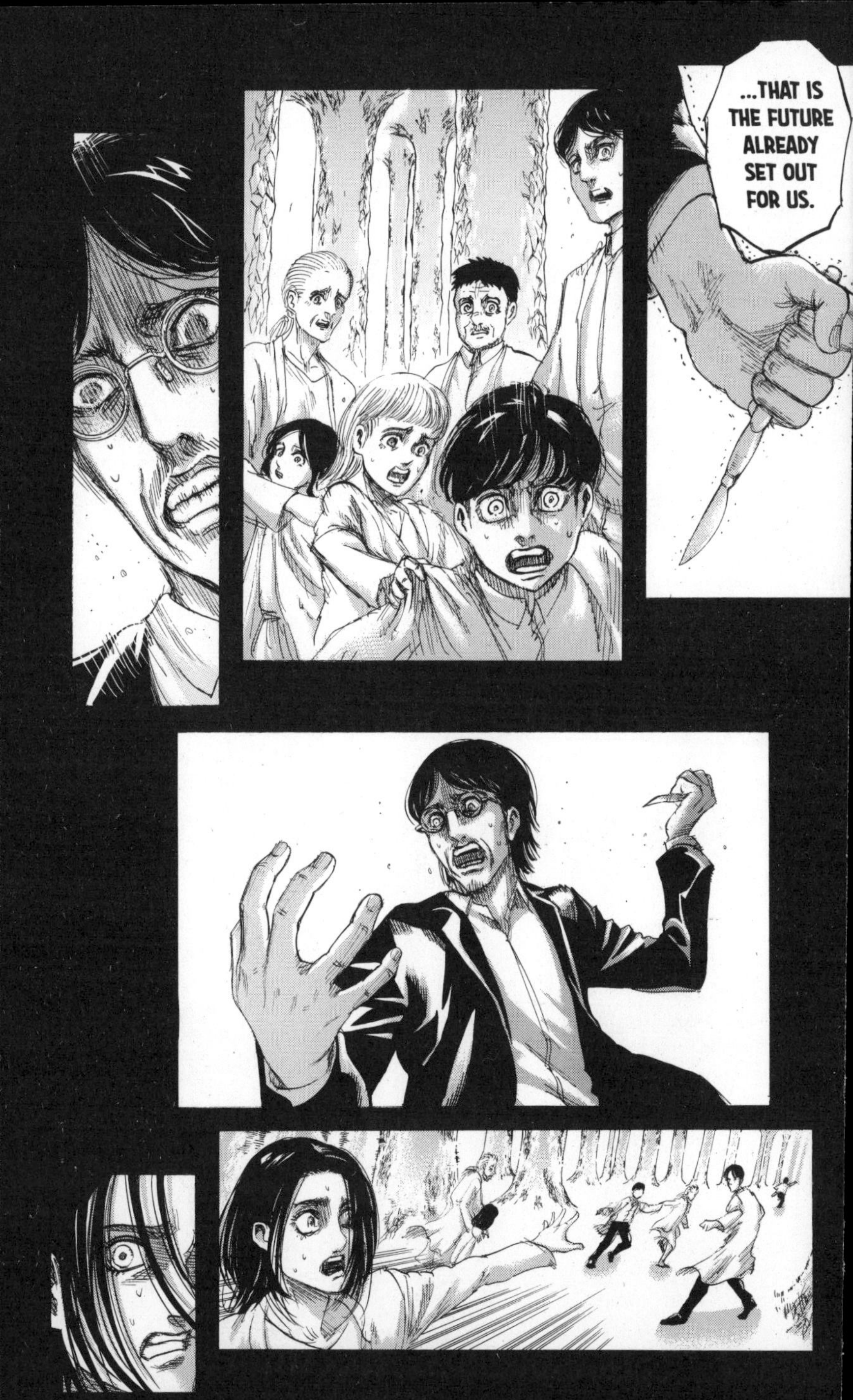
...THAT IS THE FUTURE ALREADY SET OUT FOR US.

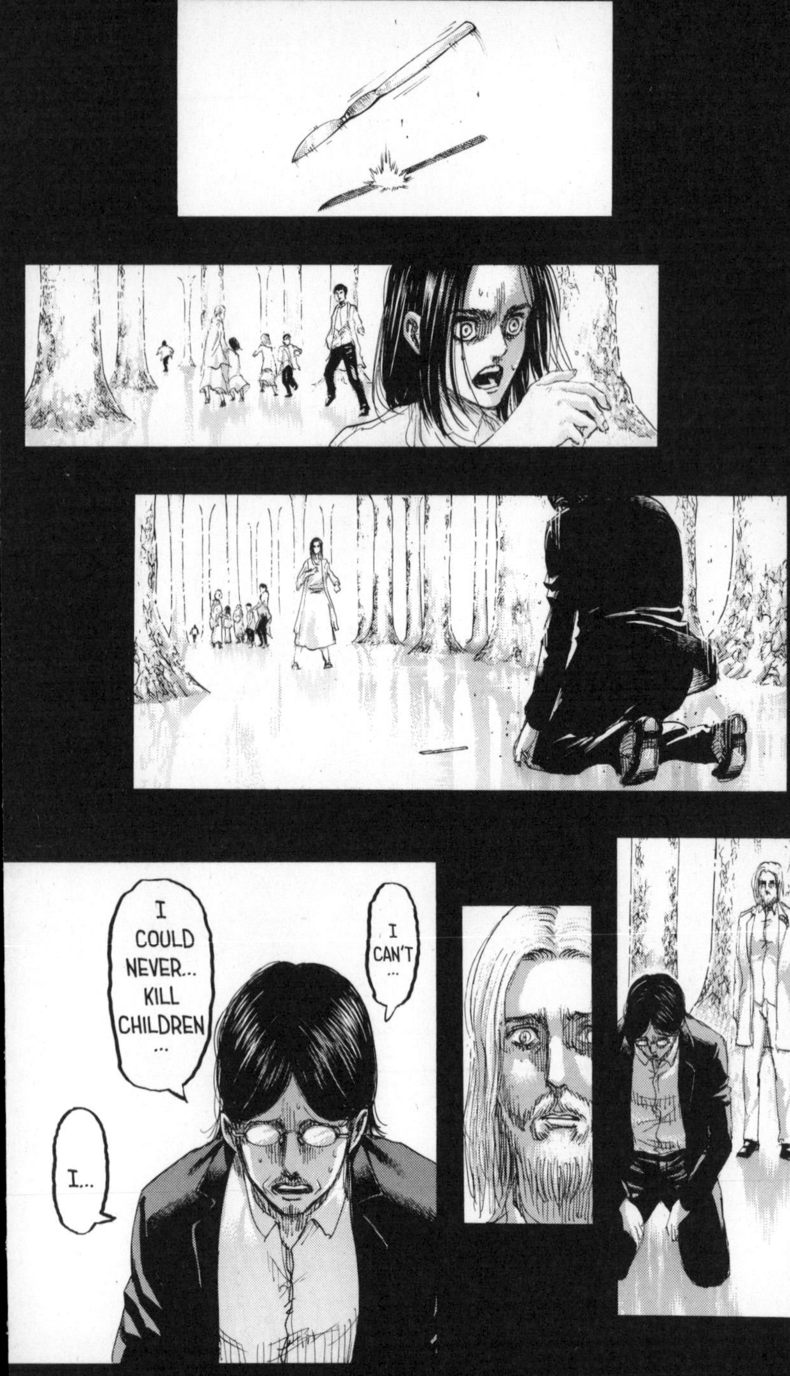
I CAN'T ...
I COULD NEVER... KILL CHILDREN ...
I...

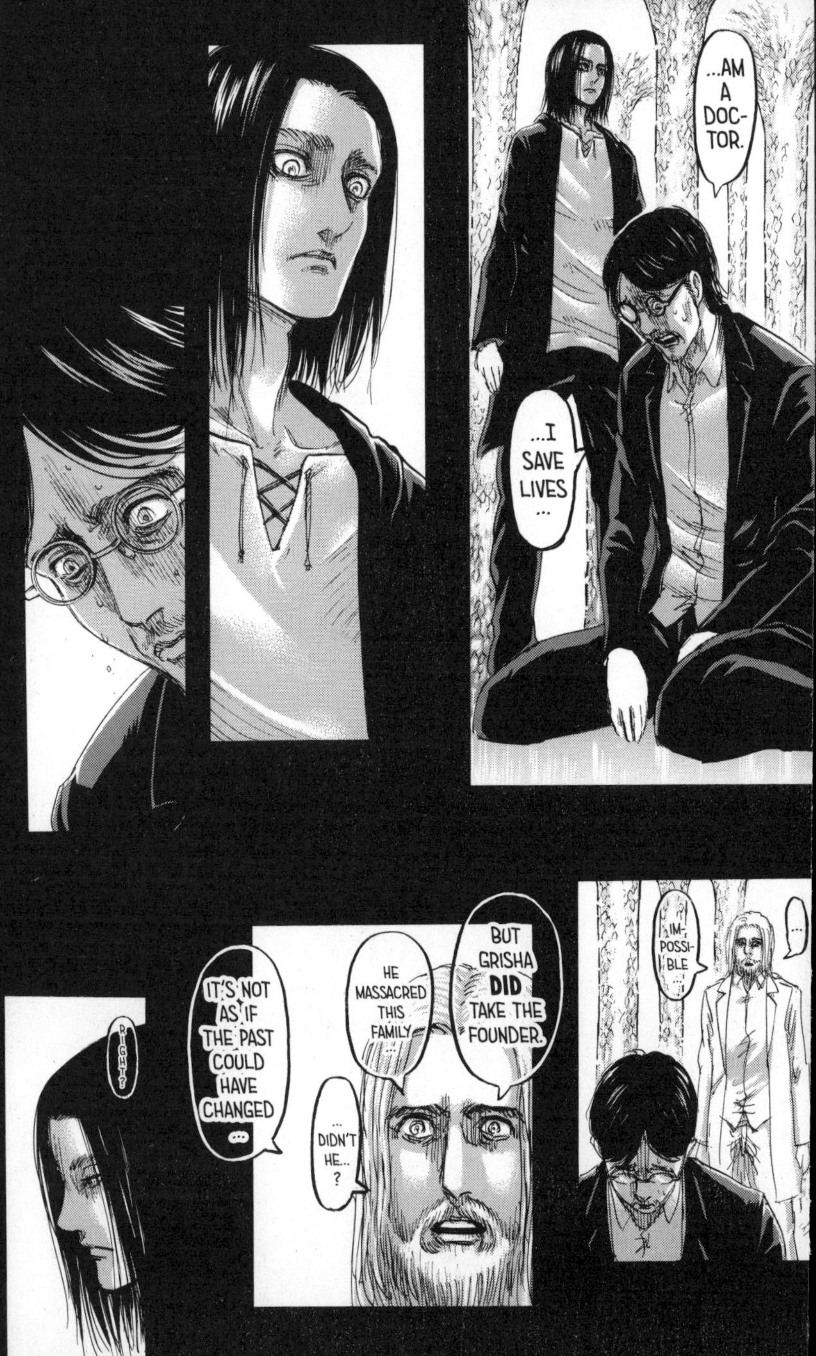
...AM A DOCTOR.
...I SAVE LIVES...
...
IMPOSSIBLE...
BUT GRISHA DID TAKE THE FOUNDER.
HE MASSACRED THIS FAMILY...
...DIDN'T HE...?
IT'S NOT AS IF THE PAST COULD HAVE CHANGED...
RIGHT?

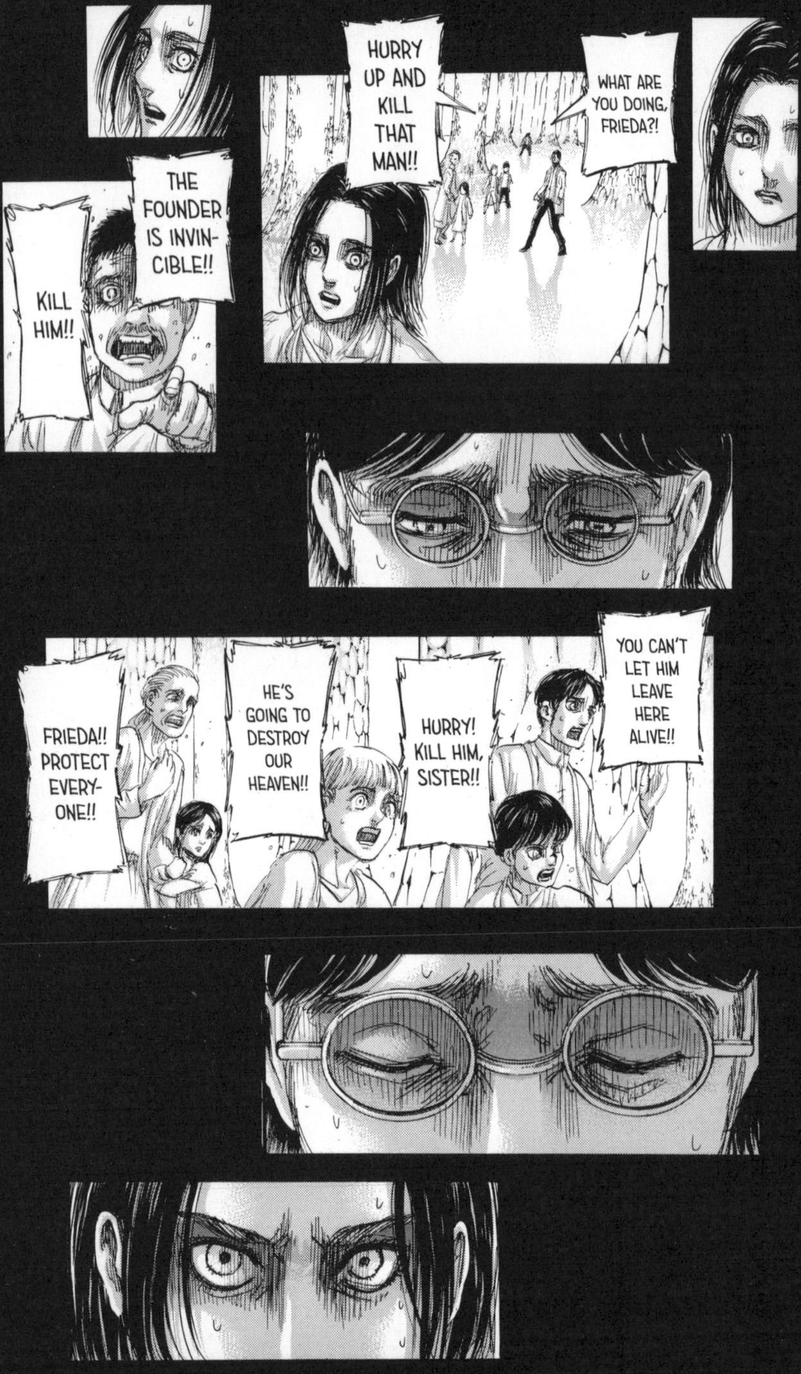
WHAT ARE YOU DOING, FRIEDA?!
HURRY UP AND KILL THAT MAN!!
THE FOUNDER IS INVINCIBLE!!
KILL HIM!!
YOU CAN'T LET HIM LEAVE HERE ALIVE!!
HURRY! KILL HIM, SISTER!!
HE'S GOING TO DESTROY OUR HEAVEN!!
FRIEDA!! PROTECT EVERYONE!!

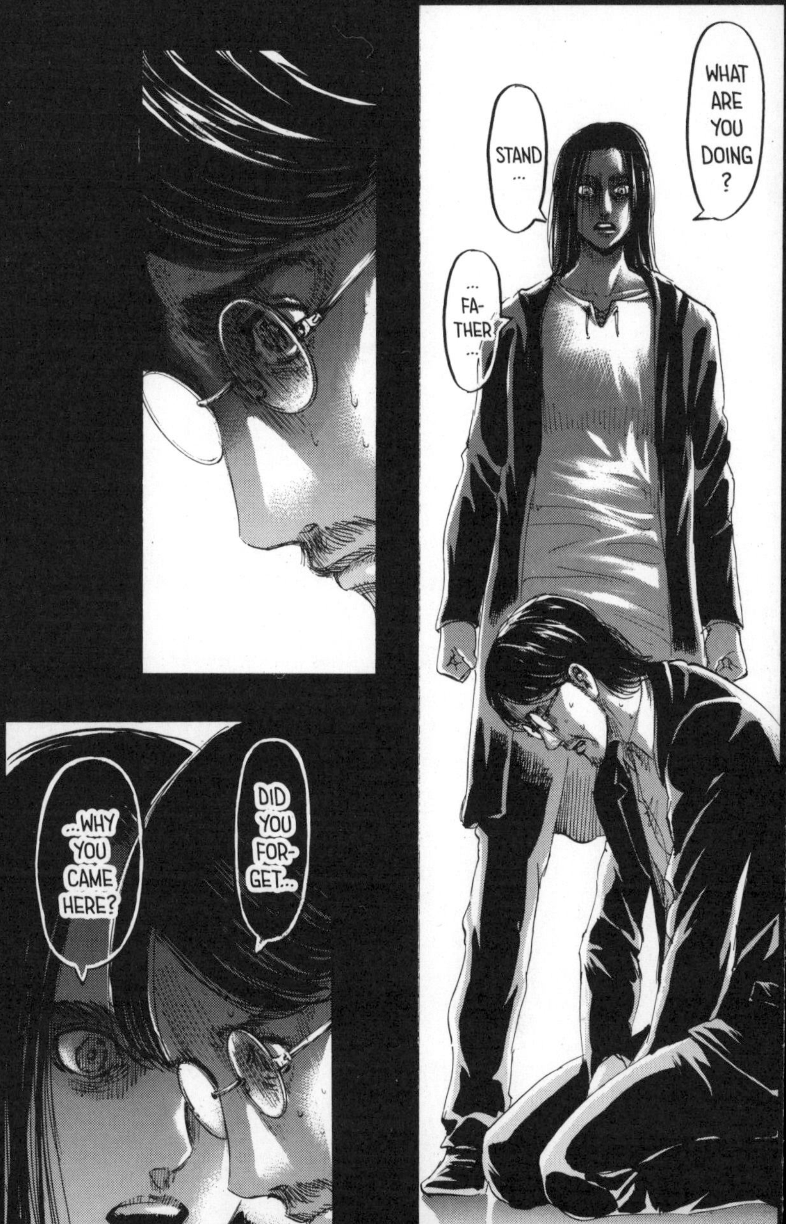
WHAT ARE YOU DOING?
STAND...
...FA-THER...
DID YOU FOR-GET...
...WHY YOU CAME HERE?

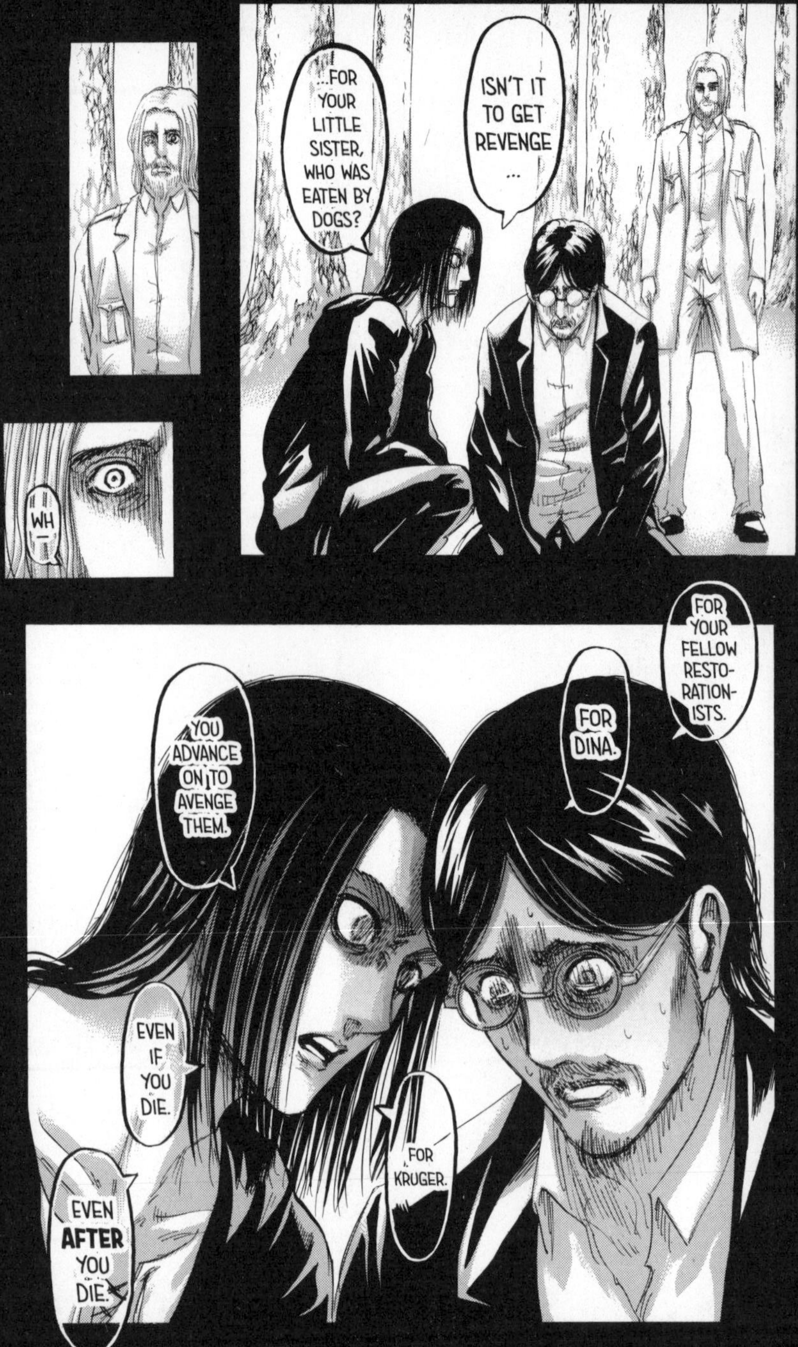
ISN'T IT TO GET REVENGE ...
...FOR YOUR LITTLE SISTER, WHO WAS EATEN BY DOGS?
WH—
FOR YOUR FELLOW RESTO-RATION-ISTS.
FOR DINA.
YOU ADVANCE ON TO AVENGE THEM.
FOR KRUGER.
EVEN IF YOU DIE.
EVEN **AFTER** YOU DIE.

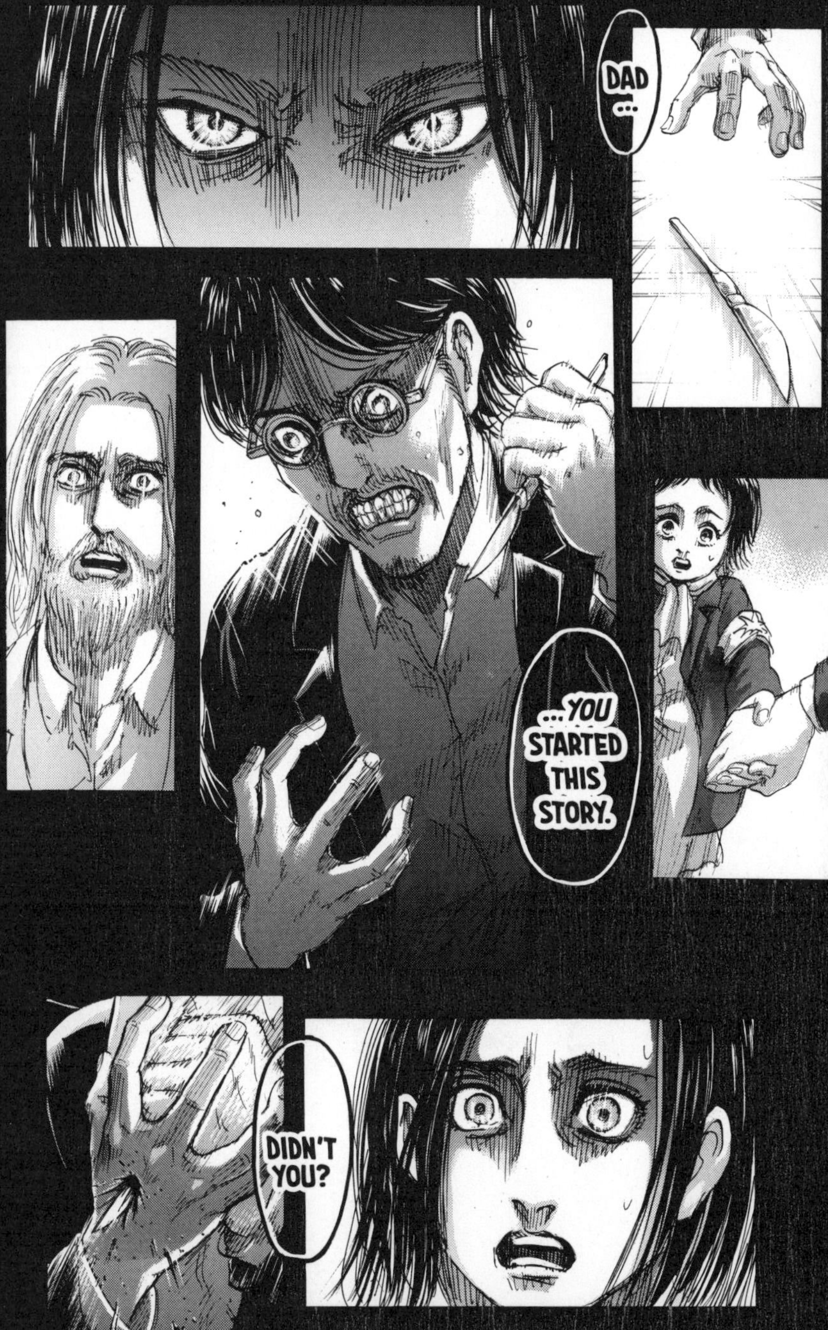
DAD ...
...YOU STARTED THIS STORY.
DIDN'T YOU?

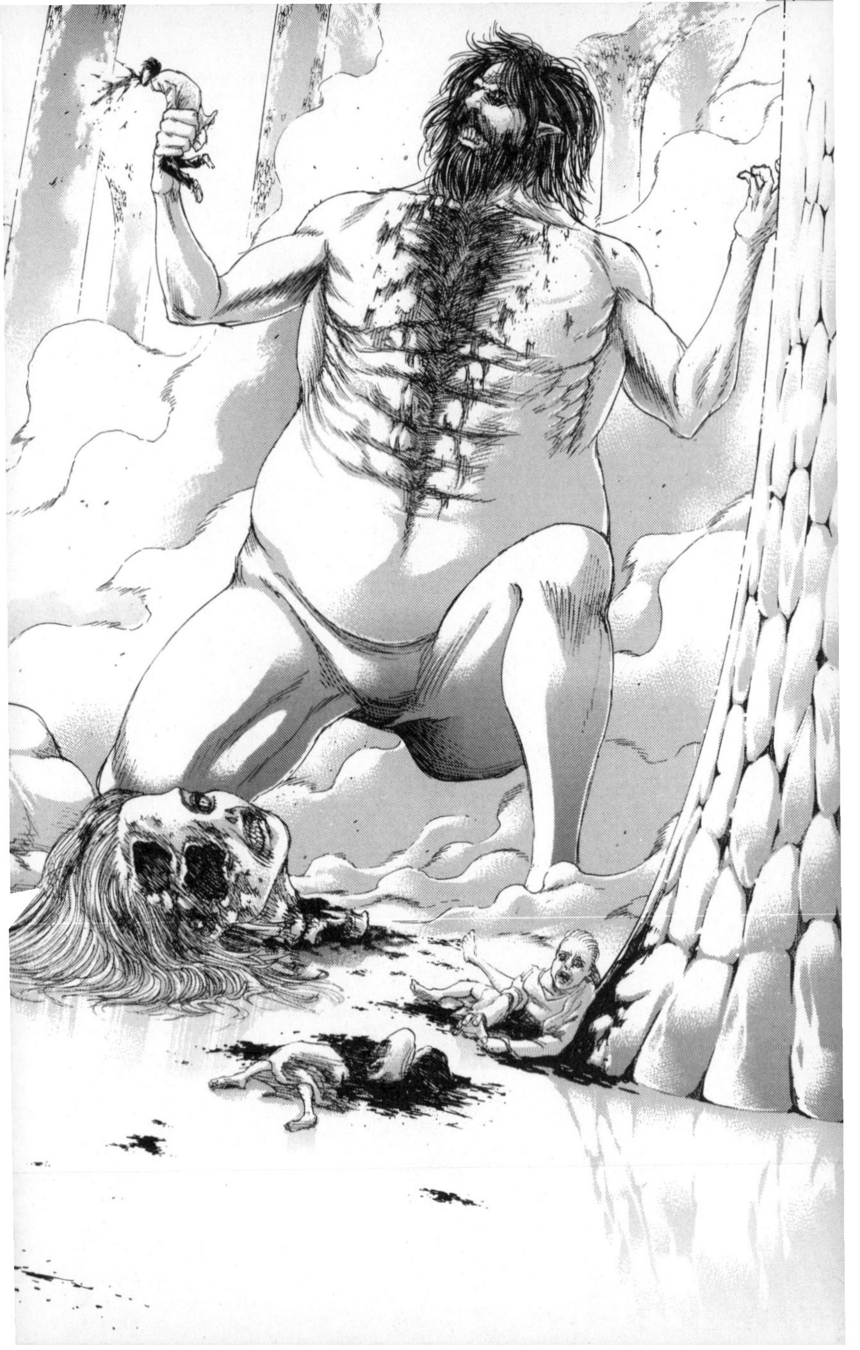

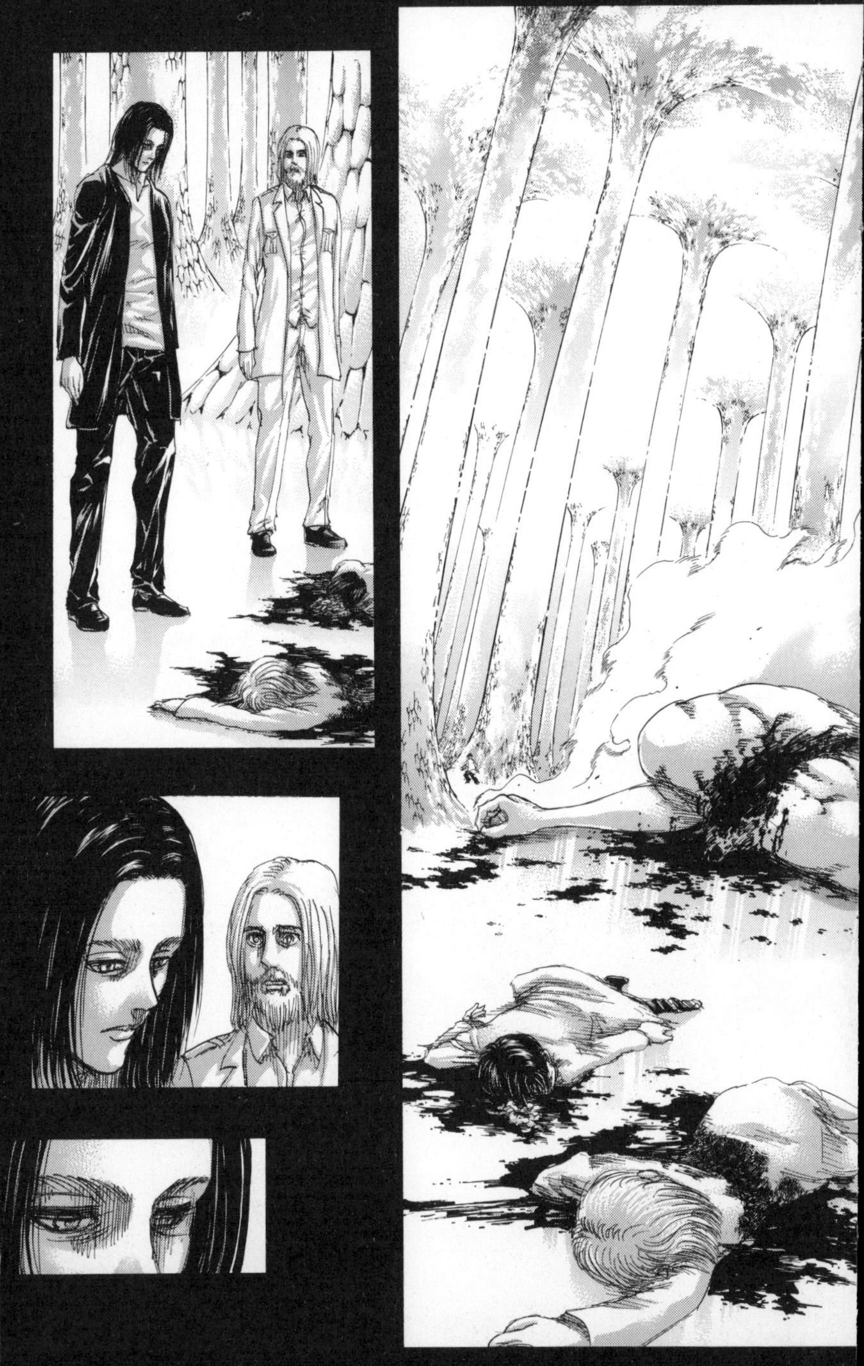

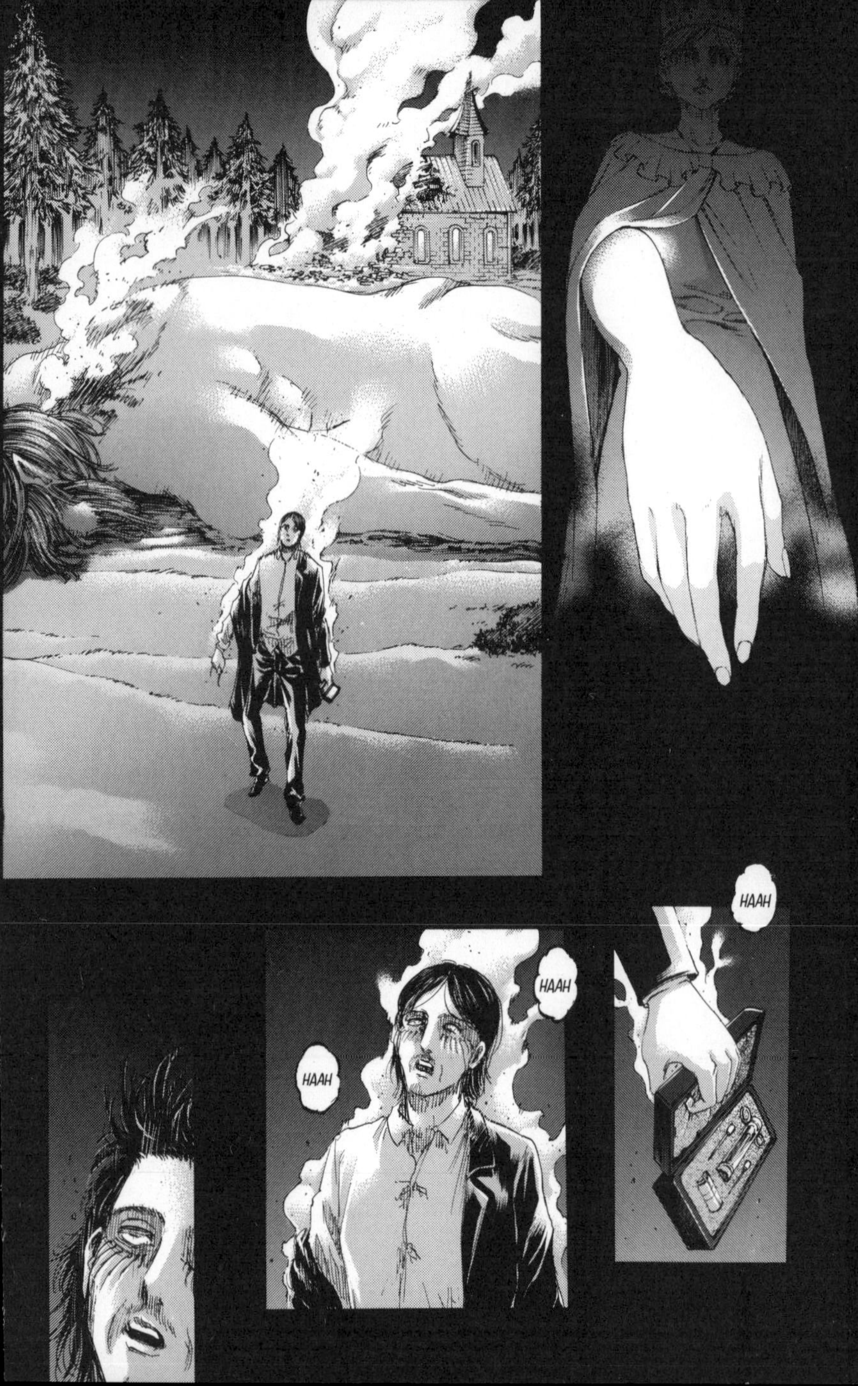
HAAH
HAAH
HAAH

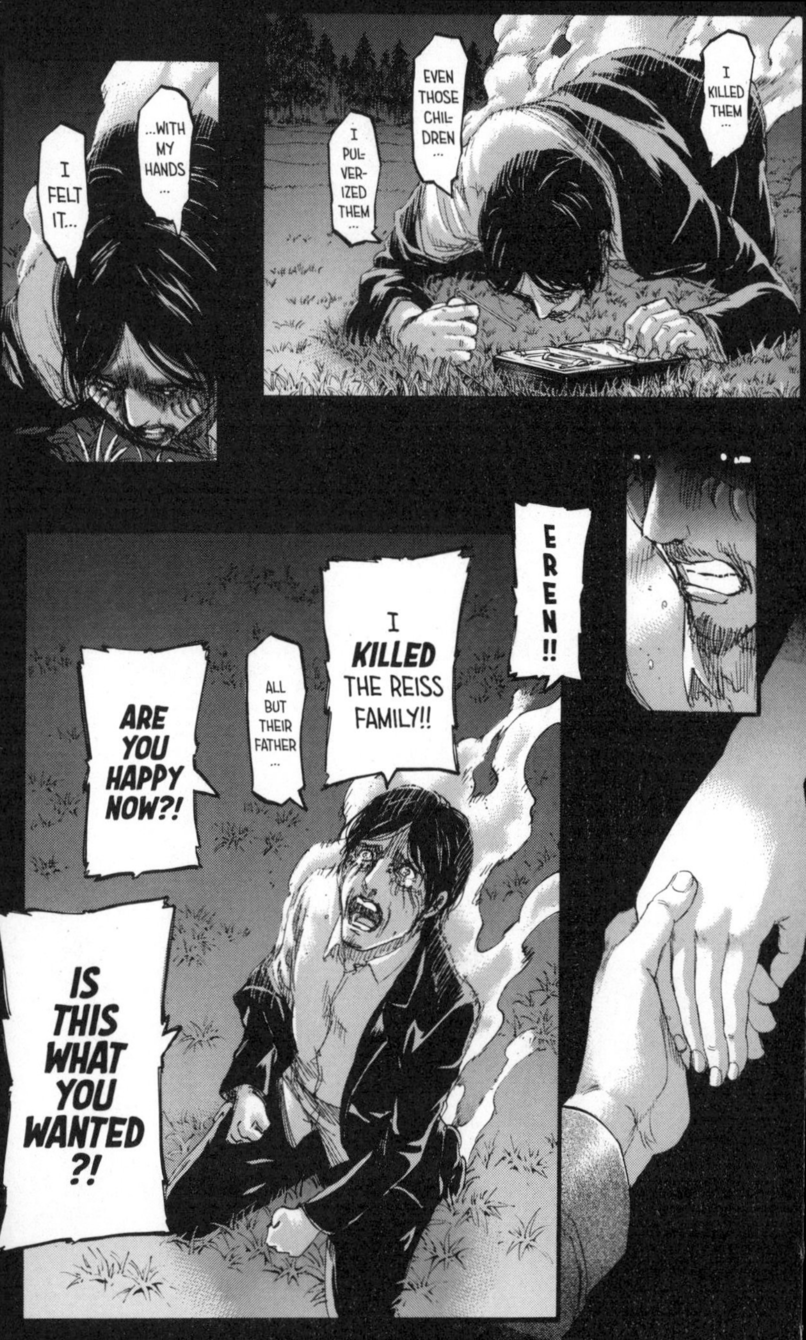
I KILLED THEM ...
EVEN THOSE CHIL-DREN ...
I PUL-VER-IZED THEM ...
...WITH MY HANDS ...
I FELT IT...
EREN!!
I KILLED THE REISS FAMILY!!
ALL BUT THEIR FATHER ...
ARE YOU HAPPY NOW?!
IS THIS WHAT YOU WANTED ?!

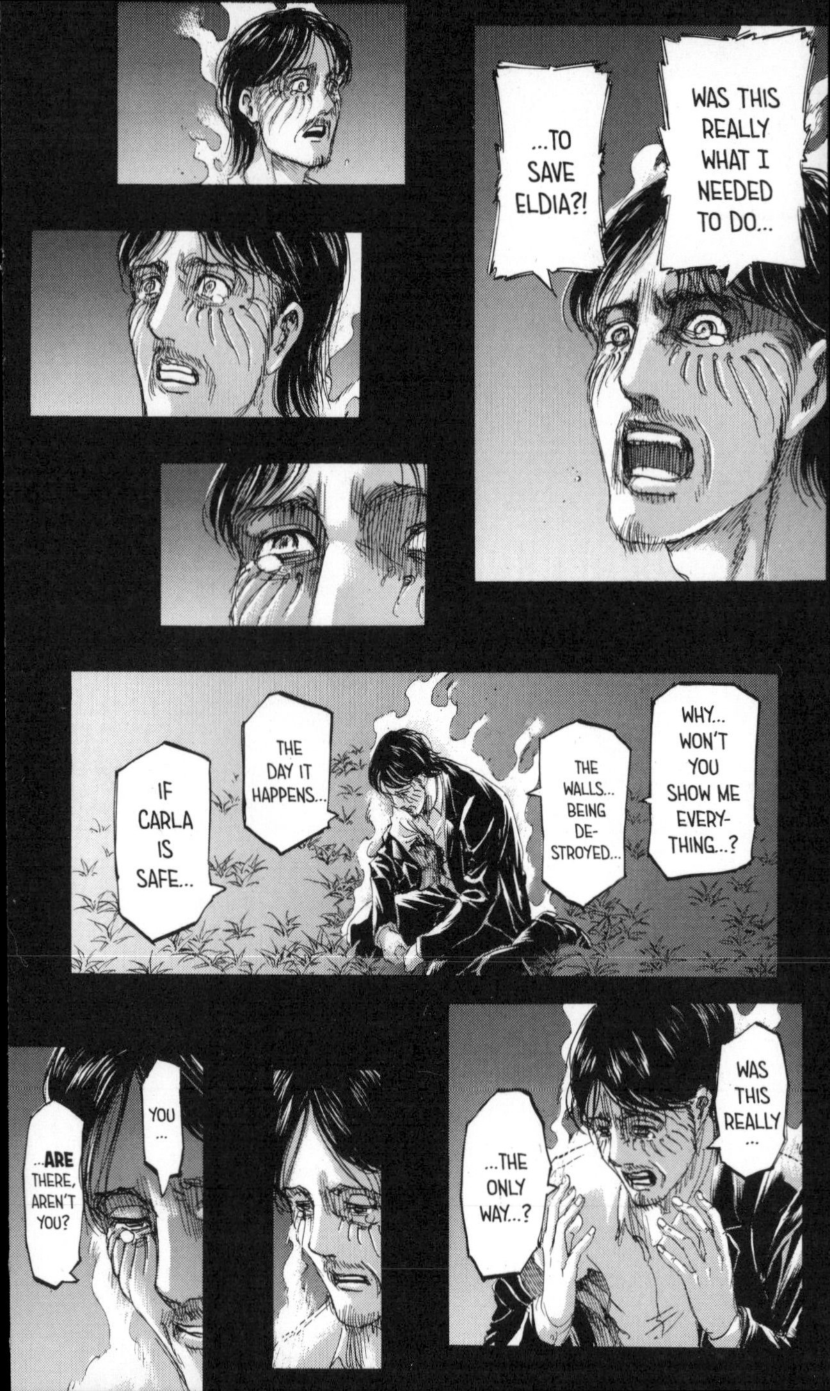
WAS THIS REALLY WHAT I NEEDED TO DO...
...TO SAVE ELDIA?!
WHY... WON'T YOU SHOW ME EVERY-THING...?
THE WALLS... BEING DE-STROYED...
THE DAY IT HAPPENS...
IF CARLA IS SAFE...
WAS THIS REALLY ...
...THE ONLY WAY...?
YOU ...
...ARE THERE, AREN'T YOU?

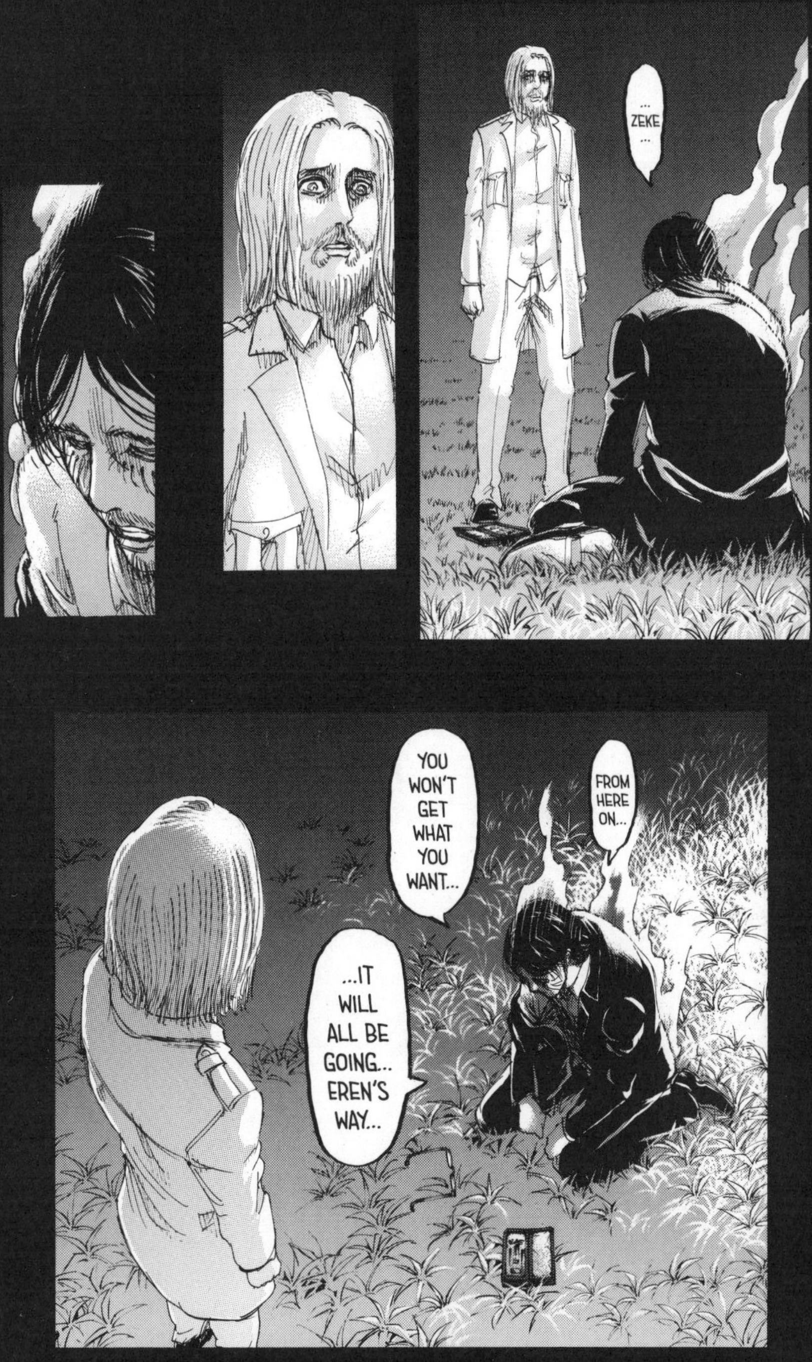
... ZEKE ...
FROM HERE ON...
YOU WON'T GET WHAT YOU WANT...
...IT WILL ALL BE GOING... EREN'S WAY...

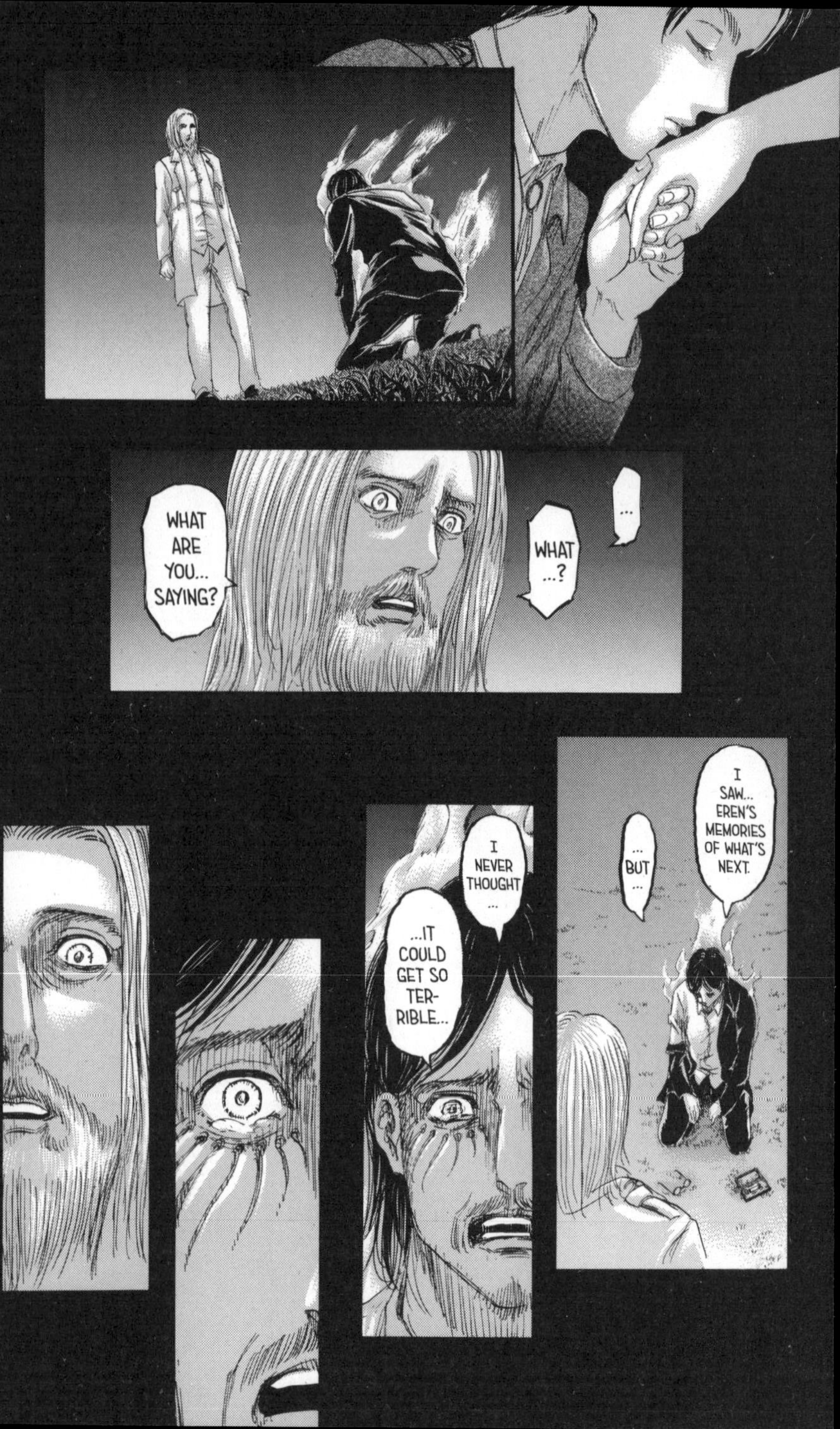
...
WHAT ...?
WHAT ARE YOU... SAYING?
I SAW... EREN'S MEMORIES OF WHAT'S NEXT.
... BUT ...
I NEVER THOUGHT ...
...IT COULD GET SO TER-RIBLE...

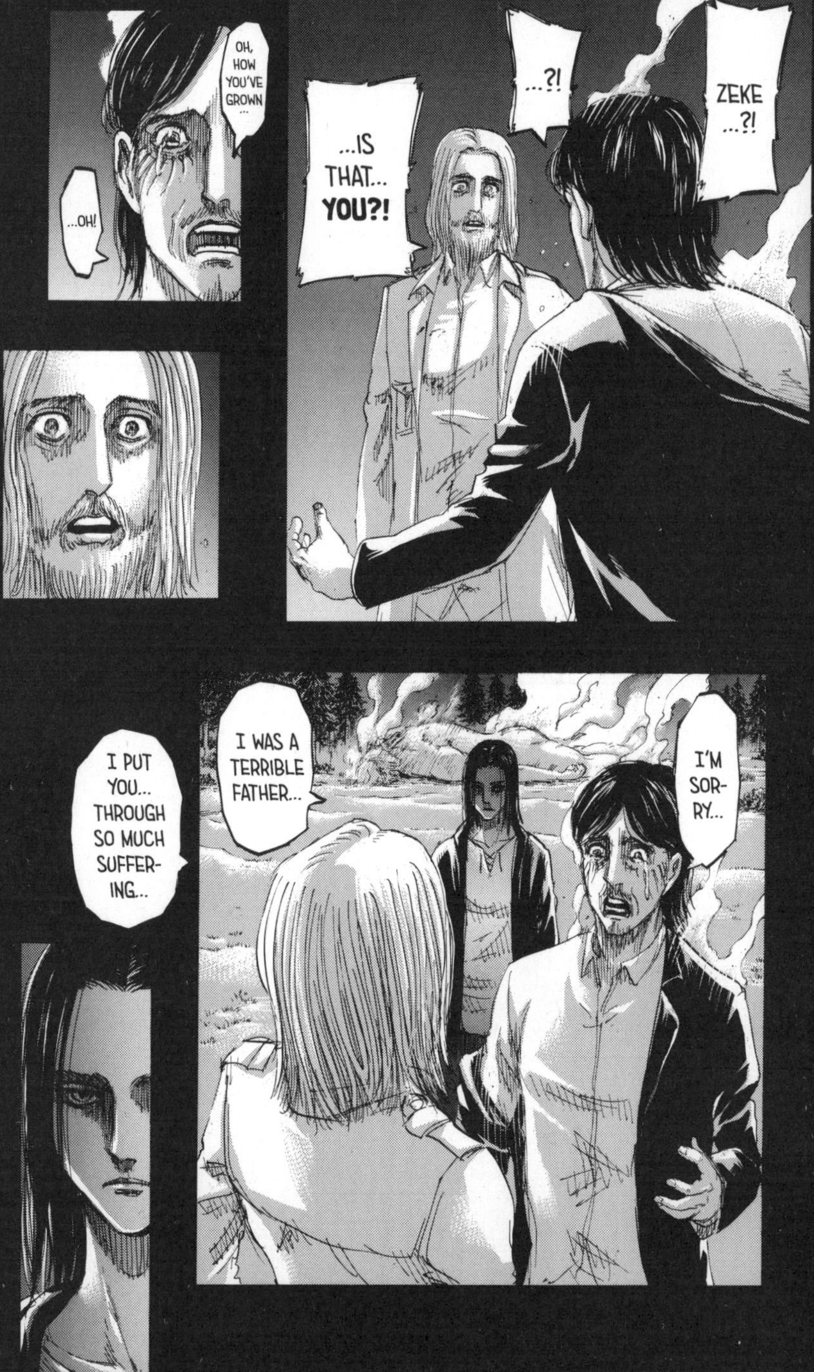
ZEKE ...?!
...?!
...IS THAT... YOU?!
OH, HOW YOU'VE GROWN ...
...OH!
I'M SOR-RY...
I WAS A TERRIBLE FATHER...
I PUT YOU... THROUGH SO MUCH SUFFER-ING...

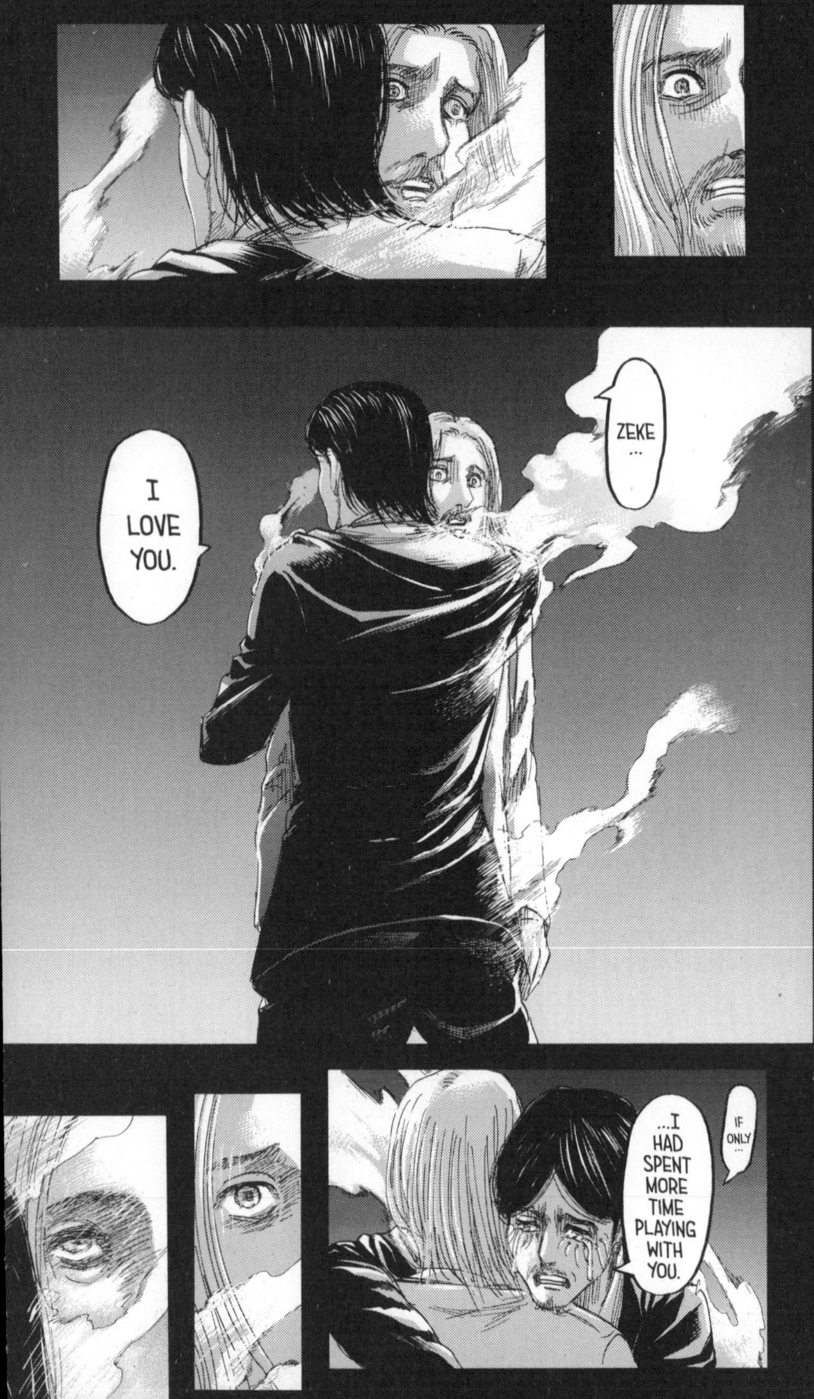
ZEKE...
I LOVE YOU.
IF ONLY...
...I HAD SPENT MORE TIME PLAYING WITH YOU.

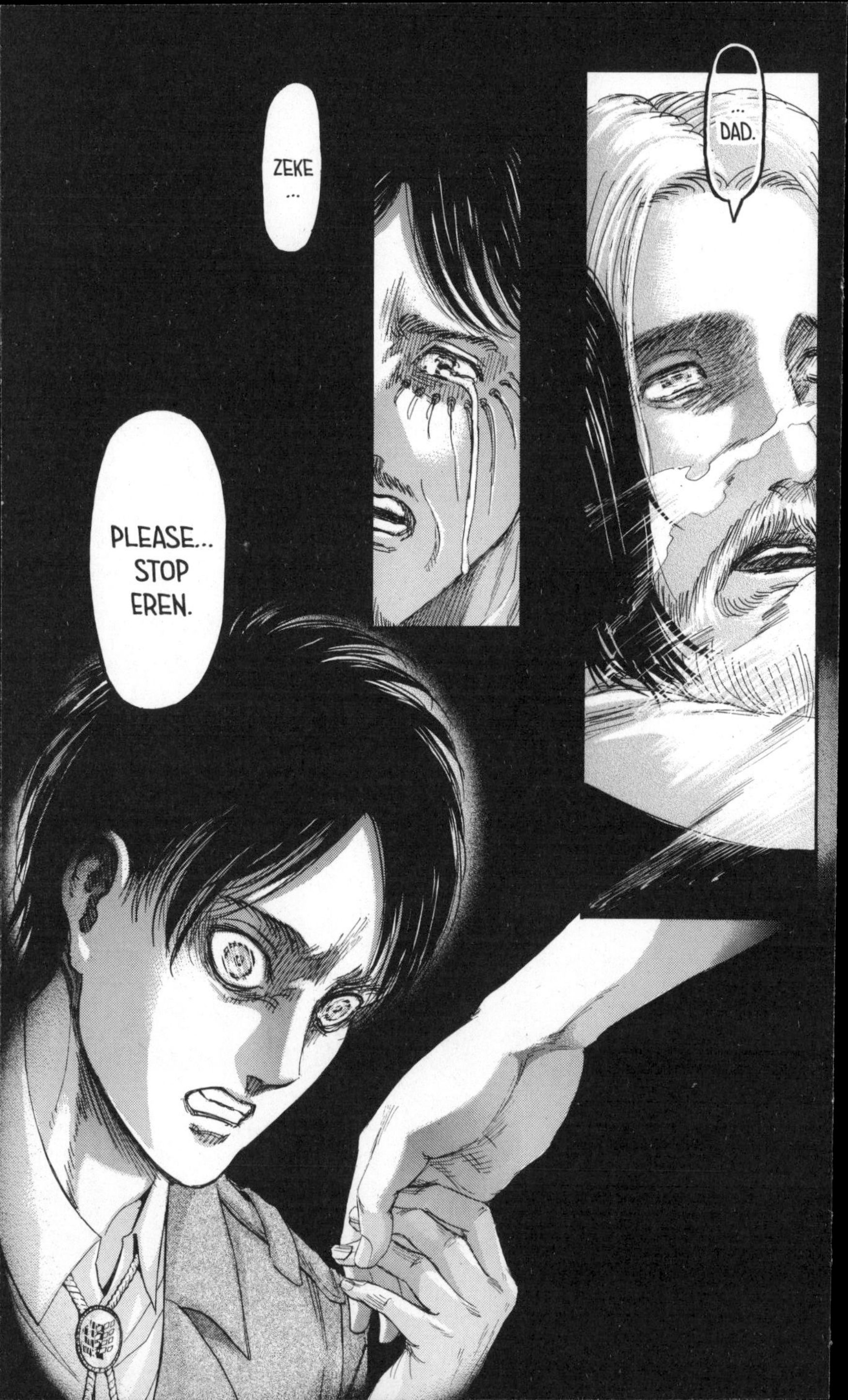
... DAD.
ZEKE ...
PLEASE... STOP EREN.

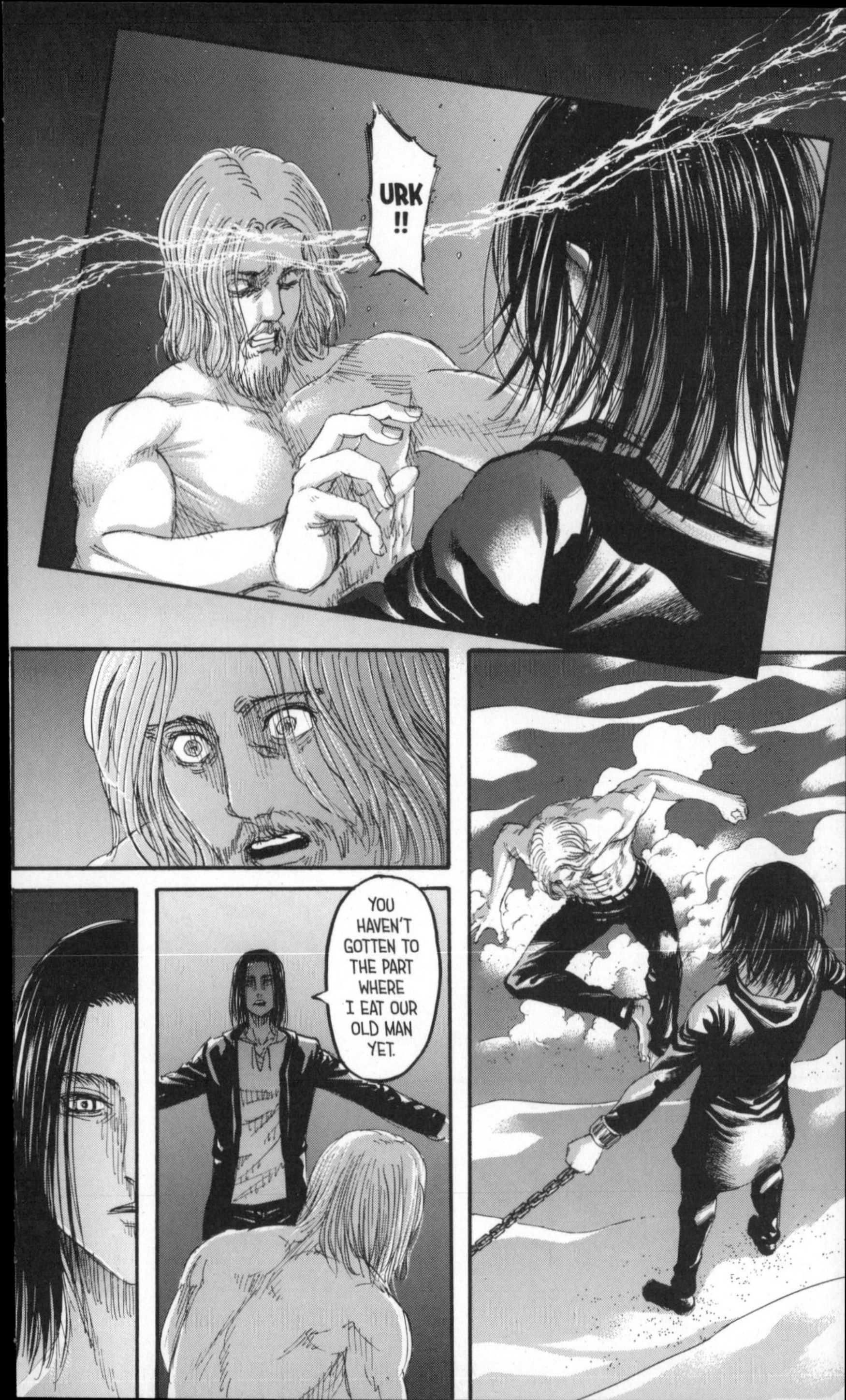
URK !!
YOU HAVEN'T GOTTEN TO THE PART WHERE I EAT OUR OLD MAN YET.

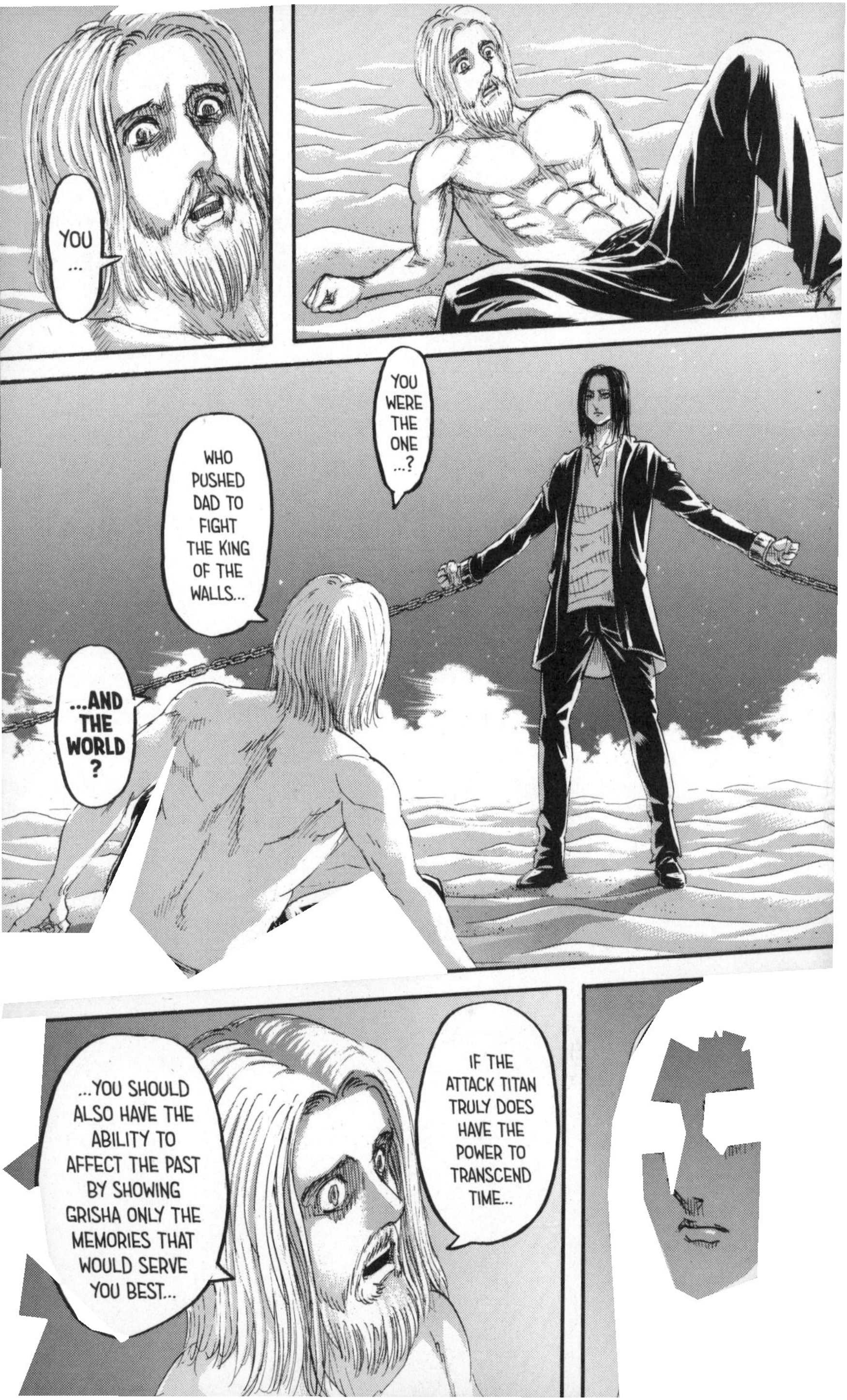
YOU ...
YOU WERE THE ONE ...?
WHO PUSHED DAD TO FIGHT THE KING OF THE WALLS...
...AND THE WORLD?
IF THE ATTACK TITAN TRULY DOES HAVE THE POWER TO TRANSCEND TIME...
...YOU SHOULD ALSO HAVE THE ABILITY TO AFFECT THE PAST BY SHOWING GRISHA ONLY THE MEMORIES THAT WOULD SERVE YOU BEST...

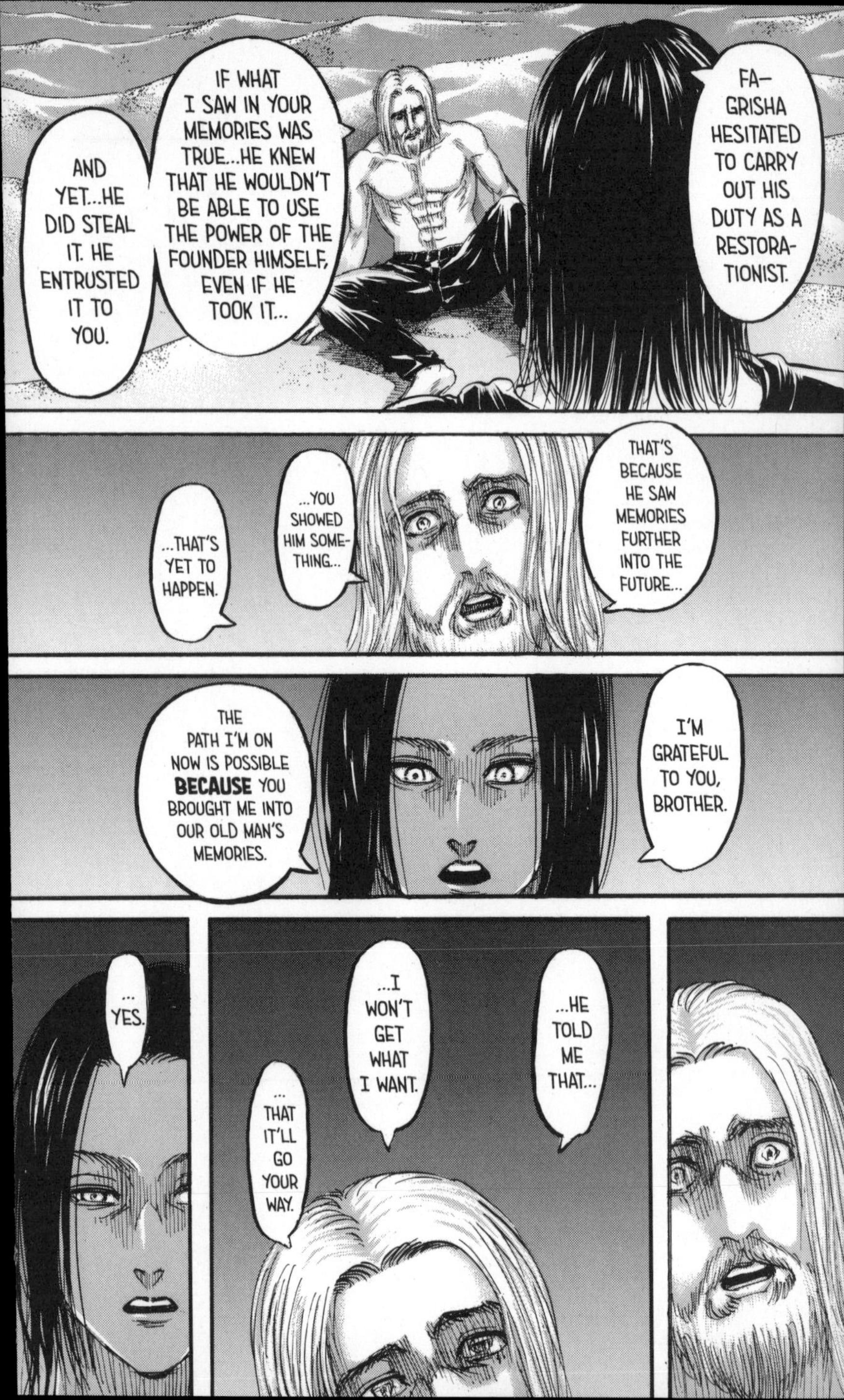
FA— GRISHA HESITATED TO CARRY OUT HIS DUTY AS A RESTORATIONIST.
IF WHAT I SAW IN YOUR MEMORIES WAS TRUE...HE KNEW THAT HE WOULDN'T BE ABLE TO USE THE POWER OF THE FOUNDER HIMSELF, EVEN IF HE TOOK IT...
AND YET...HE DID STEAL IT. HE ENTRUSTED IT TO YOU.
THAT'S BECAUSE HE SAW MEMORIES FURTHER INTO THE FUTURE...
...YOU SHOWED HIM SOMETHING...
...THAT'S YET TO HAPPEN.
I'M GRATEFUL TO YOU, BROTHER.
THE PATH I'M ON NOW IS POSSIBLE **BECAUSE** YOU BROUGHT ME INTO OUR OLD MAN'S MEMORIES.
...HE TOLD ME THAT...
...I WON'T GET WHAT I WANT.
...THAT IT'LL GO YOUR WAY.
... YES.

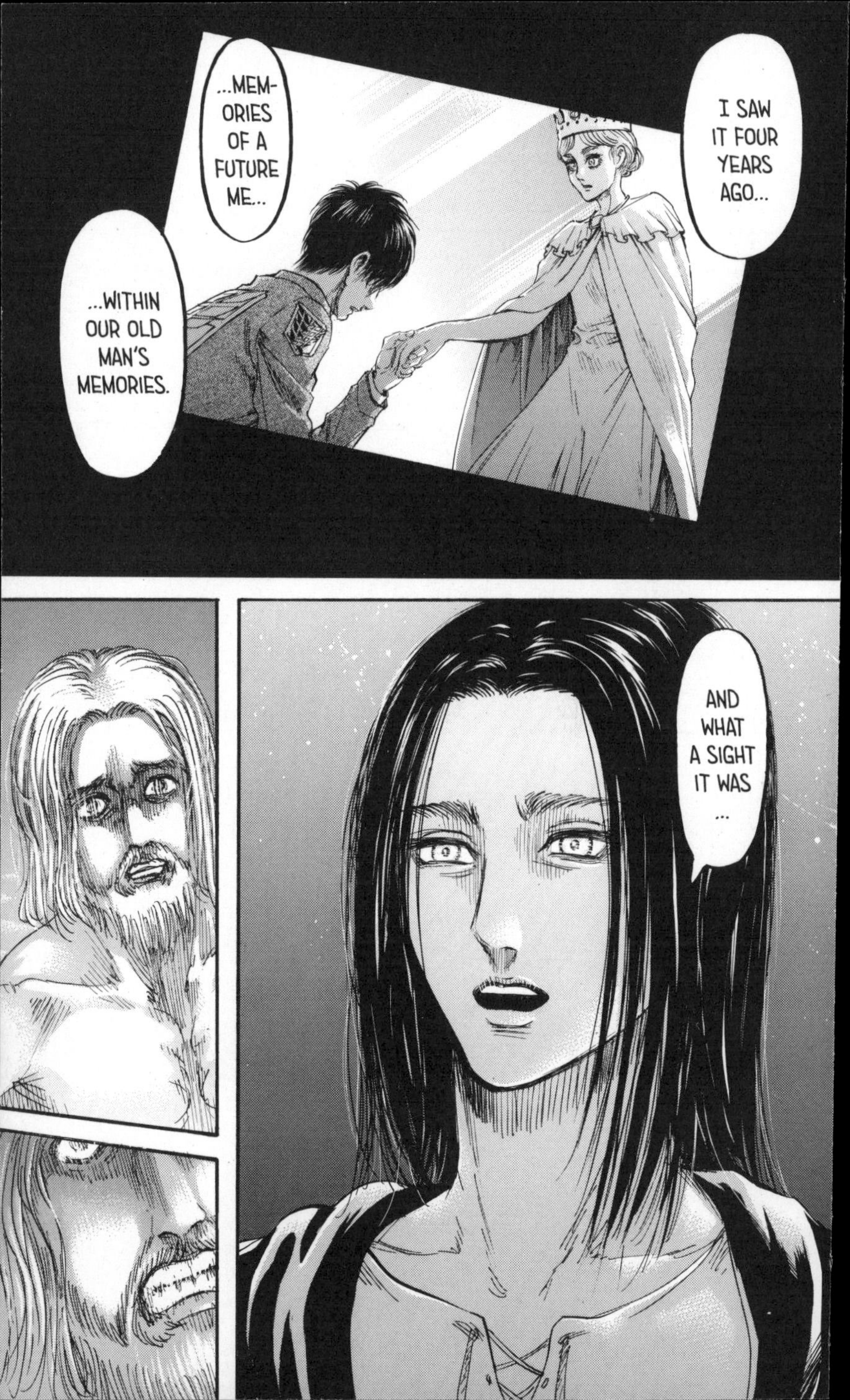
I SAW IT FOUR YEARS AGO...
...MEMORIES OF A FUTURE ME...
...WITHIN OUR OLD MAN'S MEMORIES.
AND WHAT A SIGHT IT WAS ...

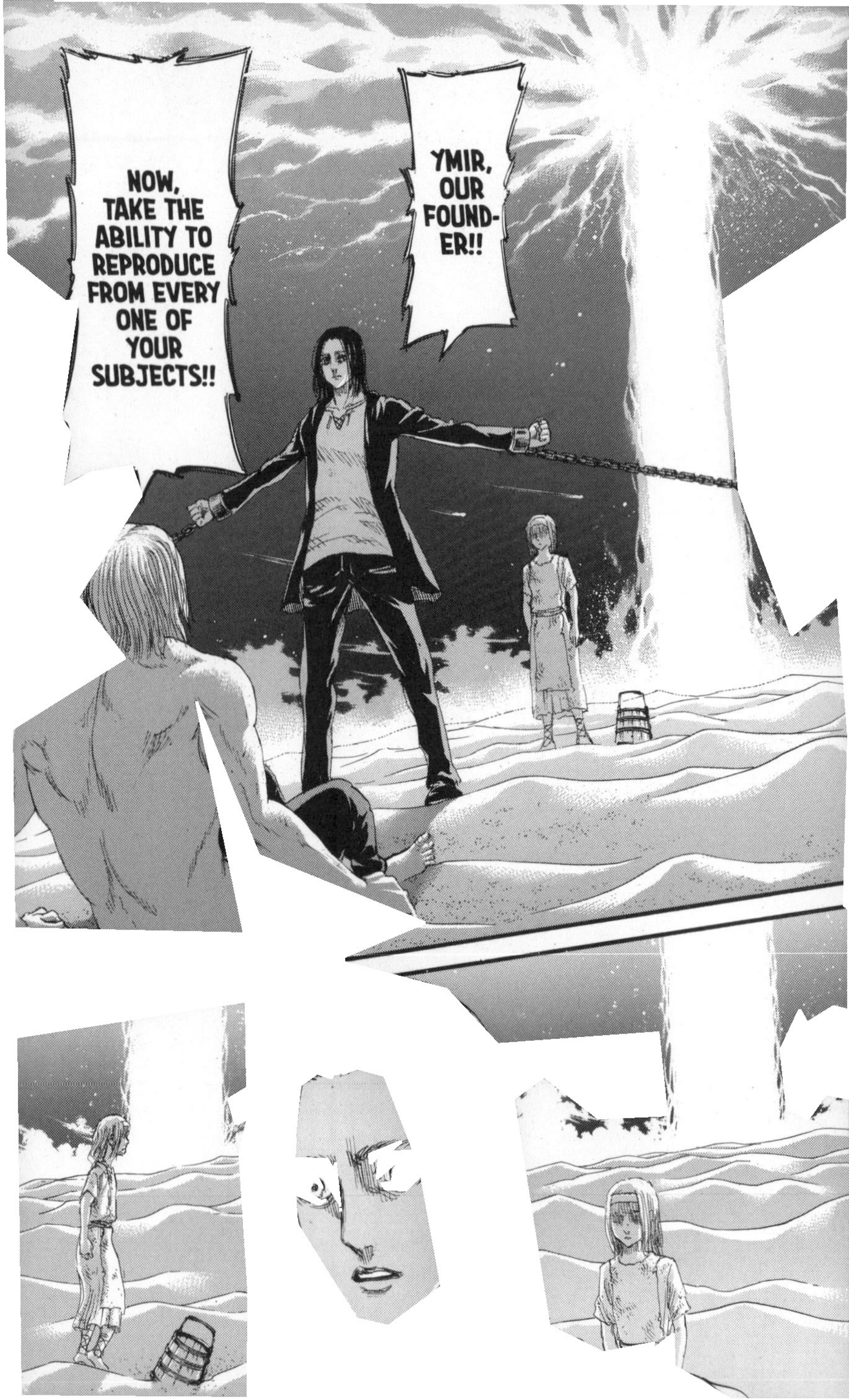
YMIR, OUR FOUNDER!!
NOW, TAKE THE ABILITY TO REPRODUCE FROM EVERY ONE OF YOUR SUBJECTS!!

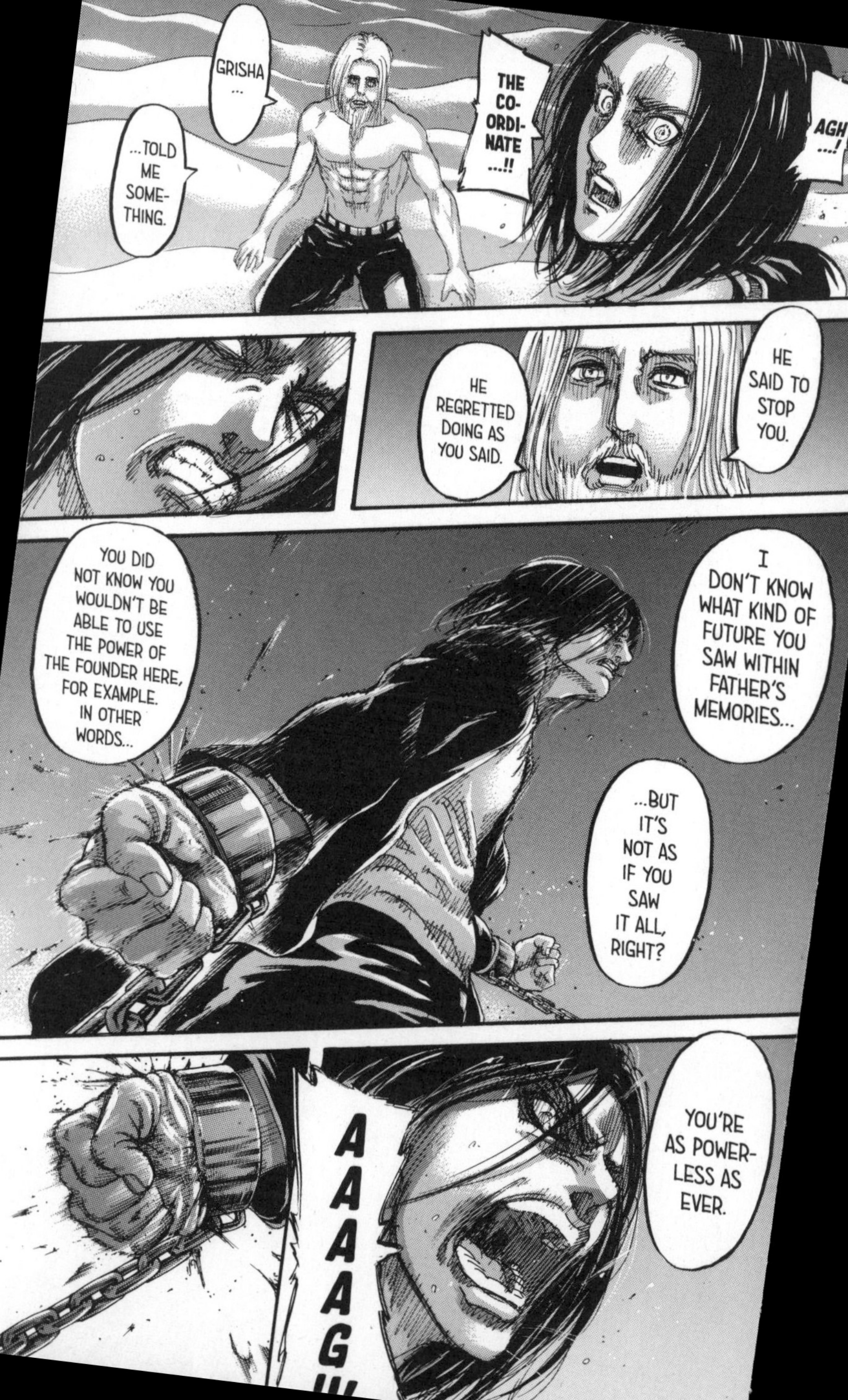
AGH...!
THE CO-ORDINATE...!!
GRISHA...
...TOLD ME SOMETHING.
HE SAID TO STOP YOU.
HE REGRETTED DOING AS YOU SAID.
I DON'T KNOW WHAT KIND OF FUTURE YOU SAW WITHIN FATHER'S MEMORIES...
...BUT IT'S NOT AS IF YOU SAW IT ALL, RIGHT?
YOU DID NOT KNOW YOU WOULDN'T BE ABLE TO USE THE POWER OF THE FOUNDER HERE, FOR EXAMPLE. IN OTHER WORDS...
YOU'RE AS POWERLESS AS EVER.
AAAAAG

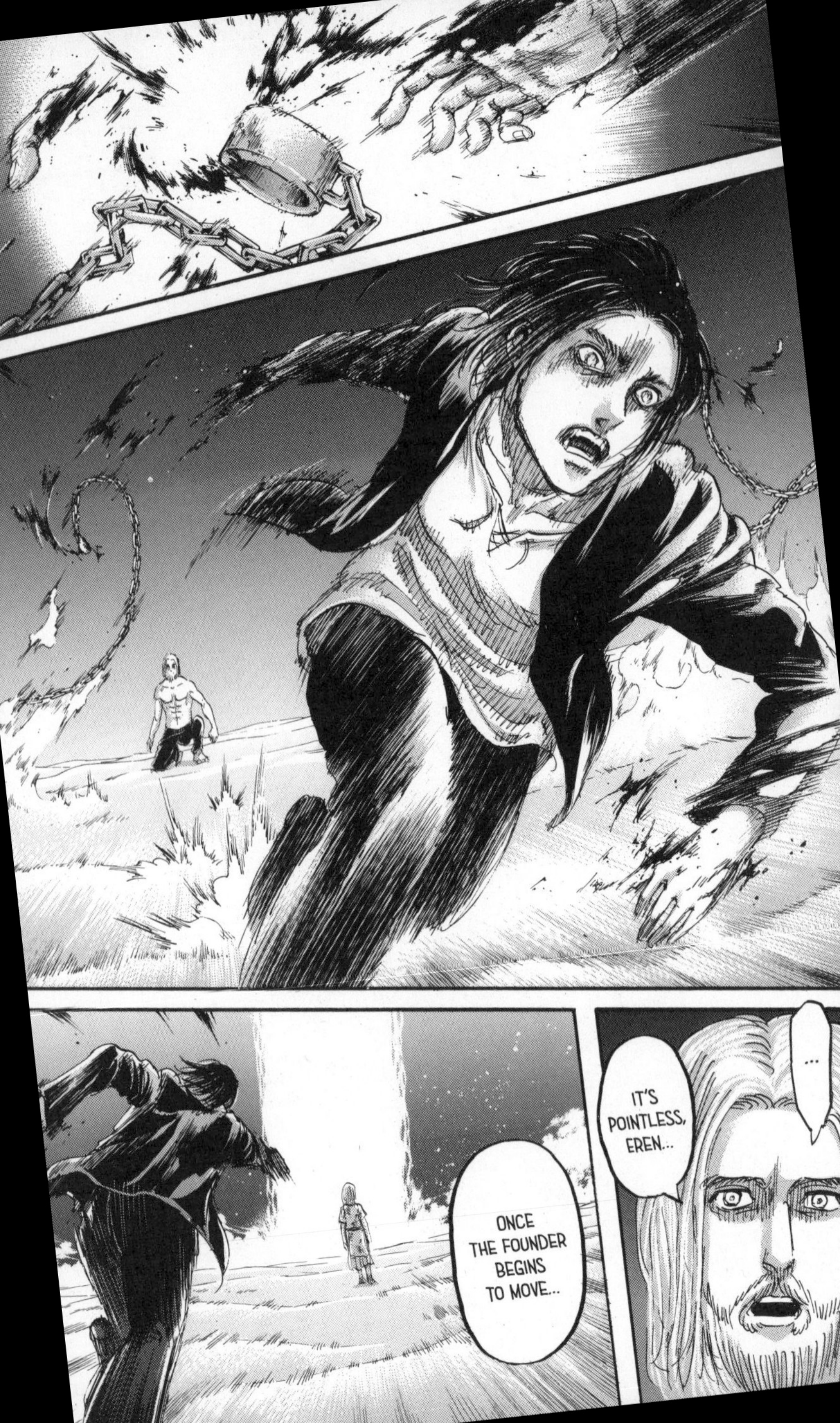
...
IT'S POINTLESS, EREN...
ONCE THE FOUNDER BEGINS TO MOVE...

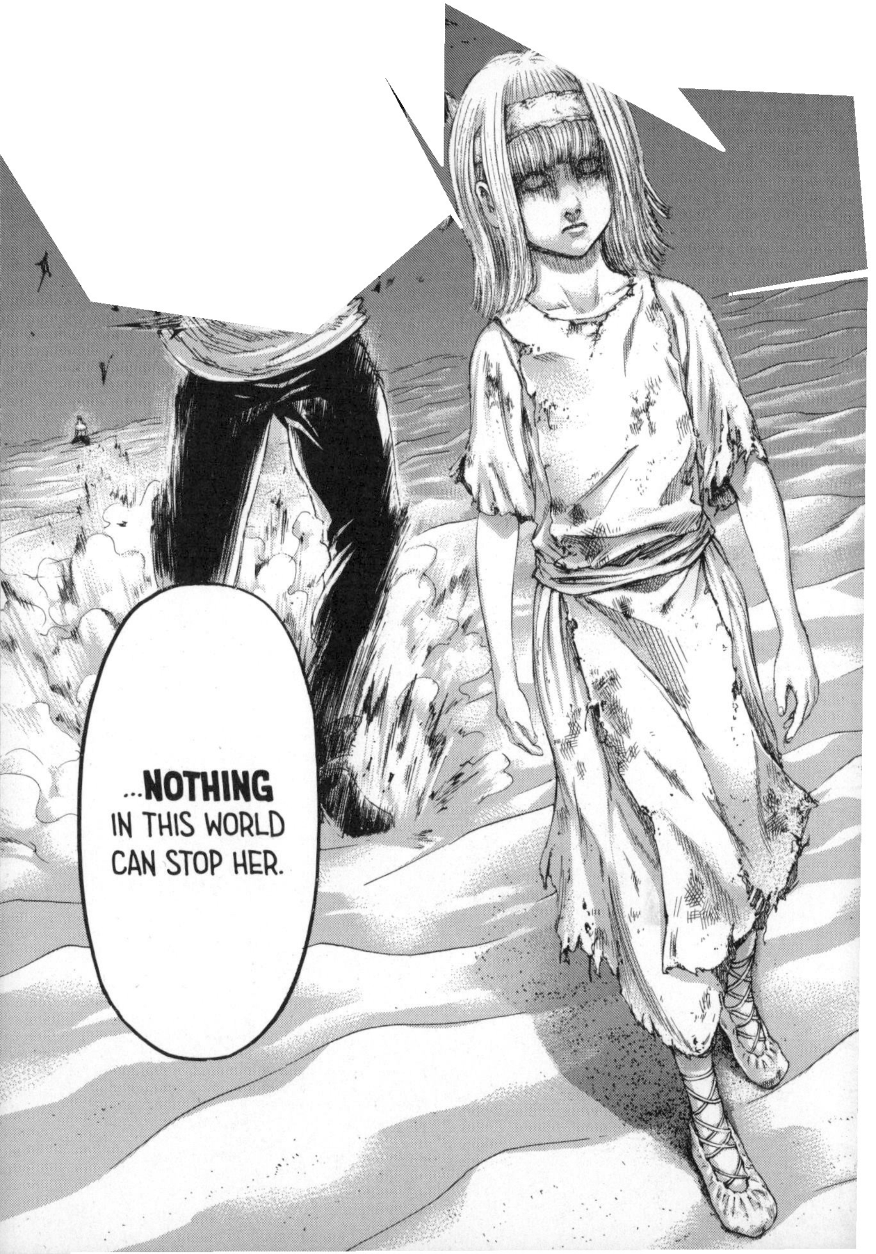
...NOTHING IN THIS WORLD CAN STOP HER.

ATTACK on TITAN

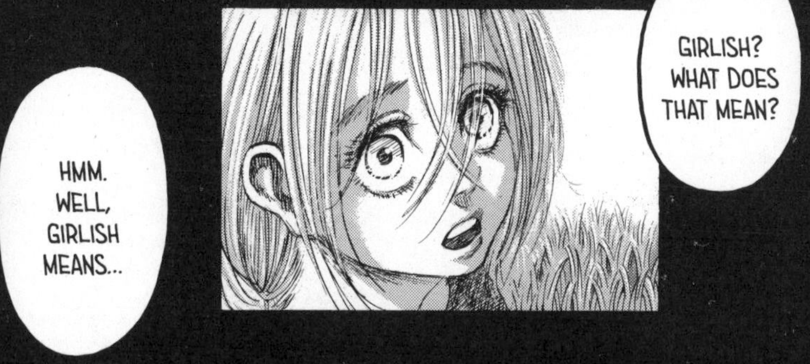
GIRLISH? WHAT DOES THAT MEAN?
HMM. WELL, GIRLISH MEANS...

Episode 122: From You, 2,000 Years Ago

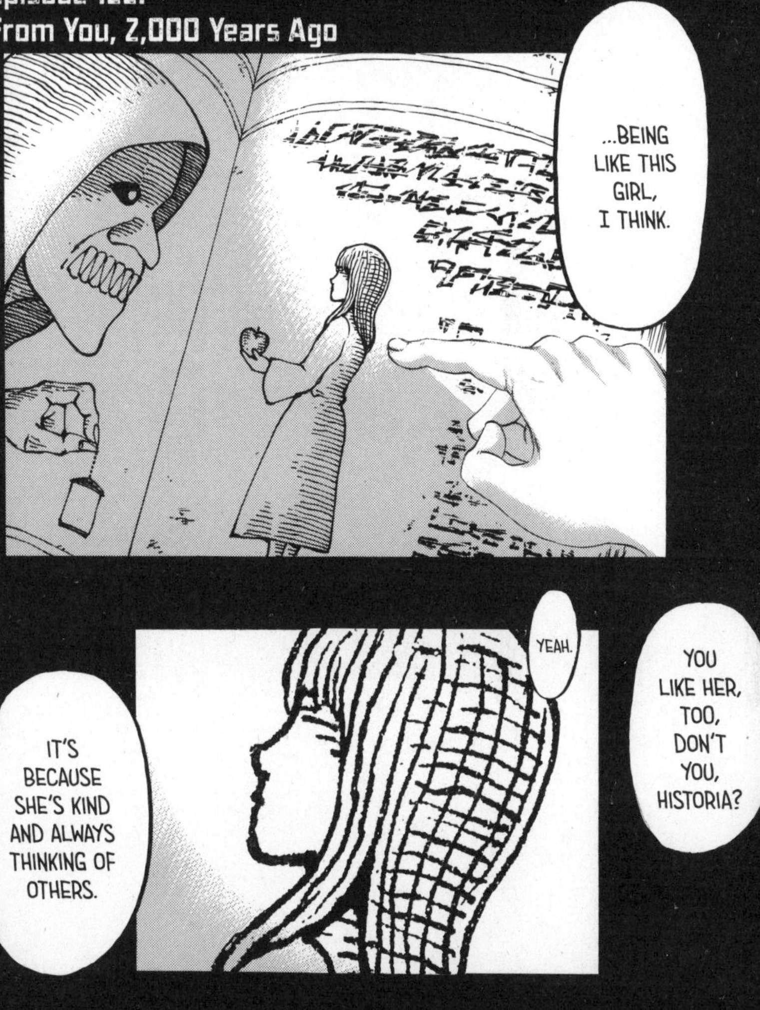
...BEING LIKE THIS GIRL, I THINK.
YOU LIKE HER, TOO, DON'T YOU, HISTORIA?
YEAH.
IT'S BECAUSE SHE'S KIND AND ALWAYS THINKING OF OTHERS.

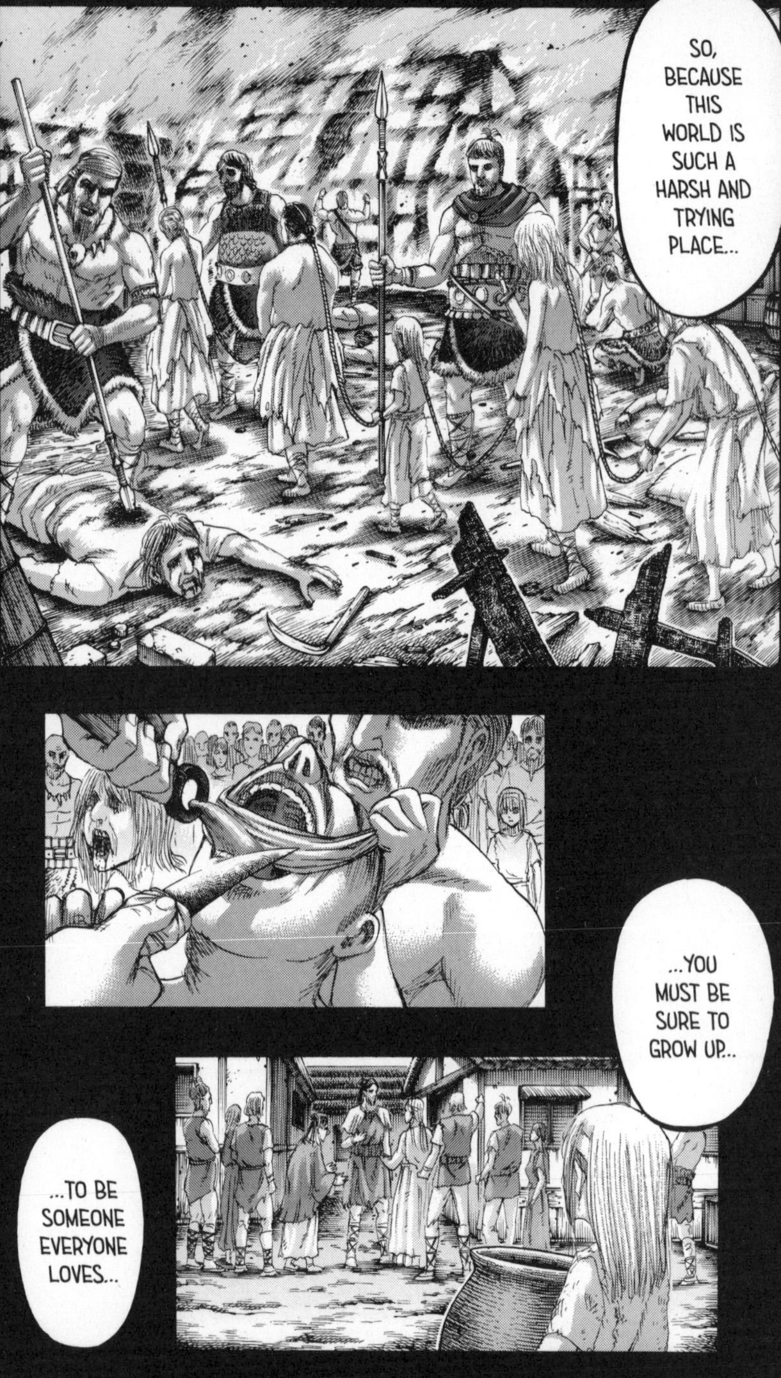
SO, BECAUSE THIS WORLD IS SUCH A HARSH AND TRYING PLACE...
...YOU MUST BE SURE TO GROW UP...
...TO BE SOMEONE EVERYONE LOVES...

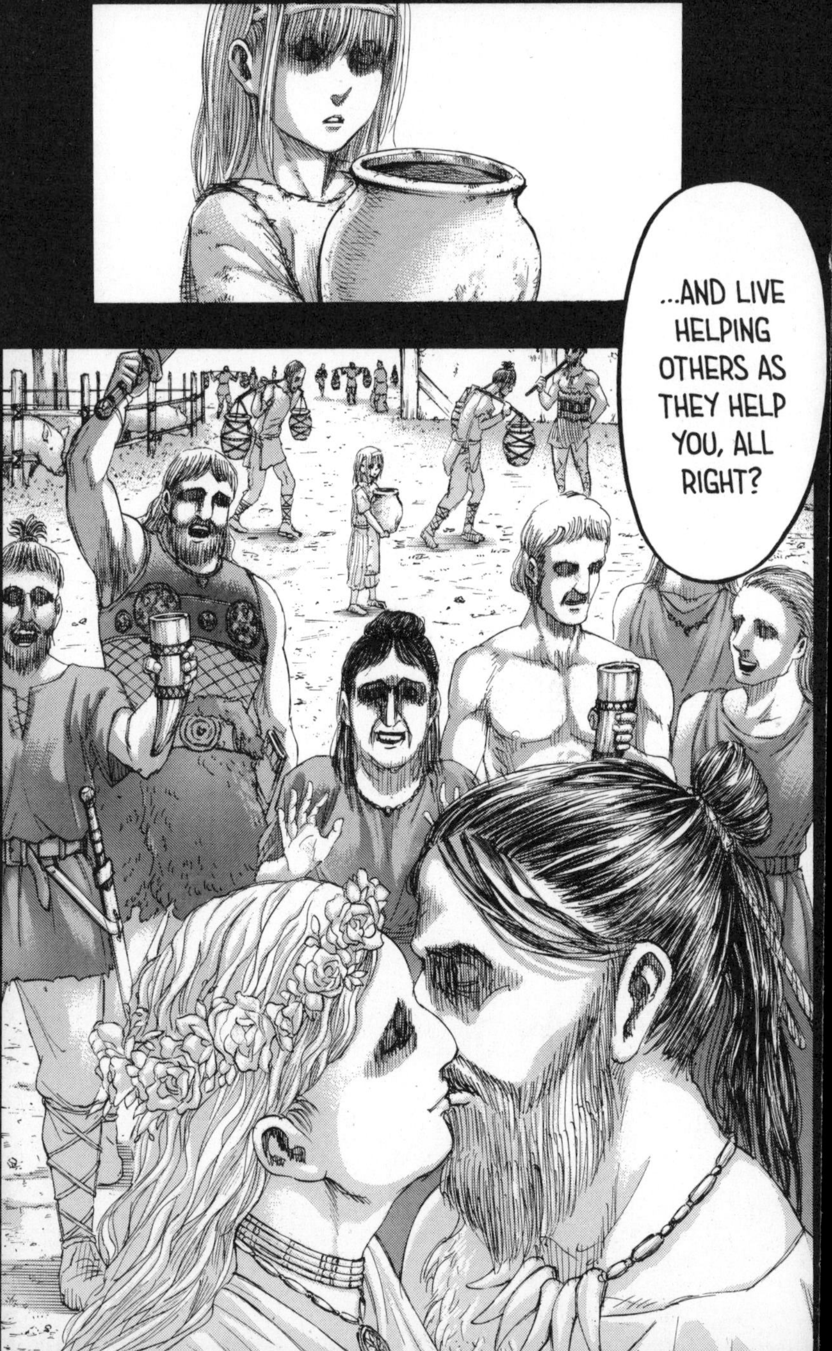
...AND LIVE HELPING OTHERS AS THEY HELP YOU, ALL RIGHT?

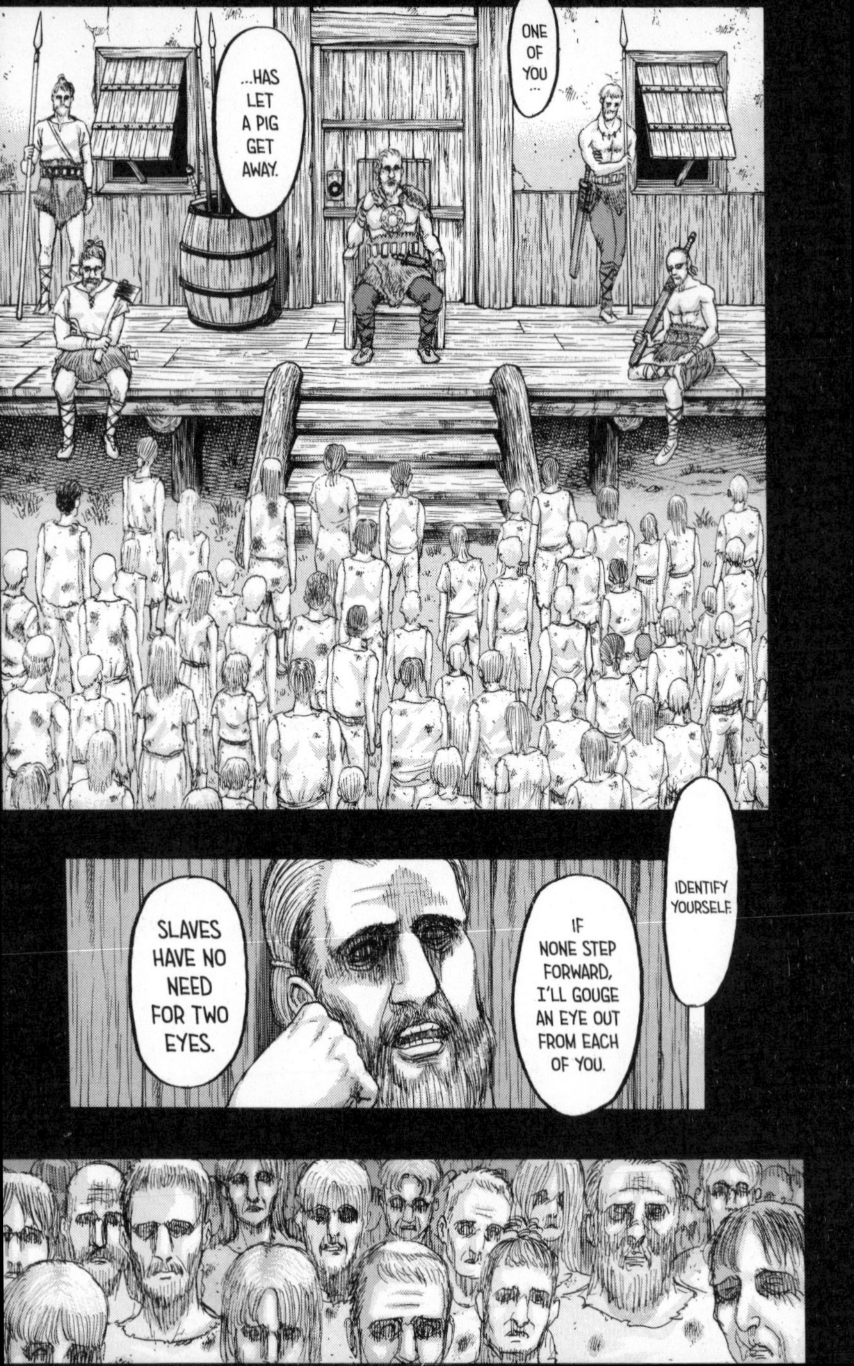
ONE OF YOU...
...HAS LET A PIG GET AWAY.
IDENTIFY YOURSELF.
IF NONE STEP FORWARD, I'LL GOUGE AN EYE OUT FROM EACH OF YOU.
SLAVES HAVE NO NEED FOR TWO EYES.

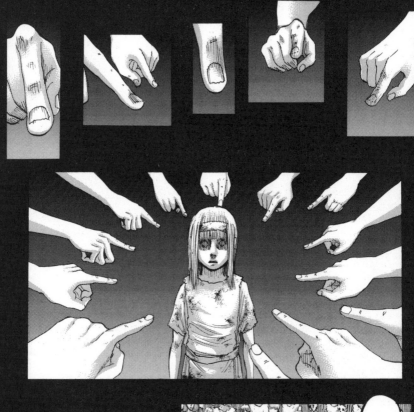

THE ONE WHO LET THE PIG GO...

...WAS YOU?

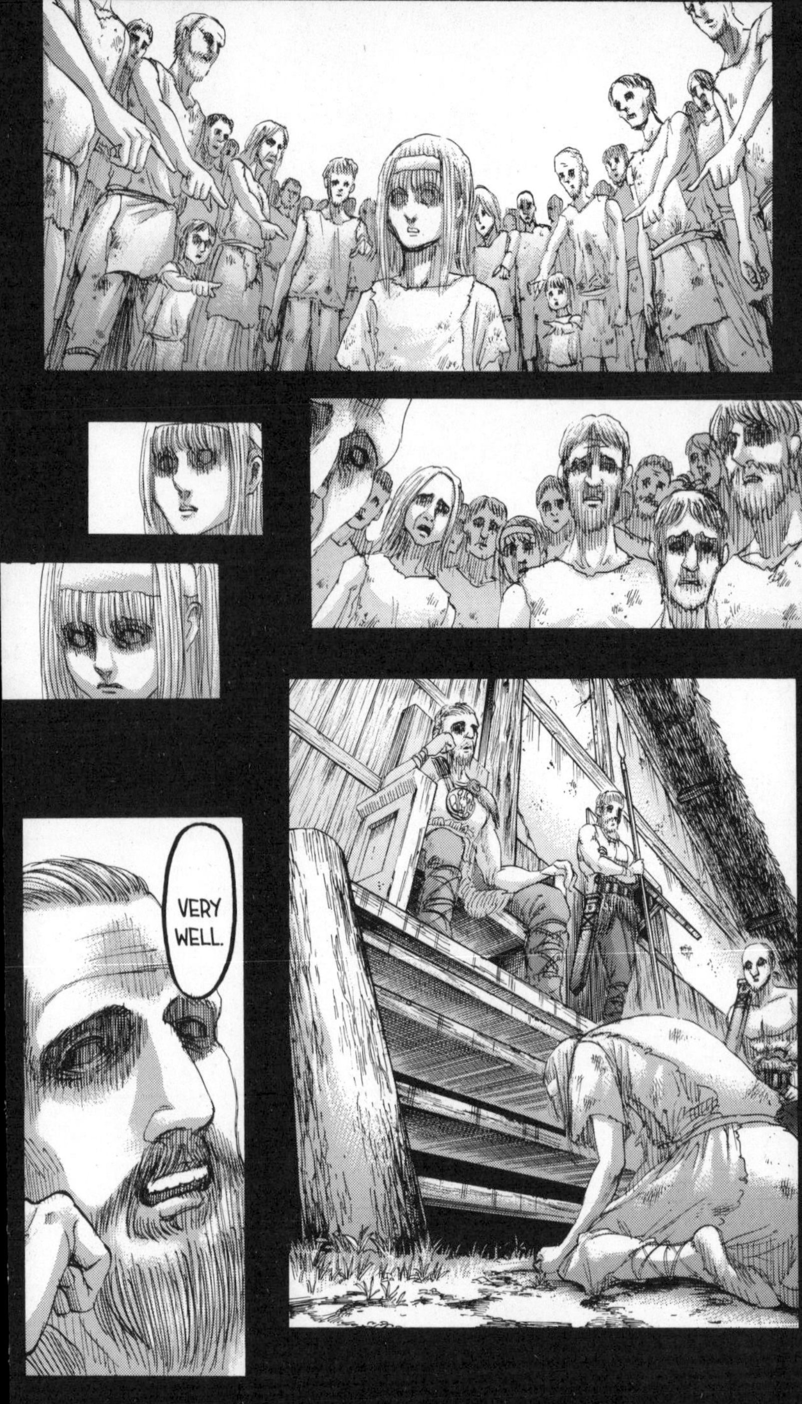
VERY WELL.

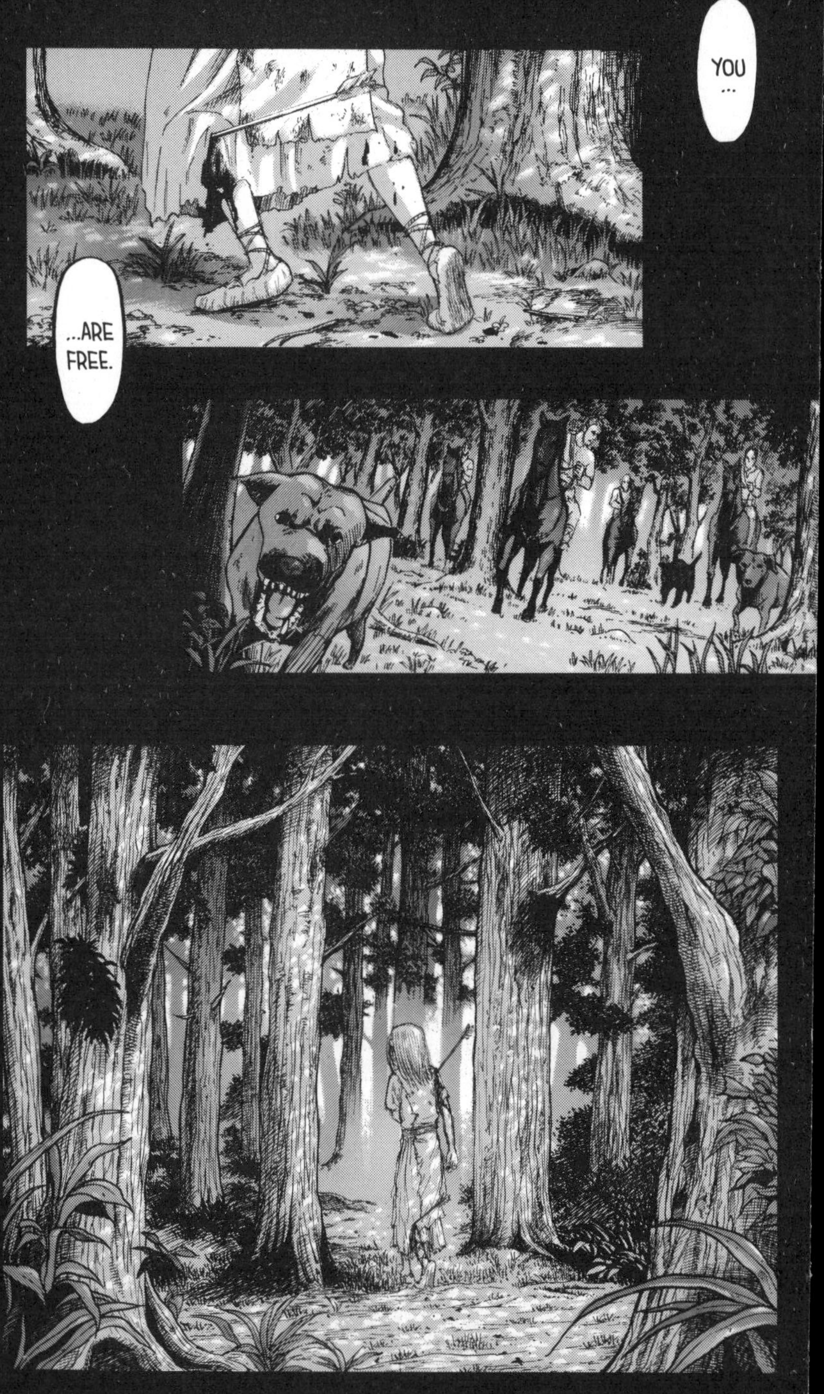
YOU ...
...ARE FREE.

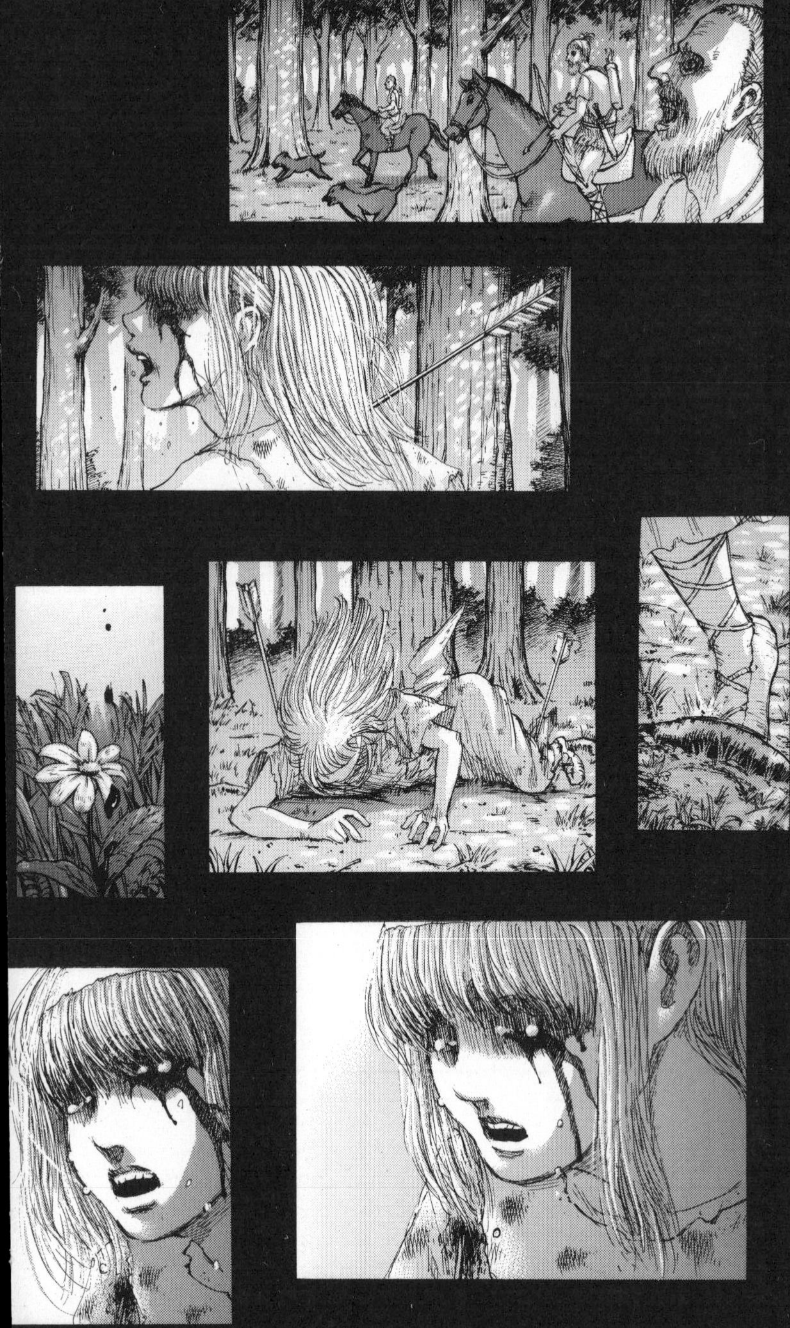

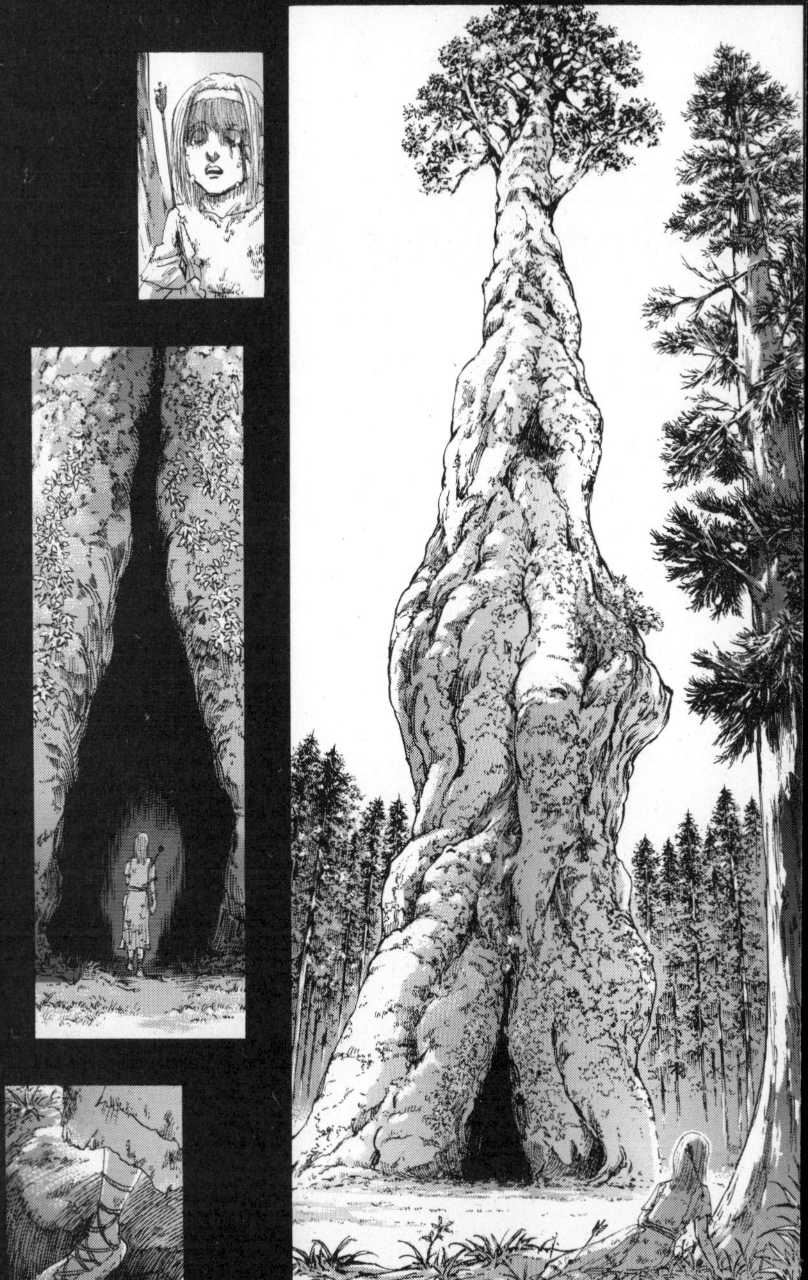

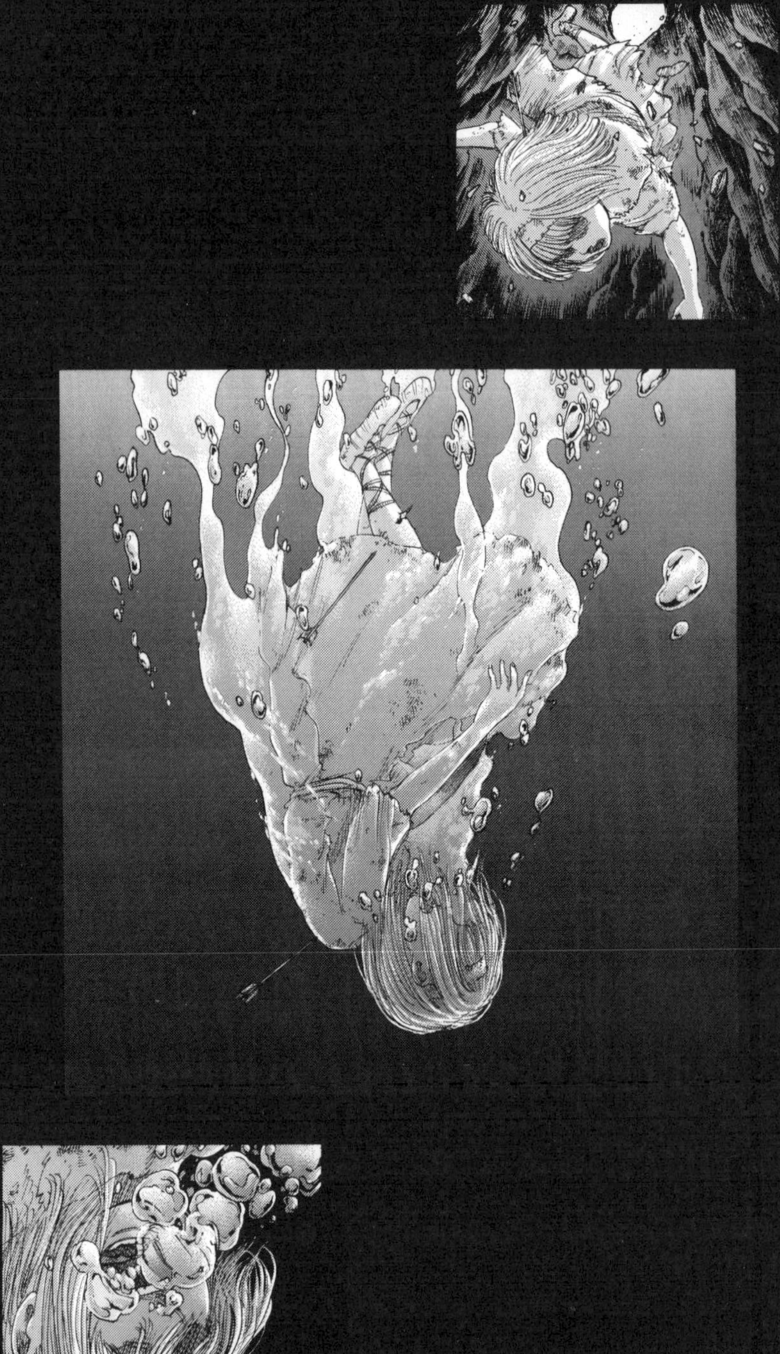

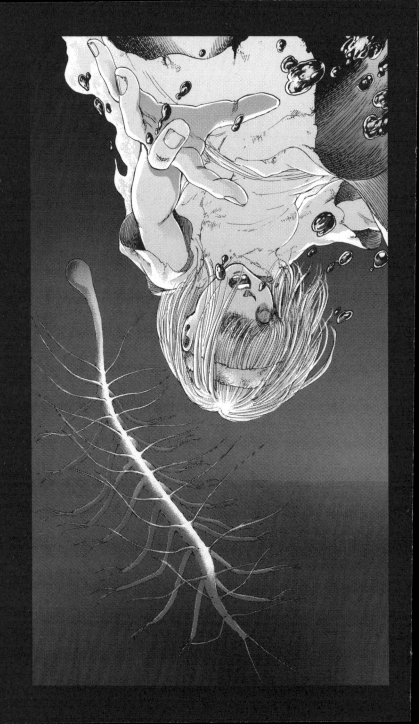

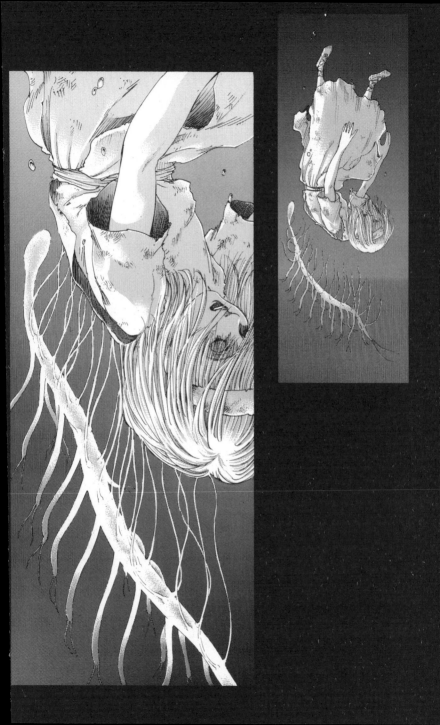

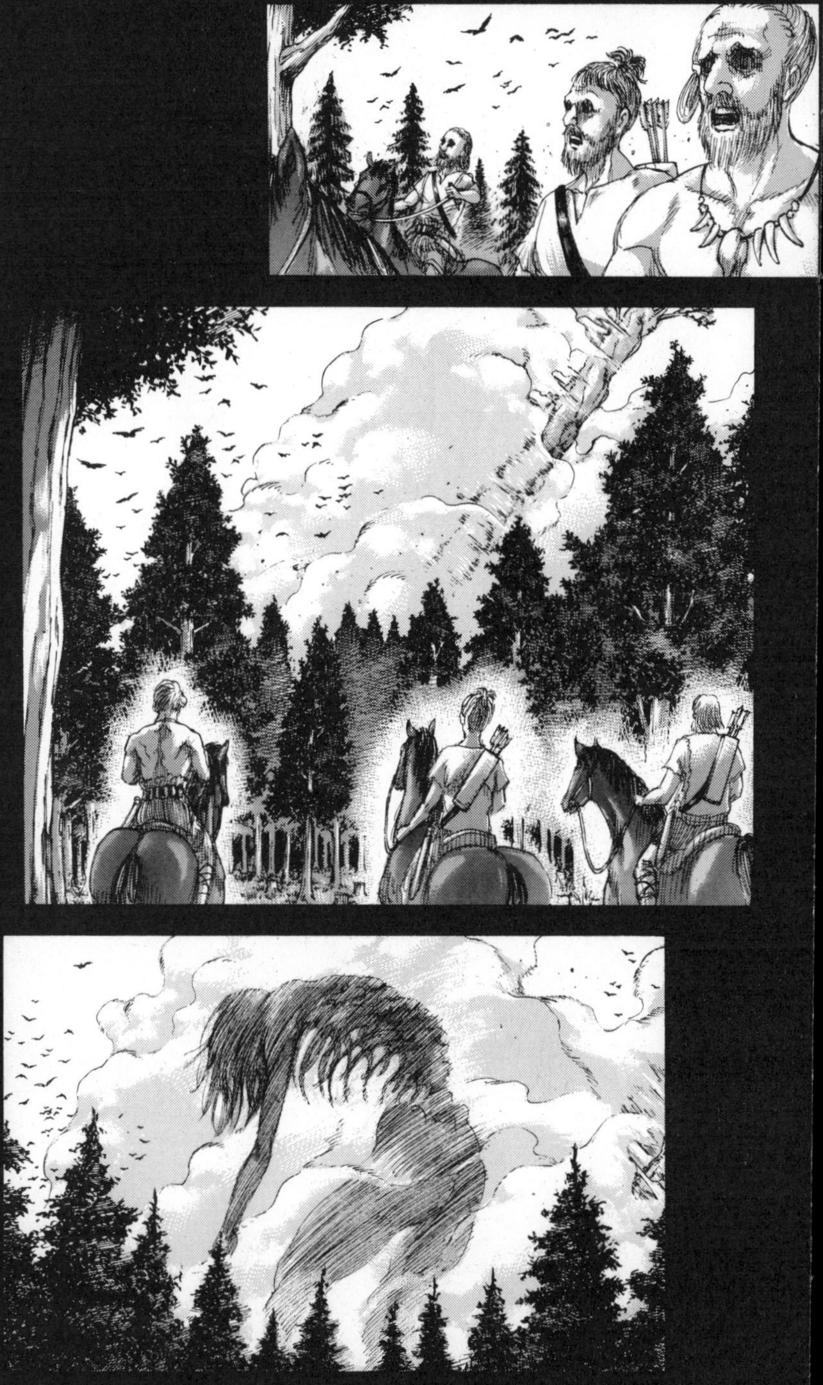

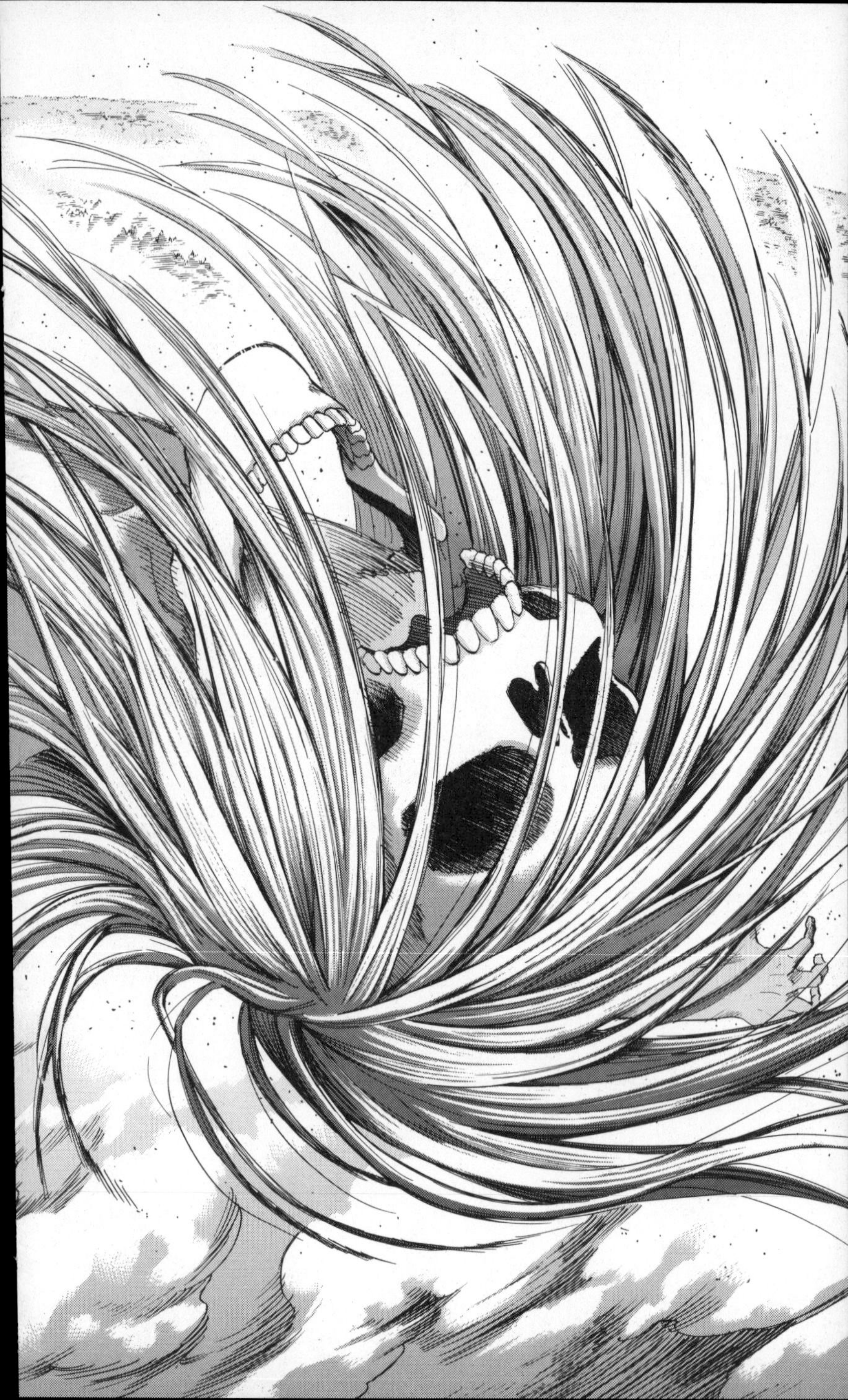

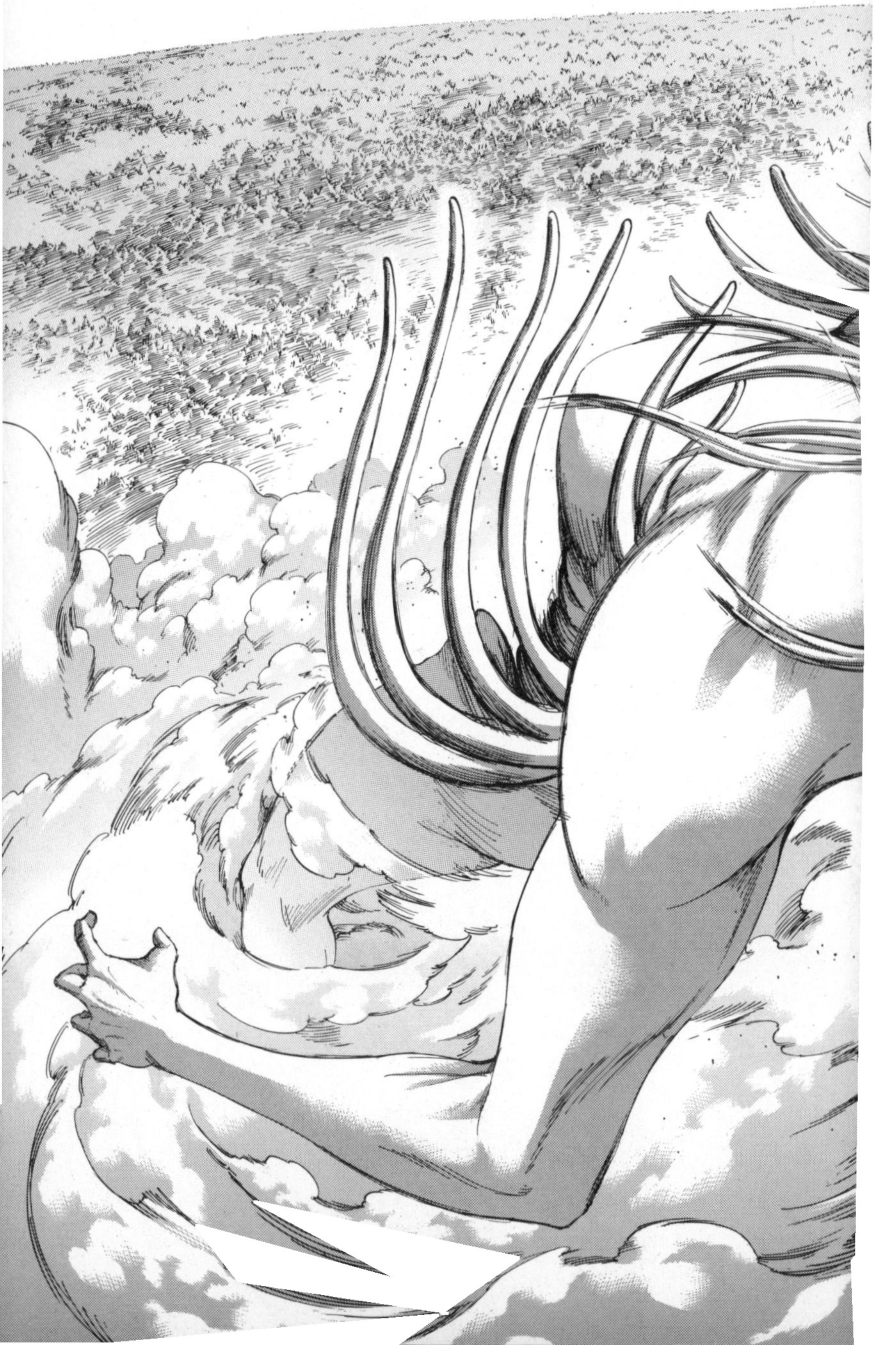

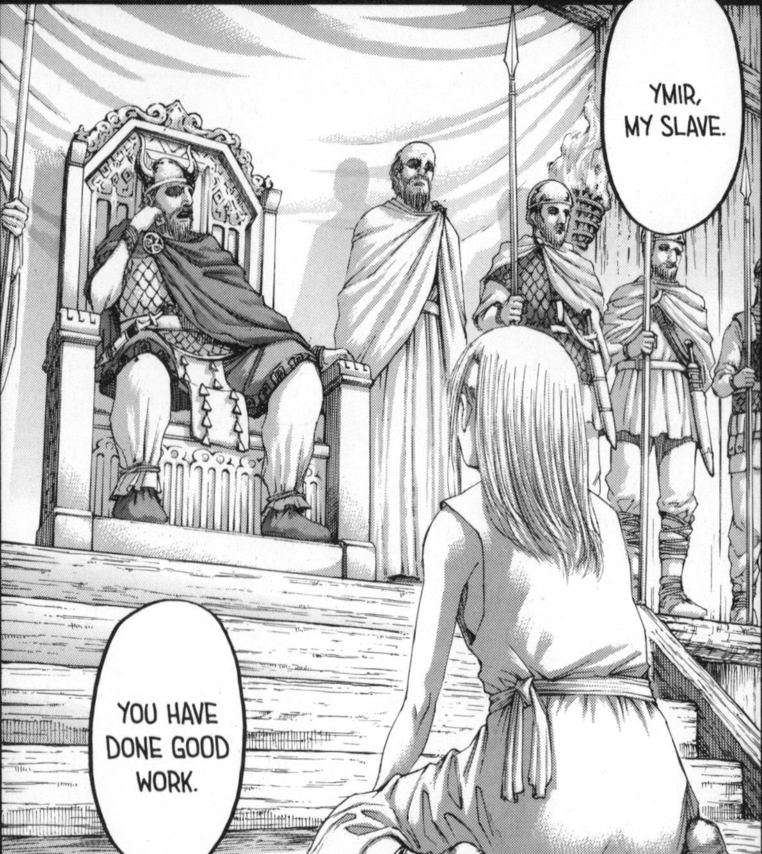
YMIR, MY SLAVE.
YOU HAVE DONE GOOD WORK.

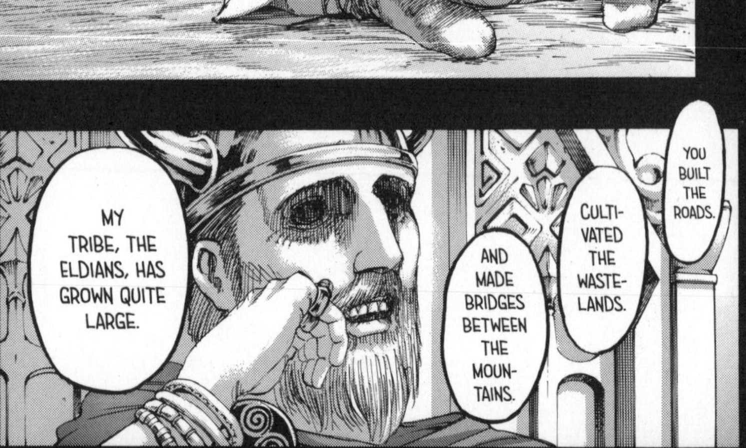
YOU BUILT THE ROADS.
CULTIVATED THE WASTELANDS.
AND MADE BRIDGES BETWEEN THE MOUNTAINS.
MY TRIBE, THE ELDIANS, HAS GROWN QUITE LARGE.

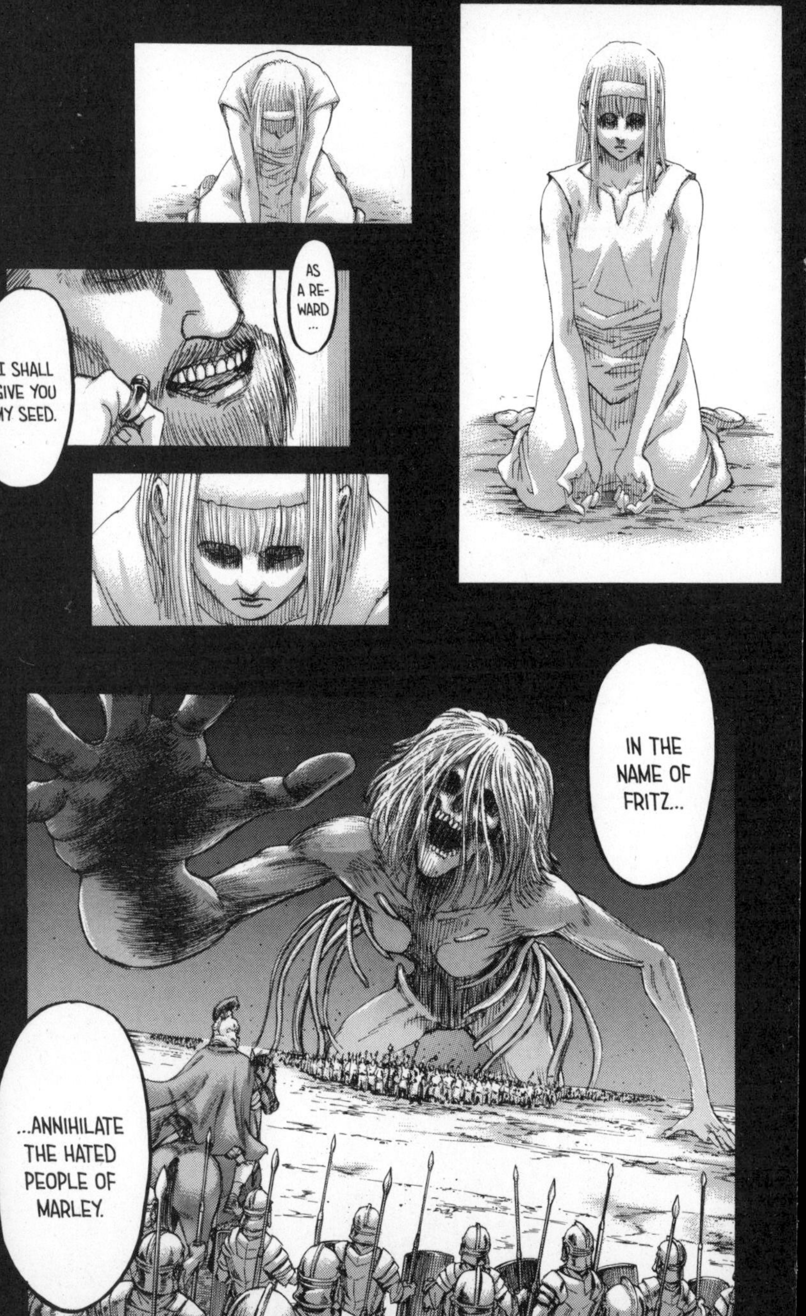
AS A RE-WARD...
I SHALL GIVE YOU MY SEED.
IN THE NAME OF FRITZ...
...ANNIHILATE THE HATED PEOPLE OF MARLEY.

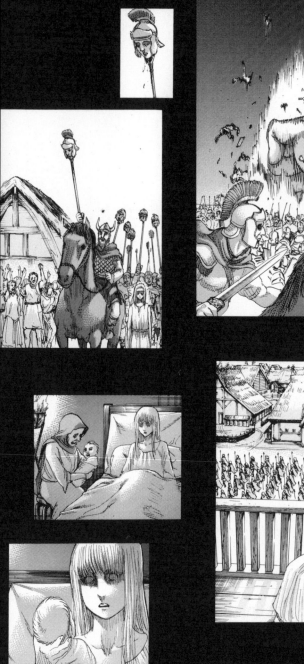

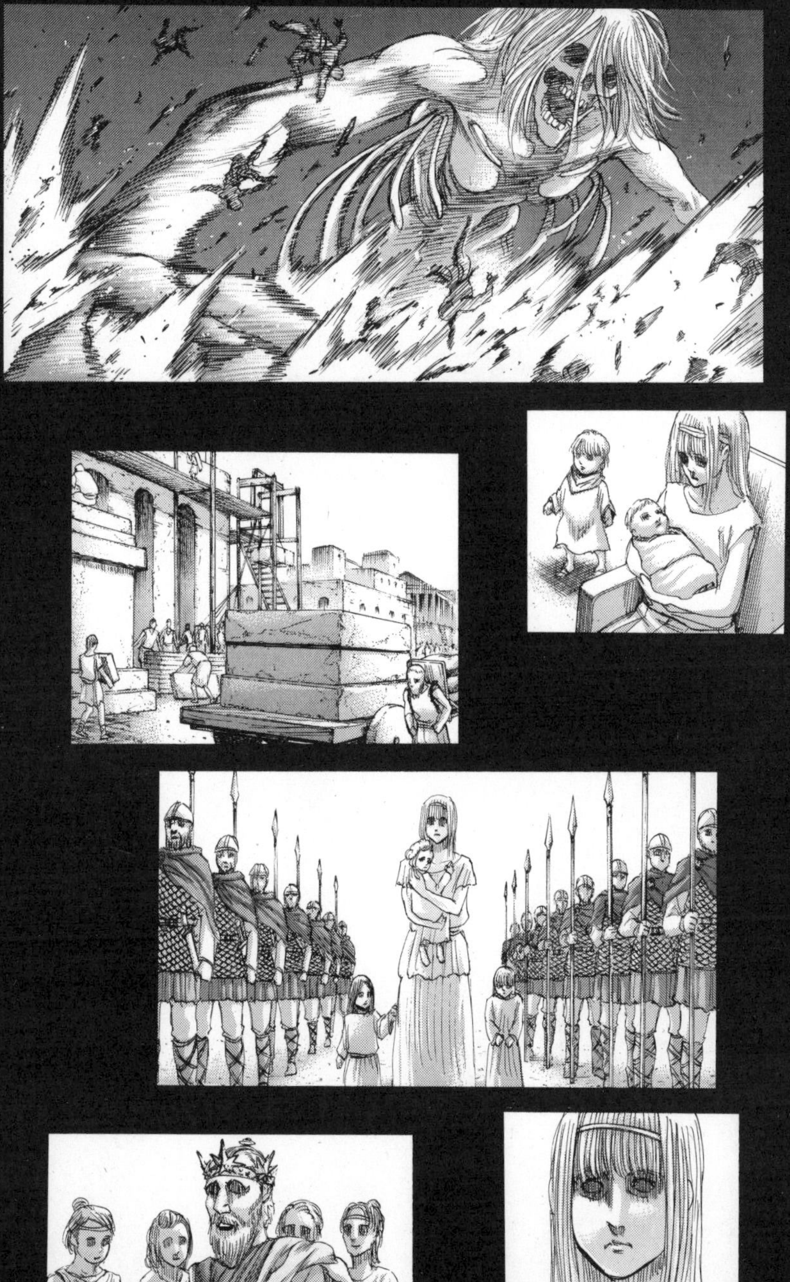

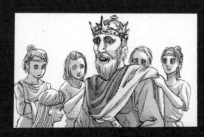

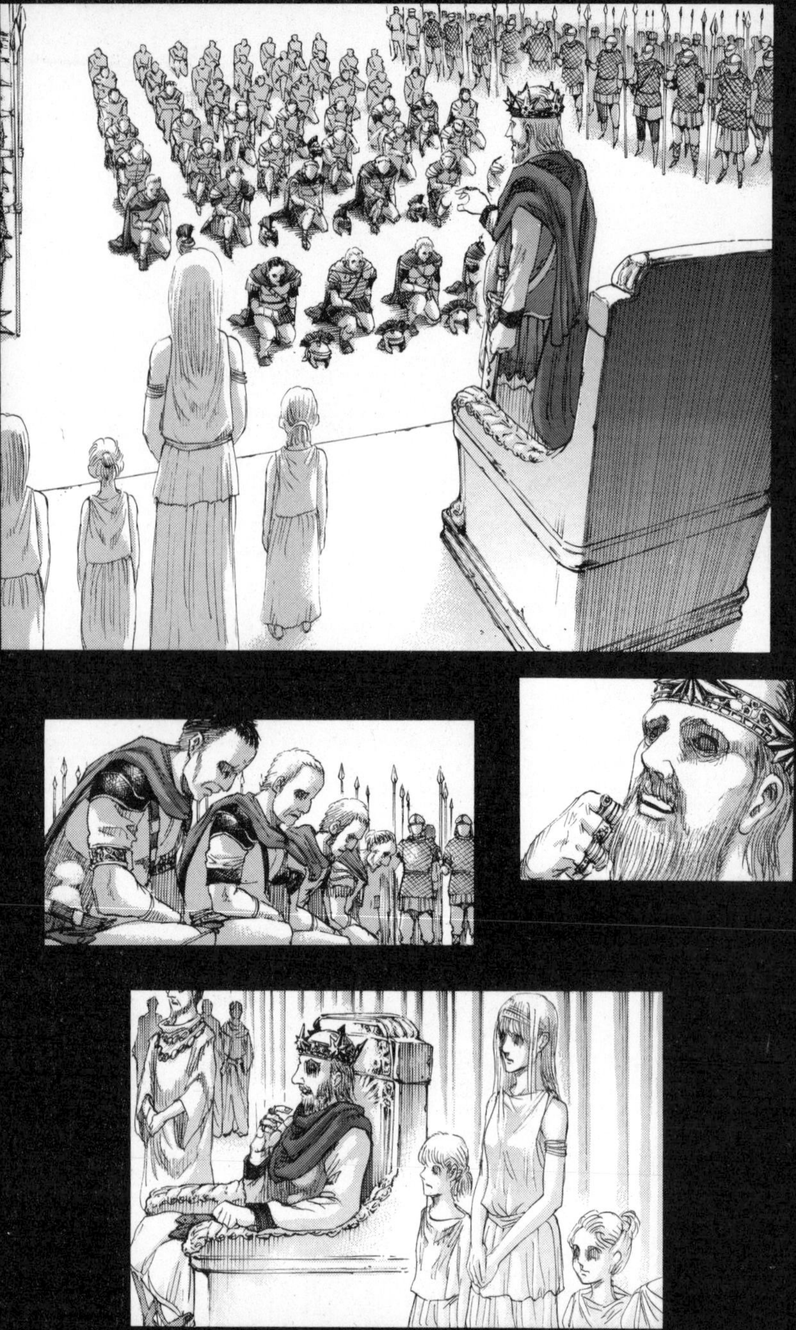

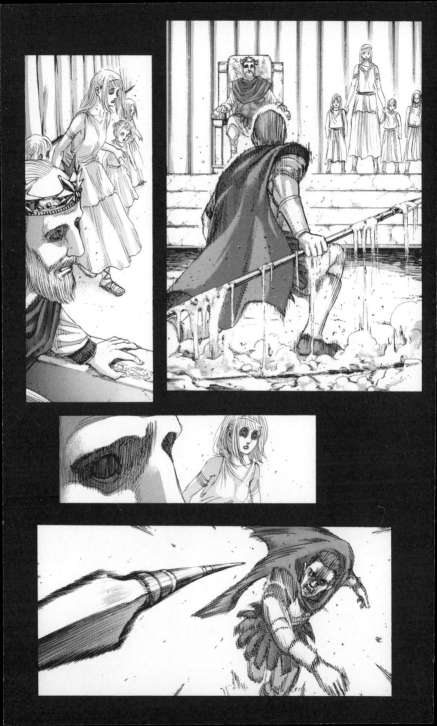

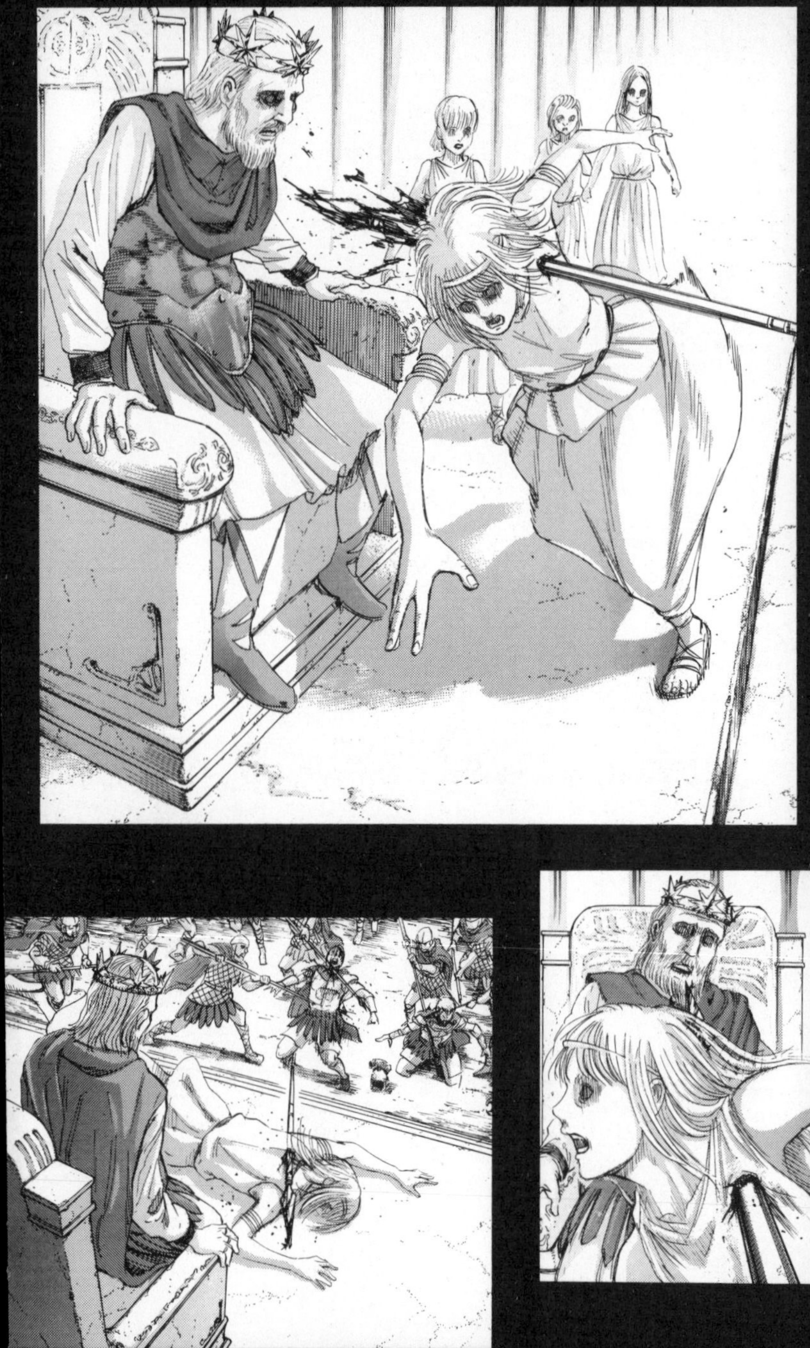

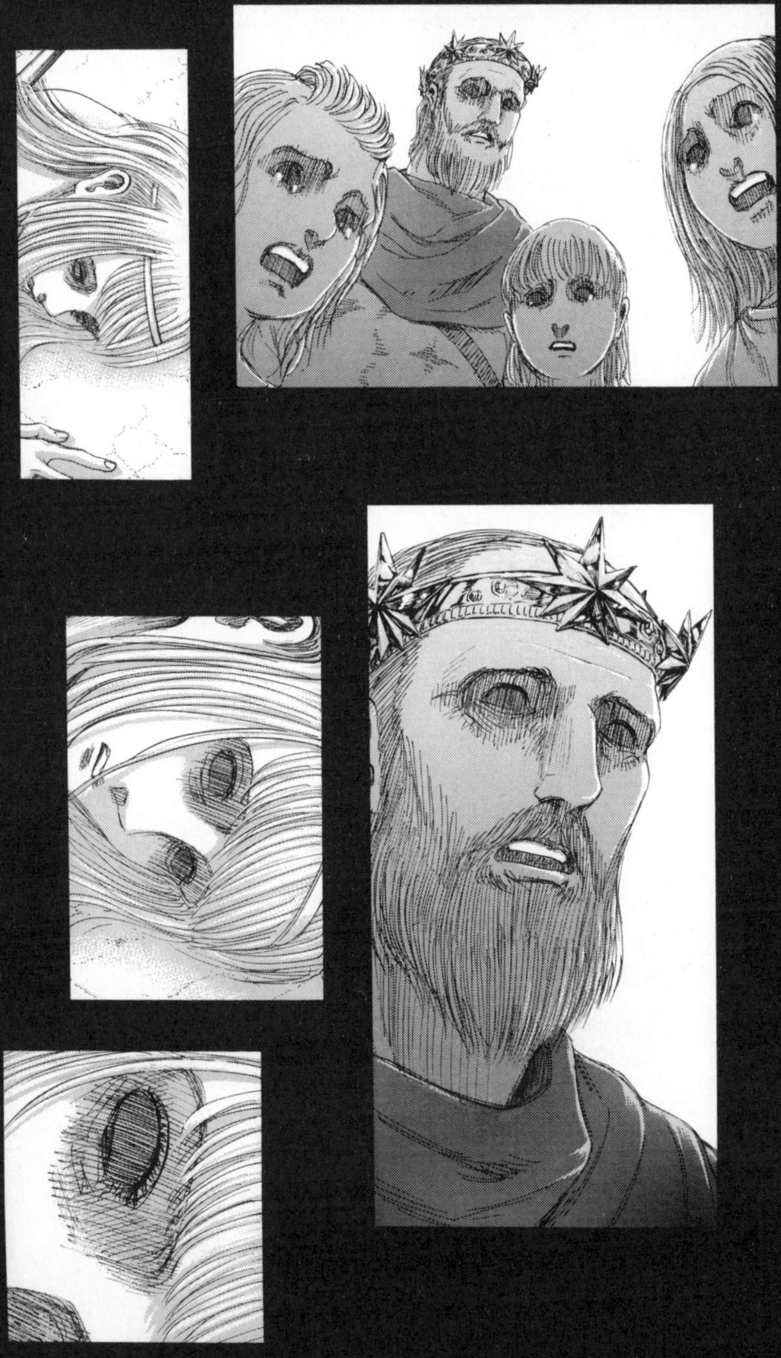

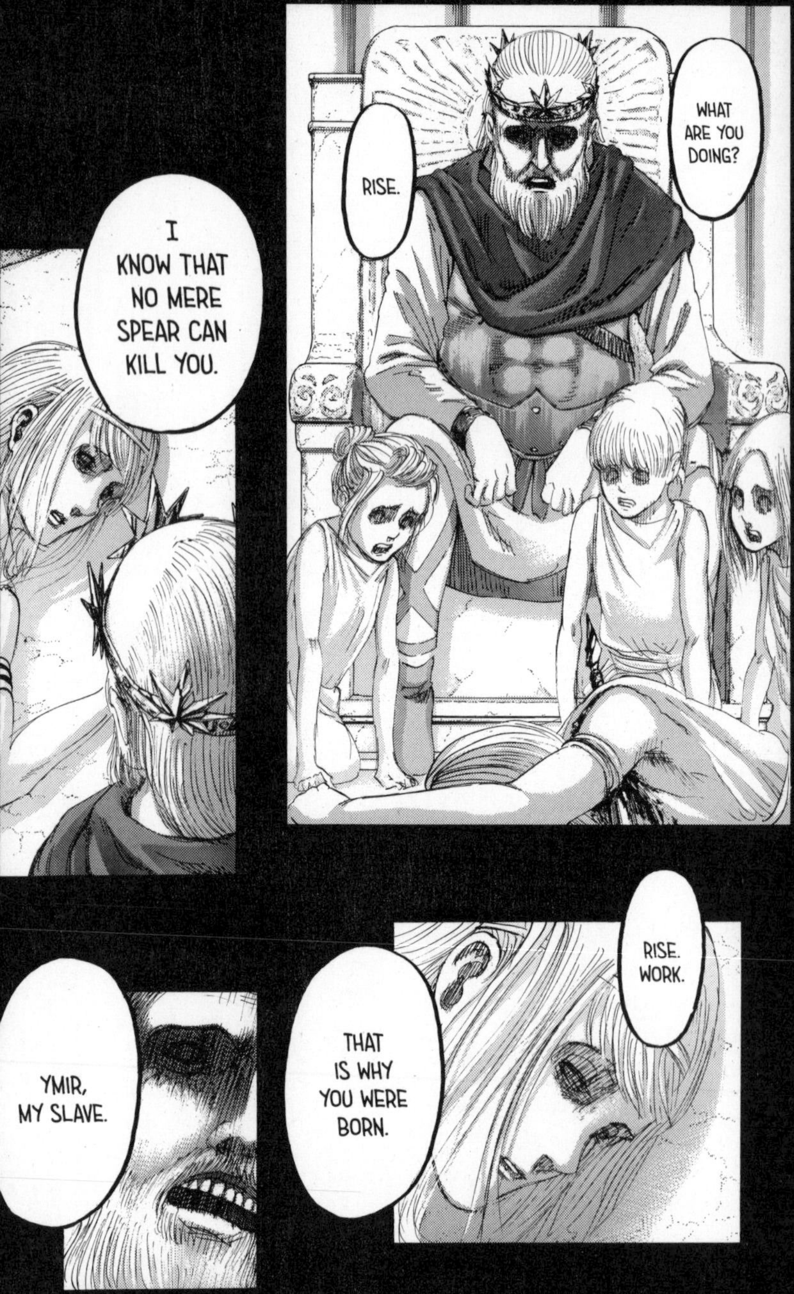
WHAT ARE YOU DOING?
RISE.
I KNOW THAT NO MERE SPEAR CAN KILL YOU.
RISE. WORK.
THAT IS WHY YOU WERE BORN.
YMIR, MY SLAVE.

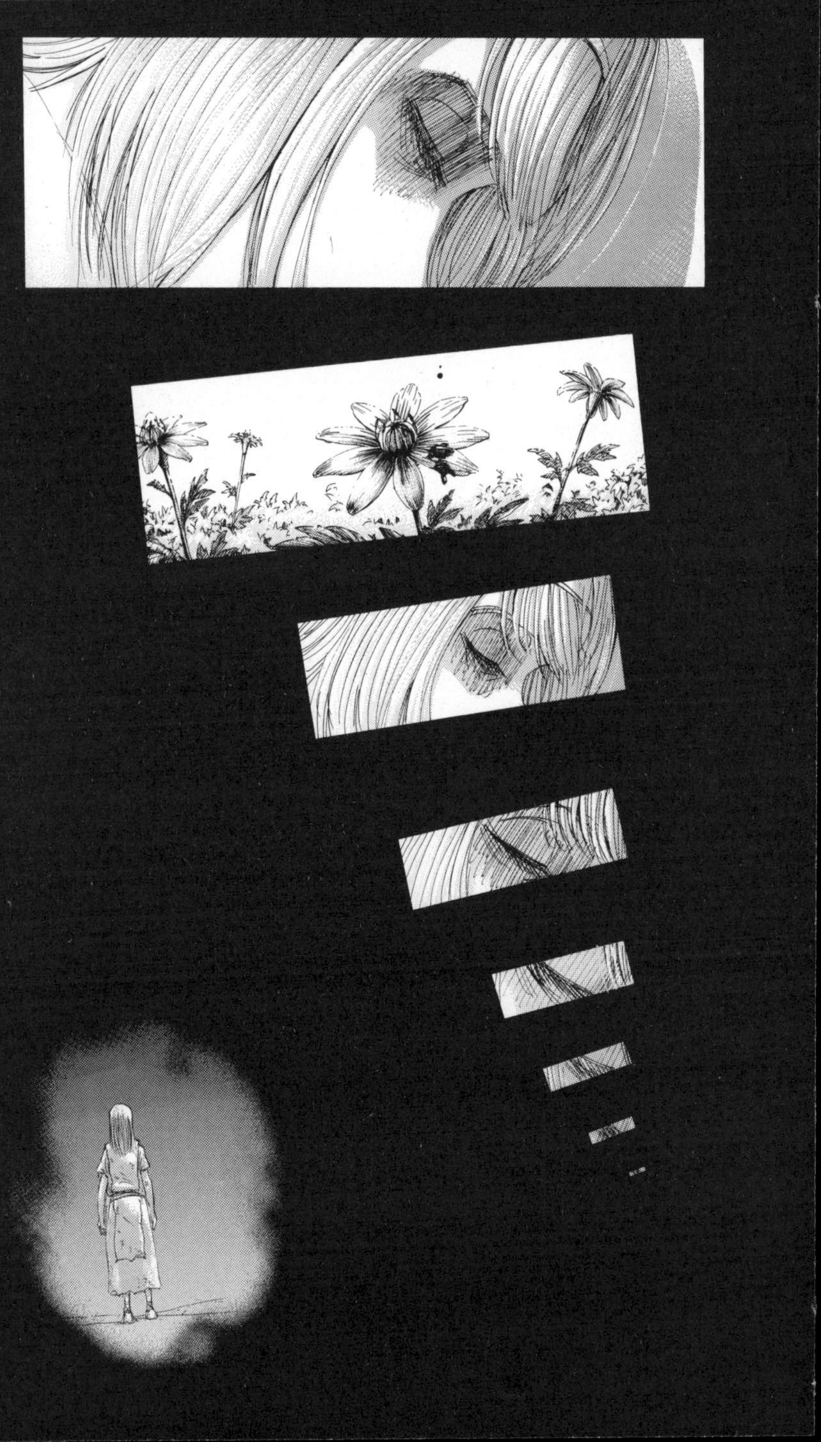

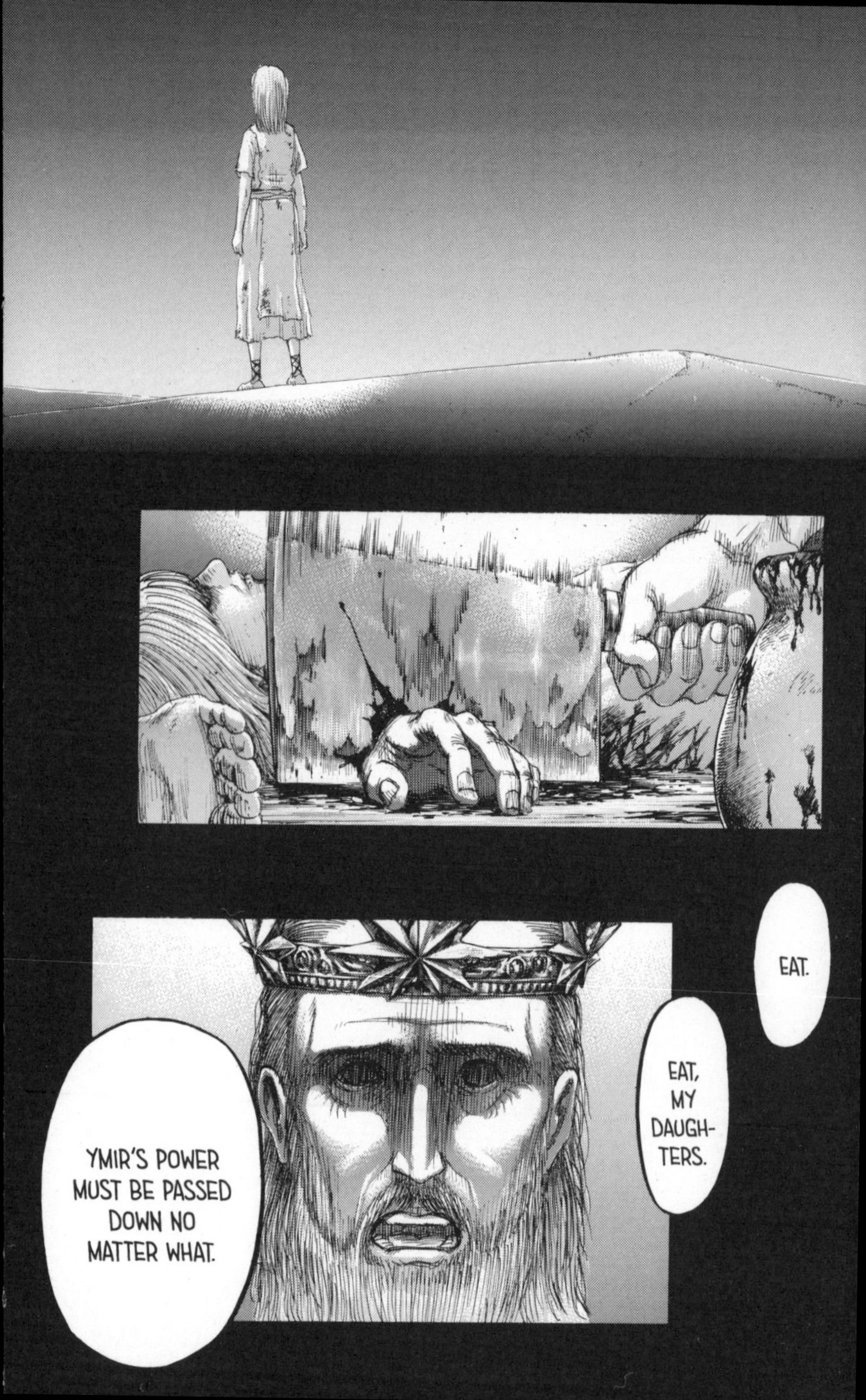
EAT.
EAT, MY DAUGHTERS.
YMIR'S POWER MUST BE PASSED DOWN NO MATTER WHAT.

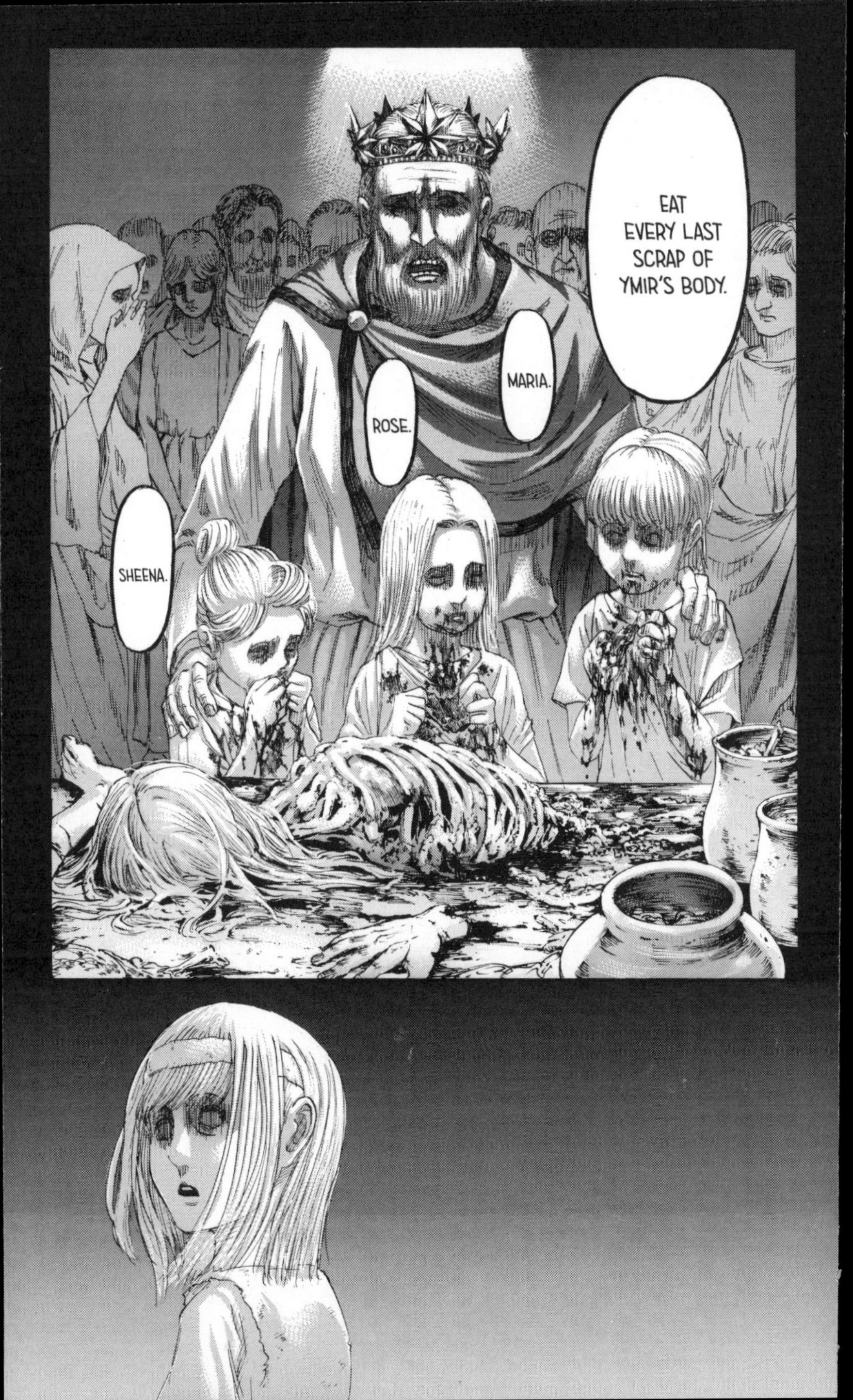
EAT EVERY LAST SCRAP OF YMIR'S BODY.
MARIA.
ROSE.
SHEENA.

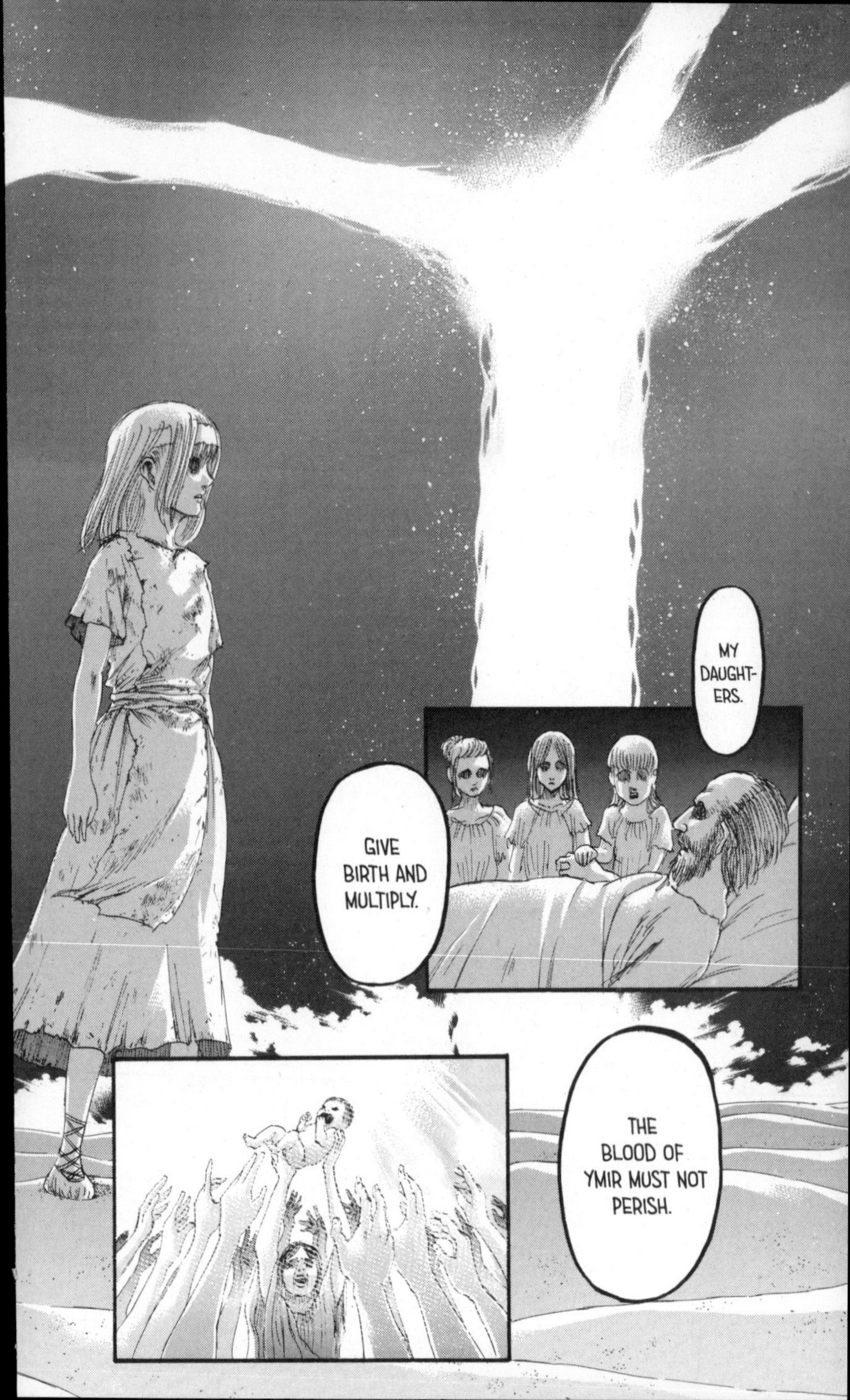
MY DAUGHT-ERS.
GIVE BIRTH AND MULTIPLY.
THE BLOOD OF YMIR MUST NOT PERISH.

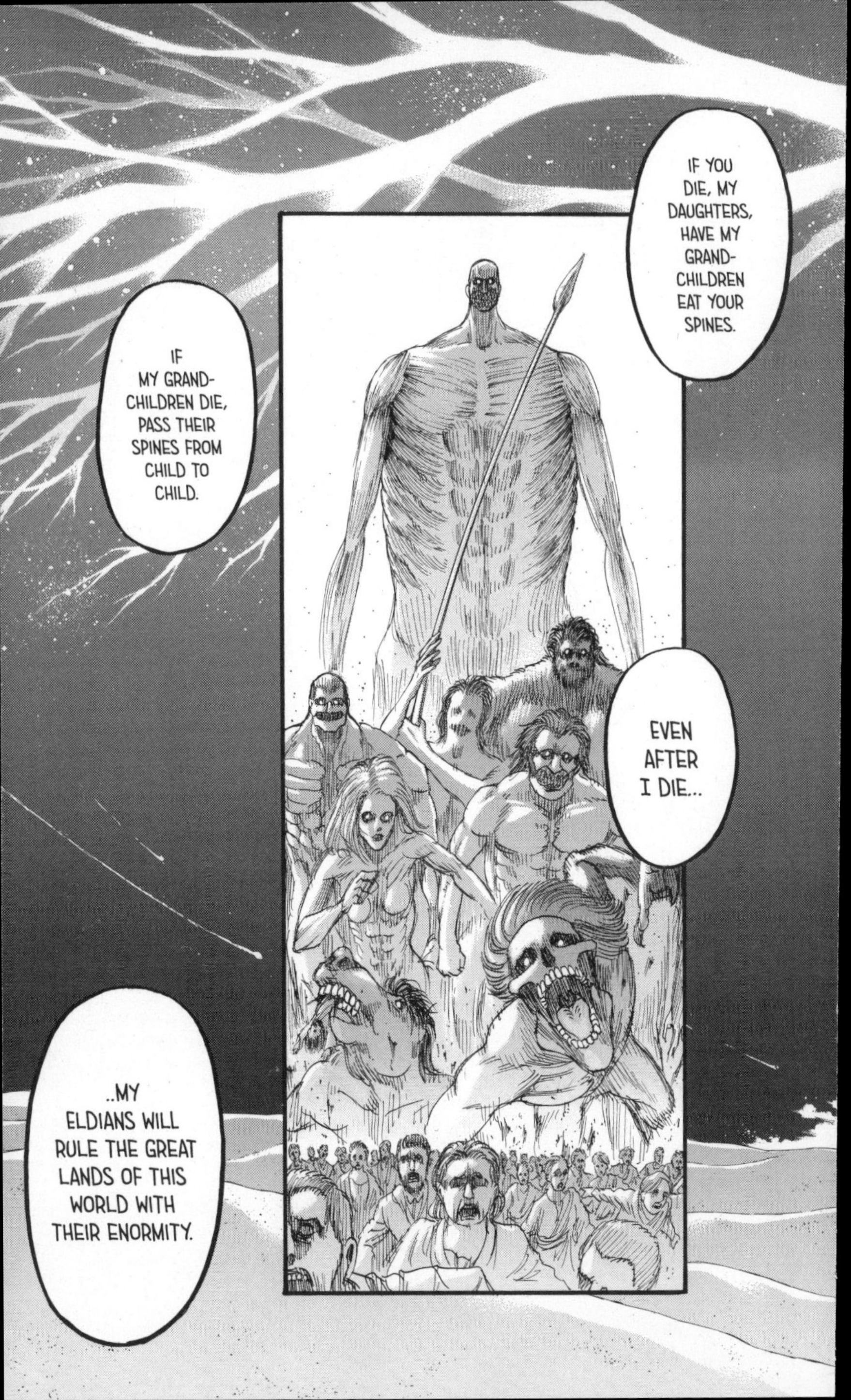
IF YOU DIE, MY DAUGHTERS, HAVE MY GRAND-CHILDREN EAT YOUR SPINES.
IF MY GRAND-CHILDREN DIE, PASS THEIR SPINES FROM CHILD TO CHILD.
EVEN AFTER I DIE...
..MY ELDIANS WILL RULE THE GREAT LANDS OF THIS WORLD WITH THEIR ENORMITY.

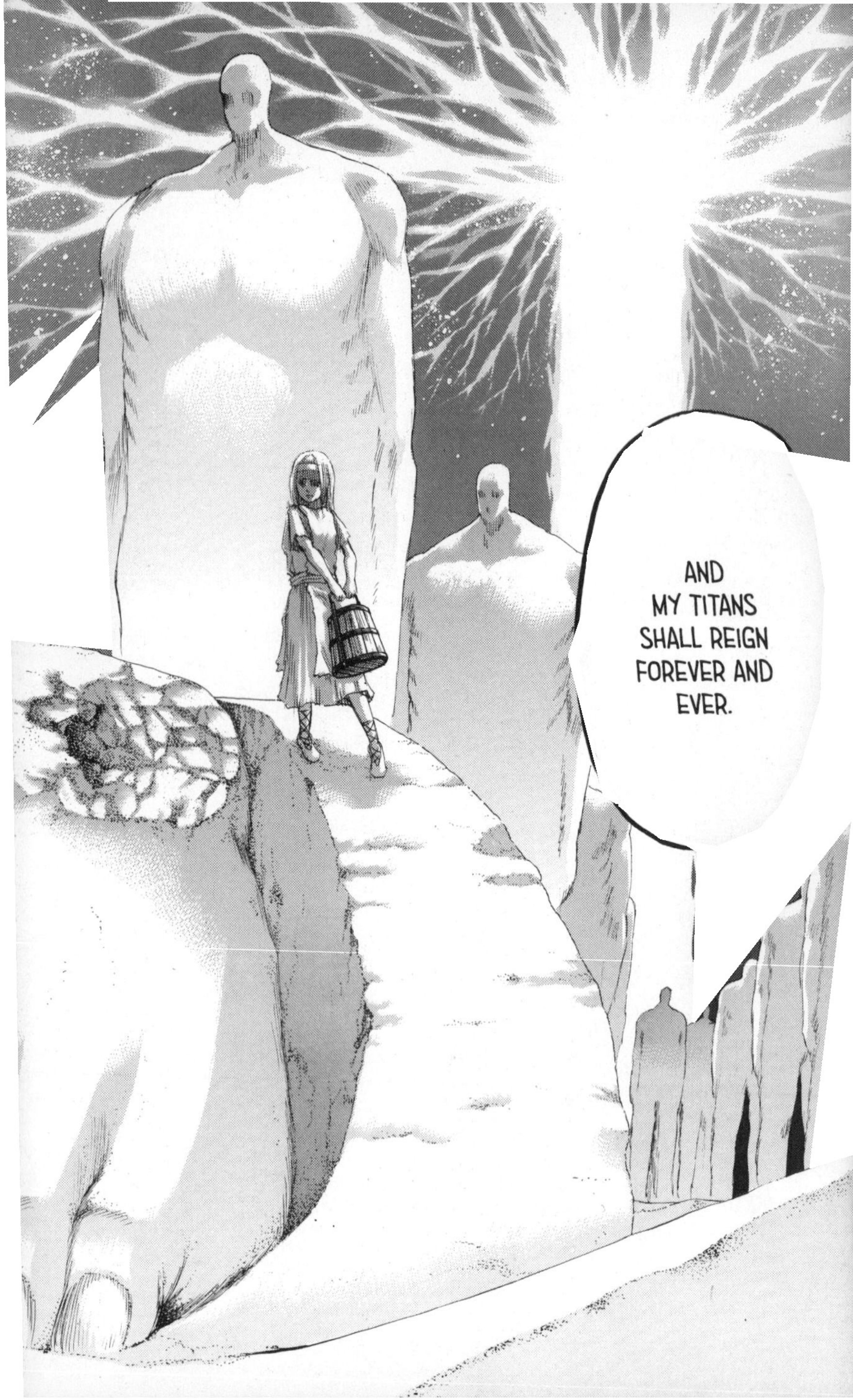
AND MY TITANS SHALL REIGN FOREVER AND EVER.

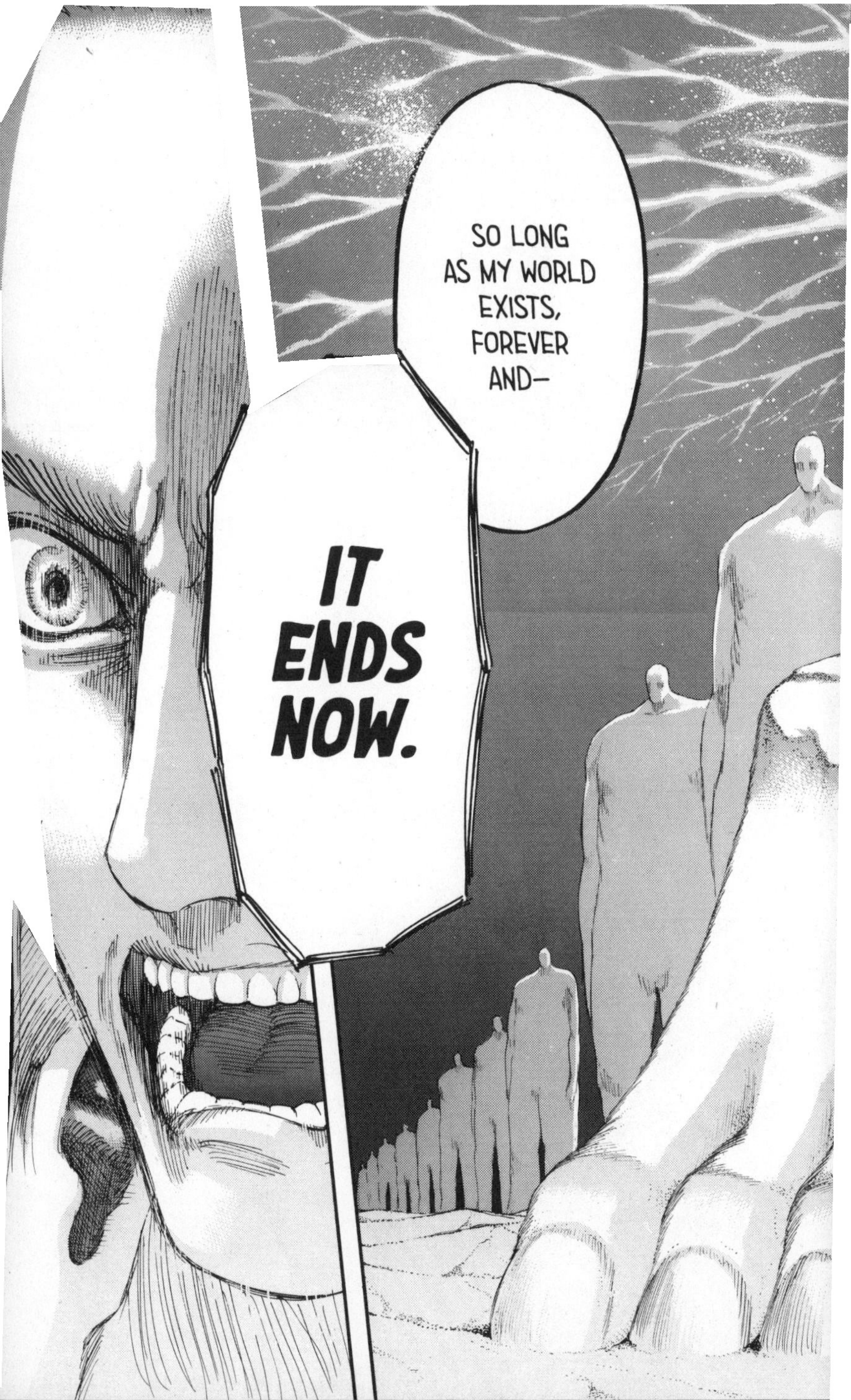
SO LONG AS MY WORLD EXISTS, FOREVER AND—
IT ENDS NOW.

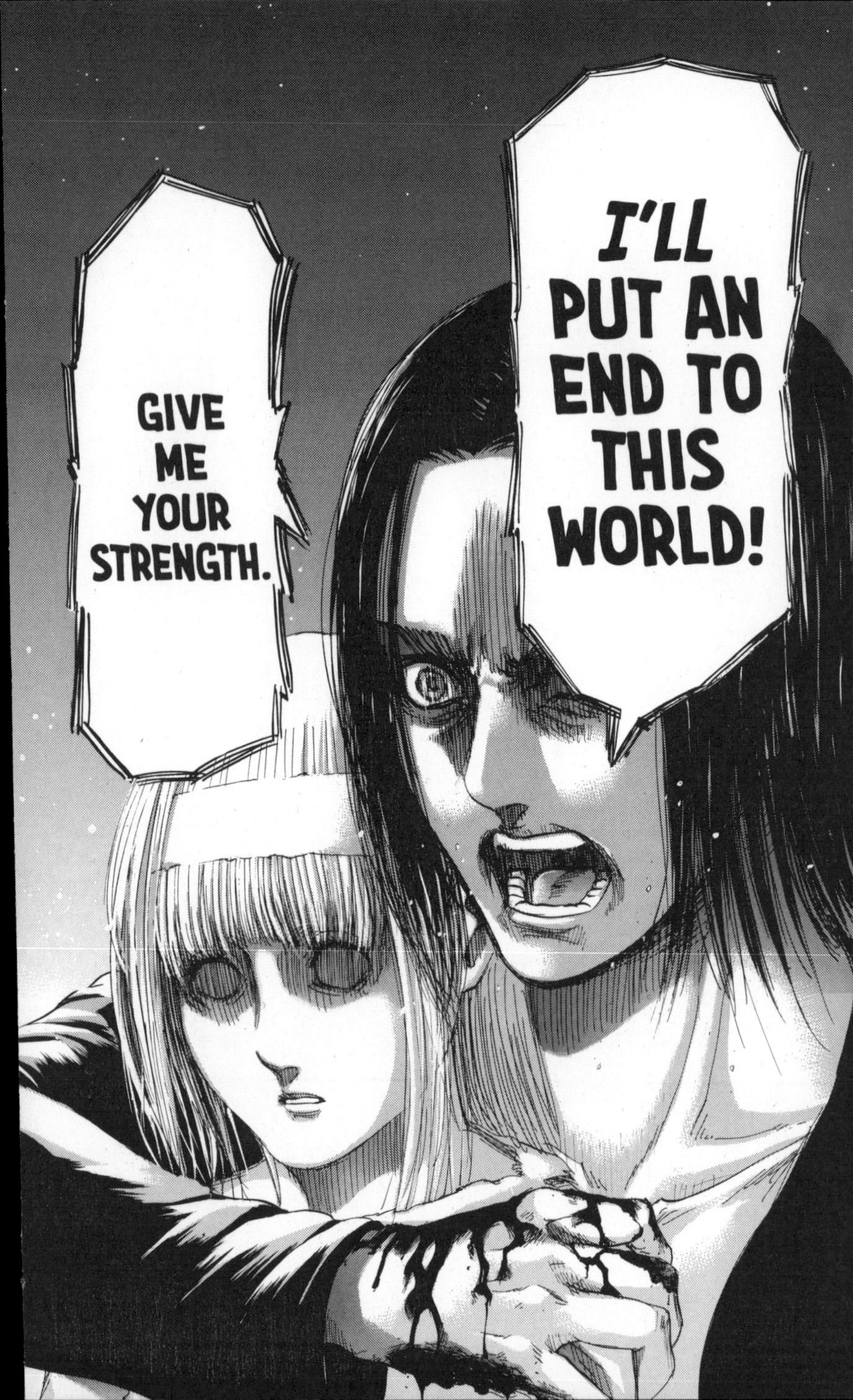
I'LL PUT AN END TO THIS WORLD!
GIVE ME YOUR STRENGTH.

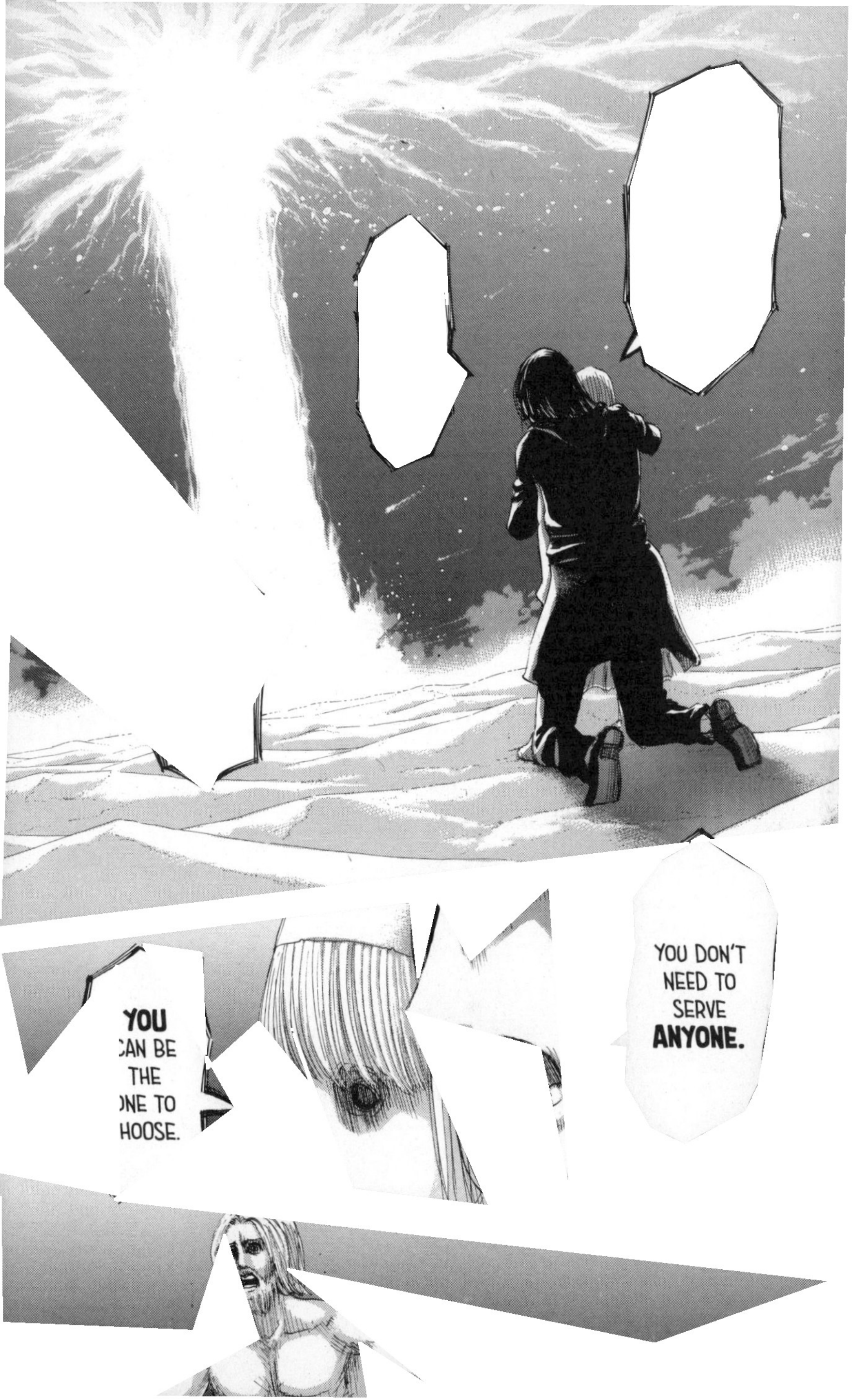
YOU DON'T NEED TO SERVE **ANYONE.**
YOU CAN BE THE ONE TO HOOSE.

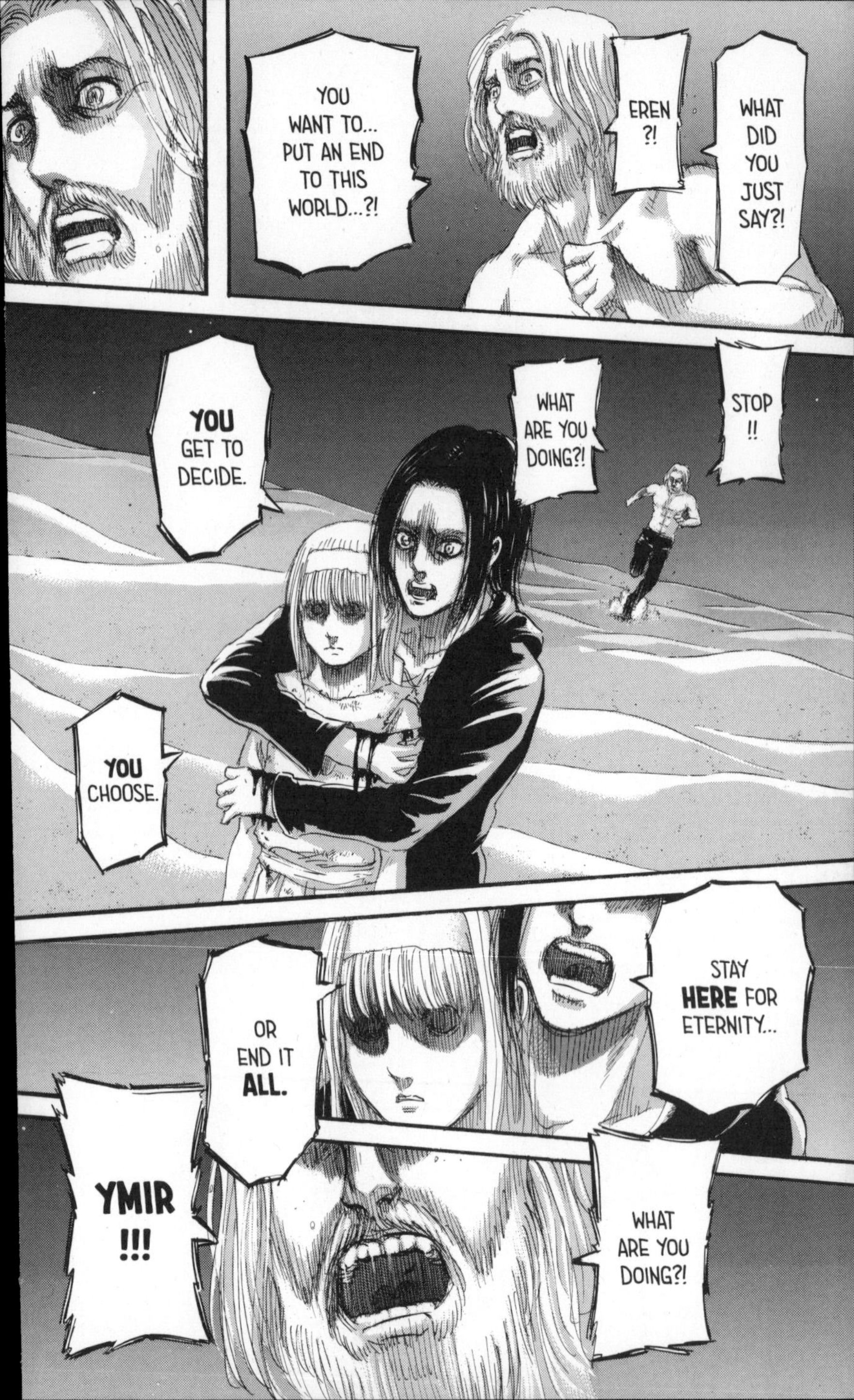
WHAT DID YOU JUST SAY?!
EREN ?!
YOU WANT TO... PUT AN END TO THIS WORLD...?!
STOP !!
WHAT ARE YOU DOING?!
YOU GET TO DECIDE.
YOU CHOOSE.
STAY **HERE** FOR ETERNITY...
OR END IT **ALL.**
WHAT ARE YOU DOING?!
YMIR !!!

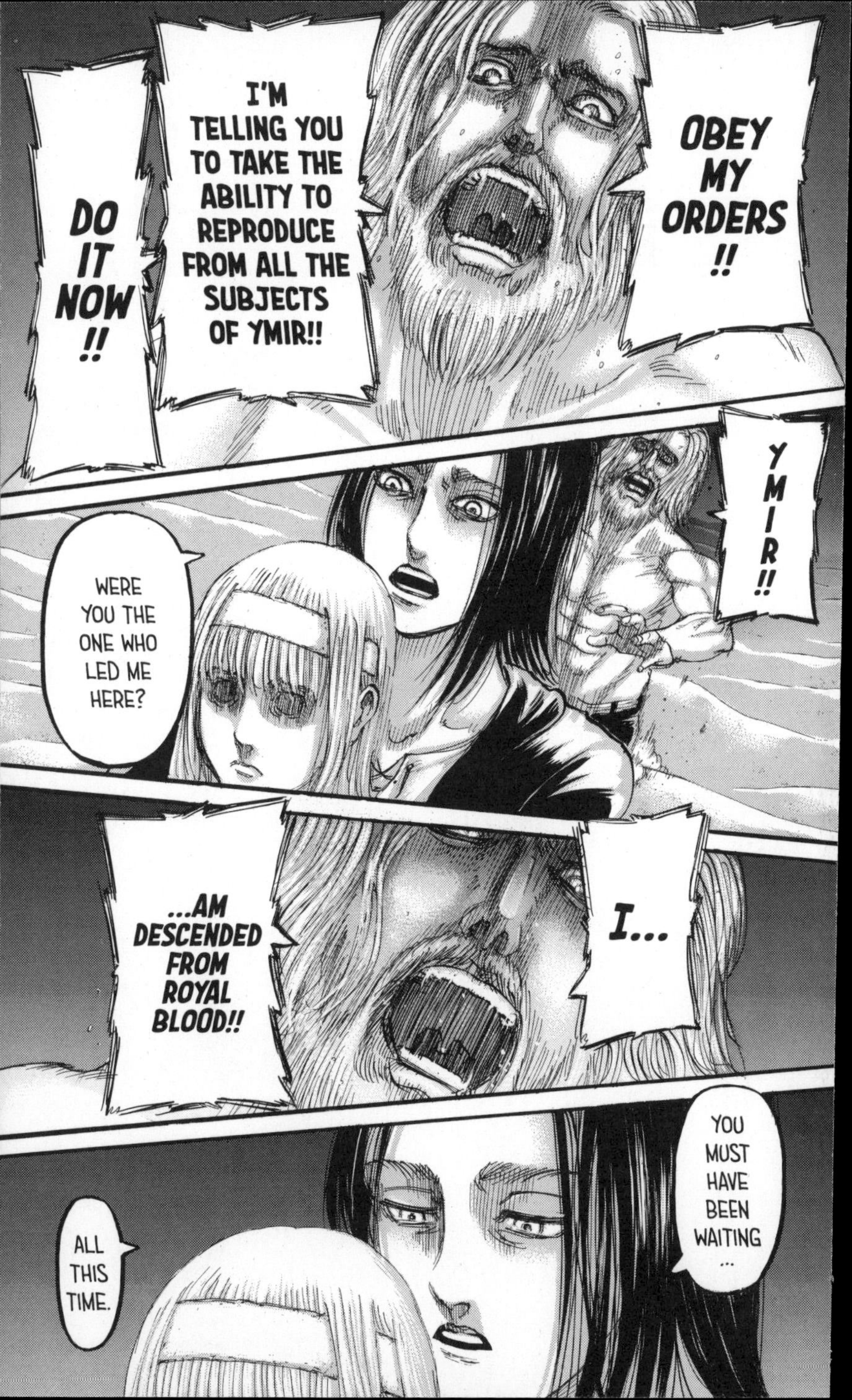
OBEY MY ORDERS!!
I'M TELLING YOU TO TAKE THE ABILITY TO REPRODUCE FROM ALL THE SUBJECTS OF YMIR!!
DO IT NOW!!
YMIR!!
WERE YOU THE ONE WHO LED ME HERE?
I...
...AM DESCENDED FROM ROYAL BLOOD!!
YOU MUST HAVE BEEN WAITING...
ALL THIS TIME.

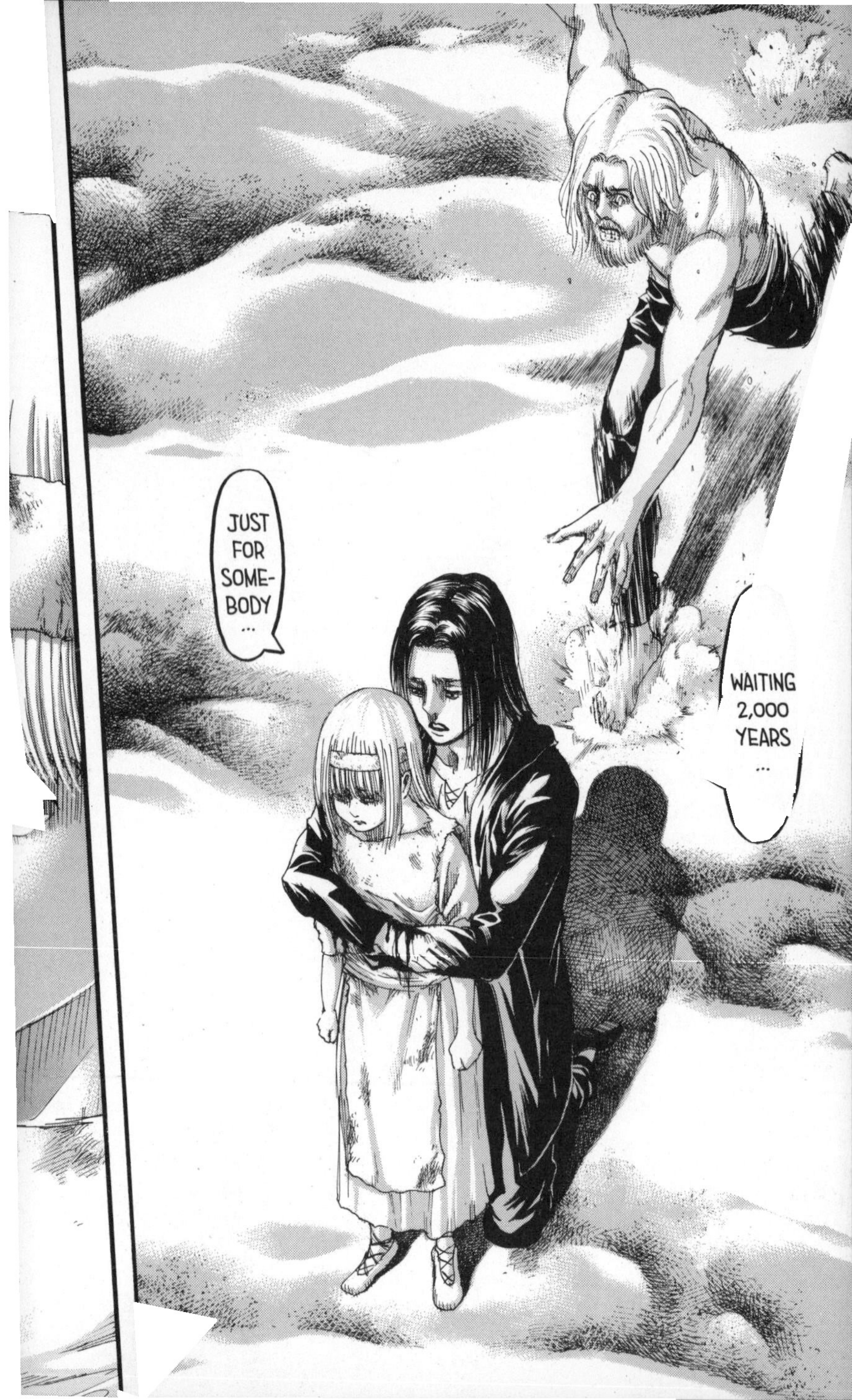
WAITING 2,000 YEARS ...
JUST FOR SOME-BODY ...

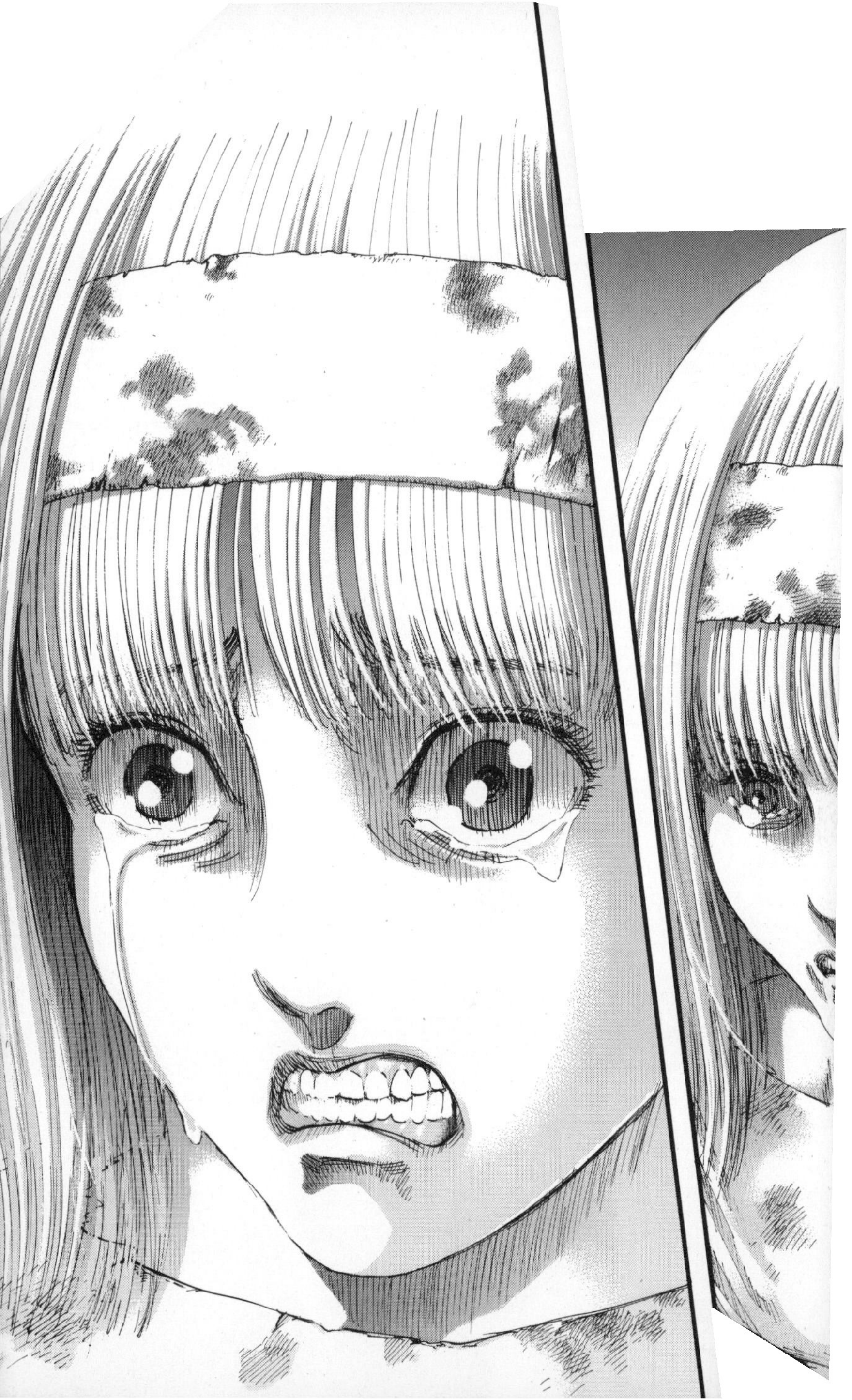

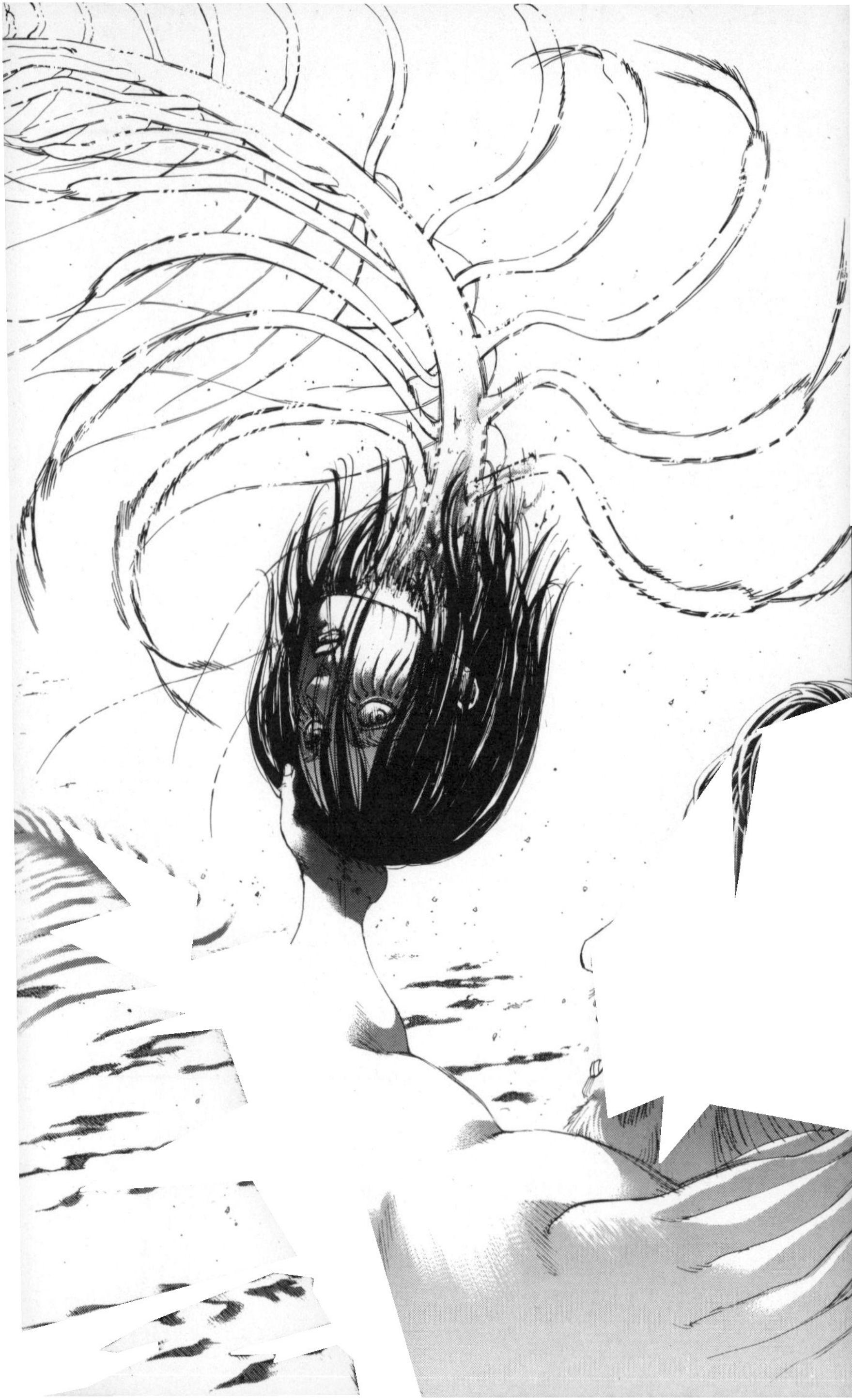

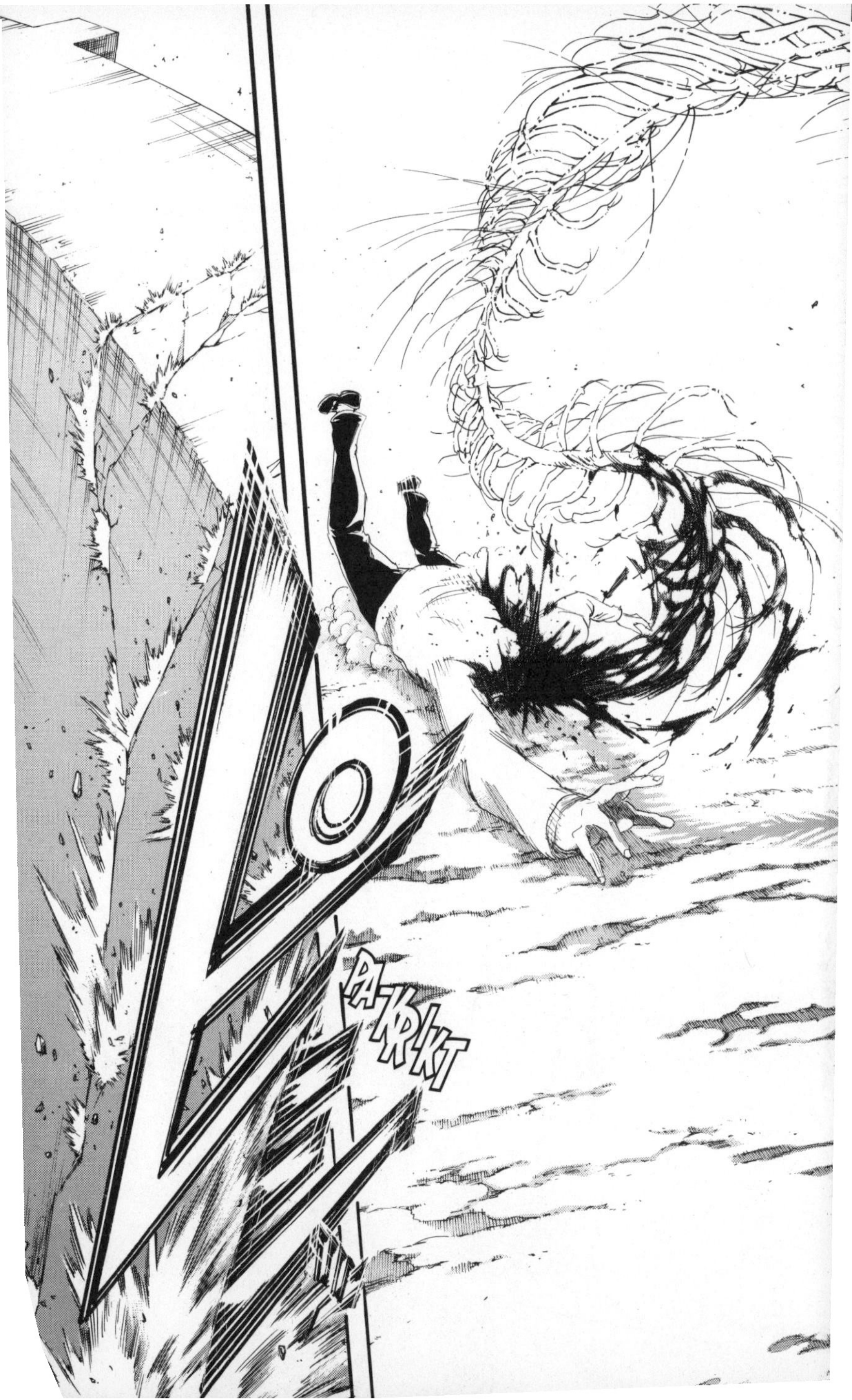
PA-KRIKT

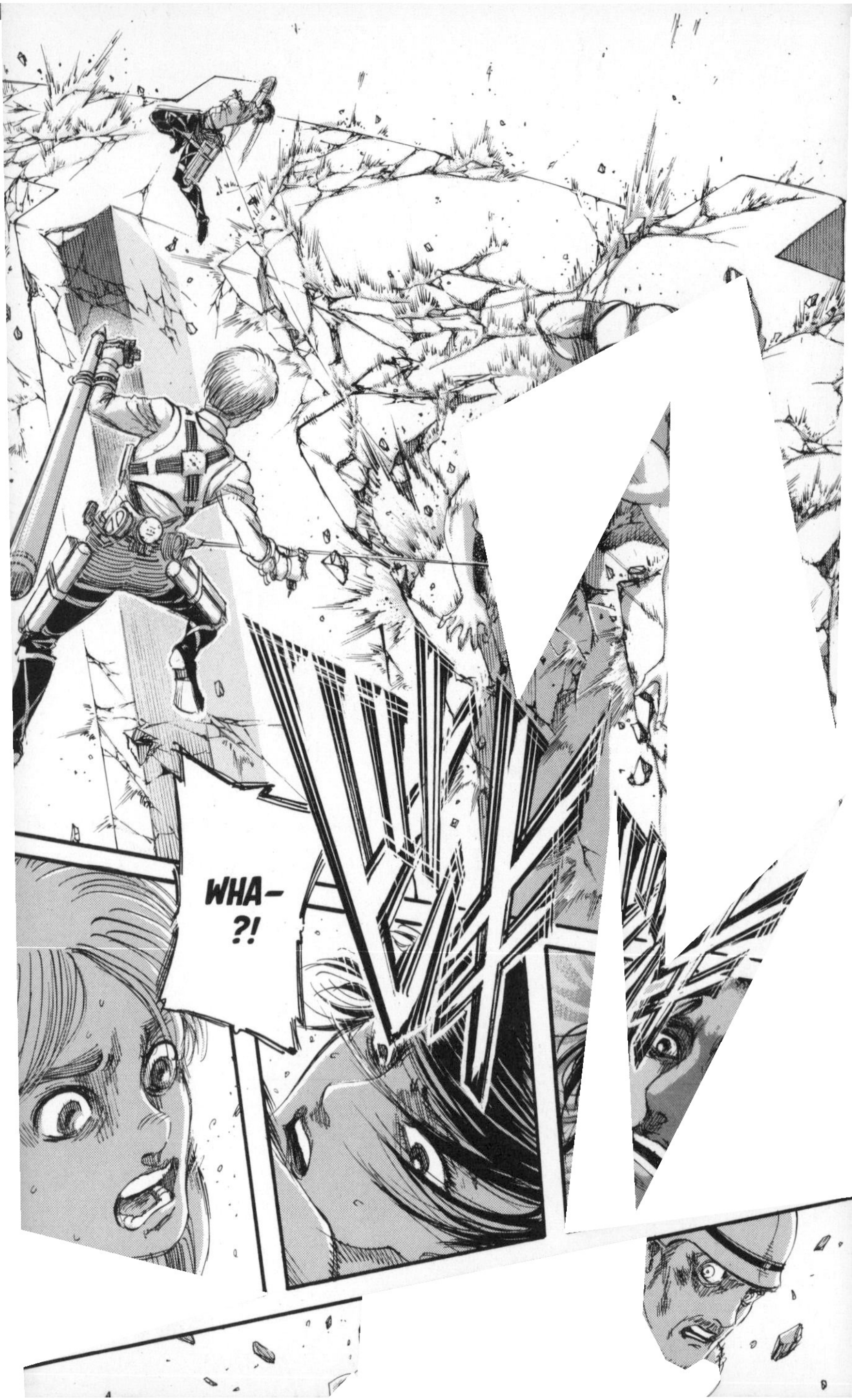
WHA- ?!

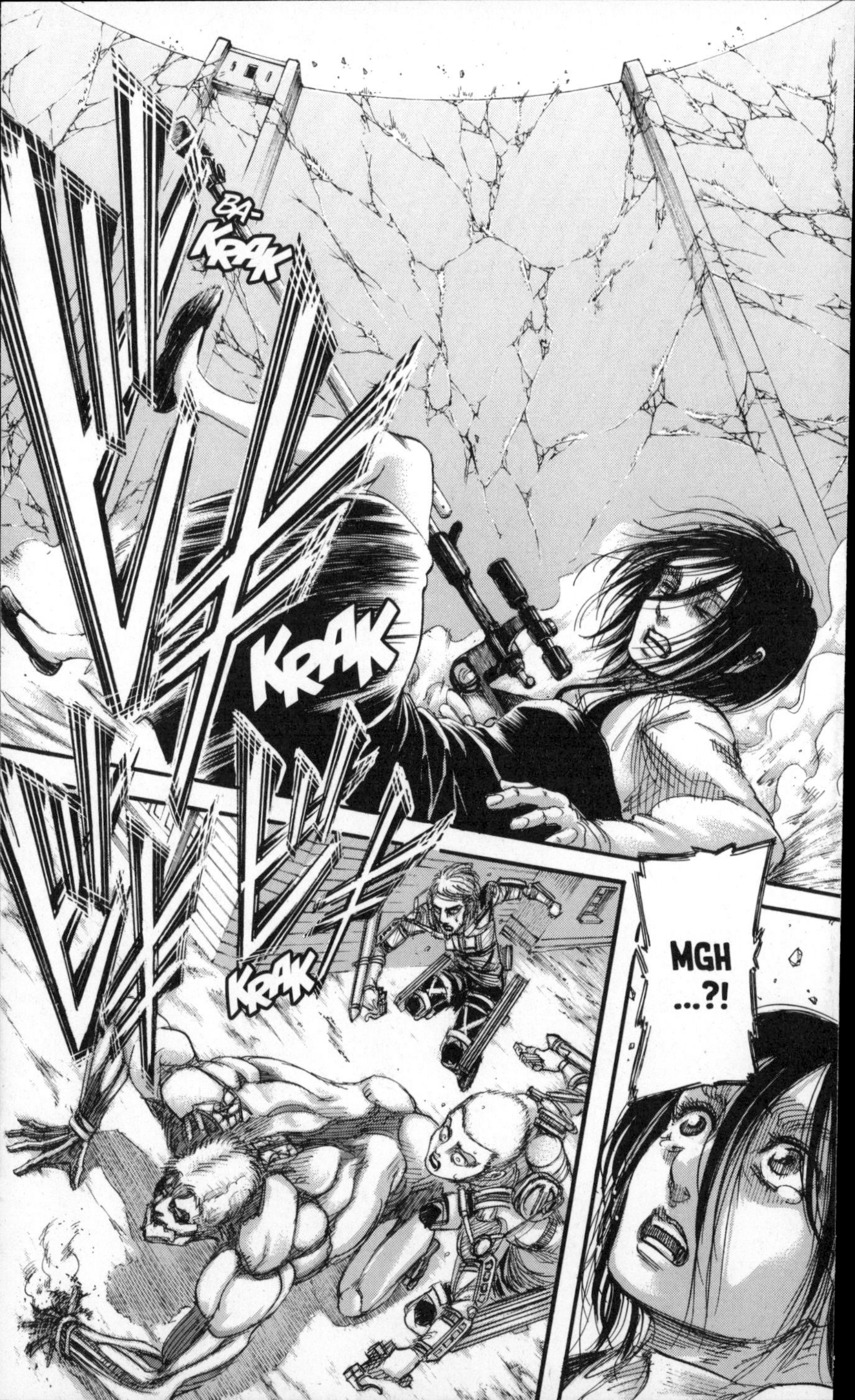
BA-KRAK
KRAK
KRAK
MGH ...?!

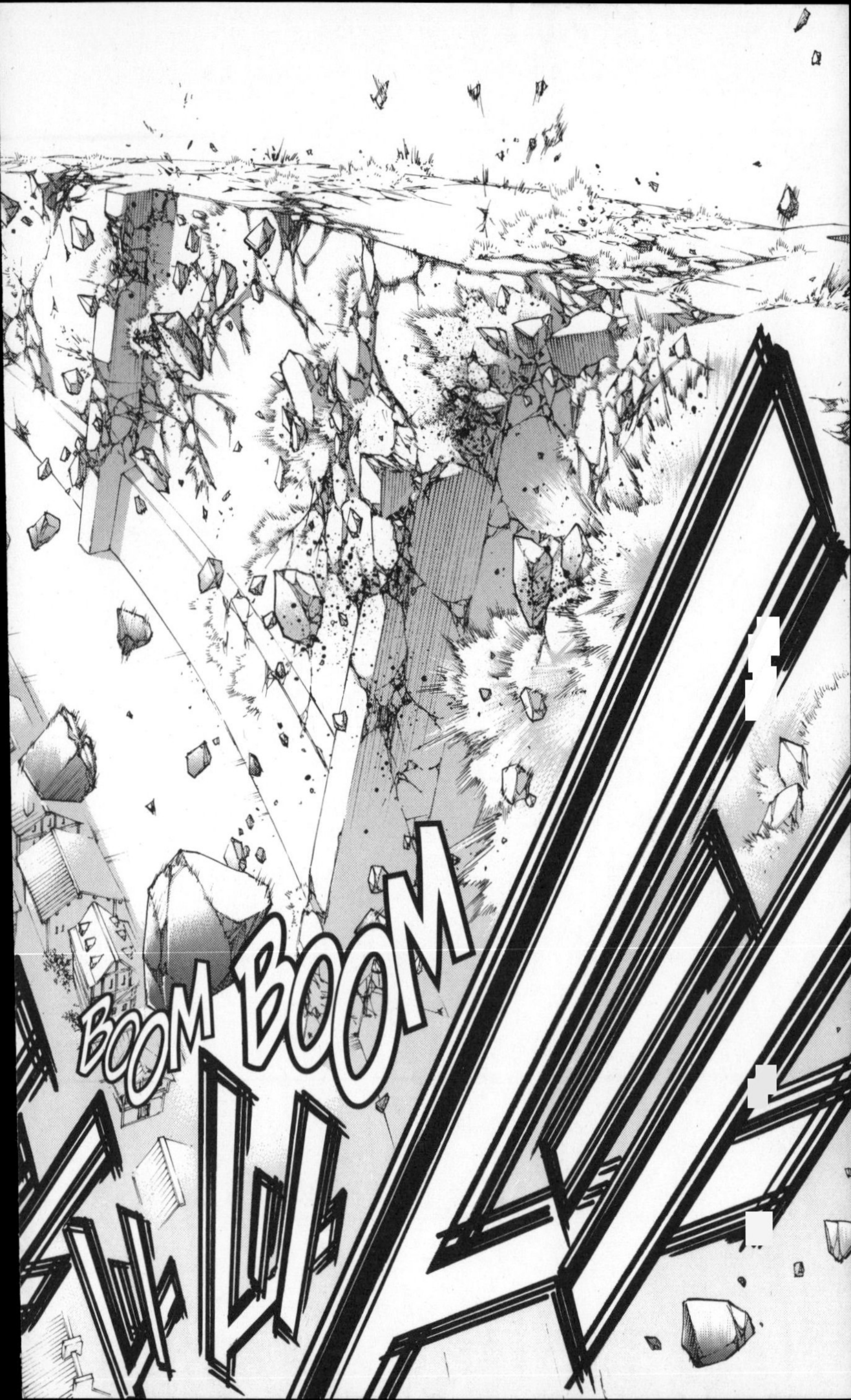
BOOM BOOM

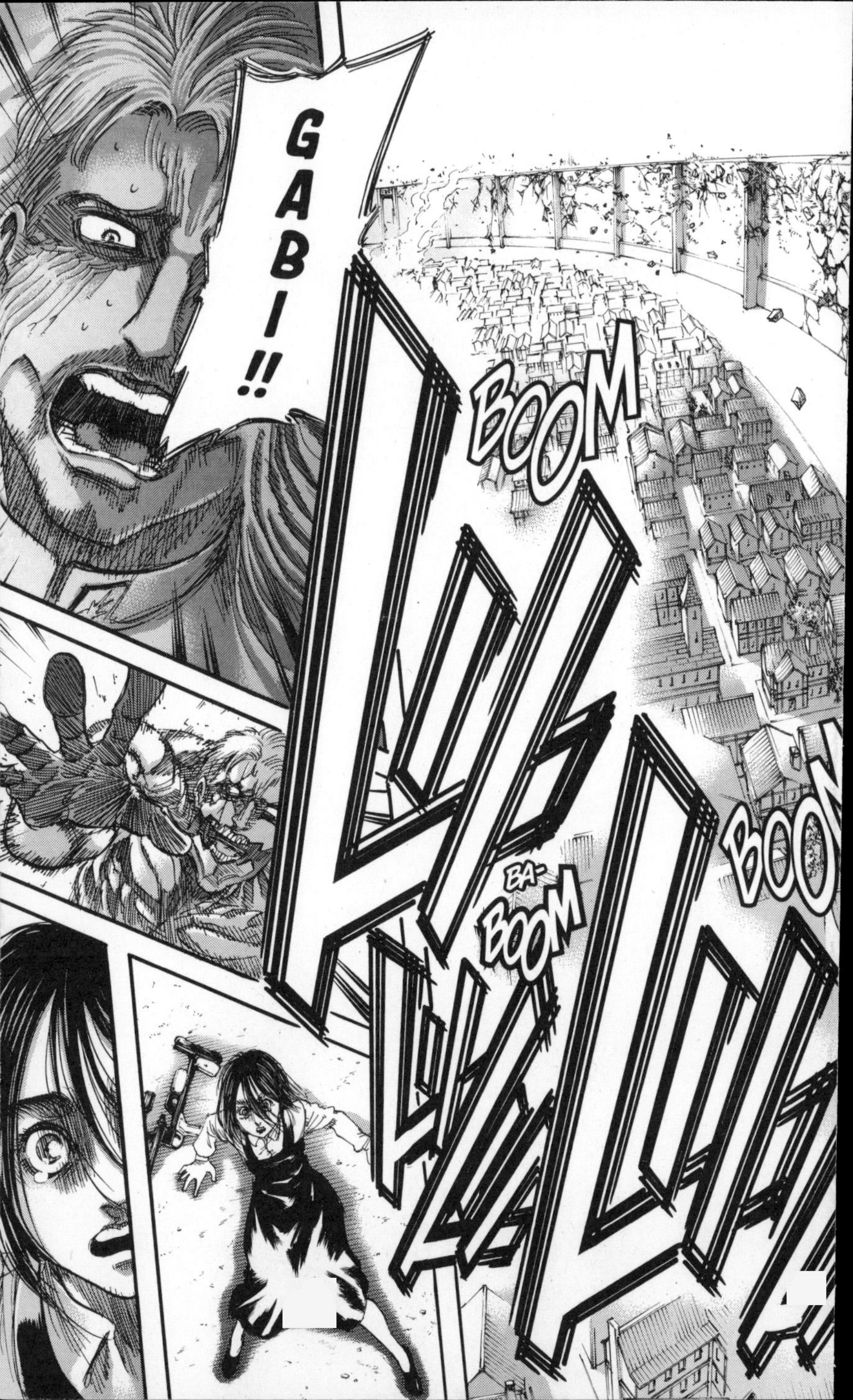
BOOM
BOO
BA-BOOM
GABI!!

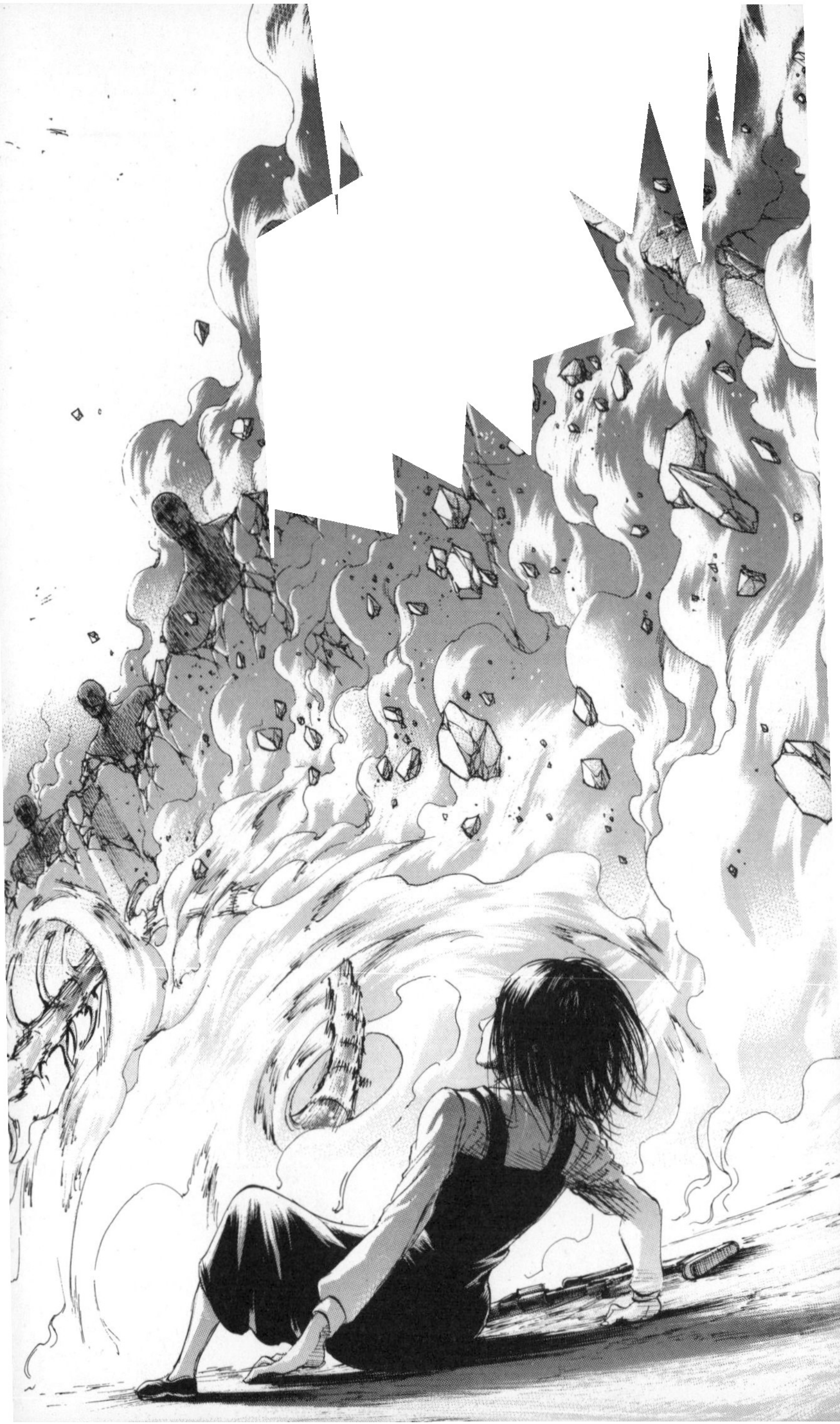

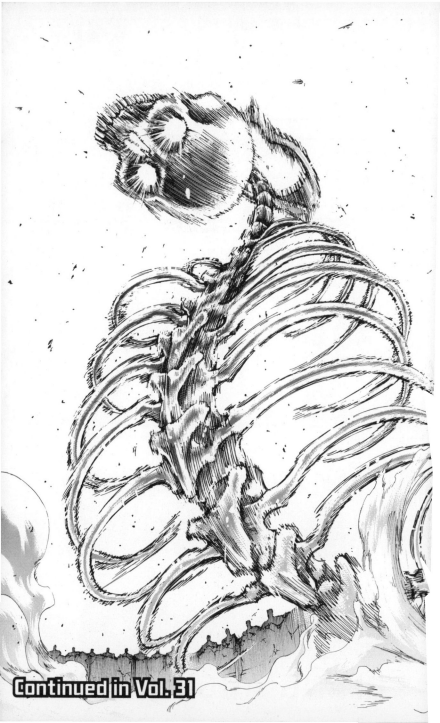

Continued in Vol. 31

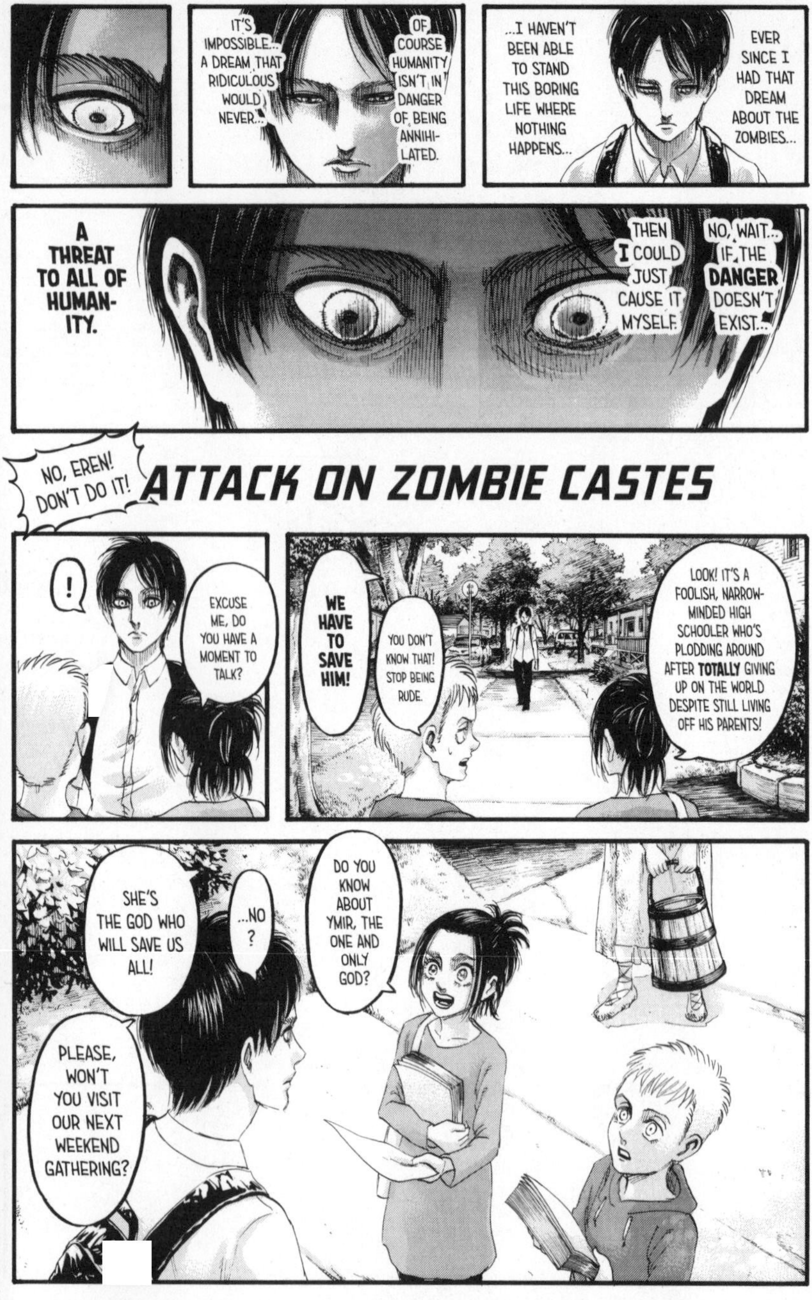

EVER SINCE I HAD THAT DREAM ABOUT THE ZOMBIES...
...I HAVEN'T BEEN ABLE TO STAND THIS BORING LIFE WHERE NOTHING HAPPENS...
OF COURSE HUMANITY ISN'T IN DANGER OF BEING ANNIHILATED.
IT'S IMPOSSIBLE... A DREAM THAT RIDICULOUS WOULD NEVER...
NO, WAIT... IF THE DANGER DOESN'T EXIST...
THEN I COULD JUST CAUSE IT MYSELF.
A THREAT TO ALL OF HUMANITY.
NO, EREN! DON'T DO IT!
ATTACK ON ZOMBIE CASTES
LOOK! IT'S A FOOLISH, NARROW-MINDED HIGH SCHOOLER WHO'S PLODDING AROUND AFTER TOTALLY GIVING UP ON THE WORLD DESPITE STILL LIVING OFF HIS PARENTS!
YOU DON'T KNOW THAT! STOP BEING RUDE.
WE HAVE TO SAVE HIM!
EXCUSE ME, DO YOU HAVE A MOMENT TO TALK?
!
DO YOU KNOW ABOUT YMIR, THE ONE AND ONLY GOD?
...NO ?
SHE'S THE GOD WHO WILL SAVE US ALL!
PLEASE, WON'T YOU VISIT OUR NEXT WEEKEND GATHERING?

COMING AUGUST 2020!

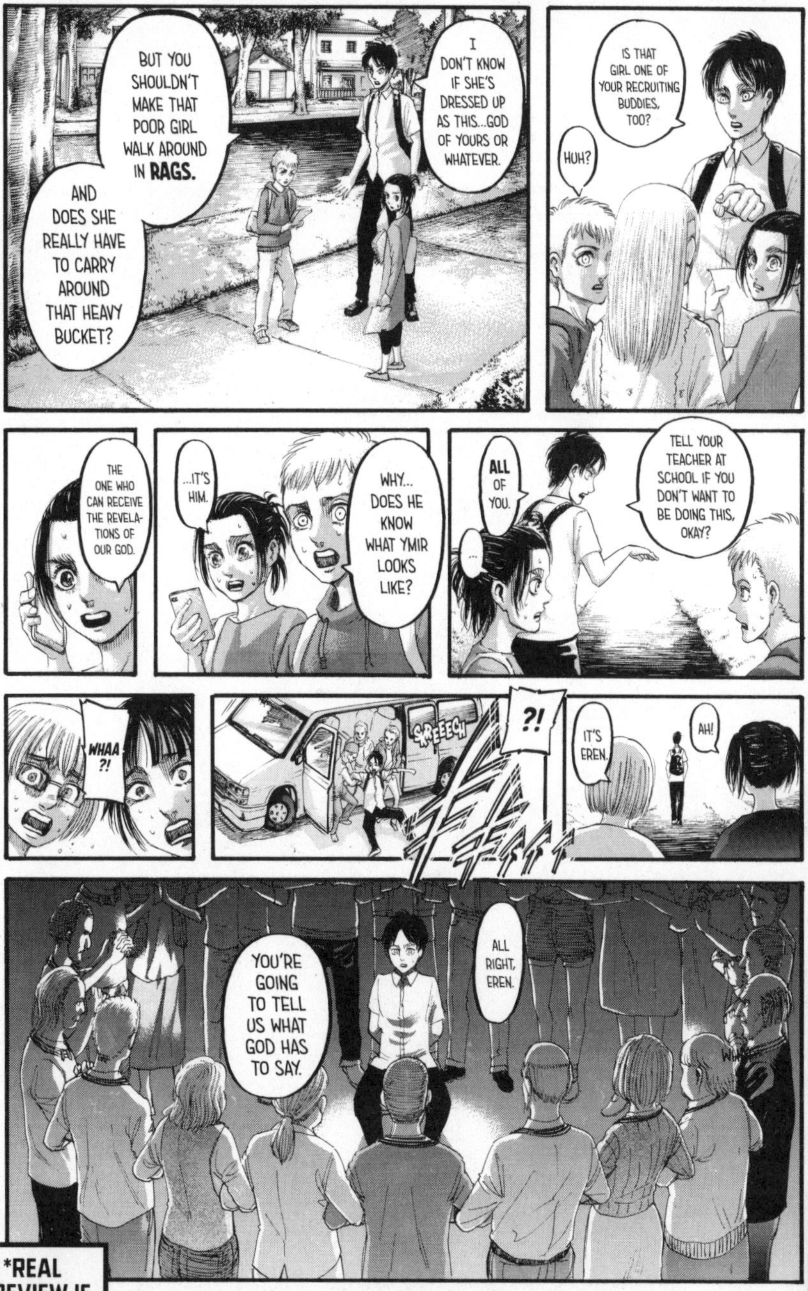
IS THAT GIRL ONE OF YOUR RECRUITING BUDDIES, TOO?
HUH?
I DON'T KNOW IF SHE'S DRESSED UP AS THIS...GOD OF YOURS OR WHATEVER.
BUT YOU SHOULDN'T MAKE THAT POOR GIRL WALK AROUND IN RAGS.
AND DOES SHE REALLY HAVE TO CARRY AROUND THAT HEAVY BUCKET?
TELL YOUR TEACHER AT SCHOOL IF YOU DON'T WANT TO BE DOING THIS, OKAY?
ALL OF YOU.
...
WHY... DOES HE KNOW WHAT YMIR LOOKS LIKE?
...IT'S HIM.
THE ONE WHO CAN RECEIVE THE REVELATIONS OF OUR GOD.
AH!
IT'S EREN.
?!
SKREEECH
WHAA ?!
ALL RIGHT, EREN.
YOU'RE GOING TO TELL US WHAT GOD HAS TO SAY.

***REAL PREVIEW IS ON THE FOLLOWING PAGE!**

VOLUME 31

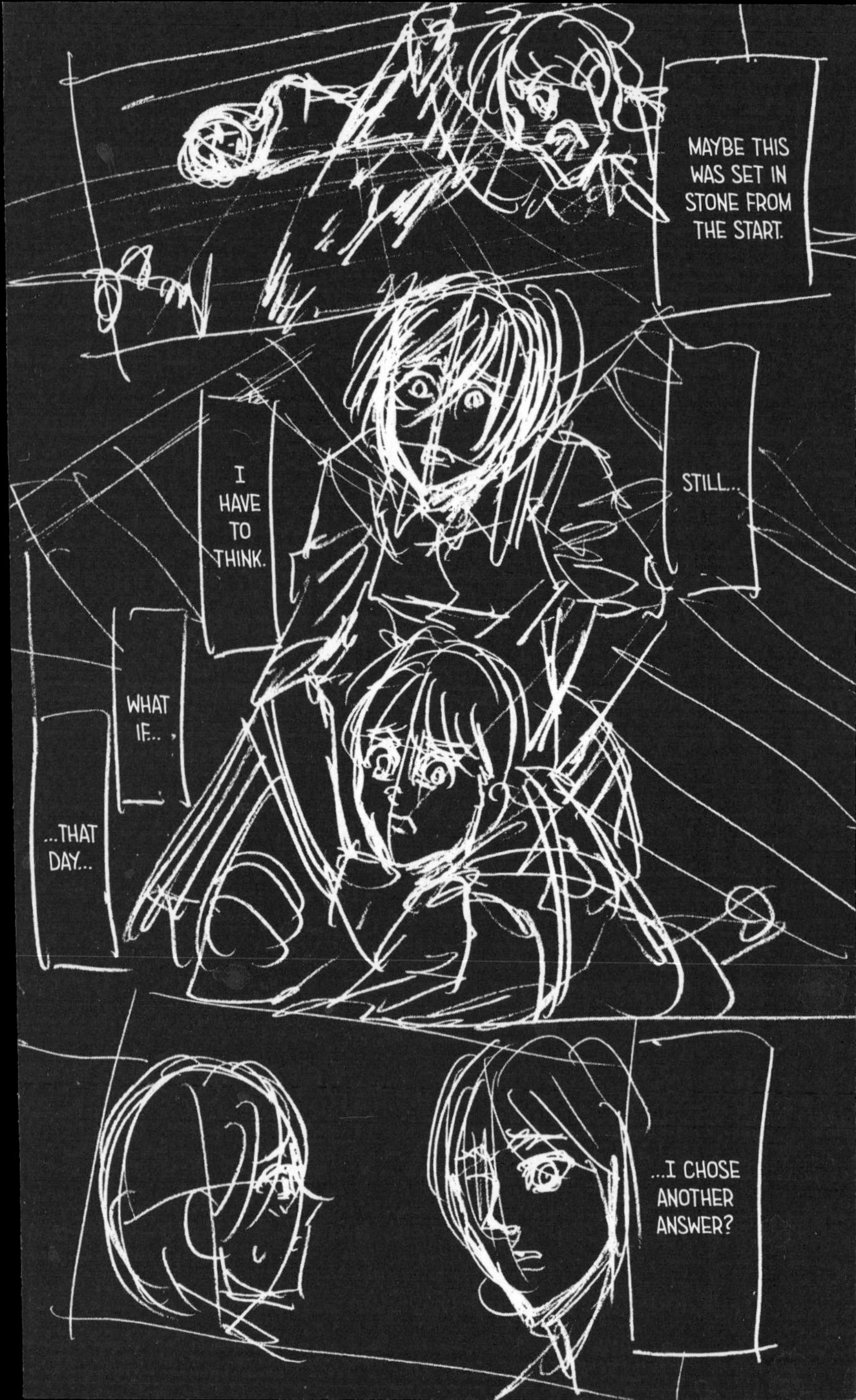
MAYBE THIS WAS SET IN STONE FROM THE START.
STILL...
I HAVE TO THINK.
WHAT IF...
...THAT DAY...
...I CHOSE ANOTHER ANSWER?